# Story of A Soul

## The Autobiography

of

## *Saint Thérèse of Lisieux*

A Study Edition

Je chanterai éternellement les Miséricordes du Seigneur !...

Armoiries de Jésus et de Thérèse

Jours de Grâces, accordés par le Seigneur à sa petite épouse

Naissance 2 Janvier 1873 — Baptême 4 Janvier 1873 — Sourire de la Sainte Vierge Mai 1883. Première Communion 8 Mai 1884 — Confirmation 14 Juin 1884 — Conversion 25 Décembre 1886 — Audience de Léon XIII 20 Novembre 1887 — Entrée au Carmel 9 Avril 1888. Prise d'habit 10 Janvier 1889 — Notre grande richesse 12 Février 1889 — Examen canonique. Bénédiction de Léon XIII. Septembre 1890 — Profession 8 Septembre 1890 — Prise de voile 24 Septembre 1890 — Offrande de moi-même à l'Amour 9 Juin 1895.

The coat of arms Thérèse designed and placed at the end of Manuscript A, together with her list of the important dates in her life (see page 437).

# Story of A Soul

### The Autobiography
### of
### *Saint Thérèse* of Lisieux

## Translated From the Original Manuscripts
## by John Clarke O.C.D.

## A Study Edition
## Prepared by Marc Foley O.C.D.

**ICS Publications**
**Institute of Carmelite Studies**
**Washington, D.C.**
**2005**

ICS Publications
2131 Lincoln Road, NE
Washington, DC 20002

www.icspublications.org
1-800-832-8489

**Library of Congress Cataloging-in-Publication Data**

Thérèse, de Lisieux, Saint, 1873-1897.
    [Histoire d'une âme. English]
    Story of a soul : the autobiography of Saint Thérèse of Lisieux /
translated from the original manuscripts by John Clarke.— Study ed. /
prepared by Marc Foley.
    p. cm.

    Includes bibliographical references and index.
    SBN 0-935216-38-3
    1. Thérèse, de Lisieux, Saint, 1873-1897. 2. Christian saints—France—
Lisieux—Biography. 3. Lisieux (France)—Biography. I. Foley, Marc, 1949-
II. Title.
    BX4700.T5A5 2005      282'.092—dc22      2005009446

# Table of Contents

## Manuscript A

# Manuscript B

# Manuscript C

# Appendices

# Introduction to the Third Edition

The growth of ICS Publications—indeed, its very existence—
is due in no small part to the book you now hold in your hands.
When the Institute of Carmelite Studies first decided in 1973 to
republish the Kavanaugh-Rodriguez translation of St. John of the
Cross, then out of print, no one could have guessed the outcome.
The success of that initial volume, however, revealed an audience
eager for more Carmelite spirituality.

ICS member Father John Clarke, O.C.D., a devotee of the
Little Flower and experienced translator, then proposed undertaking a new translation of St. Thérèse's autobiography, more faithful
to what the Saint had actually written than any of the existing
English-language versions. So limited were the funds that the first
ICS Publications edition of *Story of a Soul* in 1975 had to be typeset by volunteers, and lacked even the benefit of the French accents.
Rapid sales, however, allowed for a new edition the following year,
complete with accents, indices, and a new cover. This second edition quickly became our best-seller, and has remained so for the
past 20 years, far outstripping all other releases, and now used
throughout the English-speaking world.

In translating *Story of a Soul*, as he explains in the following
pages, Father John used *Histoire d'une âme: manuscrits autobiographiques* (Editions du Cerf & Desclée de Brouwer, 1972), a
more popular one-volume version of the critical text established by
Fr. François-Marie in the 1956 facsimile edition of *Manuscrits
autobiographiques*. Following the wishes of her superiors, Thérèse
herself had written out the story of her brief life in ink and pencil,

with few emendations, at odd moments as her health declined, on whatever paper was available (often of poor quality), and with no thought of eventual publication. Not surprisingly, as the facsimile edition reveals, the autograph is sometimes difficult to read, and shows countless variations in capitalizations, underlinings, the size, position, and slant of the letters, and so on (with some occasional corrections in a later hand). Because these variations could not be reproduced on a typeset page, Fr. François chose to represent all these indications of emphasis with *italics*, while capitalizing those words which the Saint had underlined two or more times. The 1992 "Nouvelle Edition du Centenaire" adopted slightly different typographic conventions, but in either case scholars can now check printed versions of Thérèse's autobiography against the facsimile.

More importantly, because Thérèse herself did not divide her work into chapters and numbered paragraphs, scholars have had to develop a standard method for identifying the original site of particular quotations. Increasingly, they use a system devised for the facsimile edition: Within the three manuscripts (A, B, and C) each leaf is numbered consecutively, followed by an indication of the "recto" (front) or "verso" (back) side of the page, and the line on which the text appears. Thus the words "my vocation is Love" (see p. 194 below) appear in the manuscript at Ms B, 3v°, 25 (that is, on line 25 of the verso side of the third leaf in Manuscript B).

For this third ICS Publications edition, Jude Langsam, O.C.D.S. has accomplished the almost impossible task of resetting the pages in a new typeface while incorporating the new referencing system (in superscript brackets) and keeping the pagination virtually the same as before. Accordingly, students of St. Thérèse will still be able to locate texts identified by page number in our previous editions, and at the same time can now find quotations identified by manuscript, page, and line number. Thus the "[2r°]" in the upper left-hand corner of page 13 below indicates that the text of Thérèse's autobiography starts on the "recto" or front side of the second leaf in Manuscript A. The beginning of every fifth line on the original autograph page is indicated by a bracketed superscript number, until one reaches the back of the same leaf with " [2v°]" (at the bottom left-hand corner of the body text on page 13). Readers should note that the enumeration of pages and lines does not always follow in the expected order, particularly where Thérèse's autograph jumps to a different page (see, e.g., pp. 17-20) or where she wrote across the bottom of facing pages (see, e.g., pp. 110-111). Nevertheless, with a little patience the sequence quickly becomes clear.

Finally, besides a number of small corrections and the addition of her "coat of arms," we have also included a short bibliography of resources on Thérèse. Further studies of the Saint and her writings will no doubt appear in profusion during the centenary celebration of her death in 1996–1997.

Thanks are due to John Sullivan, O.C.D., of ICS, and Françoise de Chassey of Editions du Cerf, for the contractual arrangements and their unfailing cooperation; to Regis Jordan, O.C.D., for the initial typesetting and layout; to Jude Langsam, O.C.D.S, for her skilled editing and page design; to William L. O'Neill, C.PP.S., for his bibiliography; to Matthias Montgomery, O.C.D., and Salvatore Sciurba, O.C.D., for several emendations; to our proofreaders; and most of all to the late John Clarke, O.C.D., for making this treasure available to us.

Steven Payne, O.C.D.
*Editorial Director, ICS Publications*

# Introduction to the First Edition

"I feel that my mission is about to begin, my mission to make God loved as I love Him, to teach souls my little way."

These words were spoken by St. Thérèse of the Child Jesus on July 17, 1897, a few months before her death on September 30, 1897. When her sister, Mother Agnes of Jesus, asked her "And what is this little way you want to teach to souls?" Thérèse answered: "It is the way of spiritual childhood, the way of trust and absolute surrender."

"After my death, you must not speak to anyone about my manuscript before it is published; you must speak only to Mother Prioress about it. If you act otherwise, the devil will lay more than one trap to hinder God's work, a very important work!"

She said this to Mother Agnes on August 1, 1897. There is a sense of urgency in the statement, a kind of "hurry up" or things just won't get done.

What Thérèse was talking about and what she was closely associating with her "mission" and her "little way" was the publication of her writings. These contained her teaching as she had actually lived it out in her own human experience. We come across certain specific explanations of this "little way" in several places in her manuscripts, but the entire book is a lesson in how to live this "way of trust and absolute surrender." The book that you now hold in your hands contains this lesson.

This book may be looked on, then, as St. Thérèse's legacy to the world, her personal message to "little ones." We know that her words during her last illness about a "mission" and a "little way" were not just the wanderings of a sick mind. Two popes solemnly endorsed these words within twenty-five years after her death, and both these popes tried their best during the process of her beatification and canonization to bring her teachings to the attention of the faithful and to urge their practice.

"In spiritual childhood is the secret of sanctity for all the faithful of the Catholic world," stated Benedict XV in his allocution on the heroicity of Sister Thérèse's practice of virtue, August 14, 1921. He continued: "There is a call to all the faithful of every nation, no matter what their age, sex, or state of life, to enter wholeheartedly into the Little Way which led Sister Thérèse to the summit of heroic virtue. It is our desire that the secret of sanctity of Sister Thérèse of the Child Jesus be revealed to all our children." And his successor, Pope Pius XI, on April 29, 1923, stated: "We earnestly desire that all the faithful should study her in order to copy her, becoming children themselves; since otherwise they cannot, according to the words of the Master, arrive at the kingdom of heaven."

We find the pope making reference here to the words of Jesus regarding this teaching on spiritual childhood. These words we recall from several places in the Gospels: "Amen, I say to you, unless you be converted and become as little children, you shall not enter into the kingdom of heaven" (Matthew 18:3). "Whoever, therefore, shall humble himself as this little child, will be greatest in the kingdom of heaven" (Matthew 18:4). And elsewhere: "Allow the little ones to come to me and forbid them not, for of such is the kingdom of heaven" (Mark 10:14). "Amen, I say to you, whoever shall not receive the kingdom of God as a little child shall never enter into it" (Mark 10:15).

Although St. Thérèse was well acquainted with these familiar quotations from the New Testament because she meditated upon the Gospels frequently, it is interesting to note that when she teaches her "little way" explicitly, she uses texts from the Old Testament. There are three in particular which became the foundation of this teaching:

"Whoever is a little one, let him come to me" (Proverbs 9:4). "For to him that is little, mercy will be shown" (Wisdom 6:7). "As one whom a mother caresses, so will I comfort you; you shall be carried at the breasts, and upon the knees they shall fondle you" (Isaiah 66:12-13).

These texts do not exhaust the Old Testament teaching on this matter. We have such texts as the following: "The declaration of your word gives light and understanding to little ones" (Psalm 118:130). "The testimony of the Lord is faithful, giving wisdom to little ones" (Psalm 18:8). "The Lord is the keeper of little ones" (Psalm 114:6).

When we consider meditatively these teachings so frequently repeated in both the Old and the New Testaments, we cannot help but feel that it must be tremendously important to become a "little one," to enter into the state of spiritual childhood. In his teaching on the matter, Benedict XV reasoned this way: "When a teacher adopts various methods to inculcate the same lesson, does he not thereby seek to emphasize its value in his sight? If Jesus Christ used so many devices to drive home this lesson to His disciples, it is because He wishes, by one means or another, to ensure their thorough understanding of it. From this we must conclude it was the divine Master's express desire that His disciples should see that THE WAY OF SPIRITUAL CHILD-HOOD IS THE PATH WHICH LEADS TO ETERNAL LIFE."

What better teacher can we have than the one set up by God Himself, namely, St. Thérèse of the Child Jesus? And where can we find these teachings best expressed if not in her own writings which she wanted to see published immediately after her death for this very purpose? *Story of a Soul* has a very interesting history. [As of 1974, when this Introduction was written, it] has been in circulation for the past seventy-five years and has been read and pondered by millions of Thérèse's devoted admirers. Its title, *Story of a Soul*, is the original French title, *Histoire d'une Ame*, which was inspired by the very first words Thérèse penned when she began her writing: "It is to you, dear Mother, to you who are doubly my Mother, that I come to confide the story of my soul."

This story, the humble, simple, and joyful acknowledgement of God's mercy and love in her own uncomplicated life, captured the interest and attention of its readers from the first time it appeared in print. In fact, we can say that Thérèse's book, like the simple and direct message of the Gospels, can be the source of a deep religious inspiration for those who read it with an open mind. Shortly after its first publication in 1898, one man openly and candidly admitted: "I have read this book three times already, and each time it has made me a better man." This statement has been repeated over and over again in various ways by its many readers.

And yet the writer of this book, St. Thérèse of the Child Jesus, at the time this man made this statement, was unknown, unpraised, unimportant. She had finished writing her book only a few months before her death on September 30, 1897, when she was not yet twenty-five years old. She had spent fifteen years of her life in the comparative safety of a devout, Catholic household, and the remaining nine years in the quiet atmosphere of a cloistered community of some twenty Carmelite nuns at Lisieux, Normandy. What made this young, inexperienced girl write the story of her soul? Did she actually think that she had something worthwhile to teach the world? The answer to these questions lies, I think, in the mysterious designs of divine Providence. When we consider the seemingly accidental way in which this book was written, and when we further consider the spiritual impact it has had on all types of people in all nations, we are literally forced to say: The hand of God is here.

We come now to the presentation of a little history regarding the origin of Thérèse's writings. Thanks to the recent publication (1973) of the Process of Beatification and Canonization of Sister Thérèse of the Child Jesus, we have some precise information regarding these writings. It has been known now for a long time, in fact, ever since 1914, that the book published in 1898 under the title: *Histoire d'une Ame (Story of a Soul)* was not, as it appeared, the pouring out of Thérèse's soul to Mother Marie de Gonzague, her Prioress. It was rather a collection of three different manuscripts, addressed to three different persons, during three different years, namely, 1895, 1896, and 1897.

If you glance at the Table of Contents in this book, you will find three general divisions of its material: Manuscript A, Manuscript B, and Manuscript C. I shall deal with each of these manuscripts, trying to give some background on how each came into existence. I think an understanding of this leads to a greater appreciation of Thérèse's message.

The first manuscript, Manuscript A, was addressed to Mother Agnes, Thérèse's older sister Pauline and Prioress of the Carmel from 1893 to 1896. We shall listen to her testimony at the Diocesan Process when she was asked to speak specifically about the origin and composition of the manuscript entitled: The springtime story of a little white flower written by herself and dedicated to the Reverend Mother Agnes of Jesus. Her answer was:

"At the beginning of the year 1895, two and half years before the death of Sister Thérèse, I was with my two sisters (Marie and Thérèse) one winter evening. Sister Thérèse was telling me about several incidents in her childhood, and Sister Marie of the Sacred Heart (my older sister Marie) said: 'Ah, Mother, what a pity we don't have this in writing; if you were to ask Sister Thérèse to write her childhood memories for you, what pleasure this would give us!' I answered: 'I don't ask anything better.' Then turning to Sister Thérèse, who was laughing because she thought we were teasing, I said: 'I order you to write down all your childhood memories.'"

Thérèse, we learn, was somewhat surprised by this command, and she asked humbly: "What can I write that you don't already know?" However, she undertook the work out of obedience and evidently without reluctance because she writes: "It is with great happiness, then, that I come to sing the mercies of the Lord with you, dear Mother."

Mother Agnes continues: "She wrote during her free time and gave me her copybook on January 20, 1896, for my feast day. I was at evening prayer. When passing by to go to her place, Sister Thérèse knelt down and handed me this treasure. I acknowledged it with a simple nod of my head and placed it at my side without opening it. I did not read it until after the elections that took place in the spring of that year. I noticed the Servant of God's virtue: after her act of obedience, she was no longer preoccupied with the matter, never asking me whether I had read it or what I thought of it. One day, I told her that I hadn't had time to read any of it; she appeared in no way troubled."

We have some further testimony from Thérèse's sister Céline (Sister Geneviève), who testified at the same Diocesan Process that she composed her chief work *(Histoire d'une Ame)* at the order of Mother Agnes. She continues: "She had no ulterior motive when she began her manuscript. She wrote simply through obedience, trying above all to relate incidents specific to each member of the family in order to please all through the account of the memories of her youth. Her manuscript was really a 'family souvenir,' destined exclusively for her sisters. This explains the familiar style and certain childish details from which her pen would have recoiled if she had foreseen that this writing would ever go outside the family circle. She wrote by fits and starts, during the rare free moments left her by the Rule and her occupations among the novices. She did not make a rough draft, but she wrote what came into her mind, and yet her manuscript contains no erasure marks."

In this account of her childhood memories, Thérèse distinguishes "three separate periods." The first "extends from the dawn of my reason until the departure of our dear Mother for heaven" (August 28, 1877). Although this represents a very short period of time, Thérèse states that it "is not the least filled with memories." She uses many of the letters her mother had written to Pauline during this period of her childhood. The second period lasts for a little more than nine years, and Thérèse, much affected by the death of her Mother, refers to these years as "the most painful of the three periods." She tells us that she had withdrawn into herself and become excessively given to tears and to sensitiveness. This period covers the five years she spent at the Benedictine Abbey as a day-boarder, and she calls these "the saddest years in my life." The last period begins when Thérèse is in her fourteenth year, still subject to much crying, etc., but there is a sudden change because of a certain grace she received on Christmas night, 1886. This changed her character completely. She refers to it as her "conversion."

The account of her childhood memories comes to an end with her trip to Rome and her subsequent entrance into Carmel. There is not much information given on her religious life, and, in fact, Thérèse apologizes for "abridging" it the way she did. However, she does not fail to give an account of how she finally surrendered totally to God's Merciful Love through her great Act of Oblation, June 9, 1895.

Manuscript B was addressed to Sister Marie of the Sacred Heart, who testified at the Process: "I asked her myself during her last retreat (September 1896) to put in writing her little doctrine as I called it." We must remember that Thérèse had her first hemoptysis (coughing up of blood due to a lung hemorrhage) in the very early hours of the morning of Good Friday, April 3, 1896. She referred to this occurrence as the "first call" of Jesus. "It was like a sweet and distant murmur announcing the arrival of the Bridegroom." A few months afterward, she confided to her sister Marie a consoling dream she had on May 10, in which she saw and heard Venerable Mother Anne of Jesus confirm the presentiment she had of her approaching end. Convinced that her sister was not to live too long, Marie wrote a note to her on September 13, 1896, in which she states: "I am writing to you, not because I have something to say to you but in order to get something from you, from you who are so close to God, from you who are His privileged little spouse, to whom He confides His secrets. The secrets of Jesus to Thérèse are very sweet and I want to hear them again. Write me a short note; this will probably by your last retreat...." She concludes by saying that Thérèse has permission to answer immediately.

Thérèse did answer within the next three days, for there is a letter extant from Marie, dated September 16, 1896, acknowledging receipt of the manuscript. In very small writing, on three sheets of folded paper, Thérèse reveals the secrets of her own heart. There are many corrections on this manuscript which show that it was written in great haste and in a state of extreme fatigue.

A text as compact as Manuscript B, the jewel of all Thérèse's writings, cannot be summed up except in this exclamation: "Then, in the excess of my delirious joy, I cried out: O Jesus, my Love ... my vocation, at last I have found it ... MY VOCATION IS LOVE! Yes, I have found my place in the Church, and it is You, O my God, who have given me this place; in the heart of the Church, my Mother, I shall be Love. Thus I shall be everything, and thus my dream will be realized."

Manuscript C is addressed to Mother Marie de Gonzague, elected Prioress in the Spring elections on March 21, 1896. Mother Agnes stated at the Process that when she read over Thérèse's first manuscript and realized that the latter had written nothing about her religious life, she regretted it very much. However, she was no longer the Prioress and could no longer tell her sister to make up for the deficiency. She had to win Mother Marie de Gonzague over to her cause, and she succeeded in doing this.

"On the night of June 2, 1897, four months before the death of Sister Thérèse, I went to see Mother Prioress. I said to her: 'Mother, it is impossible for me to sleep until I confide a secret to you: When I was Prioress, Sister Thérèse wrote down the memories of her childhood in order to please me and through obedience. I read this over again the other day; it's very good, but you will not be able to obtain much information to write her circular (obituary notice) after her death, for there is almost nothing in it about her religious life. If you were to tell her to do so, she could write something of a much more serious nature, and I don't doubt that you will have something better than I do.'"

There is a great deal of feminine diplomacy in this approach, but it did succeed and the following morning Mother Marie de Gonzague told Thérèse to continue her writing. We have therefore the final manuscript made up of two rather lengthy chapters. Thérèse was to spend only a few hours a day, during the space of a month, in the writing of this last manuscript. Mother Agnes testified that she ceased writing during the first week of July because of the progression of her illness. Thérèse admits that she was interrupted frequently during the writing and was unable to arrange her thoughts properly. In spite of the difficulties under which she labored, she has succeeded in producing a very beautiful piece of literature. There is much in these concluding chapters that reveals the real Thérèse. In them we find so many lights she had on various Scripture passages, especially on the virtue of charity; we find, too, that in her dealings with the other nuns there was much of the human element that she had to overcome by great struggles. Her great trial of faith removes her forever from that category of sanctity in which she has been so often placed, the sweet sentimentality that none of us appreciates.

When we read the above material, we can readily see that not a single one of these manuscripts was ever written with a view to worldwide publication. The first was composed as a "family souvenir," and it did contain "certain childish details from which Thérèse's pen would have recoiled if she had foreseen that this writing would ever go outside the family circle." The second manuscript was done exclusively for Marie at her own request; it too was a kind of "souvenir" of Thérèse's last retreat. The third was made for Mother Marie de Gonzague, its purpose being to supply her with information for composing a "circular" after Thérèse's death.

When Thérèse was given a premonition of her future mission during those last months of her life, a mission that was to last until the end of time, and when she realized that her manuscripts would be closely associated with the spread of this mission, at least in part, we can understand why she saw the need for a revision in her manuscripts. She supplied for this by appointing her sister Pauline, Mother Agnes of Jesus, as "mon historien." She gave her permission to add, to delete, to make any changes necessary.

After Thérèse's death, Mother Agnes carried out her sister's directive as quickly as possible: "After my death, you must speak to no one about my manuscript before it is published; you must speak only to Mother Prioress about it. If you act otherwise, the devil will lay more than one trap to hinder God's work, a very important work!" When Mother Agnes approached the Prioress for permission to publish all three manuscripts, the latter agreed but laid down as a "conditio sine qua non" that all three must be rearranged in such a way as to seem to be addressed to herself. Mother Agnes agreed with the condition. The publication one year later, September 30, 1898, of the book entitled *Histoire d'une Ame* read beautifully because of Mother Agnes's masterly work of editing. It also appeared as a composite whole that contained the intimate outpourings of Sister Thérèse's soul to her Mother Prioress, Marie de Gonzague. The subsequent editions retained this format until the Diocesan Process held in 1910. The judges on this tribunal, on hearing about Mother Marie's directive, insisted that all future editions of *Histoire d'une Ame* indicate clearly the individual direction of each of the manuscripts, namely, to Mother Agnes of Jesus, to Sister Marie of the Sacred Heart, and finally to Mother Marie de Gonzague. This was done with the 1914 editions.

As the fame of St. Thérèse of Lisieux grew and special studies of her works were undertaken, it was only natural that theologians would be satisfied only with her original, unedited manuscripts. Requests were made for their publication. Permission was finally granted by the Bishop of Bayeux and Lisieux in August 1947. Shortly thereafter Mother Agnes received the following letter from Very Reverend Marie-Eugène, Definitor General of the Discalced Carmelite Order: "The Church has spoken. The sainthood and the doctrinal mission of St. Thérèse of the Child Jesus are universally recognized. From now on she belongs to the Church and to history. To avoid and to refute partial or mistaken interpretations of her doctrine and in order that her doctrine and her soul should be still more deeply understood, the documents that you have so generously given us are insufficient. Only the original texts can allow us to discover the movement of her thought, its living rhythm, and disclose all the light contained in her definitions, which are usually so firm and precise."

When Mother Agnes sat down and read this letter, she was

somewhat overwhelmed by the demand that was being made on her. After all, she was now an old woman in her late eighties, eighty-six to be exact, and as a consequence she was both tired and somewhat fearful. While she was willing to have Thérèse's original works finally published, the undertaking seemed too much for her strength. She obtained a delay from Rome. She instructed her sister Céline, Sister Geneviève, to take charge of this work after her own death: "After my death I order you to do it in my name."

Mother Agnes lived for another four years and died on July 28, 1951. A year later steps were taken to obtain permission for the publication of the Manuscripts. This was given by Rome on September 19, 1952. Mother Agnes was not wrong when she felt the work was far too much for her, for it took Father François de Sainte Marie, O.C.D., four long years to make all the necessary preparations for the photostatic publication of Thérèse's three original manuscripts. This publication was printed the next year, 1957.

When he sent his copy of Thérèse's original manuscripts to the printer, Father François had been very careful about what he did. He realized that there was a demand for Thérèse's original writings without any additions or deletions, etc., and this is exactly what he scrupulously provided. The result: *Sainte Thérèse de l'Enfant Jésus — Manuscrits autobiographiques*. This contained no additions, no deletions, practically no paragraphs, no division into chapters, no prologue, no epilogue. There was a certain starkness about the book that made it very unattractive to the ordinary reader, and especially to the old friends of Thérèse who had come to know her in the pages of *Histoire d'une Ame*. These old friends missed the homey atmosphere of that old book. They wanted it back. This is why there was a new publication in French of Thérèse's work. It was published in 1972. A note on the formation of the book explains the reasons for its publication:

"For the occasion of the centenary of St. Thérèse's birth, January 2, 1973, many people expressed the desire for a new edition of the Autobiographical Manuscripts. While retaining the scientific tone of the Manuscripts, this new edition should meet the needs of the ordinary person and appear under the form of a biography of Thérèse similar to the *Histoire d'une Ame [Story of a Soul]*. The team that produced this book answered this twofold request: (1) fidelity to the authentic text as it came from Thérèse's pen; (2) fidelity to the first edition of *Histoire d'une Ame* (1898), which Mother Agnes had conceived as a complete biography of Thérèse for the ordinary reader."

This book is a translation of the French publication made in 1972 to fill these specifications. With reference to the first specification, fidelity to the authentic text as it came from Thérèse's pen, readers may feel certain that what they are reading is what she herself wrote. Many portions of her original manuscripts had to be deleted for good reasons, and even Thérèse realized this when she told her sister, Mother Agnes of Jesus, to delete what was necessary. These portions are contained in this book, and I feel that their contents make her personality even more attractive. In them, without constraint, she expresses herself as she really was, and appears even more human.

With reference to the second specification, fidelity to the first edition of *Histoire d'une Ame* (1898), which Mother Agnes conceived as a complete biography of Thérèse for the ordinary reader, a glance at the format of this book will make this evident. First, its division into eleven chapters is the same as that made by Mother Agnes; second, the addition of a Prologue explaining family origins and an Epilogue explaining Thérèse's illness, last agony, and death was also Mother Agnes's idea; finally, there are some long footnotes of certain additions made to Thérèse's texts by Mother Agnes in order to elucidate some points of family history.

In closing, I would like to assure Thérèse's readers that I have tried to be absolutely faithful in translating into English what she beautifully expressed in French. After her friends have waited so long to read her in the original manuscripts, it would be a shame, I think, to give them an interpretation of her words rather than an exact rendition. Consequently, I have deliberately retained her own choice of words because this best expressed her feelings; I have retained her exclamation points even though we seldom use them; I have capitalized words that she capitalized because they had a special significance for her; I have retained throughout the text her habit of direct address to the one to whom she is writing; finally, Thérèse frequently emphasized her thought by either underlining words and sentences or writing them in larger script; this has been duplicated here through the use of italics or capital letters. All Scripture quotations are italicized.

"O Jesus! why can't I tell all *little souls* how unspeakable is Your condescension? I feel that if You found a soul weaker and littler than mine, You would be pleased to grant it still greater favors, provided it abandoned itself with total confidence to Your infinite Mercy. I beg You to cast Your Divine Glance upon a great number of *little* souls. I beg You to choose a legion of *little* Victims worthy of Your LOVE!"

St. Thérèse of the Child Jesus.

John Clarke, O.C.D.
*September 8, 1974*

# Prologue

"There is nothing as mysterious as those preparations attending man on the threshold of life. Everything is played out before we are twelve."

In what concerns St. Thérèse of the Child Jesus and the Holy Face, everything was not really played out until September 30, 1897, when, consumed by tuberculosis, she expired at the age of twenty-four years and nine months.

And still her contemporary, Charles Péguy, was speaking about her too, so true is it that a human destiny is rooted in a soil, an epoch, a family, and is dependent on a heredity and a history. As John Donne wrote: "No man is an island." Thérèse did not descend from heaven like an angel, but was born on Norman soil, dependent on her ancestors and her country.

Before the whole world was to honor St. Thérèse of Lisieux and her "Way of Childhood," a child already existed, namely, Thérèse Martin of Alençon.

She is truly the mysterious fruit of those secret preparations. Had her parents followed the inclinations of their heart, "the greatest saint of modern times" would never have seen the light of day.

Descended from a family of soldiers, and the son of a soldier attached to successive barracks (Avignon, Strasbourg), Louis Martin was born at Bordeaux on August 22, 1823. He was acquainted with the life of army camps and was raised in the atmosphere of the Napoleonic legend, though his father joined the royalist armies during the Hundred Days. Captain under the Restoration, the future grandfather of Thérèse took up residence at Alençon in 1830.

Orderly, methodical, of a solitary and meditative temperament, his son Louis learned the watchmaking trade, which requires much patience and precision. At the age of 22 he dreamed of a much more solitary life and presented himself as a candidate at the monastery of the great St. Bernard. He was refused because he did not have any knowledge of Latin. After a sojourn in Paris, he settled down as a watchmaker at Alençon and lived with his parents on rue du Pont-Neuf. For the next eight years he led a quasi-monastic life that was filled with travel, prayer, reading, fishing — his favorite pastime — and frequenting the company of his friends in the Catholic Club.

Alençon, the chief town of Orne, had a population of 13,600 inhabitants at this time. It was a quiet little town, perfectly suitable for this quiet man. It owed its fame solely to the art of its lacemakers, who export the famous "Point d'Alençon" to all parts of France and especially to Paris.

Zélie Guérin was born into a family of peasant background on December 23, 1831. She, too, was brought up in a military atmosphere as her father was present at Wagram and terminated his career in the gendarmes. He retired in 1844 to Alençon, 36 rue Saint-Blaise, opposite the Prefecture.

Reared by this overbearing father and by a mother who showed her little affection, Zélie one day wrote her brother: "My childhood and youth were as dismal as a winding sheet; although my mother spoiled you, she was very severe with me as you know. Even though she was very good, she did not know how to take me, and I suffered very much interiorly" (family correspondence, November 7, 1865). She expressed her love for this brother Isidore, who was studying to be a pharmacist, and for her sister Elise, her confidante, who entered the Visitation convent at Le Mans under the name Sister Marie-Dosithée. She carried on a correspondence with them right up until her death, a correspondence that revealed her restless and often melancholic temperament, but her lively character too, her eagerness for work, her faith under every trial, her good sense, and even her humor.

She dreamed of the religious life just as Louis Martin did, and like him, she was categorically refused when she sought permission to join the Sisters of the Hôtel Dieu at Alençon. Then she took up the manufacture of the "Point d'Alençon," opening an "office" of her own with her sister's help. A clever worker, she was to be supremely successful.

Refused entrance into the religious life, the watchmaker of 35 and lacemaker of 27 met and after a short engagement were married at Alençon in the Church of Notre-Dame, July 13, 1858.

They settled down on the rue du Pont-Neuf and lived for a period of ten months as brother and sister. The intervention of a confessor, however, made them change their mind, and nine children were born into this home from 1860 to 1873. Mme. Martin wrote before the birth of her last child, Thérèse: "I love children even to the point of folly and was born to have some of my own. But soon the time for this will be ended since I will be 41 this month, and this is the time when one is a grandmother!"

Five daughters only were to survive, for this was the epoch in which infant mortality was still unconquered. In poor health, weakened by a breast cancer that was declared incurable only in 1876, Mme. Martin hesitantly resigned herself to entrusting her fifth child and those who followed to nurses who were more or less conscientious. For fifteen years there was a rhythm between births and deaths. The parents were to witness two little boys and two little girls depart for heaven. One of the girls was the delightful Hélène who reached the age of five. Her mother wrote of her:

"Since I lost this child, I experience an intense desire to see her once more. However, those who remain need me and for their sake I ask God to leave me a few more years on earth. I was saddened over the death of my two little boys but much more over the loss of this one, for I had begun to enjoy her company. She was so good, so affectionate, and so advanced for her years! There is not a moment of the day when I am not thinking of her" (March 27, 1870).

The war of 1870 and its aftermath — they had to lodge nine German soldiers — did not interrupt the increase in this family nor its entrance to lower middle class status through the mother's incessant toil. She used to rise early and retire late, and was now aided in her work by her husband, who had sold his watchmaking and jewelry business. The Martins moved and came to live on rue Saint-Blaise in a house that one can still visit today.

Family life held a privileged position. They were content only when together. Marie, the eldest and the father's favorite, and Pauline, lively, mischievous, and the mother's confidante, were exiled each year to the Visitation at Le Mans. The two boarders lived there happily under the vigilant eye of their aunt, Sister Marie-Dosithée. She reported to their mother on the girls' scholastic progress, their conduct, and she appreciated very much their different temperaments. Each return for summer vacation set off explosions of joy, and each return to school brought on a torrent of tears!

"Poor Léonie," the least talented, frequently ill, was the sole worry of her mother. Céline, "the intrepid," was soon to become the inseparable companion of Thérèse.

Walks to the "Pavilion" or into the Norman countryside, trips to Semallé, visits to the family of Uncle Guérin, a pharmacist in Lisieux, train journeys to Le Mans to visit Aunt Marie-Dosithée, all these left their impressions on the Martin children, who remembered these simple joys all their lives. The seven deaths that put the family into mourning between 1859 and 1870 — three grandparents and four children — did not extinguish the affectionate ardor uniting the members.

What could have been austere and unbending in the father's personality was compensated for by the indulgent kindness he showed for his noisy brood who could have upset his love for silence and peace. He did not disdain enlivening the family evenings by reciting the poems of famous authors of the day, the romanticists, singing old-fashioned tunes in his beautiful voice and making miniature toys, much to the admiration of his daughters.

The mother, frequently worried over the future — she felt her strength ebbing — managed her household with the "really incredible and prodigious courage of the strong woman! Adversity does not get her down nor does prosperity make her proud," wrote her sister on October 25, 1868. Her realism, lively candor, and loving consideration all made her the soul of the family.

There reigned in the Martin family a solid faith that saw God in all life's events, paying Him a permanent homage: family prayers together, morning attendance at Mass, frequent reception of Holy Communion — rare in an epoch when Jansenism continued its ravages — Sunday Vespers, retreats. Their whole life revolved around the liturgical year, pilgrimages, a scrupulous regard for fasts and abstinences. Yet there was nothing stiff and bigoted in this family that was unacquainted with formality. They could be active and contemplative, feeding abandoned children, tramps, and the aged. Zélie took time out of her few short hours of nightly rest to attend to an ailing housemaid, while Louis went out of his way to help the disinherited, the epileptic, the dying. Both parents taught their children to respect the poor.

The mother loved to see her children dressed attractively, and when Sister Marie-Dosithée was concerned at hearing that Marie was enjoying herself with girls of her own age, she said: "Must they shut themselves up in a cloister? In the world we cannot live in seclusion! There is something to take and something to leave in everything the 'holy girl' tells us" (November 12, 1876).

When she was four months pregnant, Mme. Martin announced to the Guérins "an event that will probably take place toward the end of the year," that is, in 1872. She writes also that she hopes the child will be born in good health. Such is the first mention of the existence of the one whom they were already calling "little Thérèse" in memory of a Thérèse who died when five months old.

And then comes the good news: "My little daughter was born yesterday, Thursday, at 11:30 at night. She is very strong and healthy, and they say she weighs eight pounds; let's put it at six pounds, and that is not bad! She seems very nice. I suffered only a half-hour, and what I experienced before is not to be counted. She will be baptized on Saturday, and you will be the only ones missing to make the celebration complete. Marie will be the godmother, and a little boy, almost her age, the godfather" (January 3, 1873).

Everything went as announced by Mme. Martin. The only unexpected thing was this note brought to rue Saint-Blaise by a child; its father had written this short poem:

| | |
|---|---|
| Souris et grandit vite | Smile and grow quickly |
| Au bonheur, Tout t'invite, | Everything promises you happiness. |
| Tendre soins, tendre Amour | Tender care, tender Love |
| Oui, souris à l'Aurore, | Yes, smile at the Dawn, |
| Bouton qui viens d'éclore | Bud that just blossomed, |
| Tu seras Rose un jour. | One day you will be a Rose. |

She was hardly born when Marie-Françoise-Thérèse Martin knew suffering: at two weeks she just missed being carried off by intestinal troubles; at three months, there was still a more serious danger: "She is very bad and I have no hope whatsoever of saving her. The poor little thing suffers horribly since yesterday. It breaks your heart to see her" (March 1, 1873).

The crisis over, the mother was forced, on the doctor's advice, to entrust Thérèse to a friendly nurse. For a whole year, nursed by the strong and vivacious Rose Taillé, the little one led the life of a little peasant. At Semallé she grew into a big baby, tanned by the sun. There she drank in a zest for life among the flowers and the animals. Her mother wrote on July 20, 1873: "Her nurse brings her out to the fields in a wheelbarrow, seated on top a load of hay; she hardly ever cries. Little Rose says that one could hardly find a better child."

Blond, blue-eyed, very attractive, precocious, lively, very touchy, capable of violent outbursts of temper, stubborn, Thérèse very quickly became the favorite. She was "devoured by kisses" by the whole family, and this especially because they were deprived of her presence. "All my life God was pleased to surround me with love, and my first memories are imprinted with the most tender smiles and caresses!"

Thérèse was to write at the age of 23: "Ah! how rapidly the sunny years of my early childhood passed by, but what a sweet impression they left on my soul! Everything on earth smiled at me. I found flowers under each of my steps, and my happy disposition contributed also to making my life pleasing."

Her mother's death broke up this happiness and necessitated the departure of the family to Lisieux. But let Thérèse herself tell us.

# Thérèse's Family and Cousins

**The Family**

Louis Martin and Zélie Guérin married on July 13, 1858. They had the following children:

* Marie, born February 22, 1860, became a Carmelite October 15, 1886 (Sister Marie of the Sacred Heart), died January 19, 1940.
* Pauline, born September 7, 1861, became a Carmelite October 2, 1882 (Mother Agnes of Jesus), died July 28, 1951.
* Léonie, born June 3, 1863, became a Visitandine January 28, 1899 (Sister Françoise-Thérèse), died June 16, 1941.
* Hélène, born October 13, 1864, died February 22, 1870.
* Joseph-Louis, born September 20, 1866, died February 14, 1867.
* Joseph-Jean-Baptiste, born December 19, 1867, died August 24, 1868.
* Céline, born April 28, 1869, became a Carmelite September 14, 1894 (Sister Geneviève of the Holy Face), died February 25, 1959.
* Mélanie-Thérèse, born August 16, 1870, died October 8, 1870.
* Thérèse, born January 2, 1873, became a Carmelite April 9, 1888 (Sister Thérèse of the Child Jesus and the Holy Face), died September 30, 1897.

**Cousins of Thérèse**

Fanny Martin, aunt of Thérèse, married on April 11, 1842, François-Adolphe Leriche (born in 1818, died May 25, 1843). They had a child:

- Adolphe Leriche, born January 7, 1844, died December 7, 1894.

Isidore Guérin, uncle of Thérèse, married on September 11, 1866, Céline Fournet (born March 15, 1847, died February 13, 1900). They had the following children:

- Jeanne, born February 24, 1868, died April 25, 1938, who married on October 1, 1890, François La Néele, a doctor.
- Marie, born August 22, 1870, died April 14, 1905, became a Carmelite at Lisieux August 15, 1895 (Sister Marie of the Eucharist).
- A son, born dead, October 16, 1871.

# Manuscript Dedicated
## to
# Reverend Mother Agnes of Jesus

# Manuscript A

# Chapter I

# *ALENÇON*
# *(1873-1877)*

The Mercies of the Lord
Surrounded by Love
The Trip to Le Mans
My Character
I Choose All!

[2r°]                    **J.M.J.T.**                    **January 1895**
**Jesus+**

Springtime story of a little white flower written by herself and dedicated to the Reverend Mother Agnes of Jesus.

I t is to you, dear Mother, to you who are doubly my Mother, that I come to confide the story of my soul. The day you asked me to do this, it seemed to me it would distract my heart by too much concentration on myself, but since then Jesus has made me feel that in obeying simply, I would be pleasing Him; [5]besides, I'm going to be doing only one thing: I shall begin to sing what I must sing eternally: *"The Mercies of the Lord."*[1]

Before taking up my pen, I knelt before the statue of Mary[2] (the one that has given so many proofs of the maternal preferences of heaven's Queen for our family), and I begged her to guide my [10]hand that it trace no line displeasing to her. Then opening the Holy Gospels my

---

[1] Psalm 88:2.

[2] The "Virgin of the Smile," which is in the present shrine of St. Thérèse. The Martin family held it in special veneration. In January 1895 it was in the room outside her cell.

13

eyes fell on these words: "And going up a mountain, he called to him men of his *own choosing*, and they came to him" (St. Mark, chap. III, v. 13). This is the mystery of my vocation, my whole life, and especially the mystery of the privileges Jesus showered on my [15]soul. He does not call those who are worthy but those whom He *pleases* or as St. Paul says: "God will have mercy on whom he will have mercy, and he will show pity to whom he will show pity. So then there is question not of him who wills nor of him who runs, but of God showing mercy" (Ep. to the Rom., chap. IX, v. 15 and 16).

I wondered for a long time [20]why God has preferences, why all souls don't receive an equal amount of graces. I was surprised when I saw Him shower His extraordinary favors on saints who had [2v°] offended Him, for instance, St. Paul and St. Augustine, and whom He forced, so to speak, to accept His graces. When reading the lives of the saints, I was puzzled at seeing how Our Lord was pleased to caress certain ones from the cradle to the grave, allowing no obstacle in their way when coming to Him, helping them with [5]such favors that they were unable to soil the immaculate beauty of their baptismal robe. I wondered why poor savages died in great numbers without even having heard the name of God pronounced.

Jesus deigned to teach me this mystery. He set before me the book of nature; I understood how [10]all the flowers He has created are beautiful, how the splendor of the rose and the whiteness of the Lily do not take away the perfume of the little violet or the delightful simplicity of the daisy. I understood that if all flowers wanted to be roses, nature would lose her springtime beauty, and the fields would no longer be decked out with little wild flowers.

[15]And so it is in the world of souls, Jesus' garden. He willed to create great souls comparable to Lilies and roses, but He has created smaller ones and these must be content to be daisies or violets destined

to give joy to God's glances when He looks down at his feet. Perfection consists in [20]doing His will, in being what He wills us to be.

I understood, too, that Our Lord's love is revealed as perfectly in the most simple soul who resists His grace in nothing as in the most excellent soul; in fact, since the nature of love is to humble oneself, if all souls resembled those of the holy Doctors who illumined the Church [3r°] with the clarity of their teachings, it seems God would not descend so low when coming to their heart. But He created the child who knows only how to make his feeble cries heard; He has created the poor savage who has nothing but the natural law to guide him. [5]It is to their hearts that God deigns to lower Himself. These are the wild flowers whose simplicity attracts Him. When coming down in this way, God manifests His infinite grandeur. Just as the sun shines simultaneously on the tall cedars and on each little flower as though it were alone on the earth, so Our Lord is occupied particularly with each [10]soul as though there were no others like it. And just as in nature all the seasons are arranged in such a way as to make the humblest daisy bloom on a set day, in the same way, everything works out for the good of each soul.

Perhaps you are wondering, dear Mother, with some astonishment where I am going from here, for up till now I've said nothing that resembles [15]the story of my life. But you asked me to write under no constraint whatever would come into my *mind*. It is not, then, my life, properly so-called, that I am going to write; it is my *thoughts* on the graces God deigned to grant me. I find myself at a period in my life when I can cast a glance on the past; my soul has [20]matured in the crucible of exterior and interior trials. And now, like a flower strengthened by the storm, I can raise my head and see the words of Psalm 22 realized in me: "The Lord is my Shepherd, I shall not want; he makes me lie down in green pastures. He leads me beside still waters; he restores my soul. Even though I walk through the valley of [3v°] the shadow of

death, I fear no evil; for thou art with me..."[3] To me the Lord has always
been "merciful and good, slow to anger and abounding in steadfast
love" (Ps. 102, v. 8).

It is with great happiness, then, that I come to [5]sing the mercies
of the Lord with you, dear Mother. It is for *you alone* I am writing the
story of the *little flower* gathered by Jesus. I will talk freely and without any worries as to the numerous digressions I will make. A mother's
heart understands her child even when it can but stammer, and so I'm
sure of being understood [10]by you, who formed my heart, offering it
up to Jesus!

It seems to me that if a little flower could speak, it would tell simply what God has done for it without trying to hide its blessings. It
would not say, under the pretext of a false humility, it is not beautiful
or without perfume, that the sun has taken away its splendor and the
storm [15]has broken its stem when it knows that all this is untrue. The
flower about to tell her story rejoices at having to publish the totally
gratuitous gifts of Jesus. She knows that nothing in herself was capable of attracting the divine glances, and His mercy alone brought about
everything that is good in her.

It was He who had her born in a [20]holy soil, impregnated with a
*virginal perfume*. It was He, too, who has her preceded by eight Lilies
of dazzling whiteness. In His love He wished to preserve His little
flower from the world's poisoned breath. Hardly had her petals begun
to unfold when this divine Savior transplanted her to Mount Carmel
where already two Lilies, who had taken care of her in the springtime
of her life, spread [4r°] their sweet perfume. Seven years have passed
by since the little flower took root in the garden of the Spouse of
Virgins, and now *three* Lilies bloom in her presence. A little farther off

---

[3] Psalm 22: 1–4

another lily expands under the eyes of Jesus. The two [5]stems who brought these flowers into existence are now reunited for all eternity in the heavenly Fatherland. There they have found once again the four Lilies the earth had not seen develop. Oh! may Jesus deign not to allow a long time to pass on these strange shores for the flowers left in exile. May the Lilyplant be soon complete in Heaven![4]

[10]I have just summed up in a few words, dear Mother, what God did for me. Now I will go into detail about the years of my childhood. I realize that here where others would see nothing but a tedious recital, your *motherly heart* will find some facts that are charming. Besides, the memories I'm about to evoke are also yours since [15]my childhood unfolded near you, and I have the good fortune to belong to Parents without equal who surrounded us both with the same cares and the same tenderness. Oh! may they bless the littlest of their children and help her to sing the divine mercies!

[20]In the story of my soul, up until my entrance into Carmel, I distinguish three separate periods. The first is not the least fruitful in memories in spite of its short duration. It extends from the dawn of my reason till our dear Mother's departure for Heaven.

[4v°] God granted me the favor of opening my intelligence at an early age and of imprinting childhood recollections so deeply on my memory that it seems the things I'm about to recount happened only yesterday. Jesus [5]in His love willed, perhaps, that I know the matchless Mother He had given me, but whom His hand hastened to crown in heaven.

---

[4] In this figurative language Thérèse describes her family. When she was writing, there were "three Lilies" with her in Carmel, viz., Marie, Pauline, and Céline; another, Léonie, was in the Visitation convent at Caen. Thérèse describes her two parents as "the two stems reunited for all eternity."

God was pleased all through my life to surround me with *love,* and the first memories I have are stamped with smiles and the most [10]tender caresses. But although He placed so much *love* near me, He also sent much love into my little heart, making it warm and affectionate. I loved Mama and Papa very much and showed my tenderness for them in a thousand ways, for I was very expressive. The means I employed at times were [15]strange, as this passage from one of Mama's letters proves:

"Baby is a little imp; she'll kiss me and at the same time wish me to die. 'Oh, how I wish you would die, dear little Mother!' When I scold her she answers: 'It is because I want you to go to heaven, and you say we must die to get there!' [20]She wishes the same for her Father in her outbursts of affection for him."[5]

[5r°] And here's another passage from a letter dated June 25, 1874. I was only a year and a half: "Your Father just installed a swing, and Céline's joy knows no bounds. But you should see the little one using it; it's funny to see her trying to conduct herself as a big girl. There's no danger of her letting the rope go. [5]When the swing doesn't go fast enough, she cries. We attached her to it with a rope, but in spite of this I'm still uneasy to see her perched so high.

"A strange thing happened to me regarding the little one. I'm in the habit of attending the 5:30 Mass in the morning, but at first I didn't dare leave her alone. Seeing she didn't wake up early I decided to leave her. I'd place her [10]in my bed and set the cradle alongside the bed so that she couldn't fall out. One day, I forgot the cradle. I returned and the little one was no longer in the bed; at the same moment I heard a whimper; I looked and saw her in a sitting position in a chair at the head of

---

[5] Letter of Mme. Martin to Pauline, December 5, 1875. [See p. ix above for explanation of manuscript reference numbers here. — Ed.]

my bed. She was sleeping fitfully as she was uncomfortable with her head resting on a cushion.

"I can't [15]understand how she fell onto the chair in a sitting position since she was in the bed. I thanked God, feeling it was providential as she could have tumbled onto the floor. Her good Angel watched over her and the souls in purgatory protected her. I pray every day to them for her. This is my explanation for it; explain it the way you like."

[20]At the end of the letter Mama added: "The little one has just placed her hand on my face and kissed me. This poor little thing doesn't want to leave me; she's continually at my side. She likes going into the garden, [5v°] but when I'm not there she won't stay but cries till they bring her to me."[6]

Here is a passage from another letter:

"Little Thérèse asked me the other day if she would go to Heaven. I told her 'Yes' if she were good. She answered: 'Yes, but if I'm not good, I'll go to hell. But [5]I know what I will do. I will fly to you in Heaven, and what will God be able to do to take me away? You will be holding me so tightly in your arms!' I could see in her eyes that she was really convinced that God could do nothing to her if she were in her mother's arms."[7]

"Marie loves her little sister very much. She finds her very good, and it would be [10]difficult for her to think otherwise since this poor little thing has a great fear of causing Marie any trouble. Yesterday, knowing she is very happy to be given a rose, I wanted to cut one for

---

[6] In a letter to Pauline, November 1985, Mme. Martin wrote: "She will not climb the stairs all alone, but cries at each step: 'Mama, Mama!' If I forget to say: 'Yes, my child,' she stops and won't go any further" (Histoire d'une Ame).

[7] Letter of Mme. Martin to Pauline, October 29, 1876.

her. She began begging me not to do so because Marie had forbidden this. Her face was red with emotion. In spite of this, I gave her two roses, but she did not dare go into the house. It was useless for me to tell her the roses belonged to me. 'No,' she [15]insisted, 'they belong to Marie!'

"She becomes emotional very easily. As soon as she does anything wrong, everybody must know it. Yesterday, not meaning to do so, she tore off a small piece of wallpaper. She wanted to tell her Father immediately, and you would have pitied her to see her anxiety. When he returned four hours later and everybody had forgotten about it, she ran at once to Marie, saying: 'Marie, [20]hurry and tell Papa I tore the paper.' Then she awaited her sentence as if she were a criminal. There is an idea in her little head that if she owns up to something, she will be more readily forgiven."[8]

---

[8] Letter of Mme. Martin to Pauline, May 21, 1876. *Histoire d'une Ame* adds: "Coming on our dear little Father's name, I very naturally recall certain happy memories. When he came home I used to run and sit on one of his boots; then he would carry me in this way all around the house and out into the garden. Mama said laughingly to him that he carried out all my wishes; and he answered: 'Well, what do you expect? She's the Queen!' Then he would take me in his arms, lift me very high, set me on his shoulder, kiss and caress me in many ways.

"I cannot say, however, that Papa spoiled me. I remember very well how one day when I was swinging contentedly, he passed by and called out to me: 'Come and kiss me, my little Queen!' Contrary to my usual custom, I didn't want to budge, and I answered boldly: 'Come and get it, Papa!' He paid no attention to me and was right to do so. Marie was there. She said: 'You naughty little girl! How bad it is to answer one's father in this way!' Immediately I jumped off my swing for the correction was not lost on me! The whole house resounded with my cries of sorrow. I climbed the stairs quickly, and this time I

[4v°, cont'd.] I was very fond of my *godmother*.[9] Without appearing to do so, I paid close attention to what was said and done around me. It seems to me I was judging things then as I do now. I was listening carefully to what Marie was teaching Céline in order to do what Céline did. [6v°] After Marie came out of the Visitation,[10] to obtain permission to go into the room where she was giving Céline her lessons, I was very good and did everything she wanted. She gave me a lot of gifts, and in spite of their insignificant value these pleased me a lot.

---

didn't call 'Mama' each step, for I thought of nothing but finding Papa and being reconciled to him. This was done very quickly.

"I could not stand the thought of having offended my beloved parents. Acknowledging my faults was the work of an instant as this following incident recounted by my mother shows: 'One morning, I wanted to kiss little Thérèse before going downstairs. She seemed to be in a deep sleep, and I didn't dare awaken her; but Marie said to me: "Mama, she's only pretending to be asleep; I'm sure of it!" Then I leaned over to kiss her forehead, but she immediately hid under her blanket and said with the tone of a spoiled child: "I don't want anybody to see me!" I was very much displeased and let her feel it. Two minutes later I heard her crying and very soon, to my great surprise, I saw her at my side! She had left her bed all by herself and had come downstairs in her bare feet, hindered somewhat by her long nightdress. Her face was bathed in tears, and throwing herself at my knees, she said: "Mama, I was naughty; forgive me!" Pardon was quickly granted. I took my angel in my arms, pressed her to my heart, and covered her with kisses.' " (Letter of Mme. Martin to Pauline, February 13, 1877.)

[9] Marie, Thérèse's oldest sister.
[10] She made her studies there.

[5]I was very proud of my two sisters, but the one who was my *ideal* from childhood was Pauline. When I was beginning to talk, Mama would ask me: "What are you thinking about?" and I would answer invariably: "Pauline!" Another time, I was moving my little finger over the windowpanes and I said: "I'm writing Pauline!"

I had often heard it [10]said that surely Pauline would become a *religious*, and without knowing too much about what it meant I thought: "I too *will be a religious*." This is one of my first memories and I haven't changed my resolution since then! It was through you, dear Mother, that Jesus chose to espouse me to Himself. You were not with me then, but already a bond was formed between our [15]souls. You were my *ideal*; I wanted to be like you, and it was your example that drew me toward the Spouse of Virgins at the age of two. What sweet reflections I would like to confide to you! But I have to continue the story of the little flower, her complete and general story, for if I were to go into detail about my relationship with you, I would have to leave everything [20]else aside!

Dear little Léonie held a warm place in my heart. She was very fond of me and in the evenings when the family took a walk she used to take care of me. I still seem to hear those beautiful lullabies she used to sing to me to get me to sleep. She was always trying to find ways of pleasing me, and I would be sorry if I caused her any trouble.

[6v°] I remember very well her First Communion and especially the moment she picked me up in her arms and carried me into the rectory.[11] It seemed so nice to be carried by a big sister all in white like myself! In the evening they put me to bed early as I was [5]too little to stay up for the banquet, but I can still see Papa coming at dessert time, carrying a piece of cake to his little Queen.

---

[11] May 23, 1875, when Thérèse was only two and a half.

We accompanied Mama the next day or a few days after to the home of Léonie's little companion.[12] I believe that was the day our good little Mother took us behind a wall to give us a drink of[10]wine after the dinner (which we provided for Mme. Dagoreau), because she didn't want to offend the good woman and didn't want to deprive us of anything. Ah! how delicate a Mother's heart really is, and how it shows its tenderness in a thousand little cares that no one thinks about!

And [15]now I have to speak about my dear Céline, the little companion of my childhood, but the memories here are so numerous I don't know which to choose. I'm going to extract a few passages from letters Mama wrote to you at the Visitation but won't copy them out in full as it would take too long. July 1, 1873, the year of my birth, she said:

[20]"The nurse brought little Thérèse here on Thursday.[13] The little one did nothing but laugh. Céline pleased her especially and she went into peals of laughter with her. One would say she already wants to play, so that will come soon. She holds herself up on her two little legs straight as a post. I believe she will walk very early and she will be very good. She appears very intelligent and has the face of a little cherub."

[7r°] I showed my affection for dear little Céline especially after I came home from the nurse's place. We understood each other very well, only I was much more lively and less naive than she;

---

[12] Armindine Dagoreau. "I remember the poor little girl, Léonie's companion, whom our Mother dressed for her First Communion, following the custom of the better-off families. This child didn't leave Léonie for one minute that day! In the evening she was given the place of honor at the banquet" (Histoire d'une Ame).

[13] Rose Taillé (1836–1908). She lived at Semallé, about eight miles from Alençon. Thérèse was entrusted to her from March 15 or 16, 1873, until April 2, 1874.

although I was three and a half years younger, it seemed to me we were the same age.

[5]Here is a passage from one of Mama's letters showing how good Céline was and how I was just the opposite. "My little Céline is drawn to the practice of virtue; it's part of her nature; she is candid and has a horror of evil. As for the little imp, one doesn't know how things will go, she is so small, so thoughtless! [10]Her intelligence is superior to Céline's, but she's less gentle and has a stubborn streak in her that is almost invincible; when she says *'no'* nothing can make her give in, and one could put her in the cellar a whole day and she'd sleep there rather than say 'yes.'

"But still she has a heart of gold; she is very lovable and frank; [15]it's curious to see her running after me making her confession: 'Mama, I pushed Céline once, I hit her once, but I won't do it again.' (It's like this for everything she does.) Thursday evening we took a walk in the direction of the train station, and she wanted absolutely to go into the waiting room to go and see Pauline; [20]she was running on ahead with a joy that was pleasant to see, but when she saw we had to return without getting on the train to go to visit Pauline, she cried all the way home."[14]

This last part of the letter reminds me of the happiness I experienced when seeing you return from the Visitation; you, dear Mother, took me in your arms and Marie took Céline; then I gave you a thousand hugs and I leaned [7v°] over in order to admire your long braids. Then you gave me a piece of chocolate that you had kept for three months. Can you imagine what a relic that was for me!

I recall also the trip I made to Le Mans;[15] it was my first train ride. [5]What a joy to see myself on a trip alone with Mama. I don't know why

---

[14] Letter to Pauline, May 14, 1876.

[15] March 29, 1875.

I began to cry, but poor little Mother had nothing to introduce to Aunt[16] at Le Mans but a *plain* little girl all red with the tears she shed on the way. I remember nothing about the visit except the moment when Aunt [10]handed me a little white toy mouse and a little cardboard basket filled with candies, on top of which *were enthroned* two pretty sugar rings, just the right size for my finger. Immediately I exclaimed: "How wonderful! there will be a ring for Céline also!" I took my basket by the handle. I gave the other hand to Mama and we left. After a [15]few steps, I looked at my basket and saw that my candies were almost all strewn out on the street like Tom Thumb's pebbles. I looked again more closely and saw that one of the precious rings had undergone the awful fate of the candies. I had nothing now to give to Céline and so was filled with grief! I asked if I could retrace my steps, but [20]Mama seemed to pay no attention to me. This was too much and my *tears* were followed by loud *cries*. I was unable to understand why she didn't share my pain, and this only increased my grief.

Now I return to the letters in which Mama speaks to you about Céline and me. This is the best means I can use to have you understand my character. Here is a passage where my faults shine forth with great brilliance: [8r°] "Céline is playing blocks with the little one, and they argue every once in a while. Céline gives in to gain a pearl for her crown. I am obliged to correct this poor little baby who gets into frightful tantrums; when things don't go just right and according to her way of thinking, she rolls on the floor in desperation like [5]one without any hope. There are times when it gets too much for her and she literally chokes. She's a nervous child, but she is very good, very intelligent, and remembers everything."[17]

---

[16] Sister Marie-Dosithée (Marie-Louise Guérin), older sister of Mme. Martin and a religious at the Visitation Convent at Le Mans.

[17] Letter of Mme. Martin to Pauline, December 5, 1875.

You can see, dear Mother, how far I was from being a faultless little child! They weren't even able to say about me: "She's good when she's asleep" because at night I was [10]more restless than during the day, throwing off the blankets and sending them in all directions and (while still sleeping) banging myself against the wood of my little bed. The pain would awaken me and I'd cry out: "Mama, I *bumped myself!*" Poor little Mother was obliged to get up and convince herself I really had bruises on my forehead, that I really *bumped myself!* She'd cover me up and then go back to bed, [15]but in a short time I would begin *bumping myself* again, so much so they had to tie me in bed. And so every evening, little Céline came to tie me up with a lot of cords that were to prevent the little rascal from *bumping herself* and waking up her Mama; this was so successful a means that I was, from then on, *good* when *sleeping.*

There was another fault I had when wide awake, which [20]Mama doesn't mention in her letters, and this was an excessive self-love. I will give only two examples of this in order not to prolong the recital. One day, Mama said: "Little Thérèse, if you kiss the ground I'll give you a sou." A sou was a fortune at the time and to get it I didn't have to lower my dignity too much, my *little frame* didn't put much of a distance between my lips and the ground. And still my pride revolted at [8v°] the thought of "kissing the ground"; so standing up straight, I said to Mama: "Oh! no, little Mother, I would prefer not to have the sou!"

Another time we had to go to Grogny to Mme. Monnier's home. Mama told Marie to dress me in my Sky-blue frock with the lace trimmings but not to [5]leave my arms bare lest the Sun burn them. I allowed myself to be dressed with the indifference a child of my age should really have, but I thought within myself that I would look much more pretty with my arms bare.

With a nature such as my own, had I been reared by Parents without virtue or even if I had been spoiled by the maid, Louise,[18] as Céline was, I would have become [10]very bad and perhaps have even been lost. But Jesus was watching over His little fiancée; He had willed that all turn out for her good, even her faults that, corrected very early, stood her in good stead to make her grow in perfection. As I had an excessive *self-love* and also a *love* of the *good*, as soon as I began to think seriously (which I did when still very little), it was enough for one to tell me a [15]thing wasn't *good* and I had no desire to repeat it twice.

I see with pleasure that in Mama's letters I gave her great consolation when growing up. Having nothing but good example around me, I naturally wanted to follow it. This is what she wrote in 1876: "Even Thérèse wants to do little acts of penance at times.[19] [20]She's a charming child, very alert, very lively, but she is very sensitive. Céline and she are very fond of each other, and are sufficient unto themselves for passing the time. Every day as soon as they've eaten dinner Céline takes her little rooster; she catches Thérèse's little hen with one swoop of her hand, something I can never do, but she's so lively she gets it in one bound. Then they come with their little pets and sit before the [9r°] fireplace and amuse themselves for long hours at a time. (It was little Rose who gave me the hen and the rooster, and I gave the rooster to Céline.)

"The other day Céline slept with me and Thérèse had slept on the second floor in Céline's bed; she had begged Louise to take her downstairs to dress her. [5]Louise went up to get her but found the bed empty.

---

[18] Louise Marais (1849–1923), maid in the Martin family from 1865 until the death of Mme. Martin.

[19] "It's funny to see Thérèse put her hand in her pocket a hundred times a day to pull a bead of her chaplet every time she makes a sacrifice of some kind" (Histoire d'une Ame).

Thérèse had heard Céline and had come down to be with her. Louise said: 'You don't want to get dressed?' Thérèse answered: 'Oh no! Louise, we are like the two hens, we're inseparable!' Saying this they embraced each other and both held each other tightly. [10]Then in the evening Louise, Céline, and Léonie left for the meeting of the Catholic circle and left little Thérèse all alone. She understood she was too little to go to the meeting and she said: 'If they would only let me sleep in Céline's bed!' But no, they didn't want it, so she said nothing and stayed alone with her little lamp and fifteen minutes [15]later fell into a sound sleep."[20]

Another day Mama wrote: "Céline and Thérèse are inseparable and it's impossible to see two children love each other so much. When Marie comes to get Céline for her classes, poor Thérèse begins to cry. Alas, what's going to become of her, her little friend is leaving! Marie [20]pities her and takes her along too, and the poor little thing sits in a chair for two or three hours on end; she is given some beads to thread or a little piece of cloth to sew, and she doesn't dare budge but heaves deep sighs. When her needle becomes unthreaded, she tries to rethread it; and it's funny to see her, not being able to succeed and still not daring to bother Marie. Soon you can see two big tears rolling down her cheeks. Marie [9v°] consoles her very quickly, threads the needle, and the poor little angel smiles through her tears."[21]

I remember that I really wasn't able to be without Céline. I'd sooner leave the table without taking my dessert than not to [5]follow her as soon as she got up. Begging for help to get down, I would turn in my highchair, and then we would go out and play together. Sometimes we went with the Mayor's little daughter, and I liked this because of the park and all the beautiful toys she showed us. But most

---

[20] Letter of Mme. Martin to Pauline, November 8, 1876.
[21] Ibid., March 4, 1877.

of the time I went there only to please Céline, much [10]preferring to stay in our own little garden to *scrape the walls* and get all the little shiny stones there, then we would go and *sell* them to Papa who bought them from us in *all seriousness.*

On Sunday, as I was too little to go to the services, Mama stayed with me; I was very good, walking around on [15]tiptoe during the Mass; but as soon as I saw the door open, there was an explosion of joy! I would throw myself in front of my *pretty* little sister, "*adorned like a chapel,*"[22] and say: "Oh! little Céline, hurry, give me the blessed bread!" Sometimes she didn't have it because she arrived too late. What to do? I [20]wasn't able to be without it as this was "*my Mass.*" A way was soon found. "You haven't any blessed bread? Then make some!" No sooner said then done. Céline got a chair, opened the cupboard, took the bread, cut off a slice, and then very *gravely* recited a *Hail Mary* over it, and then she gave it to me. After making a sign of the Cross I would eat it with *great devotion,* finding it *tasted* [10r°] the same as the *blessed bread.*

We carried on *spiritual conferences* together frequently. Here is a sample taken from one of Mama's letters: "Our two little dears, Céline and Thérèse, are angels of benediction, little cherubs. Thérèse is the joy and happiness of Marie and even her glory; it's incredible [5]how proud she is of her. It's true she has very rare answers for one her age; she surpasses Céline in this who is twice her age. Céline said the other day: 'How is it that God can be present in a small host?' The little one said: 'That is not surprising, God is all powerful.' 'What does all [10]powerful mean?' 'It means He can do what He wants!'"[23]

---

[22] "An expression my Father used" (note of Mother Agnes).
[23] Letter of Mme. Martin to Pauline, May 10, 1877.

One day, Léonie, thinking she was too big to be playing any longer with dolls, came to us with a basket filled with dresses and pretty pieces for making others; her doll was resting on top. "Here, my little sisters, *choose*; I'm [15]giving you all this." Céline stretched out her hand and took a little ball of wool that pleased her. After a moment's reflection, I stretched out mine saying: "I choose all!" and I took the basket without further ceremony. Those who witnessed the scene saw nothing wrong and even Céline herself didn't dream of complaining (besides, she [20]had all sorts of toys, her godfather gave her lots of presents, and Louise found ways of getting her everything she desired).

This little incident of my childhood is a summary of my whole life; later on when perfection was set before me, I understood that to become *a saint* one had to suffer much, seek out always the most perfect thing to do, and forget self. I understood, too, there were many degrees of perfection and each soul [10v°] was free to respond to the advances of Our Lord, to do little or much for Him, in a word, to *choose* among the sacrifices He was asking. Then, as in the days of my childhood, I cried out: "My God '*I choose all!*' I don't want to be a *saint by halves,* I'm not [5]afraid to suffer for You, I fear only one thing: to keep my *own will*; so take it, for 'I *choose all*' that You will!"

I must stop now. I must speak to you no longer about my infancy but of the little four-year-old Rascal. I remember a dream I must have had around that age and it is still deeply imprinted on my imagination.[10] I dreamed one night I went to take a walk all alone in the garden. When I reached the foot of the steps leading to the garden and which have to be climbed to get into it, I stopped, seized with fright. In front of me, near the arbor, there was a barrel of lime and on this barrel two *frightful little devils* were dancing with surprising agility in spite of the flatirons they had on their feet. All of a sudden [15]they cast fiery glances at me and at the same moment appeared to be more frightened than I was, for they jumped from the barrel and went to hide in the laundry that was just opposite. Seeing they weren't so brave, I wanted to know what they were going to do, and I went up to the window. The poor little devils were there, running on the tables, not knowing what to do [20]to hide from my gaze. Sometimes they approached the window, looking out to see if I was still there and seeing me there they began running like madmen. This dream, I suppose, has nothing extraordinary about it, and still I believe God permitted me to remember it in order to prove to me that a soul in the state of grace has nothing to fear from demons who are cowards, capable of fleeing before the gaze of a little child!

[11r°] Here's another passage I find in Mama's letters. This poor little Mother evidently had a presentiment that the end of her exile was near.[24] "The little ones don't disturb me since both of them are very good; they are very special, and certainly will turn out well. You and Marie will be able to raise them [5]perfectly. Céline never commits the smallest deliberate fault. The little one will be all right too, for she wouldn't tell a lie for all the gold in the world and she has a spirit about her that I have not seen in any of you.[25]

"The other day she was at the grocery store with Céline and Louise. She was talking about her practices. She was doing this rather loudly with Céline and the woman in the store said to Louise: [10]'What does she mean by these little practices? When she's playing in the garden that's all she talks about. Mme. Gaucherin listens at the window trying to understand what this debate about practices means.'

---

[24] Her sickness, cancerous in nature, appeared for the first time in 1865 in a mild form; it got worse in 1876.

[25] Letter to Pauline, March 22, 1877.

"The little one is our whole happiness. She will be good; one can already see the germ of goodness in her. She speaks only about God and wouldn't miss [15]her prayers for anything. I wish you could see her recite the little poems she learned. Never have I seen anything so cute. She gets the exact expression and tone all by herself. But it is especially when she says: 'Little child with the golden hair, where do you believe God is?' When she comes to the words: 'He is up there in the blue heavens,' she raises her eyes with an [20]angelic expression. It's so beautiful that one doesn't grow tired of asking her to recite it, for there is something heavenly in her face!"[26]

How happy I really was at that age, dear Mother! I had already begun to enjoy life; virtue had its charming qualities for me, and I was, it seems to me, in the same dispositions then as I am now, enjoying a firm [11v°] control over my actions.

Ah! how quickly those sunny years passed by, those years of my childhood, but what a sweet imprint they have left on my soul! I recall the days Papa used to bring us to the *pavilion*;[27] the smallest details [5]are impressed in my heart. I recall especially the Sunday walks when Mama used to accompany us. I still feel the profound and *poetic* impressions that were born in my soul at the sight of fields enamelled with *cornflowers* and all types of wild flowers. Already I was in love with the *wide open spaces*. Space and the [10]gigantic fir trees, the

---

[26] Letter of March 4, 1877. In the original French, the actual words of the poem are: "Petit enfant à tête blonde, où crois-tu [donc] qu'est le bon Dieu?" "Il est là-haut dans le Ciel bleu."

[27] The Pavilion was a small piece of property acquired by M. Martin before his marriage, on Rue des Lavoirs (today called Rue du Pavillon Sainte-Thérèse).

branches sweeping down to the ground, left in my heart an impression similar to the one I experience still today at the sight of nature.

We frequently met poor people on these long walks, and it was always little Thérèse who was put in charge of bringing them alms, which made her quite happy. [15]Very often Papa, finding the walk too long for his little Queen, brought her back to the house before the others (which displeased her very much). And to console her, Céline filled her pretty little basket with daisies and gave them to her when she got back; but alas! grandmother[28] found her granddaughter had too many, so she took a large [20]part of them for her statue of the Blessed Virgin. This didn't please little Thérèse, but she kept from saying anything, having got into the habit of not complaining ever, even when they took what belonged to her or when she was accused unjustly. She preferred to be silent and not excuse herself. There was no merit here but natural virtue. What a shame that this good inspiration has vanished!

[12r°] Oh! everything truly smiled upon me on this earth: I found flowers under each of my steps and my happy disposition contributed much to making life pleasant, but a new period was about to commence for my soul. I had to pass through the crucible of trial and to suffer from my childhood in order to [5]be offered earlier to Jesus. Just as the flowers of spring begin to grow under the snow and to expand in the first rays of the sun, so the little flower whose memories I am writing had to pass through the winter of trial.

---

[28] M. Martin's mother, who frequently visited on Sunday.

# *Alençon*

### *Background and Context.*

One winter's night in January, 1895, in Lisieux Carmel, St. Thérèse was reminiscing about old times with her two sisters Pauline (Mother Agnes of Jesus) and Marie (Sister Marie of the Sacred Heart).[1] Perhaps the occasion was in celebration of Thérèse's twenty-third birthday (January 2). But whatever the occasion may have been, Thérèse so delighted her siblings by telling them stories about her childhood that Marie said to Pauline, who was the prioress, "Mother, what a pity that we don't have all that in writing." Pauline recounts what happened next. "'I couldn't ask for anything better, I replied. Then turning to Sister Thérèse, who was laughing at what she took to be a bit of leg-pulling, I said, 'I order you to write down all your childhood memories.' "[2] Pauline had said these words in jest, but Thérèse had taken them seriously. The following January, Thérèse presented to Pauline a copy-book containing her childhood reminiscences. She had not written them for the general public but only for the eyes of her blood sisters. Fortunately, however, her reminiscences were published. What was contained in this copy-book became the first eight chapters (Manuscript A) of one of the greatest spiritual testimonies of all time, *Story of a Soul*.

Thérèse began putting down her reflections soon after Pauline had ordered her to do so; perhaps that very night, even though there are reasons to believe that she began her task toward the end of January.[3] Thérèse did not work from an outline, nor did she go back and rewrite what she had written. With only scraps of time to work, Thérèse put down on paper the memories that came to her mind. If we read *Story of a Soul* carefully, we can see the inner process of Thérèse's mind at work. Just as in conversation, the topic imperceptibly shifts from one subject to another as ideas are triggered in the minds of the speakers, so too did Thérèse's thoughts as she was writing. For example, Thérèse begins her work by telling us that she prayed before the statue of Mary "which has given so many proofs of the maternal preferences ...to our family" (S. 13)*. The word preferences triggered what follows in the next paragraph. "I wondered for a long time why God has preferences, why all souls don't receive an equal amount of graces" (S. 14). Thérèse's puzzlement over the mysterious ways of providence breaks through to a resolution in the next paragraph. "Jesus deigned to teach me this mystery. He set before me the book of nature; I understood how all the flowers He has created are beautiful, how the splendor of the rose and the whiteness of the Lily do not take away from the perfume of the little violet or the delightful simplicity of the daisy" (S. 14).

We should not interpret this linking of thoughts that we see in *Story of a Soul* as merely a  process of free association. Rather it is a stream of consciousness guided by the mind of God. "God acts upon us internally," writes St. Augustine, "where no man has in his own control what shall enter into his thoughts."[4] Thérèse

---

*All quotations of St. Thérèse are taken from the John Clarke O.C.D. translation of her works published by ICS Publications. The abbreviations used in this study are as follows: *Story of a Soul* (this edition) (S), *The Last Conversations* (LC), *The Collected Letters* (L). The number following the letter refers to the page of the ICS edition of the work cited. Thus, (S. 13) refers to page thirteen of *Story of a Soul.*

was deeply attuned to this inner guidance of God's Spirit. "Never have I heard Him speak, but I feel that He is within me at each moment; He is guiding and inspiring me with what I must say and do" (S. 276).

The reason that *Story of a Soul* has so deeply touched the hearts of countless people is that it was born out of God's wisdom. St. John of the Cross writes regarding preaching, which also applies to the written word, that "the better life of the preacher the more abundant the fruit...for the living spirit enkindles fire. But when this spirit is wanting the gain is small, however sublime the style and doctrine. Although it is true that good style, gestures, sublime doctrine, and well-chosen words are more moving and productive of effect when accompanied by this good spirit, yet without it the sermon imparts little or no devotion to the will even though it may be delightful and pleasing to the senses and the intellect." [5] *Story of a Soul* has the power to enkindle devotion in the will because Thérèse's pen was guided by the living spirit of God. Therefore, it should not be read merely for the sake of acquiring information about Thérèse's life or even acquiring a better grasp of her spiritual doctrine. Even though these goals are important, for ignorance of Thérèse's life and teaching can distort her message, they should not be ends in themselves. For as Pascal warns us, "Be aware of knowledge that does not end in love."

This volume of *Story of a Soul* is a "study"edition. I am not using "study" in the academic sense of the word but rather to denote a meditative process. Just as St. John of the Cross writes that the stanzas of his poem *The Spiritual Canticle* were "composed with a certain burning love of God," and, therefore, cannot be understood unless they are "read with the same simplicity of the spirit of knowledge and love they contain," the same holds true for *Story of a Soul.* ⁶ It must be read as it was written, with an attentiveness to the inner promptings of God's Spirit.

### Reflections and Questions.

1. Thérèse begins *Story of a Soul* with a dilemma. She believed that she was under obedience to write down her childhood memories but felt that by doing so "it would distract my heart by too much concentration on myself"(S. 13). Thérèse found a solution to her predicament in *how* she would reflect upon her past. "I am going to write...my *thoughts* on the graces God deigned to grant me" (S. 15). In short, Thérèse chose to look at her life through the lense of what *God* had done for her rather than through the lense of what she had done or failed to do. Thérèse mused upon her life from the vantage point of how God had graced it. In consequence, Thérèse was filled with gratitude. "It seems to me that if a little flower could speak, it would tell simply what God has done for it without trying to hide its blessings" (S. 16).

"It is the spirit of gratitude which draws upon us the overflow of God's grace," said Thérèse, "for no sooner have we thanked Him for one blessing than he hastens to send us ten additional favours in return. Then, when we show our gratitude for these new gifts, He multiplies His benedictions to such a degree that there seems to be a constant stream of divine grace ever coming our way."⁷ The truth contained in Thérèse's words is not that God *sends* more blessings when we are grateful but rather that we become more *aware* of the abundant blessings that we *have*. Cardinal Newman, in his sermon *Remembrance of Past Mercies*, contrasts the characteristic grace of Abraham who looked *forward* in faith, with the distinctive grace of Jacob which "was a habit of affectionate musing upon God's providences toward him in times past...In consequence, he overflowed with gratitude when he looked back upon the past; marveling at the contrast between what he was in himself and what God had been to him." [8]

Similarly, Thérèse writes that "I find myself at a period in my life when I can cast a glance upon my past; my soul has matured in the crucible of exterior and interior trials. And now, like a flower strengthened by the storm, I can raise my head and see the words of Psalm 22 realized in me: 'The Lord is my Shepherd, I shall not want; he makes me lie down in green pastures. He leads me beside still waters; he restores my soul. Even though I walk through the valley of the shadow of death, I fear no evil; for thou art with me...' To me the Lord has always been 'merciful and good, slow to anger and abounding in steadfast love' " (S.15).

*Questions.* There is much wisdom in the old admonition to count one's blessings, for the more we are aware of how much we are blessed by God, the happier we are. Conversely, when we take things for granted, our happiness decreases because our awareness of how much we are blessed is diminished. When was the last time you reflected upon how truly blessed your life is?

2. It is important to realize the vantage point *from which* Thérèse cast a glance upon her past. A year before she began writing *Story of a Soul*, the first signs that she had contracted tuberculosis manifested themselves, and by the time that Thérèse began to write, she had become aware of her impending death. In the same month that she began *Story of a Soul*, Thérèse wrote

to her sister Léonie, "this thought of the brevity of life gives me courage, it helps me bear the weariness of the road...the hour of rest is approaching" (L. 896). Two months later, Thérèse confided to Sr. Teresa of St. Augustine, "I am going to die soon."[9] Thus, Thérèse was looking back over her life with the consciousness of a person about to die.

"When that last hour shall come you will begin to have quite other thoughts of your whole past life." These words taken from *The Imitation of Christ* (Bk.1, chap. 23), a book that Thérèse had committed to memory in her youth, became for her a source of meditation on the vanity and transitoriness of life. When Thérèse was ten years old, she made her "*first entrance* into the *world*" (S. 115) when her family traveled to Alençon and spent their holidays in the châteaus of many of her father's well-to-do friends, who "knew too well how to ally the joys of this earth to the service of God" (S. 116). From Thérèse's perspective, "[t]hey didn't think about *death* enough, and yet *death* had paid its visit to a great number of those whom I knew, the young, the rich, the happy" (S. 116)! In contrast, Thérèse reflected on the vanity of life. " I love to return in spirit to the *enchanting* places where they lived, wondering where these people are, what became of their houses and gardens where I saw them enjoy life's luxuries? And I see that all is vanity and vexation of spirit under the sun, and that the *only good* is to love God with all one's heart and to be *poor in spirit* here on earth" (S. 116). How often have we *heard* the truth that our *only good* is to love God? Yet, in the face of death, we *know* this truth for the first time.

*Questions.* There is no morbidity in Thérèse's observation that "They don't think of *death* enough," for reflection upon our mortality can enhance our appreciation of life. Seeing time against the backdrop of eternity helped shape Thérèse's clear vision of life. Her abiding sense of her own mortality did not distance her from daily life but helped her to focus on what was truly essential. In Muriel Spark's novel *Memento Mori*, a group of septuagenarians and octogenarians begin to receive the same chilling telephone message from a ghostly voice: "Remember you must die." The characters have different reactions to Death's reminder, ranging from fright to anger to accepting the message as an invitation to reflect upon mortality. Henry Mortimer mused, "If I had my life over again I should form the habit of nightly composing myself to thoughts of death. I would practice, as it were, the remembrance of death. There is no other practice which so intensifies life...Without an ever-present sense of death life is insipid. You might as well live on the whites of eggs." [10] To remember entails more than calling a fact to mind; derived from the Latin *rememorari*, it means to be mindful. When we remember that we must die, we *re-member* ourselves, for we become mindful of ourselves as mortals. Just as an awareness of how we are blessed by God increases our gratitude, so too does an awareness of our mortality increase our appreciation of the preciousness of life. How different would your life be if you lived as if today were your last?

3. "Perfection consists in doing His will, in being what He wills us to be" (S. 15), or as Dante wrote, "In his will is our peace." [11] The command "Be ye perfect..." does not enjoin us to strive for a flawless performance in the various tasks of life, but to do them as God wills us. We feel driven to do an A+ job on projects in which we have overinvested our egos. But doing

God's will often demands the courage to do a C+ job because God bids us to spend our time and energy on other tasks.

There is an unhealthy striving for perfection which psychologists call perfectionism. Perfectionism is the state of *being driven* to achieve a standard of perfection in an area of life that is fueled by either the fear of failure or the need for approval. This unhealthy striving is not the type of perfection to which God calls us.

In James Hilton's novel *Goodby, Mr Chips* we see a kind, serene English schoolmaster who is at peace with himself because he has come to accept the person that God has willed him to be.

"[Brookfield] was a good school of the second rank. But if it had not been this sort of school it would probably not have taken Chips. For Chips, in any social or academic sense, was just as respectable, but no more brilliant, than Brookfield itself. It had taken him some time to realize this [because] in his early twenties he was as ambitious as most other young men at such an age. His dream had been to get a headship eventually, or at any rate a senior mastership in a really first-class school; it was only gradually, after repeated trials and failures, that he realized the inadequacy of his qualifications. About 1880, after he had been at Brookfield a decade, he began to recognize that the odds were heavily against his being able to better himself by moving elsewhere; but about that time also, the possibility of staying where he was began to fill a comfortable niche in his mind. At forty, he was rooted, settled, and quite happy." [12]

Just as Mr.Chips came to be at peace with himself when he was able to mourn his unrealistic dreams and accept his vocation as a teacher at Brookfield, so too, we can come to peace only when we accept the unique person that God has called us to be. Thérèse conveys this truth in her analogy of the garden. "I understood how all the flowers He has created are beautiful, how the splendor of the rose and the whiteness of the Lily do not take away from the perfume of the little violet or the simplicity of the daisy. I understood that if all flowers wanted to be roses, nature would lose her springtime beauty, and the fields would no longer be decked out with little wild flowers. And so it is in the world of souls, Jesus' garden. He willed to create great souls comparable to Lilies and roses, but He has created smaller ones and these must be content to be daisies or violets destined to give joy to God's glances when He looks down at His feet. Perfection consists in doing His will, in being what He wills us to be" (S. 15).

*Questions.* Is there some unrealistic or unhealthy goal that you are pursuing that is depriving you of happiness and peace? Is being driven in some area of your life preventing you from being the person that God wills you to be?

4. Of the several incidences from her childhood that Thérèse recounts in this chapter, the most significant is the time Thérèse took the basket that Léonie put before her and Céline, for it symbolizes the whole of Thérèse's life. "This little incident of my childhood is a summary of my whole life; later on when perfection was set before me, I understood that to become *a saint* one had to suffer much, seek out always the most perfect thing to do, and forget self. I understood, too, there were many degrees of perfection and each soul was free to respond to the advances of Our Lord, to do little or much for Him, in a word, to *choose* among the sacrifices He was asking. Then, as in the days of my

childhood, I cried out: "My God 'I *choose all!*' I don't want to be
a *saint by halves,* I'm not afraid to suffer for You, I fear only one
thing: to keep my *own will*; so take it, for '*I choose all*' that you
will" (S. 30).

*Choose!* Thérèse emphasizes this word several times in the
above passage because it is a central reality of life. The great
Scripture scholar William Barclay wrote that "the whole Bible is
one long sermon on the word *Choose*. 'I have set before you life
and death, blessing and curse; therefore *choose* life' (Deut.
30:19). '*Choose* this day whom you will serve' (Josh. 24:15)." [13]
Thérèse sets before us the drama of our lives from which there is
no escape. Like Thérèse, every day we are confronted with
choices either to love or not to love; we too are "free to respond
to the advances of the Lord, to do little or much for Him." Like
Thérèse, the choices that are set before us in daily life summa-
rize who we are, for each of us is a composite of the choices that
we make.

*Questions.* Thérèse's life was like our own; she lived and
worked day in and day out with highly imperfect and flawed
human beings who rubbed her the wrong way. Similarly, in our
daily lives, we all come in contact with people whom we don't
like, perhaps even hate; whom we try to avoid at all cost, and
who we wish would drop off the end of the earth. Yet, these are
the people whom God has entrusted to our care. What made
Thérèse a saint was that she *chose* to love the people whom God
placed upon her path, those whom she was attracted to and those
who repelled her. Who are the people in your life who are difficult to love? In what ways can you choose to love these people
whom God has entrusted to your care?

### Notes

1. Thérèse lived with three of her siblings in Lisieux Carmel, Marie (Sister Marie of the Sacred Heart), Pauline (Mother Agnes of Jesus), and Cèline (Sister Geneviève of the Holy Face). For additional information on members of Thérèse's family, see the *Prologue* of this book.

2. Christopher O'Mahony, ed. and trans. *St. Thérèse of Lisieux: By Those Who Knew Her,* (Dublin: Veritas Publications, 1975), 33.

3. We do not know the exact date that Thérèse began writing *Story of a Soul*; all that Thérèse wrote on the top of the first page is "January 1895." Pauline testified that she ordered Thérèse to write down her childhood memories toward the beginning of January: "One winter's evening early in 1895..." (O'Mahony ibid., 33). Conrad De Meester argues that because Thérèse was occupied in writing her third play *Joan of Arc, Accomplishing Her Mission* for Pauline's feast day (January 21), Thérèse would have only had time to begin writing down her childhood memories toward the end of January. See *The Power of Confidence* by Conrad De Meester, trans. Susan Conroy, (New York: Alba House, 1998), 158-9.

4. St. Augustine, "On the Spirit and the Letter" in *The Essential Augustine*, ed. Vernon J. Bourke, (New York: New American Library, 1961), 22.

5. St. John of the Cross, "The Spiritual Canticle," in *The Collected Works of St. John of the Cross*, trans. Kieran Kavanaugh, O.C.D. and Otilio Rodriguez, O.C.D. (Washington, D.C.: ICS Publications, 1991), 348-9.

6. Ibid., 469.

7. Sr. Geneviève of the Holy Face (Céline Martin), *A Memoir of My Sister St. Thérèse*, trans. Carmelite Sisters of New York (New York: P. J. Kenedy & Sons, 1959), 97.

8. John Henry Newman, "Remembrance of Past Mercies," in *Parochial and Plain Sermons*, (New York: Scribner, Welford, & Co., 1868), volume 5, 76 & 72.

9. O'Mahony, ibid., 192.

10. Muriel Spark, *Momento Mori*, (New York: Avon Books, 1990), 156.

11. Dante, *The Paradiso*, trans. John Ciardi, (New York: The New American Library, 1970), canto 3, line 85, p. 48.

12. James Hilton, *Goodbye, Mr. Chips*, (New York: Bantam Books, 1962), 10-11.

13. William Barclay, *The King and the Kingdom*, (Grand Rapids: Baker Book House, 1968), 152.

# Chapter II

# *LES BUISSONNETS*
# *(1877–1881)*

Her Mother's Death
Lisieux
Her Father's Tenderness
First Confession
Feasts and Sundays with the Family
Prophetic Vision
Trouville

All the details of my Mother's illness are still present to me and I recall especially the last weeks she spent on earth. Céline and I [10]were like two poor little exiles, for every morning Mme. Leriche[29] came to get us and brought us to her home where we spent the day. One morning we didn't have time to say our prayers and during the trip Céline whispered: "Should we tell her we didn't say our prayers?" "Oh! yes," I answered. So very timidly Céline told Mme. Leriche, [15]who said: "Well, my little girls, you will say them," and placing us both in a large room, she left. Céline looked at me and we said: "Oh! this is not like Mama! She always had us say our prayers with her."

When we were playing with the children, the thought of our dear Mother was with us constantly. Once Céline was given a beautiful apricot, and [20]she bent down and said to me: "We are not going to eat it; I will give it to Mama." Alas, poor little Mother was already too sick to eat the fruits of the earth; she was *to be satisfied* only in heav-

---

[29] "Our cousin through her marriage with M. Leriche, nephew of our Father; he took over Father's jewelry shop on Rue Pont-Neuf, Alençon, 1870" (Note of Mother Agnes of Jesus).

en with God's *glory* and was *to drink* the mysterious wine He spoke
about at the Last Supper, saying He would share it with us in His
Father's Kingdom.[30]

The touching ceremony of the last anointing is also deeply
impressed on my mind. I can still see the spot where I was by Céline's
side. All five of us were [12v°] lined up according to age, and Papa
was there too, sobbing.

The day of Mama's departure or the day after,[31] Papa took me
in his arms and said: "Come, kiss your poor little Mother for the last
time." Without a word I placed my lips on her forehead. [5]I don't
recall having cried very much, neither did I speak to anyone about the
feelings I experienced. I looked and listened in silence. No one had
any time to pay any attention to me, and I saw many things they
would have hidden from me. For instance, once I was standing before
the lid of the coffin which had been placed upright in the hall. I
stopped for a long time gazing at it. [10]Though I'd never seen one
before, I understood what it was. I was so little that in spite of
Mama's small stature, I had to raise my head to take in its full height.
It appeared *large* and *dismal*.

Fifteen years later, I was to stand before another coffin, Mother
Geneviève's.[32] It was similar in size. I imagined myself back once
again in the [15]days of my childhood and all those memories flooded
into my mind. True, it was the same Thérèse who looked, but she'd
*grown up* and the coffin appeared smaller. I had no need to *raise* my
head to see and, in fact, no longer *raised* it but to contemplate *heaven*

---

[30] Matthew 26:29.

[31] Mme. Martin died at 1:00 a.m., August 28, 1877.

[32] Mother Geneviève of St. Teresa, one of the foundresses of the
Lisieux Carmel.

which to me was *filled with joy*. All my trials had come to an end and the winter of my soul had passed on [20]forever.

The day the Church blessed the mortal remains of our dear Mother, now in heaven, God willed to give me another mother on earth. He willed also that I choose her freely. All five of us were gathered together, looking at each other sadly. Louise was there too, and, seeing Céline and me, she said: "Poor little things, you have no mother any more!" Céline threw her arms around Marie saying: "Well, you will be my Mama!" Accustomed to following [13r°] Céline's example, I turned instead to you, Mother, and as though the future had torn aside its veil, I threw myself into your arms, crying: "Well, as for me, it's Pauline who will be my Mama!"

As I've already said, it's from the end of this phase in my [5]life that I entered the second period of my existence, the most painful of the three, especially since the entrance into Carmel of the one whom I chose as my second "Mama." This period extends from the age of four and a half to that of fourteen, the time when I found once again my *childhood* character, and entered more and more into[10] the serious side of life.

I must admit, Mother, my happy disposition completely changed after Mama's death. I, once so full of life, became timid and retiring, sensitive to an excessive degree. One look was enough to reduce me to tears, and the only [15]way I was content was to be left alone completely. I could not bear the company of strangers and found my joy only within the intimacy of the family.

And still I continued to be surrounded with the most delicate *tenderness*. Our Father's *very affectionate* heart seemed to be enriched now with a [20]truly maternal love! You and Marie, Mother, were you not *the most tender* and selfless of mothers? Ah! if God had not showered His beneficent *rays* upon His little flower, she could never have accustomed herself to earth, for she was too weak to stand up against the rains and the storms. She needed warmth, a gentle dew, and the springtime breezes. Never were [13v°] these lacking. Jesus had her find them beneath the snow of trial!

I experienced no regret whatsoever at leaving Alençon; children are fond of change, and it was with pleasure that I came to Lisieux.[33] I recall the trip, our arrival at Aunt's home; and I can still picture [5]Jeanne and Marie waiting for us at the door. I was very fortunate in having such nice little cousins. I loved them very much, as also Aunt and especially Uncle; however, he frightened me, and I wasn't as much at ease in his home as I was at Les Buissonnets,[34] for there my life was truly happy.

In the morning you used to come to me and [10]ask me if I had raised my heart to God, and then you dressed me. While dressing me you spoke about Him and afterward we knelt down and said our

---

[33] On November 15, 1877, M. Martin decided to live at Lisieux in order to bring his daughters in closer contact with his wife's family. M. and Mme. Guérin had two children: Jeanne, who was nine, and Marie, seven. M. Guérin owned a pharmacy at Place St. Pierre.

[34] *Histoire d'une Ame* states: "The next day, November 16, we were brought to our new home, Les Buissonnets, which was situated in a quiet section next to a park named 'Jardin de l'Étoile.' The house appeared very charming to me: a belvédère from which a view extended far into the distance, an English garden in front, and a large vegetable garden in the rear of the house, all this was a new joy to my young imagination. In fact, this smiling habitation became the theatre of many sweet joys and unforgettable family scenes. Elsewhere, as I said above, I was an exile, I wept, I felt I no longer had a mother! There, my heart expanded and I smiled once more at life."

prayers together. The reading lesson came later and the first word I was able to read without help was "heaven." My dear godmother took charge of the writing lessons and you, Mother, all the rest. I enjoyed no great facility in learning, [15]but I did have a very good memory. Catechism and sacred history were my favorite subjects and these I studied with joy. Grammar frequently caused me to shed many tears. You no doubt recall the trouble I had with the masculine and feminine genders!

As soon as my classes were over, I climbed up to the belvédère[35] and showed my badge and my marks to Papa. How happy I was when I could[20]say: "I got *full marks*, and it's *Pauline* who said so *first!*" For when I asked you if I had five full marks and until you said "Yes," the marks seemed lower in my own eyes. You gave me points for good conduct and when I collected a certain number I got a prize and a free day. I recall these free days [14r°] seemed longer than the others; this pleased you as it was a sign I didn't like being idle. Each afternoon I took a walk with Papa. We made our visit to the Blessed Sacrament together, [5]going to a different church each day, and it was in this way we entered the Carmelite chapel for the first time. Papa showed me the choir grille and told me there were nuns behind it. I was far from thinking at that time that nine years later I would be in their midst!

After the walk (during which Papa bought me a little [10]present worth a few sous) we returned to the house; then I did my homework and the rest of the time I stayed in the garden with Papa, jumping around, etc., for I *didn't know* how to play with dolls. It was a great joy for me to prepare mixtures with little seeds and pieces of bark I found on the ground, and I'd bring them to Papa [15]in a pretty little

---

[35] The belvédère was the little summer room on the top floor where M. Martin used to study.

cup. Poor Papa stopped all his work and with a smile he pretended to drink. Before giving me back the cup he'd ask me (on the sly) if he should throw the contents out. Sometimes I would say "Yes," but more frequently I carried away my precious mixture, wanting to use it several times.

I loved cultivating my little flowers [20]in the garden Papa gave me. I amused myself, too, by setting up little altars in a niche in the middle of the wall. When I completed my work, I ran to Papa and dragged him over, telling him to close his eyes and not open them till I told him. He did all I asked him to do and allowed himself to be led in front of my little garden, then I'd cry out: "Papa, open your eyes!" He would open them [14v°] and then go into an ecstasy to please me, admiring what I believed was really a masterpiece! I would never come to an end if I really wanted to portray a thousand little actions like this which crowd into my memory. How could I possibly express the tenderness which *"Papa"* showered upon his [5]little queen? There are things the heart feels but which the tongue and even the mind cannot express.

They were beautiful days for me, those days when my "dear King" took me fishing with him. I was very fond of the countryside, flowers, birds, etc. Sometimes I would try to fish with my little line, but I preferred to go *alone* and [10]sit down on the grass bedecked with flowers, and then my thoughts became very profound indeed! Without knowing what it was to meditate, my soul was absorbed in real prayer. I listened to distant sounds, the murmuring of the wind, etc. At times, the indistinct notes of some military music reached me where I was, filling my heart with a sweet melancholy. Earth then seemed to be a place of exile and I could dream only of [15]heaven.

The afternoon sped by quickly and soon we had to return to Les Buissonnets. Before leaving, I would take the lunch I had brought in my little basket. The *beautiful* bread and jam you had prepared had changed its appearance: instead of the lively colors it had earlier, I now saw only a light rosy tint and the bread had become old and crumbled. [20]Earth again seemed a sad place and I understood that in heaven alone joy will be without any clouds.

Speaking of clouds, I remember one day when the beautiful blue sky became suddenly overcast and soon the thunder began to roll and the lightning to flash through the dark clouds. I saw it strike a short distance away, and, far from being frightened, I was thrilled with delight because God [15r°] seemed to be so close! Papa, however, was not as delighted as his little Queen. It wasn't because the storm frightened him but because the grass and the tall daisies (taller than I) were beginning to sparkle with precious stones. We had to cross several fields before coming to [5]a road, and Papa, fearing the diamonds would soak his little girl, picked her up and carried her on his back in spite of his bundle of lines.

During the walks I took with Papa, he loved to have me bring alms to the poor we met on the way. On one occasion we [10]met a poor man who was dragging himself along painfully on crutches. I went up to give him a coin. He looked at me with a sad smile and refused my offering since he felt he wasn't poor enough to accept alms. I cannot express the feeling that went through my heart. I wanted to console this man and [15]instead I had given him pain or so I thought. The poor invalid undoubtedly guessed at what was passing through my mind, for I saw him turn around and smile at me. Papa had just bought me a little cake, and I had an intense desire to give it to him, but I didn't dare. However, I really wanted to give him something he couldn't refuse, so great was the sympathy I felt toward him. I [20]remembered having heard that on our First Communion Day we can obtain whatever we ask for, and this thought greatly consoled me. Although I was only six years old at this time, I said: "I'll pray for this poor man the day of my First Communion." I kept my promise five years later, and I hope God answered the prayer He inspired me to direct to Him in favor of one of His suffering members.

[15v°] I loved God very much and offered my heart to Him very often, making use of the little formula Mother had taught me. However, one evening in the beautiful month of May I committed a fault that merits the penalty of being confessed. It gave me [5]good reason to humble myself and I believe I had perfect contrition for it.

Since I was too little to attend May devotions, I remained at home with Victoire,[36] carrying out my devotions with her before *my little May altar*. This I had arranged according to my taste; everything was so small, the candlestick, the flower pots, etc. *Two tapers* lit it up perfectly. Sometimes Victoire [10]would surprise me with a gift of two candle stubs. But this was rare. All was in readiness one evening for us to commence our prayers, so I said to her: "Victoire, will you begin the Memorare? I'm going to light the tapers." She pretended to begin but said nothing and looked at me, laughing. I watched my *precious tapers* burning away rapidly and [15]begged her to recite the prayer, but she still said nothing. Then rising from my knees, I shouted at her and told her she was very wicked. Laying aside my customary gentleness, I stamped my foot with all my might. Poor Victoire stopped laughing. She looked at me in amazement and then showed me the two candle stubs she'd brought along. [20]After shedding tears of anger, I poured out tears of repentance, having a firm purpose of not doing it again!

Another time there was another incident with Victoire, but this time I had no repentance because I had kept calm. I wanted an inkstand that was on the shelf of the fireplace in the kitchen; being too lit-

---

[36] Victoire Pasquier was a servant of the Martin family at Lisieux.

tle to take it down, I very *nicely* asked Victoire to [16r°] give it to me, but she refused, telling me to get up on a chair. I took a chair without saying a word but thinking she wasn't too nice; wanting to make her feel it, I searched out in my little head what offended me the most. She often called me [5]"a little brat" when she was annoyed at me and this humbled me very much. So *before jumping off* my chair, I turned around with *dignity* and said: "Victoire, you are a brat!" Then I made my escape, leaving her to meditate on the profound statement I had just made. The result wasn't long in coming, for soon I heard her shouting: "M'amz'elle Marie Thérèse just [10]called me a brat!" Marie came and made me ask pardon, and I did so without having contrition. I thought that if Victoire didn't want to stretch her *big arm* to do me a *little service*, she merited the title *brat*.

And still Victoire was very fond of me and I was also fond of her. One day, she drew me out of a *great peril* into which I had [15]tumbled through my own fault. She was ironing the clothes and she had at her side a bucket filled with water. I was watching her and at the same time swinging on a chair, which was a habit of mine. All of a sudden, the chair slipped from under me and I fell, not on the floor, but into the bucket! My feet met my head and I filled the bucket like a little [20]chick fills an eggshell! Poor Victoire gaped at me with great surprise, having never seen anything like it in her life. I wanted to extricate myself from my bucket as quickly as possible, but impossible! My prison fit me so perfectly I couldn't make a single move. With a little trouble she saved me from my *great peril* but not my dress and all the rest of my clothes which she had to change. I was soaked to the skin!

Another time I fell into the fireplace where fortunately there was no fire [16v°] lighted at the time. Victoire had to draw me out and shake off the ashes that covered me completely. These incidents hap-pened to me on a Wednesday when you were at singing practice with

Marie. It was on Wednesday also that Father Ducellier[37] came to pay
a visit. Victoire[5]told him nobody was home except Thérèse, and so he
came out into the *kitchen* to see me and look over my homework; I
was very proud to receive my *confessor*, for I had made my first confession to him a short time before. What a sweet memory for me!

Oh! dear Mother, with what care you prepared me for my first
confession, [10]telling me it was not to a man but to God I was about to
tell my sins; I was very much convinced of this truth. I made my confession in a great spirit of faith, even asking you if I had to tell Father
Ducellier I loved him with all my heart as it was to God in person I
was speaking.

[15]Well instructed in all I had to say and do, I entered the confessional and knelt down. On opening the grating Father Ducellier saw
no one. I was so little my head was below the arm-rest. He told me to
stand up. Obeying instantly, I stood and faced him directly in order to
[20]see him perfectly, and I made my confession like a *big girl* and
received his blessing with *great devotion* for you had told me that at
the moment he gave me absolution the *tears of Jesus* were going to
purify my soul. I remember the first exhortation directed to me. Father
encouraged me to be devout to the Blessed Virgin and I promised
myself to redouble my tenderness for her.[38] Coming out of the confessional I was so happy and light-hearted that I had never felt so much
joy in my [17r°] soul. Since then I've gone to confession on all the

---

[37] Priest at the Cathedral of Saint-Pierre at Lisieux.

[38] "I then passed my rosary through to have him bless it. It was evening
and on the way home when we passed under a street light I looked at
it from all sides. 'What are you looking at, Thérèse?' you asked. 'I want
to see what a blessed rosary looks like.' This amused you. I remained
a long time affected by the grace I received" *(Histoire d'une Ame)*.

great feasts, and it was truly a *feast* for me each time.

The *feasts!* what memories this word brings back to me. How I loved the *feasts!* You knew how to explain all the mysteries [5]hidden under each, and you did it so well that they were truly heavenly days for me. I loved above all the processions in honor of the Blessed Sacrament. What a joy it was for me to throw flowers beneath the feet of God! Before allowing them to fall to the ground, I threw them as high as I could and I was never so happy as when I saw my roses *touch* the sacred monstrance.

[10]If the big feasts were rare, each week brought one that was very dear to my heart, namely Sunday! What a day Sunday was for me! It was God's feast day, and feast of *rest*. First, I stayed in *bed* longer than on the other days; then Pauline spoiled her little girl by bringing her some chocolate to drink while still in *bed* and then she [15]dressed her up like a little Queen. Marie came to curl her hair and Thérèse was not always nice when Marie pulled her hair. Afterward she was very happy to take the hand of her *King* who on that day kissed her more tenderly than usual. The whole family then went off to Mass.

All along the way to church and even in the church [20]Papa's little Queen held his hand. Her place was by his side, and when we had to go down into the body of the church to listen to the sermon, two chairs had to be found side by side. This wasn't too difficult, for everyone seemed to think it so wonderful to see such a *handsome* old man with such a *little daughter* that they went out of their way to give them their places. Uncle, sitting in the warden's pews, was always happy to see us come. He used to call me his little [17v°] ray of sunshine.

I wasn't too disturbed at being looked at by people. I listened attentively to the sermons which I understood very poorly. The first I *did understand* and which *touched me deeply* was a sermon on the Passion preached by Father Ducellier and since then I've [5]understood all the others. When the preacher spoke about St. Teresa, Papa leaned over and whispered: "Listen carefully, little Queen, he's talking about your Patroness." I did listen carefully, but I looked more frequently at Papa than at the preacher, for his *handsome* face said so much to me! His eyes, at times, were filled with *tears* which he tried in vain to [10]stop; he seemed no longer held by earth, so much did his soul love to lose itself in the eternal truths. His earthly course, however, was far from completed; long years had to pass by before heaven opened to his enraptured eyes and the Lord would wipe the *tears* from the eyes of His good and faithful servant!

[15]I return once more to my Sundays. This *joyous* day, passing all too quickly, had its tinge of *melancholy*. I remember how my happiness was unmixed until Compline.[39] During this prayer, I would begin thinking that the day of *rest* was coming to an end, that the morrow would bring with it the necessity of beginning life over again, we would have to go back [20]to work, to learning lessons, etc., and my heart felt the exile of this earth. I longed for the everlasting repose of heaven, that never-ending *Sunday* of the *Fatherland!*

The walks we took on Sundays before returning to Les Buissonnets left a feeling of sadness in my soul, for then the family was not complete. Papa, to please Uncle, used to permit Marie or Pauline to spend Sunday evenings at his home; [18r°] I was happy when I was there with one of them. I preferred this to being invited all alone because then they paid less attention to me. I listened with great pleasure to all Uncle had to say, but I didn't like it when he asked me questions. I was very much [5]frightened when he placed me on his knee and sang Blue Beard in a formidable tone of voice. I was happy to see Papa coming to fetch us. When we were on the way home, I

---

[39] The liturgical night prayer of the Church.

would gaze upon the *stars* that were twinkling ever so peacefully in the skies and the sight carried me away. There was especially one cluster of *golden pearls* that attracted my attention and gave me great joy [10]because they were in the form of a -T-. I pointed them out to Papa and told him my name was written in heaven. Then desiring to look no longer upon this dull earth, I asked him to guide my steps; and not looking where I placed my feet I threw back my head, giving myself over completely [15]to the contemplation of the star-studded firmament!

What shall I say of the winter evenings at home, especially the Sunday evenings? Ah! how I loved, after the *game of checkers* was over, to sit with Céline on Papa's knees.[40] He used to sing, in his beautiful voice, airs that filled the soul with profound thoughts, or else, [20]rocking us gently, he recited poems that taught the eternal truths. Then we all went upstairs to say our night prayers together and the little Queen was alone near her King, having only to look at him to see how the saints pray. When prayer was ended we came according to age to bid Papa good night and receive his kiss; the *Queen* naturally came last and the *King* [18v°] took her by the two *elbows* to kiss her and she would cry out in a high-pitched tone: "Good night, Papa, good night and sleep well!" Every evening was a repetition of the same thing.

Then my little Mama took me in her arms and brought me to Céline's bed. I would say: "Was I very [5]good today, Pauline? Will the *little angels fly around me?*" The answer was invariably "Yes," otherwise I would have cried the whole night. After she and Marie had kissed me, *Pauline* went downstairs and poor little Thérèse was left all alone in the dark; in vain did she [10]picture the *little angels flying around her*; fright soon took over, the darkness filled her with fear, for she could no longer see the stars twinkling away serenely.

---

[40] Marie or Pauline read from Dom Gueranger's *Liturgical Year*; then a few pages of an interesting and instructive book.

I consider the overcoming of my fears as a grace I received through you, dear Mother; you used to send me [15]in the evening to a far-off room in search of an object. Had I not been so well guided, I would have been very nervous, whereas now it is difficult to frighten me. I wonder at times how you were able to raise me with so much *love* and tenderness without spoiling me, for it's true you never allowed an [20]imperfection to pass, you *never* scolded me without a reason, and you never went back on something once you made a decision. I knew this so well, I wouldn't have been able nor would I have wanted to do anything you had forbidden. Papa himself was obliged to conform to your will, for without *Pauline's* consent I didn't even take a walk, and when Papa told me to come I'd answer: "*Pauline* doesn't want it." [19r°] Then he'd come and ask your permission and to please him, Pauline would say "Yes," but little Thérèse saw by her look that she wasn't saying it with all her heart, and she'd begin to cry and would not be consoled until Pauline said "Yes" and *kissed her with all her heart!*

[5]When little Thérèse was sick, which happened every winter,[41] it isn't possible to explain the maternal tenderness she received. Pauline then made her sleep in her bed (incomparable favor) and gave her everything she wanted. One day Pauline drew a *beautiful little knife* from under her pillow and giving it to her little girl [10]left her in an indescribable ecstasy. "Ah! Pauline," she cried, "you love me so much you're willing to deprive yourself of your little knife with the *mother of pearl star!* Since you love me so much, would you sacrifice your *watch* to prevent me from *dying?*" — "I would give you [15]my

---

[41] "The colds turned into bronchitis, but later this was cured completely. At Carmel she hardly ever had colds" (note of Mother Agnes of Jesus.).

watch not only to prevent you from dying, but to see you get well soon I'd sacrifice it immediately." When I heard Pauline's words, my astonishment and gratitude were so great I couldn't express them. In the summer, I had stomach aches at times, and Pauline again took tender care of me. To amuse me she [20]*would drive* me all around the garden in a *wheelbarrow* and then, making me get off, she'd put in a little daisy plant and *drive* this *very carefully* to my little garden where she'd plant it with great ceremony.

It was Pauline, too, who received all my intimate confidences and cleared up all my doubts. Once I was surprised that God didn't [19v°] give equal glory to all the Elect in heaven, and I was afraid all would not be perfectly happy. Then Pauline told me to fetch Papa's large tumbler and set it alongside my thimble and filled both to the brim with water. She asked me which one was fuller. I told her [5]each was as full as the other and that it was impossible to put in more water than they could contain. My dear Mother helped me understand that in heaven God will grant His Elect as much glory as they can take, the last having nothing to envy in the first. And it was in this way that you brought the most sublime mysteries down to my level of understanding and [10]were able to give my soul the nourishment it needed.

How glad I was to see the day of the distribution of prizes arrive each year! In this as in all other matters, *justice* was strictly observed and I received only the rewards I deserved. All alone, standing before the *august assembly*, I listened to my sentence being read by "the King of France and Navarre"; my heart [15]was beating rapidly as I received my prizes and the crown. It was like a picture of the Last Judgment! Immediately after the distribution, the little Queen took off her white dress and they quickly dressed her in disguise in order to take part in the *grand pageant* that followed.

Ah! how joyous were these family feasts! How far I was [20]then from foreseeing the trials awaiting my dear King when seeing him so happy! One day, however, God showed me in a truly extraordinary *vision* the *living* image of the trial He was pleased to prepare for us in advance.[42]

Papa was on a trip for several days and was not expected to return for [20r°] two more days. It could have been about two or three o'clock in the afternoon; the sun was shining brightly and all nature seemed to be rejoicing. I was all alone at the window of an attic which faced the large garden; I was looking straight ahead, my mind occupied with joyful thoughts, when I saw a man dressed exactly like Papa standing in front of [5]the laundry which was just opposite. The man had the same height and walk as Papa, only he was *much more stooped*. His head was covered with a sort of apron of indistinct color and it hid his face. He wore a hat similar to Papa's. I saw him walking at a regular pace along [10]my little garden. Immediately a feeling of supernatural fright invaded my soul, but in an instant I reflected that surely Papa had returned and was hiding to surprise me; then I called out very loudly— "Papa! Papa!"—my voice trembling with emotion. But the mysterious personage, appearing not to hear, continued his steady pace without [15]even turning around. Following him with my eyes, I saw him go toward the grove that divides the wide path in two, and I waited to see him reappear on the other side of the tall trees, but the prophetic vision had vanished! All this lasted but an instant but was engraved so deeply on my heart that today, after fifteen years, it is as present to me as though I were still seeing the vision [20]before my eyes.

---

[42] This vision took place in broad daylight, not in a dream; it occurred in the summer of 1879 or 1880. He was on business trip at Alençon.

Marie was with you, Mother, in a room adjoining the one where I was; hearing me call Papa, she experienced fright also, feeling, as she told me later, that something extraordinary must have happened. Without allowing me to see her emotion, she ran to me and asked what possessed me to call Papa, who was still at Alençon. I [20v°] told her what I had just seen. To calm me down, Marie said it was no doubt Victoire who hid her head in her apron to frighten me, but when asked about it, Victoire said she hadn't left her kitchen. Besides, I was very sure I'd seen a man and this man [5]had Papa's appearance. Then all three of us went behind the screen of trees, but when we found no mark indicating the passage of anyone, you told me to think no more about it.

It was not within my power to think no more about it. Very often my imagination presented again the mysterious scene I had witnessed. Very often, too, [10]I tried to lift the veil that was hiding its meaning from me because I kept in the bottom of my heart the conviction that this vision had a meaning which was one day to be revealed to me. That day was a long time in coming; but after fourteen years God Himself tore away the mysterious veil.

I had permission to be with Sister Marie of the Sacred Heart,[43] and we were talking as [15]always about the things of the other life and our childhood memories. I recalled to her the vision I had seen at the age of six or seven, and all of a sudden, while I was describing the details of the strange scene, we understood simultaneously what it meant. It was indeed *Papa* whom I had seen advancing, bent over with age. It was indeed Papa, who was bearing on his venerable counte-

---

[43] According to a custom then in usage in Carmel, the Sisters had "permission" on certain feast days to converse privately with one another.

nance and [20]white hair the symbol of his *glorious* trial.[44] Just as the adorable Face of Jesus was veiled during His Passion, so the face of His faithful servant had to be veiled in the days of his sufferings in order that it might shine in the heavenly Fatherland near its Lord, the Eternal Word!

It is from the midst of this ineffable glory where he reigns in heaven that our dear Father obtained for us the grace to understand the vision [21r°] his little Queen had at an age when illusions are not to be feared. It is from the midst of glory he obtained this sweet consolation of understanding that God, ten years before our great trial, was already showing it to us. He was doing this as a Father who gives His children a glimpse of the [5]glorious future He is preparing for them and is pleased to have them consider in advance the priceless riches which will be their heritage.

Ah! why was it to me that God gave this light? Why did He show such a small child a thing she couldn't understand, a thing which, if she had understood, would have [10]made her die of grief? Why? This is one of the mysteries we shall understand only in heaven and which we shall eternally admire!

How good God really is! How He parcels out trials only according to the strength He gives us. Never, as I've said already, [15]would I have been able to bear even the thought of the bitter pains the future held in store for me. I wasn't even able to think of Papa *dying* without trembling. Once he had climbed to the top of a ladder and as I was standing directly below, he cried out: "Move away, little one, if I fall, I'll crush you!" When I heard this, [20]I experienced an interior revulsion

---

[44] The paralysis that affected M. Martin's mental faculties during the five last years of his life and necessitated a stay in the psychiatric hospital. See chapter 7 for more details.

and instead of moving away I clung to the ladder, thinking: "At least, if Papa falls, I'll not have the grief of seeing him die; I'll die with him!"

I cannot say how much I loved Papa; everything in him caused me to admire him. When he explained his ideas to me (as though I were a big girl), I told him very simply that surely if he said this [21v°] to the great men of the government, they would take him to make him *King*, and then France would be happy as it had never been before. But in the bottom of my heart I was happy that it was only myself who [5]*knew* Papa *well*, for if he became *King of France and Navarre*, I knew he would be unhappy because this is the lot of all monarchs; but above all he would no longer be my King alone!

I was six or seven years old when Papa brought us to Trouville.[45] Never will I [10]forget the impression the sea made upon me; I couldn't take my eyes off it since its majesty, the roaring of its waves, everything spoke to my soul of God's grandeur and power. I recall during the walk on the seashore a man and a woman were looking at me as I ran [15]ahead of Papa. They came and asked him if I were his little daughter and said I was a very pretty little girl. Papa said, "Yes," but I noticed the sign he made to them not to pay me any compliments. It was the first time I'd heard it said I was pretty and this pleased me as I didn't think I was. You always [20]took great care, Mother, to allow me to come in contact with nothing that could destroy my innocence, and you saw to it, too, that I heard nothing capable of giving rise to vanity in my heart. As I listened to what you and Marie said, and as you had never directed any compliments to me, I gave no great importance to the words or admiring glances of this woman.

[22r°] In the evening at that moment when the sun seems to bathe itself in the immensity of the waves, leaving a *luminous trail*

---

[45] August 8, 1878; Thérèse was only five years and eight months old.

behind, I went and sat down on the huge rock with *Pauline*. Then I recalled the touching story of the "Golden Trail."[46] I contemplated [5]this luminous trail for a long time. It was to me the image of God's grace shedding its light across the path the little white-sailed vessel had to travel. And near Pauline, I made the resolution never to wander far away from the glance of Jesus in order to travel peacefully toward the eternal shore!

My life passed by tranquilly and happily. The affection with which I was [10]surrounded at Les Buissonnets helped me grow. I was undoubtedly big enough now to commence the struggle, to commence knowing the world and the miseries with which it was filled.

[46] This story appears in a collection of readings called *La Tirelire aux histoires* by Madame Louise Belloc. This meditation, though, didn't take place on the 8th of August, 1878, but on another occasion sometime between 1879 and 1881.

# *Les Buissonnets*

## Background and Context.

In 1865, Zélie Martin noticed a swelling in her breast. For eleven long years, her condition was not taken seriously by doctors until it was too late. She was diagnosed with incurable breast cancer. Toward the end, when Zélie's pain was so great that she could no longer repress her cries, Thérèse and Céline (ages 4 and 7 respectively) were removed from the Martin household during the day. They spent the day at the home of Mme. Leriche, Mr. Martin's niece by marriage. Zélie's death was a brutal shock for Thérèse. It so traumatized her that Thérèse withdrew into herself and clung to her family.

On her death bed, Zélie gave her last look neither to her husband nor any of her children but to her sister-in-law Céline Guérin. "I believed that I understood that look" [Céline Guérin wrote to Thérèse] "which nothing will be able to make me forget. It is engraved within my heart. Since that day, I have tried to replace her whom God had taken away from you, but, alas! nothing can replace a Mother"(L. 745)! Céline Guérin understood that Zélie was asking her to take care of her children. The Guérins took this request very seriously. Isidore Guérin was named the deputy guardian of the Martin children, and the Guérins proposed to the Martins that they move to Lisieux where they lived. The Martins agreed.

The move to Lisieux proved to be a good one for the Martin family. Both *Story of a Soul* and the family correspondence paint an idyllic picture of the Martin family during its early years in Lisieux. Thérèse's account of herself during this time gives the impression that these were some of the happiest years of her life.

The whole atmosphere that surrounded the Martin family in Lisieux was much more joyous and serene than the one they had lived in at Alençon. What made the difference? There is no one factor that accounts for this change, for a psychic atmosphere like a physical one is composed of many particles. Let us explore some of the elements that constituted the new atmosphere that the Martin family enjoyed in Lisieux.

Before the Martin family arrived in Lisieux, Isidore procured a spacious well-lighted house for them to rent. It was cloistered by a ring of trees and walls, and sequestered on the outskirts of town. "From the house you are not seen from any direction," wrote Isidore to Louis, "and you see no road but simply a delightful panorama of the town"(L. 128). What added to this contemplative atmosphere was the beauty of the grounds. "It is a charming house, cheerful and gay," wrote Marie to her father, " with a large garden in which Céline and Thérèse will be able to play" (L. 130). Their new home, which was promptly christened Les Buissonnets ("little bushes") by the Martin children because of the little bushes that surrounded the house, was adjacent to a beautiful spacious park, the *Jardin de l'Etoile* which was a source of sheer delight for Thérèse. "This baby loves flowers so much...she's very soon going to pick all there are of lilies of the valley in the *"jardin de l'Etoile"* (L. 135). Thérèse, who was deeply nourished by the beauty of nature, came home to herself at Les Buissonnets.

Not only was Les Buissonnets sequestered from public view, so was the Martin family. Except for church functions, the Martins rarely participated in the social life of Lisieux. They spend most evenings at home gathered around the family hearth listening to Louis either singing, reading from Dom Guéranger's

*The Liturgical Year*, or reciting "...from memory long passages [of poetry] principally from Lamartine and Victor Hugo." [1]

The peaceful, bucolic atmosphere that permeated Les Buissonnets was in stark contrast to the noisy urban atmosphere that had surrounded the Martin household in Alençon. Their house opened on to a busy city street and was a thoroughfare for customers and employees associated with Zélie's lace business. Because their living space was also a place of employment, privacy and silence were at a premium.

Thérèse lived a very sheltered life and an overprotected existence at Les Buissonnets, yet, that is what she needed to survive those early years that immediately followed her mother's death. "Ah! If God had not showered His beneficent rays upon His little flower," writes Thérèse, commenting on her family's care for her after the death of her mother, "she could never have accustomed herself to earth, for she was too weak to stand up against the rains and the storms. She needed warmth, a gentle dew, and the springtime breezes" (S. 49-50). But as we will see in the next chapter, the medicinal atmosphere of Les Buissonnets came at a price.

### Reflections and Questions.

1. Thérèse was so traumatized by the death of her mother that she withdrew into herself and felt secure only within the confines of her family. "I, once so full of life, became timid and retiring, sensitive to an excessive degree. One look was enough to reduce me to tears, and the only way I was content was to be left alone completely. I could not bear the company of strangers and found my joy only within the intimacy of the family" (S. 49).

All of us are like Thérèse. In order to feel secure we cling to the familiar. The circle of the familiar that we draw around our lives may not be our family of origin as it was for Thérèse; nevertheless, we all have our comfort zones. Fear and cribbing anxiety result when we cross over the rim of the familiar into uncharted territory, and irritation and anger erupt when the unannounced guest, the unplanned for event, the unexpected interruption rupture our routines and trespass upon our settled lives. The instinct for security is ingrained within us, but so is a drive to grow. [2]

Our fear of the unknown is in conflict with the fear that we will come to the end of our lives and find out that we have never lived. Our instinct for security often kills what it attempts to preserve; the person who saves his life will lose it. The tragedy of what fear can do to us is expressed poignantly in Edgar Lee Masters' poem "George Gray." In this poem, George Gray is reflecting upon the image carved on his gravestone as a symbol of his life.

> I have studied many times
> The marble which was chiseled for me –
> A boat with a furled sail at rest in a harbor.
> In truth it pictures not my destination
> But my life.
> For love was offered me and I shrank from its
>         disillusionment;
> Sorrow knocked at my door, but I was afraid;
> Ambition called to me, but I dreaded the chances.
> Yet all the while I hungered for meaning in my life.
> And now I know that we must lift the sail
> And catch the wind of destiny

Whenever they drive the boat.
To put meaning in one's life may end in madness,
But life without meaning is the torture
Of restlessness and vague desire –
It is a boat longing for the sea and yet afraid. [3]

Like all of us, Thérèse was afraid of leaving the safe harbor of her life, but as we will see, she chose to do God's will in spite of her fears. May the same be said of us.

*Questions.* At what times in your life have you been confronted with the choice of doing the will of God in spite of your fears?

2. "I preferred to go alone and sit down on the grass bedecked with flowers, and then my thoughts became very profound indeed! Without knowing what it was to meditate, my soul was absorbed in real prayer. I listened to distant sounds, the murmuring of the wind, etc. At times, the indistinct notes of some military music reached me where I was, filling my heart with a sweet melancholy. Earth then seemed to be a place of exile and I could dream only of heaven" (S. 52). Let us compare Thérèse's experience with that of another four-year old child and then extract from them some common elements about the nature of prayer.

In the following excerpt from Thomas Wolfe's short story "The Lost Boy," Eugene is reflecting upon and trying to recapture an experience of the core of his being which he links with a longing for something or someone that he cannot name but can only label as "Absence."

"He could remember how it got hot in the afternoons, and how he would feel a sense of absence and vague sadness in the afternoons, when everyone had gone away. The house would seem so lonely, and sometimes he would sit inside, on the second step of the hall stairs and listen...He would sit there and listen. He could hear the girl next door practice her piano lessons in the afternoon, and hear the street car coming by between the backyard fences, half a block away... And he felt that if he could only sit there on the stairs once more, in solitude and absence in the afternoon, he would be able to get it back again. Then would he be able to remember all that he had seen and been – the brief sum of himself, the universe of his four years, with all the light of Time upon it – that universe was so short to measure, and yet so far, so endless, to remember. Then would he be able to see his own small face again, pooled in the dark mirror of the hall, and peer once more into the grave eyes of the child that he had been, and discover there in his quiet three-years' self the lone integrity of "I," knowing: "Here is the House and here House listening; here is Absence, Absence in the afternoon; and here in this House, this Absence, is my core, my kernel here am I!" [4]

Both Thérèse and Eugene were alone but present to the world around them when they were drawn into their deepest selves and the presence of God. They listened to distant sounds, the murmuring of the wind, a street car a half a block away, some indistinct notes of military music and a piano from next door, when suddenly they there moved by a great yearning. Thérèse's heart was filled with a "sweet melancholy" for heaven, and Eugene longed to recover something that he felt that he had lost – his "I," the core of his being.

All of us have had similar experiences. It might have been

that Friday night when you were driving home from a weary week at work when, suddenly, a shaft of golden light shot through the steel grey sky, and for a moment you were raised above the humdrum of life and knew that all was well. Or you may have been washing dishes at the sink, when you heard your child playing outside, and you were inexplicably filled with a feeling of awe in the face of the mystery of life. A strain of music, a waft of a fragrance, an old photograph album, etc., are the sacramental means by which we are touched by God. They are the means by which this opaque world of ours becomes transparent and we behold a glimpse of Eternity and an intimation of Immortality. Or as William Blake puts it, "To see a World in a grain of Sand/And a Heaven in a Wild Flower/Hold Infinity in the palm of your hand/And Eternity in an hour." [5]

It is important to note that Thérèse did not label her thoughts and feelings about heaven that were engendered by what she saw and heard (eg. flowers and music) as prayer, at the time she experienced them but only upon reflection. "Without knowing what it was to meditate, my soul was absorbed in real prayer..." So too, we may be apt not to label a train of thought or a change of mood that comes upon us during our daily rounds as prayer because it is not connected with something explicitly religious. But St. John of the Cross tells us that we encounter God in creation because creation is God's handiwork. Furthermore, John tells us that the longing, the "sweet melancholy," the feeling of "Absence" that results from our encounters with creation is an experience of God, a glimpse of God that fills us with desire to see God face to face. "The soul [is] wounded with love through a trace of the beauty of her Beloved, which she has known through creatures, and [thus is] anxious to see the invisible beauty that caused this visible beauty ..."(italic added).[6] Thus, the God whom we long for is in the longing. Therefore, we should attend to those moments in daily life when we are touched by God through his creation, for in doing so, we are attending to God.

*Questions.* An interviewer once said to Karl Rahner that he had never had an experience of God. Rahner replied heatedly, "I don't believe you; I just don't accept that. You have had, perhaps, no experience of God under this precise label God but you have had or have now an experience of God – and I am convinced that this is true of every person... This inner experience of God is naturally and necessarily very difficult to describe. What love is, what fidelity is, what longing is, what immediate responsibility is – are all things that are difficult to reflect upon and to express. We begin to stutter, and what we say sounds very strange, laborious, and clumsy. But that is no proof that a person has not experienced fidelity, responsibility, joy, true love, and so on. So it is with the experience of God." [7] What are some of the experiences of God's presence that you have had in your own life that you have not labeled as an experience of the Sacred?

3. As Thérèse recounts the time that she stood before her mother's coffin, the memory of standing before Mother Geneviève's coffin comes to her mind, and she reflects upon the vast difference between the two experiences. As a four year old child who had just lost her mother, the coffin "appeared *large* and *dismal*" (S. 48). In contrast, as an adult, who had "grown up...the coffin appeared smaller...[and now, the reality of death, seen through faith, was an occasion] to contemplate heaven" (S. 48). As Thérèse looks back upon her four year old self, who had

been shattered by the death of her mother, she stands in amazement that she has survived this loss. "All my trials had come to an end and the winter of my soul had passed on" (S. 49). Like Thérèse, there are moments when we take a backward glance upon our lives and stand in amazement that we were able to survive a devastating loss. "Black grief closed over my heart," wrote St. Augustine on the death of a friend. "Everything I had shared with my friend turned into hideous anguish without him. My eyes sought him everywhere, but he was missing; I hated all things because they held him not...All this is over now, Lord, and my hurt has been assuaged with time." [8]

Like Thérèse and Augustine, all of us have experienced losses, which at the time, we felt that we did not have the strength to bear. For when we are overwhelmed with black grief, it is beyond the power of imagination to believe that the winter of our soul will ever pass. But all things are passing, and time heals all wounds. Thérèse experienced time's healing hand as she cast a backwards glance upon her mother's death, but she also experienced something else, the faith that pierces the dark veil of death. "I had no need to raise my head to see and, in fact, no longer raised it but to contemplate heaven which to me was filled with joy" (S. 48).

In less than a year after Thérèse had penned these words, the thought of heaven would not fill her soul with joy but with anguish. During her night of faith, when she doubted the existence of heaven, she wrote, "that the thought of heaven, up until then so sweet to me, was no longer anything but the cause of struggle and torment" (S. 333). Yet, in the midst of her darkness, when she felt that she lived "in a country that is covered with thick fog" (S. 333), God's light would periodically "shine through even in the midst of the darkest storm...[and for a brief moment] heaven was calm and serene and I believed I felt there was a heaven and that this heaven is peopled with souls who actually love me, who consider me their child" (S. 297, 299). Thérèse is describing an experience of God's love that pierces through our pain during times of our deepest darkness and for a moment, we know that love is eternal.

On a cold winter morning, as he and his fellow inmates were marching to their work site in Auschwitz, Vickor Frankl had such an experience.

We stumbled on in the darkness, over big stones and through large puddles, along the road leading from the camp. The accompanying guards kept shouting at us and driving us with the butts of their rifles. Anyone with very sore feet supported himself on his neighbor's arm. Hardly a word was spoken; the icy wind did not encourage talk. Hiding his mouth behind his upturned collar, the man marching next to me whispered suddenly:

"If our wives could see us now! I do hope they are better off in their camps and don't know what is happening to us."

That brought thoughts of my own wife to mind. And as we stumbled on for miles, slipping on icy spots, supporting each other and again, dragging one another up and onward, nothing was said, but we both knew: each of us was thinking of his wife. Occasionally I looked at the sky, where the stars were fading and the pink light of the morning was beginning to spread behind a dark bank of clouds. But my mind clung to my wife's image, imagining it with an uncanny acuteness. I heard her answering me, saw her smile, her frank and encouraging look. Real or not, her look was then more luminous than the sun which was beginning to rise.

A thought transfixed me: for the first time in my life I saw the truth as it is set into song by so many poets, proclaimed as the final wisdom by so many thinkers. The truth – that love is the ultimate and highest goal to which man can achieve. Then I grasped the meaning of the greatest secret that human poetry and human thought and belief have to impart: The salvation of man is through love and in love. I understood how a man who has nothing left in this world still may know this bliss, be it only for a brief moment in the contemplation of his beloved. In a position of utter desolation...for the first time in my life I was able to understand the meaning of the words, "The angels are lost in perpetual contemplation of an infinite glory."

I sensed my spirit piercing through the enveloping gloom. I felt it transcend that hopeless, meaningless world. At that moment a light was lit in a distant farmhouse, which stood on the horizon as if painted there, in the midst of the miserable grey of a dawning morning of Bavaria. *"Ex lux in tenebris lucet"*– and the light shineth in the darkness. [9]

*Questions.* When you look back upon your life, have you ever stood in amazement that you survived a devastating loss? Have you ever experienced God's love in the midst of your deepest darkness?

## Notes

1. Sister Geneviève of the Holy Face (Céline Martin), *The Father of the Little Flower*, translated by Michael Collins, S.M.A., (Dublin: M.H. Gill and Sons Ltd., 1955), 34.

2. For a good analysis of the relationship between the desire for security verses a drive toward growth see Abraham Maslow's *Toward a Psychology of Being*, (Princeton: D.Van Nostrand Company, Inc.,1968), especially pages 44-59. "Every human being has both sets of forces within him. One set clings to safety...tending to regress backward, hanging on to the past, afraid to grow...afraid to take chances, afraid to jeopardize what he already has, afraid of independence, freedom and separateness. The other set of forces impels him forward toward wholeness of Self and uniqueness of Self, toward full functioning of all his capacities, toward confidence in the face of the external world at the same time that he can accept his deepest, real, unconscious Self." p.46.

3. Edgar Lee Masters, "George Gray" in *Spoon River Anthology*, (New York: Signet Classic, 1992), 65.

4. Thomas Wolfe, "The Lost Boy" in *The Hills Beyond*, (Chicago: Ivan R. Dee, Inc, 1941), 34-38.

5. William Blake, "Auguries of Innocence," in *William Blake: The Complete Poems*, (New York: Penguin Books, 1988), 506.

6. St. John of the Cross, "The Spiritual Canticle," in *The Collected Works of St. John of the Cross*, trans. Kieran Kavanaugh, O.C.D. and Otilio Rodriguez, O.C.D. (Washington, D.C.: ICS Publications,1991), stanza 6, 497.

7. Harvey D. Egan, Karl Rahner: *Mystic of Everyday Life*, (New York: Crossroads Publishing Company, 1998), 34.

8. St. Augustine, *The Confessions*, trans. Maria Boulding, O.S.B., (Hyde Park, N.Y.: New City Press, 1997), Bk. 4, par. 9, p. 62-63.

9. Viktor E. Frankl, *Man's Search for Meaning*, (New York: Simon & Schuster, 1984), 48-52.

# Chapter III

# *THE DISTRESSING YEARS (1881–1883)*

Pupil at the Abbey
Holidays
Céline's First Communion
Pauline at Carmel
Strange Sickness
The Blessed Virgin's Smile

I was eight and a half when Léonie left boarding school and I replaced her at the Abbey.[47] I have often heard it said that the time spent at [15]school is the best and happiest of one's life. It wasn't this way for me. The five years I spent in school were the saddest in my life, and if I hadn't had Céline with me, I couldn't have remained there and would have become sick in a month. The poor little flower had become accustomed to burying her fragile roots in [20]a *chosen soil* made purposely for her. It seemed hard for her to see herself among flowers of all kinds with roots frequently indelicate; and she had to find in this *common soil* the food necessary for her sustenance!

You had instructed me so well, dear Mother, that when I went to boarding school I was the most advanced of the children of my age. I was placed, as a result, in [22v°] a class where the pupils were all older than I. One of them was about thirteen or fourteen and she wasn't too intelligent, but she was really adept at influencing the students

---

[47] A boarding school conducted by the Benedictine nuns and established at the beginning of the 16th century, near the Abbey of Notre-Dame-du-Pré, Lisieux.

and even the teachers. When she noticed I was so young, almost always first in the class, and loved by all the Sisters, [5]she experienced a jealousy pardonable in a student. She made me pay in a thousand ways for my little successes.

As I was timid and sensitive by nature, I didn't know how to defend myself and was content to cry without saying a word and without complaining *even to you* about what I was suffering. I didn't have enough [10]virtue, however, to rise above these miseries of life, so my poor little heart suffered very much. Each evening I was back at home, fortunately, and then my heart expanded. I would jump up on Papa's lap, telling him about the marks they were giving me, and his kiss made me forget my [15]troubles. How happy I was to announce the results of my *first composition*, one in sacred history, where I missed getting the maximum grade by *one point* only, and this because I didn't know the name of Moses' father. I was then the first and was wearing a beautiful silver badge. Papa rewarded me by giving me a *pretty little coin* worth [20]four sous. I placed it in a box which was to receive a new coin of the same *value* every Thursday. It was from this box that I drew my offerings on the big feasts when there were special collections for the Propagation of the Faith or similar works. Pauline, delighted with her little student's success, gave her a [23r°] pretty hoop to encourage her in her studies. The poor little thing needed these family joys very much, for without them life at the boarding school would have been too hard.

Each Thursday afternoon was a holiday, but this wasn't [5]like Pauline's holidays; and I wasn't in the belvédère with Papa. I had to play, not with Céline, which pleased me very much when I was alone with her, but with my little cousins and the little Maudelondes.[48] This

---

[48] First cousins of Jeanne and Marie Guérin. Mme. Maudelonde, the

was a real penance for me because I didn't know how to play like other children and as a consequence [10]wasn't a very pleasant companion. I did my best, however, to imitate them but without much success. I was very much bored by it all, especially when we spent the whole afternoon *dancing quadrilles*. What I really liked, though, was going to the park,[49] for there I was first in everything, gathering flowers in great profusion and, knowing how to [15]find the prettiest, I excited the envy of my companions.

What pleased me was when by chance I was alone with little Marie and, not having Céline Maudelonde dragging her into *ordinary games*, she left me free to choose, and I chose a game that was entirely new. Marie and Thérèse became two [20]*hermits*, having nothing but a poor hut, a little garden where they grew corn and other vegetables. Their life was spent in continual contemplation; in other words, one *hermit* replaced the other at prayer while she was occupied in the active life. Everything was done with such mutual understanding, silence, and so religiously that it was just perfect. When Aunt came to fetch us to go for our walk, we continued the game even on the street. The two hermits recited [23v°] the rosary together, using their fingers in order to screen their devotion from the inquisitive public; however, one day the younger hermit forgot herself completely: having received a piece of cake for lunch, she made a big sign of the Cross over it before eating it, causing [5]people to laugh.

Cousin Marie and I were always of the same opinion and our tastes were so much the same that once our *union of wills* passed all

sister of Mme. Guérin (1843–1926), had two sons and three daughters: Marguerite-Marie, Céline, and Hélène.

[49] The park was called Le jardin de l'étoile.

bounds. Returning one evening from the Abbey, I said to Marie: "Lead me, I'm going to close my eyes." "I want to close mine too," she replied. [10]No sooner said than done; without *arguing*, each did her *will*. We were on a sidewalk and there was nothing to fear from vehicles; having savored the delights of walking without seeing, the two little scamps fell *together* on some cases placed at the door of a store, or rather[15]they tipped them over. The merchant came out in a rage to lift up his merchandise, while the two blind ones lifted themselves up alone and walked off at *great strides*, eyes *wide open*, listening to the just reproaches of Jeanne who was as angry as the merchant! To punish us she decided to separate us, and since that day [20]Marie and Céline went together while I made the trip with Jeanne. This put an end to our great *union of wills*. And this wasn't a bad idea since the two older ones, Jeanne and Céline, were never of the same opinion and used to argue all the way home. Peace was then complete.

I have said nothing of my close relationship with Céline and [24r°] if I had to recount everything I would never come to an end. At Lisieux the roles had changed, for Céline had become a naughty little rascal and Thérèse was no longer anything but a sweet little girl, much given to crying. This did not prevent Céline [5]and Thérèse from loving each other more and more, but at times there were little arguments. These were not of a serious nature and basically they were both of the same mind. I can truly say that *never* did my little sister cause me any *trouble*, but was always a ray of sunshine for me, giving me much joy and consolation. Who can [10]say with what intrepidity she defended me at the Abbey when I was accused of something? She took such a good care of my health that I was wearied with her at times. What never wearied me, though, was *to see her at play*. She arranged our group of little dolls and conducted class like a truly clever teacher. [15]She took care that her girls were always good, while mine were often put out of class because of bad behavior. She used to tell me all the new things she had just learned in class, which amused me very much; I looked upon her as a fountain of knowledge.

I had received the name: "Céline's little girl," [20]and when she was irritated with me, her greatest sign of displeasure was to say: "You're no longer my little girl; that's over with, and I'll *always remember it!*" All I had to do was to start crying like a Magdalene, begging her to consider me still as her "little girl." Very soon she kissed me and promised me *to remember nothing.* To console me once she took one of her dolls and [24v°] said: "My dear, embrace your Aunt!" The doll was in such a rush to embrace me tenderly that her two little arms went up *my nose.* Céline, who hadn't done it purposely, looked at me stupefied; the doll was dangling from my nose. Aunt, of course, was not long in warding [5]off the excessively tender embraces of her *niece* and began laughing heartily at such a strange incident.

It was most amusing to see us buying our New Year's presents together at the bazaar, carefully staying out of each other's way. Having ten sous to spend, we had to buy at least five or six different objects, and the [10]contest was to see who would buy the most *beautiful things.* Delighted with our purchases, we waited impatiently for the first day of the year in order to offer each other our *magnificent presents.* The one who awakened before the other rushed to wish her a Happy New Year, and then they gave each other the gifts; each went into ecstasy over the treasures we bought for ten sous!

[15]These little gifts afforded us almost as much pleasure as *Uncle's beautiful presents.* But this was only the beginning of these joys. That day we were dressed as quickly as possible, and then we were on the watch to jump up on Papa's neck; as soon as he came out of his room our shrieks of joy resounded through the whole house and this poor little Father appeared happy to [20]see us so content. The gifts

Marie and Pauline gave their little girls also gave them *great joy*,
though the gifts had no great value. Ah! it was because we were not
*blasé* at this age; our soul in all its freshness was expanding like a
flower content to receive the morning's dew. Our petals were swayed
by the same breeze; what gave one joy or pain did [25r°] exactly the
same to the other. Yes, our joys were in common. I felt this especially
on the beautiful day when Céline made her First Communion. I wasn't
going to the Abbey as yet because I was only seven, but I have preserved a very sweet memory of the preparation [5]you, my dear Mother,
had Céline make. You took her, each evening, on your knees and spoke
to her of the great action she was about to perform; I listened eagerly
in order to prepare myself also, but very often you told me to go away
as I was too little. Then my heart was very heavy and I thought [10]four
years was not too long to prepare to receive God.

One evening, I heard you say that from the time one received
one's First Communion, one had to commence living a new life, and I
immediately made the resolution not to wait for that day but to commence the very same time as Céline. Never had I felt I loved her as
much [15]as I did during her three-day retreat; for the first time in my life,
I was separated from her and I didn't sleep in her bed. The first day,
forgetting she was not going to return, I kept a small bunch of cherries
that Papa had brought me in order to eat them with her. When I didn't
see her returning home, I was really sad. Papa [20]consoled me by saying he would take me the next day to the Abbey to see my Céline and
that I would give her another bunch of cherries! The day of Céline's
First Communion left me with an impression similar to my own First
Communion. When awakening in the morning all alone in the big bed,
I felt *inundated with joy.* "It's today! The great day has arrived." I
[25v°] repeated this over and over again. It seemed it was I who was
going to make my First Communion. I believe I received great graces

that day and I consider it one of the most *beautiful* in my life.
I have fallen a little behind in recalling that delightful and
[5]sweet memory, and now I must speak of the sorrowful trial that
broke little Thérèse's heart when Jesus took away her dear *Mama*, her
tenderly loved *Pauline!*

I had said to Pauline, one day, that I would like to be a hermit
and go away with her alone in a faraway desert place. She answered
that my [10]desire was also hers and that she *was waiting* for me to be
big enough for her to leave. This was no doubt not said seriously, but
little Thérèse had taken it seriously; and how she suffered when she
heard her dear Pauline speaking one day to Marie about her coming
entrance into Carmel. I didn't know what Carmel was, but I [15]under-
stood that Pauline was going to leave me to enter a convent. I understood, too, she *would not wait for me* and I was about to lose my second *Mother!* Ah! how can I express the anguish of my heart! In one
instant, I understood what life was; until then, I had never seen it so
sad; but it appeared to me in all its reality, and [20]I saw it was nothing
but a continual suffering and separation. I shed bitter tears because I
did not yet understand the *joy* of sacrifice. I was *weak*, so *weak* that I
consider it a great grace to have been able to support a trial that
seemed to be far above my strength! If I had learned of my dear
Pauline's departure very gently, I would not have suffered as much
perhaps, but [26r°] having heard about it by surprise, it was as if a
sword were buried in my heart.

I shall always remember, dear Mother, with what tenderness
you consoled me. Then you explained the life of Carmel to [5]me and it
seemed so beautiful! When thinking over all you had said, I felt that
Carmel was the *desert* where God wanted me to go also to hide
myself. I felt this with so much force that there wasn't the least doubt
in my heart; it was not the dream of a child led astray but the *certitude*

of a [10]divine call; I wanted to go to Carmel not for *Pauline's sake* but for *Jesus alone*. I was thinking *very much* about things that words could not express but which left a great peace in my soul.

The next day, I confided my secret to Pauline; she considered my desires as the will of heaven and told me that soon I would go with her [15]to see the Mother Prioress of the Carmel and that I must tell her what God was making me feel. A Sunday was chosen for this solemn visit, and my embarrassment was great when I learned that Marie Guérin was to stay with me since she was still small enough to see the Carmelites. I had to find a way, however, to remain alone with the Prioress and this is [20]what entered my mind: I said to Marie that since we had the privilege of seeing Mother Prioress, we should be very nice and polite and to do this we would have to confide our *secrets* to her. Each one in turn was to leave the room and leave the other all alone for a moment. Marie took me on my word, and, in spite of her repugnance of confiding *secrets she didn't have*, we remained alone, one after the other, with Mother Prioress. [26v°] Having listened to my *great confidences*, Mother Marie de Gonzague believed I had a vocation, but she told me they didn't receive postulants at the age of *nine* and that I must wait till I was sixteen. I resigned myself in spite of my intense desire to enter as soon as possible and to make my First Communion [5]the day Pauline received the Habit. It was on this day I received compliments for the second time. Sister Teresa of St. Augustine came to see me and did not hesitate to say that I was pretty. I had not counted on coming to Carmel to receive praises like this, and after the visit I did not cease repeating to God that it was for [10]*Him alone* I wished to be a Carmelite.

I took great care to profit from my dear Pauline during the few weeks she still remained in the world. Every day, Céline and I bought her cake and candy, thinking that later on she would never eat these anymore; we were always by her side and never gave her a moment's [15]rest. Finally, *October* 2 arrived, a day of tears and blessings when Jesus gathered the first of His flowers, who was to be the *Mother* of those who would come to join her a few years later.

I still see the spot where I received *Pauline's* last kiss; and then Aunt brought us to Mass, while Papa went [20]to Mount Carmel to offer his *first sacrifice*. The whole family was in tears so that people who saw us coming into the church looked at us in surprise. But it was all the same to me and it didn't prevent me from crying. I believed that if everything crumbled around me, I would have paid no attention whatsoever. I looked up at the beautiful blue skies and was astonished the Sun was shining with [27r°] such brightness when my soul was flooded with sadness! Perhaps, dear Mother, you find I am exaggerating the pain I was experiencing? I readily admit that it should not have been as great, since I had the hope of finding you again in Carmel; [5]but my soul was FAR from being *mature*, and I was to pass through many crucibles of suffering before attaining the end I so much desired.

October 2 was the day set for my return to the Abbey, and I had to go there in spite of my sadness. In the afternoon, Aunt came to get us to go to Carmel and I saw *my Pauline* behind [10]the *grille*. Ah! how I suffered from this *visit* to Carmel! Since I am writing the story of my soul, I must tell my dear Mother everything, and I admit that the sufferings which preceded your entrance were nothing in comparison with those which followed it. Every Thursday we went *as a family* to Carmel and I, accustomed to talk heart to heart with *Pauline*, obtained with great [15]trouble two or three minutes at the end of the visit. It is understood, of course, that I spent them in crying and left with a broken heart. I didn't understand that it was through consideration for Aunt that you were directing your words to Jeanne and Marie instead of speaking to your little girls. I didn't understand and I said in the depths of my heart: "Pauline [20]is lost to me!" It is surprising to see how much my mind developed in the midst of suffering; it developed to such a degree that it wasn't long before I became sick.

The sickness which overtook me certainly came from the demon; infuriated by your entrance into Carmel, he wanted to take revenge on me for the wrong our family was to do him in the future. But he did not know that the [27v°] sweet Queen of heaven was watching over her fragile little flower, that she *was smiling* on her from her throne in heaven and was preparing to stop the storm the moment her flower was to break without any hope of recovery.

Toward the end of the year, I began to have a constant headache. [5]It didn't cause me much suffering. I was able to pursue my studies and nobody was worried about me. This lasted until Easter, 1883. Papa had gone to Paris with Marie and Léonie, and Aunt had taken me and Céline with her into her home. One evening Uncle took me for a walk and spoke about Mama and about past memories with a kindness that[10]touched me profoundly and made me cry. Then he told me I was too softhearted, that I needed a lot of distraction, and he was determined to give us a good time during our Easter vacation. He and Aunt would see to it. That night we were to go to the Catholic Circle meeting, but finding I was too fatigued, Aunt made me go to bed; when I was undressing, I was seized with [15]a strange trembling. Believing I was cold, Aunt covered me with blankets and surrounded me with hot water bottles. But nothing was able to stop my shaking, which lasted almost all night. Uncle, returning from the meeting with my cousins and Céline, was very much surprised to see me in this state, which he judged to be very serious. He didn't want to say this [20]in order not to frighten Aunt.

He went to get Doctor Notta the next day, and he judged, as did Uncle, that I had a very serious illness and one which had never before attacked a child as young as I. Everybody was puzzled. Aunt was obliged to keep me at her home, and she took care of me with a truly *maternal* solicitude. When Papa returned from Paris with my older sisters, Aimée[50] met them at the door with such a sad face that Marie [28r°] believed I had died. This sickness was not "unto death," but like that of Lazarus it was to give glory to God.[51] And God was glorified by the admirable resignation of my poor little *Father*, who thought his *"little girl was going crazy or was about to die."* [5]God was glorified too by *Marie's* resignation! Ah! how she suffered because of me, and how grateful I am to her for the care she lavished upon me with such unselfishness. Her heart dictated what was necessary for me and really a *mother's* heart is more *discerning* than a doctor's, for it knows how to *guess* at what is suitable for its child's sickness.

[10]Poor Marie was obliged to come and live at Uncle's because it was impossible to bring me back at the time to Les Buissonnets. However, Pauline's taking of the Habit was approaching.[52] They avoided talking about it in my presence, knowing the pain I felt, but I spoke about it often and said I would be well enough to go and see my dear Pauline. [15]In fact, God did not want to refuse me this consolation; or rather, He wished to console His dear *Fiancée* who suffered so much because of her little girl's sickness. I have noticed that Jesus doesn't want to try His children on the day of their espousals, for this day must be without any clouds, a foretaste of heaven's joys. Has He not shown us this five times?[53] [20]I was, then, able to kiss my dear

---

[50] Aimée Roger, cook for the Guérin family.

[51] John 11:4.

[52] It was to take place April 6, 1883.

[53] An allusion to the taking of the Habit of four of her sisters, besides her own.

Mother, to *sit on her knees* and give her many caresses. I was able to
contemplate her who was so beautiful under the white adornment of a
Bride. Ah! how *beautiful that day* was, even in the midst of my dark
trial, but it passed by quickly. Soon I had to climb into the carriage
which took me to Les Buissonnets, far from Pauline and from my
beloved Carmel.[54] When we reached home, they put me to bed in spite
of my assurances that [28v°] I was perfectly cured and needed no further attention. Alas! my trial was only commencing! The next day I
had another attack similar to the first, and the sickness became so
grave that, according to human calculations, I wasn't to recover from
it. I can't describe this [5]strange sickness, but I'm now convinced it
was the work of the devil. For a long time after my cure, however, I
believed I had become ill on purpose and this was a *real martyrdom*
for my soul.

    I told Marie this and with her usual *kindness* she reassured me.
I told it too in confession and my confessor tried to [10]calm me, saying
it was not possible to pretend illness to the extent that I had been ill.
God, willing no doubt to purify and especially to *humble me*, left me
with this *interior martyrdom* until my entrance into Carmel, where the
*Father* of our souls,[55] as with the wave of his hand, removed all my
doubts. Since then I am perfectly calm.

    [15]It isn't surprising that I feared having appeared sick when I
wasn't sick in reality because I said and did things that were not in my
mind. I appeared to be almost always delirious, saying things that had
no meaning. And still I am *sure* that I *was not deprived of the use of
my reason for one single instant.* I often appeared to be in a faint, [20]not

---

[54] Thérèse didn't attend the ceremony. She was brought back to Les
Buissonnets instead of her uncle's, where she became sick.

[55] Father Almire Pichon, S.J. (1843–1919).

making the slightest movement, and then I would have permitted anyone to do anything he wished, even to kill me, and yet I heard everything that was said around me and can still remember everything. Once it happened that for a long time I was without the power to open my eyes and to open them an instant when I was alone.

I believe the devil had received an *external* power over me but [29r°] was not allowed to approach my soul nor my mind except to inspire me with very great *fears* of certain things,[56] for example, very simple remedies they tried in vain to make me accept. But although God permitted the devil to come near me, [5]He also sent me visible angels. Marie was always by my bedside, taking care of me and consoling me with a mother's tenderness. Never did she show the slightest sign of annoyance, and still I gave her a lot of trouble, not even allowing her to be away from me. She had to go and eat her meals with Papa, but I never[10]stopped calling her all the time she was away. Victoire, who was taking care of me, was at times obliged to go and get my dear "Mama" as I was calling her. When Marie wanted to go out, it had to be either to attend Mass or to go to see *Pauline*, and then I said nothing.

Uncle and Aunt were very good to me; dear little [15]Aunt came every day to visit me and brought a thousand goodies. Other friends of the family came to visit me also, but I begged Marie to tell them I

---

[56] "I was absolutely terrified by everything: my bed seemed to be surrounded by frightful precipices; some nails in the wall of the room took on the appearance of big black charred fingers, making me cry out in fear. One day, while Papa was looking at me in silence, the hat in his hand was suddenly transformed into some indescribably dreadful shape, and I showed such great fear that poor Papa left the room, sobbing" *(Histoire d'une Ame).*

wanted no visits. It displeased me to *"see people seated around my bed LIKE A ROW OF ONIONS, looking at me as though I were a strange beast."* The only visit I liked was that of Uncle and Aunt. [26]Since this sickness, I cannot express how much my affection for them has increased. I understand better than ever before that they were not just ordinary relatives to us. Ah! this poor little Father was very right when he spoke the words I have just written, and repeated them so often. Later on he was to experience that he wasn't wrong, and so now from heaven he ought to protect and bless those who gave him such devoted care and attention. I, still an exile on earth and not knowing how to show my gratitude, have [30]only one means of consoling myself and that is by praying for these relatives whom I love and who were and still remain so good to me!

[20]Léonie was also very kind to me. She tried to amuse me as well as she could. I sometimes caused her some pain as she was easily able to see that Marie could be replaced by no one.

And dear Céline, what did she not do for her Thérèse? On Sundays, instead of going out for a walk, she would close herself in for hours to be with a poor little girl who was like an idiot. Really, [29v°] it took love for anyone not to fly far from me. Ah! my dear little sisters, how I made all of you suffer! No one ever caused you as much *trouble* as I, and no one ever received as much *love* as you bestowed on me. Happily, I shall have heaven to avenge myself, for my Spouse [5]is very rich and I shall draw from His treasures of *love* to repay you a hundredfold for all you suffered on my account.

My greatest consolation when I was sick was to receive a letter from *Pauline*. I read and reread it until I knew it by heart. Once, dear Mother, you sent me an hourglass and one [10]of my dolls dressed as a Carmelite; it was impossible for me to express my joy. Uncle wasn't too happy, and said that instead of making me think of Carmel, it would be better to remove it from my mind. I am quite convinced, on the contrary, that the thought of one day becoming a Carmelite made me live.

I enjoyed working for Pauline. I made her little things [15]out of cardboard and my greatest occupation was to make crowns for the Blessed Virgin out of daisies and forget-me-nots. We were at the time in the beautiful month of May, and nature was adorned with flowers and was bursting out with joy. The *"little flower"* alone was languishing and seemed forever withered.

However, she had a Sun near her, and this Sun was the *miraculous statue* of the Blessed Virgin [20]that had spoken to Mama twice,[57] and the little flower often, very often, turned her petals toward this blessed Star. One day I saw Papa enter Marie's room where I was in bed. He gave her several pieces of gold with an expression of great sadness and told her to write to Paris and have some Masses said at Our Lady of Victories so that she would cure his poor little girl. Ah! how touched I was to see my dear King's faith and love! [30r°] I would have loved to be able to tell him I was cured; but I had already given him enough false joys, and it wasn't my desires that could work a miracle, and a *miracle* was necessary for my cure.

A miracle was necessary and it was our Lady of Victories who worked it. One Sunday[58] [5]during the Novena of Masses, Marie went

---

[57] She was wrong as it was only once. After our little sister Hélène's death, Mama was disturbed at the thought of a little lie the child had told. She was praying in front of the statue, regretting she hadn't brought the child to confession and fearing she was in purgatory, when she heard these words: "She is here by my side" (note of Mother Agnes of Jesus).

[58] Pentecost Sunday, May 13, 1883.

into the garden, leaving me with Léonie who was reading near the
window. After a few moments I began calling in a low tone: "Mama,
Mama." Léonie, accustomed to hearing me always calling out like
this, didn't pay any attention. This lasted a long time, and then I called
her much louder. Marie finally returned. I [10]saw her enter, but I cannot say I recognized her and continued to call her in a louder tone:
"Mama." *I was suffering very much* from this forced and inexplicable
struggle and Marie was suffering perhaps even more than I. After
some futile attempts to show me she was by my side,[59] Marie knelt
down near my bed with Léonie and Céline. [15]Turning to the Blessed
Virgin and praying with the fervor of a mother begging for the life of
her child, *Marie* obtained what she wanted.

Finding no help on earth, poor little Thérèse had also turned
toward the Mother of heaven, and prayed with all her heart that she
take pity on her. All of a sudden the Blessed Virgin appeared *beauti-*
*ful* to me, so *beautiful* that [20]never had I seen anything so attractive;
her face was suffused with an ineffable benevolence and tenderness,
but what penetrated to the very depths of my soul was the *"ravishing*
*smile of the Blessed Virgin."* At that instant, all my pain disappeared,
and two large tears glistened on my eyelashes, and flowed down my
cheeks silently, but they were tears of unmixed joy. Ah! I thought, the
Blessed Virgin smiled at me, how happy I am, [30v°] but never will I
tell anyone for my *happiness would then disappear.* Without any

---

[59] "Marie said something in a whisper to Léonie, then disappeared,
pale and trembling. Little Léonie carried me to the window; I saw
Marie in the garden but didn't recognize her still. She was walking
slowly, extending her arms to me, smiling, and calling in her most tender voice: 'Thérèse, my little Thérèse!' This last attempt failed"
*(Histoire d'une Ame).*

effort I lowered my eyes, and I saw Marie who was looking down at me lovingly; she seemed moved and appeared to surmise the favor the Blessed Virgin had given me. Ah! it was really to her, to her touching prayers that [5]I owed the grace of the Queen of heaven's *smile.* Seeing my gaze fixed on the Blessed Virgin, she cried out: "Thérèse is cured!" Yes, the little flower was going to be born again to life, and the luminous *Ray* that had warmed her again was not to stop its favors; the Ray did not act all at once, but sweetly and gently it raised the little flower and strengthened her in such a way that five years later she was expanding [10]on the fertile mountain of Carmel.

As I said, Marie had guessed that the Blessed Virgin had given me some hidden grace. When I was alone with her and she asked me what I had seen, I was unable to resist her very tender and pressing questions; astonished at seeing my secret discovered without my having revealed it, [15]I confided it entirely to my dear Marie. Alas! just as I had felt, my happiness was going to disappear and change into bitterness. The memory of the ineffable grace I had received was a real *spiritual trial* for me for the next four years, and I was not to find my happiness again until I was kneeling at the feet of Our Lady of Victories.[60] At this time, my happiness was restored to me in *all its* [20]*fullness.* I shall talk later on about this second grace of the Blessed Virgin. At present I shall explain, my dear Mother, how my joy was changed into sadness.

Marie, after having heard the simple and sincere recital of "my grace," asked me for permission to tell it at Carmel, and I could not say no. On my first visit to this dear Carmel, I was filled with joy when seeing my *Pauline* with the habit of the Blessed Virgin. [31r°] It was a sweet moment for both of us. There were so many things to say

---

[60] November 4, 1887, the eve of her trip to Rome.

that I couldn't say anything at all, my heart was too full. Good Mother
Marie de Gonzague was there also, giving me a thousand signs of
affection; I saw the other Sisters, and in their presence [5]I was questioned about the grace I had received. They asked me if the Blessed
Virgin was carrying the Child Jesus, or if there was much light, etc.
All these questions troubled me and caused me much pain, and I was
able to say only one thing: "The Blessed Virgin had appeared *very
beautiful*, and I had seen her *smile at me*." It was her *countenance
alone* that had struck me, [10]and seeing that the Carmelites had imagined something else entirely (my spiritual trials beginning already
with regard to my sickness), I thought I *had lied*. Without any doubt,
if I had kept my secret I would also have kept my happiness, but the
Blessed Virgin permitted this torment for my soul's good, as perhaps
without it I would have had some thought of vanity, whereas [15]*humiliation* becoming my lot, I was unable to look upon myself without a
feeling of *profound horror*. Ah! what I suffered I shall not be able to
say except in heaven!

# The Distressing Years
## Background and Context.

Leaving the family nest for the first time is a precarious adventure. Cameron and Rychlak write, "The major social change [of school age children] is that, while they are still members of a family they now go forth alone into the world outside their family... the moment a child steps out of the home unaccompanied, he or she loses the status of a protected and privileged son or daughter and becomes merely another child in the neighborhood. The patterns of friendliness, aggression and defense now encountered are different and less predicable by the child than are those to which he or she has been accustomed at home. It is quite normal for a child to be a bit timid and tentative [when placed in this situation]."[1] If this is the case with children in general, how much more anxiety ridden would Thérèse have been to leave home and venture forth into the world, considering that she was already "timid and retiring [and] could not bear the company of strangers" (S. 49)?

When Thérèse was eight years old, she began attending the Benedictine boarding school for girls in Lisieux. School was a painful experience for Thérèse because she had to leave the family circle and enter the rough and tumble world of children. Going to school was the first time that Thérèse had any real interaction with children her own age, except for her cousins Jeanne and Marie Guérin, who lived near Les Buissonnets. Thérèse "didn't know how to play like other children and as a result wasn't a very pleasant companion" (S. 83) and "*didn't know* how to play with dolls" (S. 51). These may sound like very insignificant matters to us but in the world of an eight year old girl they are tantamount to saying "I didn't know how to relate to my peers." In consequence, Thérèse was shunned. Céline testified: "The other girls finding [Thérèse] ill-adapted to their games, disregarded her. She did try, but she never succeeded in pleasing them. So she suffered a lot from the rude treatment that was meted out to her. From then on, she liked to keep away and not be seen, sincerely believing herself to be inferior to the others." [2]

Because Thérèse had never experienced this pattern of aggression and did not have the tools to defend herself, she withdrew: "I didn't know how to defend myself and was content to cry without saying a word and without complaining *even to you* about what I was suffering" (S. 82). So reticent was Thérèse to share her sufferings, that her siblings were ignorant of them until many years later. As a result of these experiences, Thérèse began to exhibit signs of depression – sad affect, social withdrawal, and low self esteem. "[I]t was as if a veil had been drawn over all of the fine qualities which the Lord had bestowed on her," testified Céline. [3]

But even Thérèse's unveiled gifts worked against her. They exposed her to the hateful jealousy of one of her classmates. "One of [the students] was about thirteen or fourteen and she wasn't too intelligent, but she was really adept at influencing the students and even the teachers. When she noticed I was so young, almost always first in the class, and loved by all the Sisters, she experienced a jealousy pardonable in a student. She made me pay in a thousand ways for my little successes" (S. 81-82). Is it any wonder that Thérèse describes her five years at school as "the saddest in [her] life," (S. 81) years when she "walked sick and sad in the big yard" (S. 132)?

But what kept Thérèse from becoming seriously sick at

school was her sister Céline, who also attended the boarding school. "If I hadn't had Céline with me, I couldn't have remained there and would have become sick in a month" (S. 81). These are not empty words, for after Céline graduated from school (Céline was three years older than Thérèse), Louis removed Thérèse from school because he feared that without Céline's support, Thérèse would relapse into the sickness that she had experienced when she was ten.

There was a deep intimacy that existed between Céline and Thérèse. Céline was "the companion of my childhood"(S. 23) and "the intimate confidante of my thoughts" (S. 158). "Thérèse and I were inseparable," testifies Céline. "We looked on our elder sisters (Marie and Pauline) more as mothers, but regarded one another as sisters." [4] In the springtime of life, these two siblings shared the innocence and simplicity of childhood. "The gifts Marie and Pauline gave their little girls also gave them great joy, though the gifts had no great value. Ah!, it was because we were not *blasé* at this age; our soul in all its freshness was expanding like a flower content to receive the morning dew" (S. 86).

But even the strength of Thérèse's bond with Céline could not protect Thérèse from the devastating blow that she had received when Pauline, Thérèse's second mother, left home and entered Carmel. "Pauline was going to leave me...I was about to lose my second Mother! Ah! how can I express the anguish of my heart! In one instant, I understood what life was; until then, I had never seen it so sad; but it appeared to me in all its reality, and I saw it was nothing but a continual suffering and separation" (S. 88).

Pauline's departure compounded Thérèse's sadness and proved to be a burden too heavy to bear. Thérèse began having violent headaches almost immediately after Pauline entered Carmel (Pauline entered Carmel on October 2, 1882, the same day that Thérèse returned to school after the summer vacation.). Over time, Thérèse developed other symptoms – loss of appetite, insomnia, pains in her stomach and side. Thérèse's condition came to a crisis in the spring of 1883 when Louis Martin took Marie and Léonie to Paris for Holy Week. During this time of separation, Thérèse stayed with her aunt and uncle. "One evening Uncle took me for a walk and spoke about Mamma and about past memories with a kindness that touched me profoundly and made me cry." Later on that evening "when I was undressing, I was seized with a strange trembling...which lasted almost all night" (S. 90). For the next six weeks Thérèse was bedridden with "a nervous trembling, followed by seizures of fright and hallucinations which recurred several times a day." [5]

On Pentecost Sunday she was miraculously cured by the Blessed Virgin but remained psychologically fragile. Thérèse suffered minor relapses after her cure.

### *Reflections and Questions.*

1. When Thérèse overheard the news that Pauline was about to leave home, she was overwhelmed by the sadness of the human condition. "I didn't know what Carmel was, but I understood that Pauline was going to leave me to enter a convent. I understood, too, she would not wait for me and that I was about to lose my second Mother! Ah! how can I express the anguish of my heart! In one instant, I understood what life was; until then, I had never seen it so sad; but it appeared to me in all its reality, and I saw it was nothing but a continual suffering and separation" (S. 87).

This statement may strike us as extreme, but loss through separation is an unremitting reality of life. Judith Viorst writes, "When we think of loss, we think of the loss through death, of people we love. But loss is a far more encompassing theme in our life. For we lose not only through death, but also by leaving and being left, by changing and letting go and moving on. And our losses include not only our separations and departures from those we love, but our conscious and unconscious losses of romantic dreams, impossible expectations, illusions of freedom and power, illusions of safety – and the loss of our own younger self, the self that thought it always would be unwrinkled and invulnerable and immortal... These losses we confront when we are confronted by the inescapable fact...that our mother is going to leave us, and we will leave her; that our mother's love can never be ours alone; that what hurts us cannot always be kissed and made better; that we are essentially out here on our own; that we will have to accept – in other people and ourselves – the mingling of love and hate, of the good with the bad; that no matter how wise and beautiful and charming a girl may be, she still cannot grow up and marry her dad; that our options are constricted by anatomy and guilt; that there are flaws in every human connection; that our status on this planet is implacably impermanent; and that we are utterly powerless to offer ourselves, or those we love protection – protection from danger and pain, from the inroads of time, from the coming of age, from the coming of death; protection from our necessary losses. These losses are a part of life-universal, unavoidable, inexorable. And these losses are necessary because we grow by losing and leaving and letting go." [6]

We may not have experienced the exact loss that Thérèse

did by the death of her mother and Pauline's leaving home, but we can all identify with Thérèse's pain because we have all suffered loss in various forms.

*Questions.* Like Thérèse, have you ever felt that life is nothing but a continual suffering and separation? What gave you the strength to bear the sadness of loss at these times?

2. Because Thérèse was intelligent and loved by her teachers, she was hated by one of the students who was jealous of her."[S]he experienced a jealousy pardonable in a student. She made me pay in a thousand ways for my little successes" (S. 82). We do not know the specific ways that the older student inflicted suffering upon Thérèse, but since the older student " was really adept at influencing the students and even the teachers" (S. 81-82), we may surmise that she used her influence to turn others against Thérèse.

Thérèse's situation is easy to understand. She was the new kid on the block who was receiving the admiration of her teachers and classmates. The older student felt threatened; her influence over the students and teachers was in jeopardy. The older student also felt impotent. Thérèse was "almost always first in the class" and "[the older student] wasn't too intelligent" (S. 81-82). In such a situation, since the jealous person feels powerless to compete and unable to raise herself up, she tears the other person down. [7]

The envied person is hated because she make us feel inferior or guilty or ashamed of ourselves; she is like a mirror in which we see a portrait of what we are not. "[The] man shows you what you have fallen away from and what you might have been," says Sydney Carton to himself, as he reflects upon the reason why he so loathes Charles Darnay. [8]

We are like the older student. We make people whom we envy pay a thousand ways for their giftedness. We make them the brunt of jokes and talk behind their backs. We give them the silent treatment and "forget" to tell them information that they need to know in order for them to perform their jobs well. We attempt to destroy their good names by sowing seeds of suspicion about them in the minds of our colleagues and friends.

Envy does not work its evil out in the open; it engages in covert operations. It works behind the scenes under the guise of good. Adrian van Kaam gives us an example of the tactics of envy.

I may say something like this: "Personally I have nothing against him. Its refreshing to hear new ideas. Of course, one must always be careful with that kind of person." When I have established myself in the minds of my audience as a reasonable fellow, I can go further. "I like him, but there is something about him that makes me uneasy." First, I present an image of sense and mitigation. My listener, a "regular guy," appreciates moderation. Then I pass along a feeling of suspicion. It may catch on like a contagious disease. I suggest discreetly that something is wrong with this fellow. Nobody knows what. But I hope that this suggestion may be enough to evoke a vague uneasiness. [9]

Envy frequently uses the word *but* to sow seeds of suspicion while covering its tracks. This is because whatever comes after the word *but* calls into question what comes before it. Let us take two examples of Marc talking about two other people? "Jack is the most disorganized guy in the world. He really drives me crazy at times, *but* he is the kindest man I have ever met." "Sally is always more than willing to give a helping hand, *but* sometimes I wonder why she is so willing?" In both cases, Marc said something both positive and negative about Jack and Sally. Yet we walk away feeling different toward them. We feel a certain affection towards Jack, because even though he is painted as a muddle-head, he a kindhearted muddle-head; whereas, we feel a little bit wary about the motivation underlying Sally's "altruism." What Marc said about Jack and Sally is one thing but what he communicated about them is another. For what we communicate about another person is what follows in the wake of our words. What our speech conveys is the emotional impress that our words have upon our listeners. But whenever we spew out the venom of envy, we simultaneously poison ourselves, for whenever we look upon the good fortune of others with spite, we become spiteful in the process.

Envy (the Latin *invidia*, from vedere, to see) has traditionally been associated with the eyes. Envy is the inability to look upon the goods of others with joy. Envy drains one's life of joy and fills it with fear. St. Thomas defined envy as "sorrow for another's good" (II-II, 36). But it is a projected sorrow, the sorrow that I don't have what others have. And it is a sorrow that is shot through with fear, the fear that I am less than others.

The envious person is competitive by nature; he is always comparing himself to others, forever looking out of the corner of his eye to see if his neighbor has more, or something bigger or better. The tragedy of the envious person is like that of a child who cannot rejoice in the Christmas present that he is unwrapping because he is spying the gifts that his siblings have received.

*Questions.* In Dante's *Purgatorio,* the envious have their eyelids sewed together in the manner that wild falcons have their eyelids sewed together for the purpose of taming their fear. This image is symbolic of three aspects of envy. First, the envious are afraid of admitting that someone else is superior to them. Thus, they are squint eyed and look upon the gifts of others with grudging hatred. Jesus says, "The eye is the body's lamp. If your eyes are good your body will be filled with light. If your eyes are bad (Gk. *poneros*) your body will be in darkness" (Mt. 6: 22-3). *Poneros* means grudging or stingy. Envy is tightfisted and niggardly in giving due praise and compliments to others. Who are the people in your life from whom you withhold compliments because of envy?

Second, Dante's image speaks of envy's blindness. The envious person is blinded to the goodness of others and is deprived of the joy that flows from rejoicing in what others have. Céline once said to Thérèse, "What I envy about you are your good works." Thérèse responded by quoting Tauler. 'If I love the good that is in my neighbour as much as he loves it himself, that good is as much mine as it is his.' Through this communion I can enrich myself with all the good that there is in heaven and on earth, in the angels, in the saints and in all those who love God." [10] The behaviors that flow from envy – backbiting, detraction, etc., destroy our ability to see goodness in our neighbor. Reflect upon the misery that such behaviors bring into your life. Think of how you could be enriched if you were able to find joy in your neighbor. If our neighbor isn't a gift then he is a threat. Which is he for you?

Third, Dante's image points to one of the basic means which we must employ in the taming of envy – restraint. Just as newly caught falcons have their eyelids sewed together in order to calm their fears and make them obedient to their masters, so too must the fear of the envious be quieted so that they will not fly off in a rage and attack their neighbor. This can be done by our choosing not to act upon envious feelings, for example, not to engage in detraction and backbiting. As our mothers told us when we were children, "If you can't say anything good about another person then don't say anything at all." Exercising this sage advice with those we envy often requires all the strength that we can muster. But in doing so, we grow in charity, the remedy of envy. Who are the people in your life whom you find most difficult not to malign?

Finally, Dante offers us another exercise in dealing with envy. As the envious are huddled in a group with their eyelids sewed together, they hear a passing voice echoing the Virgin Mary's words at the wedding feast of Cana *"Vinum non habent"* ("They have no wine"). Mary's act of thoughtfulness is an example of the antidote that we must employ to quell envious behavior.

Looking out for the good of one's neighbor is healing balm for envious eyes. What acts of kindness and thoughtfulness can you choose to do for people whom you envy?

3. There is a story of a man who while on vacation in Europe, visited the Louvre. As he was leaving, he said to the attendant at the front door, "I must admit, I was not impressed." To which the attendant rejoined, "Sir, let me remind you, that the paintings

in this museum are no longer on trial, but those who view them are." The statement, "I wasn't impressed," is often said with an air of blasé superiority, but sometimes the statement is nothing but a judgment upon the speaker, an expression of a soul that has become satiated by overexposure to stimuli and, as a result, is bored with life. As Thérèse is writing about her relationship with Céline, she muses upon the freshness of childhood, undulled by sophistication, that still retains the capacity to receive with joy the simple gifts of daily life."The gifts Marie and Pauline gave their little girls also gave them great joy, though the gifts had no great value. Ah!, it was because we were not *blasé* at this age; our soul in all its freshness was expanding like a flower content to receive the morning dew" (S. 86).

As we grow older and become worldly-wise and sophisticated, we become hardened to the beauty that life sets before us. The harried, hurried, pace of modern living beats out of us the freshness of childhood's receptivity. One simple way to begin to recover this receptivity is by slowing down and pausing to look at the world around us. One day as William Wordsworth was crossing Westminster Bridge in London, a bridge that he had crossed countless times before, he stopped and looked at the city about him. He captured what he had experienced that morning in his poem "Composed Upon Westminster Bridge, Sept. 3, 1803."

> Earth has not any thing to show more fair;
> Dull would be he of soul who could pass by
> A sight so touching in its majesty.
> This city now doth like a garment wear
> The beauty of the morning; silent, bare,
> Ships, towers, domes, theatres, and temples lie

Open unto the fields, and to the sky,
All bright and glittering in the smokeless air.
Never did sun more beautifully steep
In his first splendour valley, rock, or hill;
Ne'er say I, never felt, a calm so deep!
The river glideth at his own sweet will;
Dear God! the very houses seem asleep,
And all that mighty heart is lying still! [11]

*Questions.* The purpose of a bridge is to convey us from one place to another. Stopping upon a bridge is symbolic of a contemplative stance toward life; it is choosing to pause and to drink in the beauty of the moment. Several years ago I saw an exhibition of paintings by Monet. I was struck by the fact that the subject matter of many of his paintings was of train stations, factories, and constructions sites. One painting entitled *The Train*, which showed a train in the foreground and numerous factories belching out clouds of black smoke in the background, occasioned one author to comment, "The site in this picture looks more like Gary, Indiana than anything traditionally associated with Impressionistic France." [12] How strange that people would take time to come to a museum and stand in front of a painting depicting such a commonplace sight! But is not this one example of what art invites us to do, to pause and look at what we see everyday, but never take the time to contemplate? What are the "Westminster bridges" of your daily round that contain the "morning dew" of God's beauty? Have you become blasé to them because you have not taken time to pause and look?

## Notes

1. Norman Cameron, Joseph F. Rychlak, *Personality Development and Psychopathology: A Dynamic Approach* (Second Edition), (Boston, Houghton Mifflin Company, 1985), 82.

2. Christopher O'Mahony, ed. *St. Thérèse of Lisieux: By Those Who Knew Her*, (Dublin: Veritas Publications, 1975), 111.

3. Ibid., 114.

4. Ibid., 109.

5. This is the testimony of Marcelline Husé, the Martin's maid. Quoted from Guy Gaucher *The Story of a Life: St. Thérèse of Lisieux*, trans. Anne Marie Brennan (San Francisco: Harper & Row, 1987), 46.

6. Judith Viorst, *Necessary Losses: The Loves, Illusions, Dependencies and Impossible Expectations That All of Us Have to Give Up in Order to Grow*, (New York: Fawcett Gold Medal, 1986), 2-3.

7. Even though the literature differentiates jealously from envy, I am using the terms interchangeably.

8. Charles Dickens, *A Tale of Two Cities*, (New York: Penguin Books, 2000), Book 2, chapter 4, 89.

9. Adrian van Kaam, *Envy and Originality*, (Garden City: Doubleday & Company, 1972), 39.

10. Christopher O'Mahony, ibid., 125.

11. William Wordsworth, "Composed Upon Westminster Bridge: Sept. 3, 1803," in *William Wordsworth*, ed. Stephen Gill, (Oxford: Oxford University Press, 1984), 285.

12. Paul Hayes Tucker, *Claude Monet: Life and Art*, (New Haven: Yale University Press, 2001), 56.

# Chapter IV

# FIRST COMMUNION, BOARDING SCHOOL (1883-1886)

Pictures and Reading
First Communion
Confirmation
Malady of Scruples
Madame Papinau
Child of Mary
New Separations

W hile speaking about the visit to the Carmelites, I am reminded of the first visit which took place shortly after Pauline's entrance. I forgot to speak [20] about it, but there is a detail that should not be omitted. The morning of the day I was to visit, I was thinking things over in my *bed* (for it was there I made my profound meditations, and, contrary to the bride in the Canticles, I always found my Beloved there), I wondered what name I would be given in Carmel. I knew there was a Sister Thérèse of Jesus; however, my beautiful name of Thérèse could not be taken away from me. All of a sudden, I thought [31v°] of *Little* Jesus whom I loved so much, and I said: "Oh! how happy I would be if they called me Thérèse of the Child Jesus!" I *said nothing* during the visit about the *dream* I had while wide awake. But to good *Mother Marie de Gonzague,* who was asking the Sisters what name I should be given, came the idea of [5]calling me by the name I had *dreamed* about. My joy was great and this happy meeting of minds seemed to be a singular favor from my beloved Child Jesus.

I forgot several details of my childhood before your entrance into Carmel; for instance, I haven't spoken about my love for pictures

and reading. And still, dear Mother, I owe to the beautiful pictures you
[10] gave me as rewards, one of the sweetest joys and strongest impressions that aided me in the practice of virtue. I was forgetting to say
anything about the hours I spent looking at them. The *little flower* of
the Divine Prisoner, for example, said so many things to me that I
became deeply recollected. Seeing that the name of Pauline was written under the little flower, I wanted Thérèse's name to be written there
also and I offered myself[15] to Jesus as His *little flower.*

I wasn't too good at playing games, but I did love reading very
much and would have spent my life at it. I had human *angels,* fortunately for me, to guide me in the choice of the books which, while
being entertaining, nourished both my heart and my mind. And I was
not to go beyond a certain time in my reading, which was the cause of
great sacrifices to me as I had to interrupt [20] my reading very often at
the most enticing passage. This attraction for reading lasted until my
entrance into Carmel. To state the number of books that passed
through my hands would be impossible, but never did God permit me
to read a single one of them that was capable of doing me any harm.
It is true that in reading certain tales of chivalry, I didn't always understand the *realities* of *life*; but soon God made me [32r°] feel that true
glory is that which will last eternally, and to reach it, it isn't necessary
to perform striking works but to hide oneself and practice virtue in
such a way that the left hand knows not what the right is doing.[61]

When reading the accounts of the [5]patriotic deeds of French
heroines, especially the *Venerable* JOAN OF ARC, I had a great desire
to imitate them; and it seemed I felt within me the same burning zeal
with which they were animated, the same heavenly inspiration. Then I
received a grace which I have always looked upon as one of the great-

---

[61] Matthew 6:3.

est in my life because at that age I wasn't receiving the *lights* I'm [10] now receiving when I am flooded with them. I considered that I was born for *glory* and when I searched out the means of attaining it, God inspired in me the sentiments I have just described. He made me understand my own *glory* would not be evident to the eyes of mortals, that it would consist in becoming a great *saint!* This desire could certainly appear daring if one were [15] to consider how weak and imperfect I was, and how, after seven years in the religious life, I still am weak and imperfect. I always feel, however, the same bold confidence of becoming a great saint because I don't count on my merits since I have *none*, but I trust in Him who is Virtue and Holiness. God alone, content with my weak efforts, [20]will raise me to Himself and make me a *saint*, clothing me in His infinite merits. I didn't think then that one had to suffer very much to reach sanctity, but God was not long in showing me this was so and in sending me the trials I have already mentioned.

Now I must take up my story where I left off. Three months after my cure Papa took us to Alençon. This was the first time I had gone back. My joy was very great when seeing the places where I had spent my childhood days and [32v°] especially when I was able to pray at Mama's grave and ask her to protect me always.

God gave me the grace of knowing the *world* just enough to despise it and separate myself from it. I can say it was during [5] my stay at Alençon that I made my *first entrance* into the *world.* Everything was joy and happiness around me; I was entertained, coddled, and admired; in a word, my life during those two weeks was strewn only with flowers. I must admit this type of life had its charms for me. Wisdom is right in saying: *"The bewitching of vanity overturns the innocent mind!"* [62] [10]At the age of ten the heart allows itself

---

[62] Wisdom 4:12.

to be easily dazzled, and I consider it a great grace not to have remained at Alençon. The friends we had there were too worldly; they knew too well how to ally the joys of this earth to the service of God. They didn't think about *death* enough, and yet *death* had paid its visit to a great number of those whom I knew, the young, the rich, the happy! [15] I love to return in spirit to the *enchanting* places where they lived, wondering where these people are, what became of their houses and gardens where I saw them enjoy life's luxuries? And I see that all is vanity and vexation of spirit under the sun,[63] that the *only good* is to love God with all one's heart and to be *poor in spirit* here on earth.

[20] Perhaps Jesus wanted to show me the world before His *first visit* to me in order that I may choose freely the way I was to follow. The time of my First Communion remains engraved in my heart as a memory without any clouds. It seems to me I could not have been better disposed to receive Him than I was, and all my spiritual trials had left me for nearly a whole year. Jesus wished to make me taste a joy as perfect as is possible in this vale of tears.

[33r°] Do you remember, dear Mother, the attractive little book you made for me three months before my First Communion? It aided me in preparing my heart through a sustained and thorough method. Although I had already prepared it for a long time, my heart needed a new thrust; it had to be filled with [5]*fresh flowers* so that Jesus could rest there with pleasure. Every day I made a large number of fervent acts which made up so many *flowers*, and I offered up an even greater number of aspirations which you had written in my little book for every day, and these acts of love formed flower buds.

You used to write me a nice little letter each week and this filled [10] my soul with deep thoughts and aided me in the practice of virtue.

---

[63] Ecclesiastes 2:11.

It was a consolation for your poor little girl who was making such a *great sacrifice* in accepting the fact that she wasn't being *prepared* each evening on your knees as her dear Céline had been. Pauline was replaced by Marie. I sat on her lap and listened *eagerly* to everything she said to me. [15]It seemed to me her *large and generous* heart passed into my own. Just as famous warriors taught their children the art of war, so Marie spoke to me about life's *struggles* and of the palm given to the victors. She spoke also about the eternal riches that one can so easily amass each day, and what a misfortune it was to pass by without so much as [20]stretching forth one's hand to take them. She explained the way of becoming *holy* through fidelity in little things; furthermore, she gave me a little leaflet called "Renunciation" and I meditated on this with delight.

Ah! how *eloquent* my dear godmother was! I would have liked not to be alone when listening to her profound teachings. I felt so touched that in my simplicity I believed that the greatest sinners would have been touched just like me and that, leaving all their perishable riches behind, they would no longer want to gain [33v°] any but those of heaven.

At this time in my life nobody had ever taught me how to make mental prayer, and yet I had a great desire to make it. Marie, finding me pious enough, allowed me to make only my vocal prayers. One day, one of my teachers at the Abbey asked me what I did on my [5]free afternoons when I was alone. I told her I went behind my bed in an empty space which was there, and that it was easy to close myself in with my bedcurtain and that *"I thought."* "But what do you think about?" she asked. "I think about God, about life, about ETERNITY ... I *think!"* The good religious laughed heartily at me, and later on she loved reminding me of the [10]time when I *thought,* asking me if *I was still thinking.* I understand now that I was making mental prayer without knowing it and that God was already instructing me in secret.

The three months of preparation passed by quickly, and very soon I had to go on retreat and for this had to become a real boarder, sleeping at the Abbey. I cannot [15]express the sweet memory this retreat left with me. And truly, if I suffered very much at the boarding school, I was largely repaid by the ineffable happiness of those few days spent in waiting for Jesus. I don't believe one can taste this joy anywhere else but in religious communities. The number of children was small, and it was easy to give [20] each child particular attention, and certainly our teachers gave each of us their motherly care and attention. They spent more time with me than with the others, and each night the first mistress came, with her little lantern, and kissed me in my bed, showing me much affection. One night, touched by her kindness, I told her I was going to confide a *secret* to her; and drawing out my *precious little book* that was under my pillow, I showed it to her, my eyes bright with joy.

In the morning, I found it very nice to see all the students getting up so early [34r°] and doing the same as they; but I was not yet accustomed to taking care of myself. *Marie* was not there to comb and *curl* my hair, and so I was obliged to go and timidly offer my comb to the mistress in charge of the dressing rooms. She laughed at seeing a big girl of eleven not knowing how to take care of herself, and still [5]she combed my hair but not as *gently* as Marie. I didn't dare cry, which happened every day under the *gentle* hand of *godmother.* During my retreat I became aware that I was really a child who was fondled and cared for like few other children on earth, especially among those deprived of their mothers. Marie and Léonie came each day to see me, along with Papa, [10]who brought me all sorts of pastries. In this way, I didn't suffer the privation of being far from the family, and so nothing came to darken the beautiful heaven of my retreat.

I listened with great attention to the instructions Father Domin was giving us, even writing up a summary of them. As far as my own *thoughts* were concerned, I didn't want to write any of these down as I felt I would remember them. I was [15]right. I was very happy to be able to go with the religious to recite the Divine Office. I made a spectacle of myself among my companions by wearing a *big crucifix* Léonie had given me and which I held in my cincture like the missionaries; this crucifix was the envy of the religious who thought I wanted to imitate my [20]*Carmelite sister* by carrying it. Ah! how my thoughts fled to her; and I knew that *my Pauline* was also on retreat like me, not for Jesus to give Himself to her but to give herself to Him.[64] This solitude spent in waiting for Him was doubly dear to me for this reason.

I recall that one morning they made me go to the infirmary because I was coughing very much. Since my illness, the teachers paid a lot of attention to me and for a light headache or even if they saw me paler than [34v°] usual they sent me out to take some fresh air or to rest in the infirmary. I saw my *dear Céline* coming to the Abbey. She had obtained permission to come and see me, in spite of the retreat, to give me a holy picture which pleased me very much. It was "The little flower of the Divine Prisoner." Oh! how sweet it was [5]to receive this souvenir from *Céline's* hand! How many thoughts of love had I not experienced through it!

On the evening of the great day, I received absolution for the second time. My general confession left a great peace in my soul, and God did not permit the lightest cloud to come and trouble me. In the afternoon, I begged [10] pardon from the *whole family* who came to see

---

[64] Sister Agnes of Jesus was in retreat for Profession, which was to take place the same day as Thérèse made her First Communion.

me, but I wasn't able to speak except through my tears, so much was I moved. Pauline wasn't there, but I felt she was near me in spirit. She had sent me a beautiful *holy picture* through Marie, and I never grew tired of admiring it or showing it to others to admire! I had written Father Pichon [15]to recommend myself to his prayers and to tell him that soon I would be a Carmelite and he would be my director. (This is what happened four years later, since it was to him I opened my soul.) Marie gave me a *letter from him*, and my happiness was complete! All these good things came to me together. What pleased me [20]very much in his letter was this sentence: "Tomorrow, I will ascend the altar to say Mass for you and your Pauline!" Pauline and Thérèse were becoming more and more united on May 8 since Jesus seemed to be joining them together and flooding them with His graces.

The "beautiful day of days" finally arrived. The *smallest details* of that heavenly day have left unspeakable memories in my soul! The joyous awakening at dawn, the *respectful* embraces of the teachers and our [35r°] older companions! The large room filled with *snow-white* dresses in which each child was to be clothed in her turn! Above all, the procession into the chapel and the singing of the morning hymn: "O altar of God, where the angels are hovering!"

I don't want to enter into detail here. There are certain things that lose [5]their perfume as soon as they are exposed to the air; there are deep *spiritual thoughts* which cannot be expressed in human language without losing their intimate and heavenly meaning; they are similar to "... *the white stone I will give to him who conquers, with a name written on the stone which no one KNOWS except HIM who receives it.* "[65]

[10] Ah! how sweet was that first kiss of Jesus! It was a kiss of

---

[65] Revelation 2:17.

love; I *felt* that *I was loved*, and I said: "I love You, and I give myself to You forever!" There were no demands made, no struggles, no sacrifices; for a long time now Jesus and poor little Thérèse *looked* at and understood each other. That day, it was no longer simply a *look*, it was a fusion; they were no longer two, Thérèse had vanished as a drop [15]of water is lost in the immensity of the ocean. Jesus alone remained; He was the Master, the King. Had not Thérèse asked Him to take away her *liberty*, for her *liberty* frightened her? She felt so feeble and fragile that she wanted to be united forever to the divine Strength! Her joy was too great, too deep for her to contain, and tears of consolation soon flowed, [20] to the great consternation of her companions. They asked one another: "Why was she crying? Was there something bothering her?" — "No, it was because her mother was not there or her sister whom she loves so much, her sister the Carmelite." They did not understand that all the joy of Heaven having entered my heart, this exiled heart was unable to bear it without shedding tears. Oh! no, the absence of Mama didn't cause me any sorrow on the day of my First Communion. Wasn't Heaven itself [35v°] in my soul, and hadn't Mama taken her place there a long time ago? Thus in receiving Jesus' visit, I received also Mama's. She blessed me and rejoiced at my happiness. I was not crying because of Pauline's absence. I would have been happy to see her by [5] my side, but for a long time I had accepted my sacrifice of her. On that day, joy alone filled my heart and I united myself to her who gave herself irrevocably to Him who gave Himself so lovingly to me!

In the afternoon, it was I who made the Act of Consecration to the Blessed Virgin. It was only right that I *speak* in the name of my companions to my Mother in heaven, I who [10] had been deprived at such an early age of my earthly Mother. I put all my heart into *speaking* to her, into consecrating myself to her as a child throwing itself into the arms of its mother, asking her to watch over her. It seems to me the Blessed Virgin must have looked upon her little flower and *smiled* at her, for wasn't it she who cured her with a *visible smile?* Had she not placed [15]in the heart of her little flower her Jesus, the Flower of the Fields and the Lily of the valley?[66]

In the evening of that beautiful day, I found myself once more with my family. Already in the morning at the Mass, I had embraced *Papa* and all my relatives. But now this was the real reunion and Papa took the hand of his little Queen and brought her to *Carmel*. There I saw my *Pauline* who had become the spouse of Jesus; I [20]saw her with her white veil, one like mine, and her crown of roses. Ah! my joy was without any bitterness. I hoped to be with her soon and to await *heaven* with her! I was not indifferent to the family feast which took place the night of my First Communion. The beautiful watch my King gave me was the cause of great pleasure, but my joy was tranquil and nothing came to disturb my interior peace. Marie took me with her into her room on the night which followed this beautiful day, for the most brilliant days are followed by darkness; only the day of the first, the unique, [36r°] the eternal Communion of Heaven will be endless!

The day after my First Communion was still beautiful, but it was tinged with a certain melancholy. The beautiful dress Marie had bought me, all the gifts I had received did not satisfy my heart. [5]Only Jesus could do this, and I longed for the moment when I could receive Him a second time. About a month after my First Communion, I went to confession for the Ascension and I dared ask permission to receive Holy Communion. Against all hope, the priest permitted it and so I had the happiness of kneeling at the communion railing [10] between Papa and Marie. What a sweet memory I have of this second visit of

---

[66] Canticle of Canticles 2:1.

Jesus! My tears flowed again with an ineffable sweetness, and I repeated to myself these words of St. Paul: "It is no longer I that live, it is Jesus who lives in me!"[67] Since that Communion, my desire to receive grew more and more, and I obtained permission to [15] go to Holy Communion on all the principal feasts. On the eve of each of these happy days, Marie took me on her knees and prepared me as she did for my First Communion. I remember how once she was speaking to me about suffering and she told me that I would probably not walk that way, that God would always carry me as a child.

[20] The day after my Communion, the words of Marie came to my mind. I felt born within my heart a *great desire* to suffer, and at the same time the interior assurance that Jesus reserved a great number of crosses for me. I felt myself flooded with consolations so *great* that I look upon them as one of the *greatest* graces of my life. Suffering became my attraction; it had charms about it which ravished me without my understanding them very well. Up until this time, I had suffered without *loving* suffering, but since this day [36v°] I felt a real love for it. I also felt the desire of loving only God, of finding my joy only in Him. Often during my Communions, I repeated these words of the Imitation: "O Jesus, unspeakable *sweetness,* change all the consolations of this earth into *bitterness* for me."[68] This prayer fell from [5] my lips without effort, without constraint; it seemed I repeated it not with my will but like a child who repeats the words a person he loves has inspired in him. Later I will tell you, dear Mother, how Jesus was pleased to realize my desire, and how He was always my ineffable *sweetness.* Were I to speak of this right now, I would be [10] anticipating the time of my life as a young girl, and there are many details

---

[67] Galatians 2:10.

[68] *The Imitation of Christ* III, 26:3.

about my life as a child that I have to give you.

A short time after my First Communion, I entered upon another retreat for my Confirmation,[69] I was prepared with great care to receive the visit of the Holy Spirit, and I did not understand why [15]greater attention was not paid to the reception of this sacrament of *Love*. Ordinarily, there was only one day of retreat made for Confirmation, but the Bishop was unable to come on the appointed day and so I had the consolation of having two days of solitude. To distract us our mistress brought us to Mont Cassin[70] and there I gathered very many *big daisies* for the feast of Corpus Christi. Ah! how happy my soul was! [20]Like the Apostles, I awaited the Holy Spirit's visit with great happiness in my soul. I rejoiced at the thought of soon being a perfect Christian and especially at that of having eternally on my forehead the mysterious cross the Bishop marks when conferring this sacrament. Finally the happy moment arrived, and I did not experience an impetuous wind at the moment of the Holy Spirit's descent but rather this *light breeze* which the prophet Elias heard on Mount Horeb.[71] On that day, I received the strength to *suffer*, for soon afterward the martyrdom of my soul was about [37r°] to commence. It was my dear little Léonie who acted as my godmother, and she was so much moved that she was unable all through the ceremony to hold back her tears. She received Holy Communion with me, for I had the happiness on that beautiful day to unite myself with Jesus.

---

[69] Thérèse was confirmed by Bishop Hugonin, Bishop of Bayeux, June 14, 1884.

[70] "A little hill behind the Benedictines' garden and part of their property" (note of Mother Agnes of Jesus).

[71] 1 Kings 19:12–13.

[5]After these delightful and unforgettable feasts, my life returned to its *ordinary* course, that is, I had to take up again life as a boarder and this was very painful. At the time of my First Communion, I loved this association with children of my own age, filled with good will, having made like myself the resolution of practicing virtue seriously. But now I had to come in contact with [10] students who were much different, distracted, and unwilling to observe regulations, and this made me very unhappy. I had a happy disposition, but I didn't know how to enter into games of my age level; often during the recreations, I leaned against a tree and studied my companions at a distance, giving myself up to serious reflections! I had invented a game which pleased me, and it was to bury the poor little [15] birds we found dead under the trees. Many of the students wanted to help me, and so our cemetery became very beautiful, planted with trees and flowers in proportion to the size of our little feathered friends.

I loved, too, to tell stories I made up as they came into my mind, and my companions gathered round me eagerly, and even the older ones mingled at times in the crowd of listeners. [20] The same story lasted for several days, for I liked to make it more and more interesting when I saw the impressions it produced and which were evident on my companions' faces. Soon the mistress forbade me to continue in my role as *orator,* for she preferred to see us playing and running and not discussing.

I grasped easily the meaning of things I was learning, but I had trouble learning things word for word. As far as catechism was concerned, I received permission to learn it during my recreation periods [37v°] almost every day of the year before my First Communion. My efforts were crowned with success and I was always first. If I lost my place accidentally by *forgetting one single word,* my sadness was shown by the bitter tears I shed, [5] which Father Domin didn't know

how to stop. He was very much pleased with me (not when I was crying), and used to call me his *little doctor* because my name was
Thérèse. Once, a student who followed me did not know the catechism question to ask of her companion. Father Domin, having made
the rounds of all the students in vain, came back to me and said he was
going to see if I [10] deserved my place as first. In my *profound humility* this was what I was waiting for; and rising with great assurance I
said everything that was asked of me, to the great astonishment of
everybody. After my First Communion, my zeal for catechism continued until my leaving boarding school. I succeeded very well in my
studies, was almost always [15]first, and my greatest successes were history and composition. All my teachers looked upon me as a very intelligent student, but it wasn't like that at Uncle's house where I was
taken for a little dunce, good and sweet, and with right judgment, yes,
but incapable and clumsy.

I am not surprised at this opinion which Uncle and Aunt [20]had
of me, and no doubt still have, for I hardly ever spoke, being very
timid. When I wrote anything, my *terrible scrawl* and my spelling,
which was nothing less than original, did not make much of an
impression on anyone. In the little tasks of sewing, embroideries, and
others, I succeeded well, it is true, in the estimation of my teachers;
but the stiff and *clumsy way* I *held my work* justified the poor opinion
they had of me. I look upon this as a grace: God, wanting my heart for
[38r°] Himself alone, answered my prayer already "changing into bitterness all the consolations of earth."[72] I needed this all the more as I
would not have been indifferent to praise. They often spoke highly of
the intelligence of others in my presence, but of mine they never said
a word, and so I concluded I didn't have any and was resigned to [5]see

---

[72] *The Imitation of Christ* III, 26:3.

myself deprived of it.

My heart, sensitive and affectionate as it was, would have easily surrendered had it found a heart capable of understanding it. I tried to make friends with little girls my own age, and especially with two of them. I loved them and they, in their turn, loved me insofar as they were *capable*. But alas! [10] how *narrow* and *flighty* is the heart of creatures! Soon I saw my love was misunderstood. One of my friends was obliged to go back to her family and she returned to school a few months later. During her absence, I *had thought about her,* treasuring a little ring she had given me. When I saw my companion back again my joy was great, but [15]all I received from her was a cold glance. My love was not understood. I felt this and I did not beg for an affection that was refused, but God gave me a heart which is so faithful that once it has loved purely, it loves always. And I continued to pray for my companion and I still love her. When I noticed Céline showing affection for one of her teachers, I [20]wanted to imitate her, but not *knowing* how to win the good graces of creatures, I was unable to succeed. O blessed ignorance! which has helped me avoid great evils! How can I thank Jesus for making me find *"only bitterness in earth's friendships!"* With a heart such as mine, I would have allowed myself to be taken and my wings to be clipped, and then how would I have been able to *"fly and be at rest?"*[73] How can a heart given over to the affection of creatures be intimately united with God? I feel this is not possible. Without having drunk the poisoned cup [38v°] of a too ardent love of creatures, I *feel* I cannot be mistaken. I have seen so many souls, seduced by this *false light,* fly like poor moths and burn their wings, and then return to the real and gentle light of *Love* that gives them new wings which are more brilliant and delicate, [5] so that

---

[73] Psalm 54:7.

they can fly toward Jesus, that Divine Fire "which burns without consuming."[74] Ah! I feel it! Jesus knew I was too feeble to be exposed to temptation; perhaps I would have allowed myself to be burned entirely by the *misleading light* had I seen it shining in my eyes. It was not so for me, for I encountered only bitterness where stronger souls met with joy, and [10] they detached themselves from it through fidelity. I have no merit at all, then, in not having given myself up to the love of creatures. I was preserved from it only through God's mercy!

I know that without Him, I could have fallen as low as St. Mary Magdalene, and the profound words of Our Lord to Simon resound with a great sweetness in my soul. I know that *"he* [15]*to whom less is forgiven,* LOVES *less,'"*[75] but I also know that Jesus *has forgiven me more* than *St. Mary Magdalene* since He forgave me *in advance* by preventing me from falling. Ah! I wish I could explain what I feel. Here is an example which will express my thoughts at least a little. Suppose a clever physician's child meets with a stone in his path which [20]causes him to fall and break a limb. His father comes to him immediately, picks him up lovingly, takes care of this hurt, using all the resources of his profession for this. His child, completely cured, shows his gratitude. This child is no doubt right in loving his father! But I am going to make another comparison. The father, knowing there is a stone in his child's way, hastens ahead of him and removes it but without anyone's seeing him do it. Certainly, this child, [39r°] the object of his father's tender foresight, but UNAWARE of the mis-

---

[74] St. John of the Cross, *Living Flame of Love,* st. 2, nos. 2–3. See *The Collected Works of St. John of the Cross,* trans. Kieran Kavanaugh, O.C.D., and Otilio Rodriguez, O.C.D., rev. ed. (Washington, D.C.: ICS Publications, 1991), p. 658.

[75] Luke 7:47.

fortune from which he was delivered by him, will not thank him and *will love him less* than if he had been cured by him. But if he should come to learn the danger from which he escaped, *will he not love his father more?* [5]Well, I am this child, the object of the *foreseeing love of a Father* who has not sent His Word to save the *just,* but *sinners.*[76] He wants me *to love* Him because He *has forgiven* me not much but ALL. He has not expected me to *love Him much* like Mary Magdalene, but He has willed that I KNOW how He was loved me with a [10] love of *unspeakable foresight* in order that now I may love Him unto *folly!* I have heard it said that one cannot meet a pure soul who loves more than a repentant soul; ah! how I would wish to give the lie to this statement!

I see I am far from my subject and hasten to [15]return to it. The year following my First Communion passed almost entirely without any interior trials for my soul. It was during my retreat for the second Communion[77] that I was assailed by the terrible sickness of scruples. One would have to pass through this martyrdom to understand it well, and for me to express what I suffered for [20]*a year and a half* would be impossible. All my most simple thoughts and actions became the cause of trouble for me, and I had relief only when I told them to Marie. This cost me dearly, for I believed I was obliged to tell her the absurd thoughts I had even about her. As soon as I laid down my burden, I experienced peace for an instant; but this peace passed away like a lightning flash, and soon my martyrdom began over again. What patience my dear Marie needed to listen to me [39v°] without showing any annoyance! Hardly had I returned from the Abbey when she began to curl my hair for the next day (for every day, to please Papa,

---

[76] Matthew 9:13.

[77] This retreat took place May 17–21, 1885.

the little Queen had her hair curled, to the surprise of her companions and especially the teachers, who did not see children so coddled by [5] their parents), and during the sitting, I did not stop crying while telling all my scruples. At the end of the year, Céline, having completed her studies, remained home and poor Thérèse was obliged to attend school alone. It wasn't long before she got sick, for the only attraction which held her at the boarding school was to be with her inseparable Céline, and without her never could *"her little girl"* [10] stay there. I left the Abbey, then, at the age of thirteen,[78] and continued my education by taking several lessons a week at the home of *"Mme. Papinau."* She was a very good person, *very well educated* but a little old-maidish in her ways. She lived with her mother, and it was charming to see the little household they made up together, all three of them (for the *cat* [15] was one of the *family,* and I had to put up with its purring on my copybooks and even to admire its pretty form). I had the advantage of living within the intimacy of the family; as Les Buissonnets was too far for the somewhat old limbs of my teacher, she requested that I come and take the lessons in her home. When I arrived, I usually found only [20] old lady Cochain who looked at me *"with her big clear eyes"* and then called out in a calm, sententious voice: *"Mme. Pâpinau...Ma...d'môizelle Thê...rèse est là! ..."* Her daughter answered promptly in an *infantile* voice: "Here I am, *Mama.*" And soon the lesson began. Who could believe it! In this antiquely furnished room, surrounded as I was by text books and copybooks, I was often present [40r°] at the visits of all types of persons; priests, ladies, young girls, etc. Mme. Cochain took on the burden of the conversa-

---

[78] Thérèse left the Abbey in the course of the second trimester of the 1885–86 school year.

tion as well as she could in order to allow her daughter to conduct my lesson, but on those days I didn't learn very much. With my nose in the book, I heard everything that was said around me and even [5] those things it would have been better for me not to hear because vanity slips so easily into the heart. One lady said I had pretty hair; another, when she was leaving, believing she was not overheard, asked who the very beautiful young girl was. These words, all the more flattering since they were not spoken in my presence, left in my soul a [10] pleasurable impression that showed me clearly how much I was filled with self-love. Oh! how I pity souls that are lost! It is so easy to go astray on the flowery paths of the world. Undoubtedly, for a soul a little advanced spiritually, the sweetness which the world offers is mixed with bitterness, and the immense void of the desires cannot be filled by the praises of an instant. [15]However, if my heart *had not been raised to God from the dawn of reason,* if the world had smiled on me from my entrance into life, what would have become of me? O my dear Mother, with what gratitude I sing the Mercies of the Lord! Did He not, according to the words of Wisdom: *"... draw me from the world before my spirit was corrupted by its malice and before its [20]deceitful appearances had seduced my soul?'"*[79] The Blessed Virgin, too, watched over her little flower and, not wanting her to be tarnished by contact with worldly things, drew her to *her mountain* before she blossomed. While awaiting this moment, little Thérèse grew in love for her heavenly Mother, and to prove this love she performed *an action* which *cost her very much* and which I will recount in a few words in spite of its *length.*

[40v°] Almost immediately after my entrance at the Abbey, I was received into the Association of the Holy Angels. I loved the pious practices it imposed, as I had a very special attraction to pray

---

[79] Wisdom 4:11.

to the blessed spirits of heaven, particularly to the one whom God gave as the[5] companion of my exile. A short time after my First Communion, the ribbon of the aspirant to the Children of Mary replaced that of the Holy Angels, but I left the Abbey without being received into the Association of Mary. Having left before completing my studies, I did not have permission to enter as a student; I admit this privilege didn't excite [10] my envy, but, thinking that all my sisters had been "children of Mary," I feared I would be less a child of my heavenly Mother than they were. I went very humbly (in spite of what it cost me) to ask for permission to be received into the Association at the Abbey. The mistress didn't want to refuse me, but she placed as a [15]condition that I come twice a week in the afternoon in order to prove my worthiness. Far from giving me any pleasure, this permission cost me very much. For instance, I didn't have, as did the other students, any teacher with whom I was on friendly terms and could spend several hours. I was content, therefore, to greet the one in charge, and then [20] go and work in silence until the end of the lesson. No one paid any attention to me, and I would go up to the choir of the chapel and remain before the Blessed Sacrament until the moment when Papa came to get me. This was my only consolation, for was not Jesus *my only Friend?* I knew how to speak only to Him; conversations with creatures, even pious conversations, fatigued my soul. I felt it was far more valuable to speak to God than [41r°] to speak about Him, for there is so much self-love intermingled with spiritual conversations! Ah! it was really for the Blessed Virgin alone that I was coming to the Abbey. Sometimes I felt *alone,* very much alone, and as in the days of my life as a day boarder when I walked[5]sad and sick in the big yard, I repeated these words that always gave rise to a new peace and strength in my heart:

"Life is your barque not your home!"[80] When very little, these words gave me courage, and even now, in spite of the years which have put to flight so many impressions of childish piety, the image of the barque still charms [10]my soul and helps it put up with its exile. Doesn't Wisdom say: *"Life is like a ship that plows the restless waves and leaves after it no trace of its rapid passage"?*[81] When I think of these things, my soul is plunged into infinity, and it seems to me it already touches the eternal shore. I seem to be receiving the [15]embraces of Jesus. I believe I see my heavenly Mother coming to meet me with Papa, Mama, the four little angels. I believe I am enjoying forever a real and eternal family reunion.

Before seeing my family reunited around the *Paternal hearth* of heaven, however, I [20]was to pass through many separations; the year, for instance, when I was received as a child of the Blessed Virgin, she took from me my dear Marie,[82] the only support of my soul. It was Marie who guided, consoled, and aided me in the practice of virtue; she was my sole oracle. Pauline, no doubt, had remained well ahead in my heart, but Pauline was far, very far from me! I had suffered martyrdom getting accustomed to living without her, to seeing between me and her [41v°] impassable walls. But finally I ended up by recognizing the sad reality: Pauline is lost to me, almost in the same manner as if she were dead. She always loved me, prayed for me, but in

---

[80] Verse from Lamartine's poem called "Reflection." Thérèse cites it from memory and Mother Agnes of Jesus corrects her by saying: "She made a mistake. It is: '*Time* and not *life* ...' So: 'Time is your barque, not your home.'"

[81] Wisdom 5:10.

[82] Marie entered the Carmel of Lisieux, October 15, 1886. Thérèse was received as a Child of Mary, May 31, 1887, not 1886.

my eyes *my* dear *Pauline* had become a saint who was no longer able
to understand the things [5]of earth. And the miseries of her poor
Thérèse, if she were aware of them, would only astonish her and prevent her from loving her Thérèse as much as she did. Besides, even
when I would have desired to confide my thoughts to her as at Les
Buissonnets, I could not have done so, for the visits at the Carmel
were only for Marie. Céline and I had permission to come only at the
*end,* just to [10] have the time to break our heart.

And so, in reality, I had only Marie, and she was indispensable
to me, so to speak. I told my scruples only to her and was so obedient
that my confessor never knew my ugly malady. I told him just the
number of sins Marie permitted me to confess, not one more, and
could pass [15]as being the least scrupulous soul on earth in spite of the
fact that I was scrupulous to the highest degree. Marie knew, then,
everything that went on in my soul, and she knew my desires for
Carmel. I loved her so much I couldn't live without her. Aunt invited
us to come every year, each in our turn, to her place at Trouville, and
I should have [20]loved going there, but with Marie! When I didn't have
her with me, I was very much bored. Once I did enjoy going there,
however, and it was the year of Papa's trip to Constantinople.[83] To give
us a little distraction (we were sad when we knew Papa was so far
away), Marie sent us, Céline and me, to the seashore for two weeks. I
enjoyed myself very much because I was with my Céline. Aunt provided us with all the amusements possible: donkey rides, fishing for eels,
etc. I was still very much a child [42r°] in spite of my twelve and a half
years, and I remember the joy I had putting on some pretty sky-blue
ribbons Aunt had given me for my hair; I also recall having confessed

---

[83] M. Martin left at the end of August, 1885; Thérèse was at Trouville
in mid-September.

at Trouville even this childish pleasure which seemed to be a sin to me. I had an[5] experience one evening that surprised me very much.

Marie [Guérin], who was almost always ailing, often *whimpered;* and then Aunt babied her, giving her all kinds of endearing names, but my dear little cousin continued her crying and said she had a headache. I, who had a headache almost every day[84] and didn't complain, wanted[10] to imitate Marie. So one evening, sitting in an armchair in the corner of the parlor, I set about the business of crying. Soon Jeanne and Aunt hurried over to me, asking me what was the matter. I answered like Marie: "I have a headache." It seemed that complaining didn't suit me, for I was unable to convince them that a headache would[15] make me cry; instead of babying me, they spoke to me as to an adult, and Jeanne scolded me for lacking confidence in Aunt, for she was convinced something was bothering my conscience. Getting nowhere for all my trouble, I made the resolution never to imitate others again, and I understood the fable about *"The donkey and the pet dog."*[85] I *was the donkey* that saw the caresses[20] the little dog was getting; he came and placed his clumsy hoof on the table to get his share of kisses. Although I didn't get the blows of the cudgel like the poor animal, I did get what I deserved and this cured me for life of any desire to attract attention. The one effort I had made was far too costly!

The following year, that of my dear Marie's departure for Carmel, Aunt invited me again but this time all alone, and I was so much out of my element that [42v°] after two or three days I got sick and they had to bring me back to Lisieux.[86] My sickness, which they

---

[84] Thérèse's headaches came to her especially in May, 1885. She was on vacation (without Céline) at the Chalet des Roses at Deauville.

[85] La Fontaine, *Fables*, IV, 5.

[86] This took place in July, 1886.

feared was serious, was only an attack of nostalgia for Les
Buissonnets, for hardly had I put my foot in the house when my health
returned. And it was from a child such as this that God was taking
away the only [5] support which attached me to life!

As soon as I learned of Marie's determination, I resolved to take
no pleasure out of earth's attractions. Since my leaving the boarding
school, I set myself up in *Pauline's* old painting room[87] and arranged it
to suit my taste. It was a real bazaar, an assemblage of pious objects and
[10] curiosities, a garden, and an aviary. Thus, at the far end on the wall
was a *big cross* in black wood, without a corpus, and several drawings
I liked. On another wall, a basket, decorated with muslin and pink ribbons, contained some delicate herbs and flowers. Finally, on the last
wall, was enthroned all by itself the portrait of *Pauline* at the age of ten.
[15] Beneath the portrait was a table and upon it was a *large cage* which
enclosed a *great* number of birds; their melodious song got on the
nerves of visitors but not on those of their little mistress who cherished
them very much. There was also the *"little white piece of furniture"*
filled with my school books and copybooks, and on it [20] was set a statue of the Blessed Virgin, along with vases always filled with natural
flowers, and candles. Around the statue was a number of small statues
of the saints, little baskets made out of shells, cardboard boxes, etc.!
My garden was *suspended* in front of the window, and there I cultivat-
ed pots of flowers (the rarest I could find). I also had on the inside of
"my museum" a flower stand on which I placed my privileged plant.
In front of the [43r°] window was a table covered with a green cloth,
and in the center were an *hourglass,* a small statue of St. Joseph, a
watchcase, baskets of flowers, an inkwell, etc. A few *rickety* chairs and
a beautiful *doll's* cot belonging to *Pauline* completed my furnishings.

---

[87] One of the two attics on the second floor.

Truly, this [5] poor attic was a world for me and like M. de Maistre I could compose a book entitled: "A Walk Around My Room." It was in this room I loved to stay alone for hours on end to study and meditate before the beautiful view which stretched out before my eyes. When I learned of Marie's departure, my *room* lost [10] its attraction for me and I didn't want to leave for one instant the dear sister who was to fly away soon. What acts of patience I made her practice! *Each time* I passed in front of the door of her room, I knocked until she opened it and I embraced her with all my heart. I wanted to get a supply of kisses to make up for all the time I was to be deprived of them. [15]A month before her entrance into Carmel, Papa brought us to Alençon,[88] but this trip was far from resembling the first; everything about it was sadness and bitterness for me. I cannot express the tears I shed on Mama's grave because I had forgotten to bring the bouquet of cornflowers I had gathered especially for her. I really made a big fuss over *everything!* I was just the [20] opposite of what I am now, for God has given me the grace not to be downcast at any passing thing. When I think of the past, my soul overflows with gratitude when I see the favors I received from heaven. They have made such a change in me that I don't recognize myself. It is true that I desired the grace "of having absolute control over my actions, of not being their slave but their mistress."[89] [43v°] These words of the Imitation touched me deeply, but I had to buy, so to speak, this inestimable grace through my desires; I was still only a child who appeared to have no will but that of others, and this caused

---

[88] It was actually a few days before Marie's departure.

[89] *The Imitation of Christ* III, 38:1.

[90] October 7, 1886. "She went to express her desires to the Mother Superior, who encouraged her to enter immediately and gave her the postulant's 'little habit,' which is similar to the novices in this Order" (note of Mother Agnes of Jesus).

certain people in Alençon to say I had a [5]weak character. It was during this trip that Léonie made her attempt to enter the Poor Clares.[90] I was saddened by her extraordinary entrance, for I loved her very much and I hadn't even the chance to kiss her before her departure. Never will I forget the kindness and embarrassment of this poor little Father of ours when he came to announce that Léonie had already received the habit of the Poor Clares. [10] He found this very strange, just as we did, but he didn't want to say anything when he saw how unhappy Marie was about the matter. He took us to the convent and there I experienced a sort of *contraction of my heart* such as I never felt at the sight of a monastery. This monastery produced the opposite effect which Carmel produced in me, for there everything made my heart expand. The sight of the religious didn't attract me [15]in the least, and I was not tempted to remain among them. However, poor Léonie was very attractive in her new costume, and she told us to get a good look at *her eyes* because we would no longer see them (the Poor Clares have a custom of going around with eyes downcast), but God was content with only two months of sacrifice, and Léonie returned to show us *her* blue *eyes* which were frequently [20]moist with tears.

When leaving Alençon I believed she would remain with the Poor Clares, and so it was with a heavy heart I left the *sad* street of *Demi-lune* (half moon). We were only three now and soon our Marie was also to leave. The 15th of October was the day of separation! From the happy and numerous family of Les Buissonnets there remained only the two youngest children. The doves had flown from the paternal nest, and those who remained would have loved to fly in their turn, but their wings [44r°] were still too weak for them to take flight.

God, who willed to call to Himself the smallest and weakest of all, hastened to develop her wings. He, who is pleased to show His goodness and power by using the least worthy instruments, willed to

[5]call me before calling Céline who no doubt merited this favor more. But Jesus knew how weak I was and it was for this reason He hid me first in the crevice of the rock.[91]

When Marie entered Carmel, I was still very scrupulous. No longer able to confide in her I turned toward heaven. I addressed myself to the [10]four angels who had preceded me there, for I thought that these innocent souls, having never known troubles or fear, would have pity on their poor little sister who was suffering on earth. I spoke to them with the simplicity of a child, pointing out that being the youngest of the family, I was always the most loved, the most covered with [15]my sisters' tender cares, that if they had remained on earth they, too, would have given me proofs of their affection. Their departure for heaven did not appear to me as a reason for forgetting me; on the contrary, finding themselves in a position to draw from the divine treasures, they had to take *peace* for me from these treasures and thus show me that in heaven they still knew how to love! The answer was not long in [20]coming, for soon peace came to inundate my soul with its delightful waves, and I knew then that if I was loved on earth, I was also loved in heaven. Since that moment, my devotion for my little brothers and sisters has grown and I love to hold dialogues with them frequently, to speak with them about the sadness of our exile, about my desire to join them soon in the Fatherland!

---

[91] Canticle of Canticles 2:14.

# First Communion, Boarding School
## Background and Context.

Thérèse's recovery was gradual; emotional stress brought on minor relapses. "I upset her twice," said Léonie, "in the months immediately following her cure. She fell down and remained stretched out for several minutes each time; she went completely stiff all over, but this passed off of its own accord. On these occasions, however, she did not become delirious or convulsive as she did during her illness." [1]

A year after her cure, when Thérèse was preparing to make her first holy communion, her sister Marie "explained the way of becoming holy through *fidelity in little things*" (S. 117) (italic added), which became an important element of Thérèse's "little way."

Thérèse's reception of communion was an experience of profound union with God. "I *felt* that I was *loved*...for a long time now Jesus and poor little Thérèse *looked at* and understood each other. That day, it was no longer simply a *look*, it was a fusion; they were no longer two, Thérèse had vanished as a drop of water is lost in the immensity of the ocean" (S. 121). One expression of God's mercy that Thérèse became conscious of as a result of the grace of her first communion was the realization of God's protective love in her life. "I know that without Him, I could have fallen as low as St. Mary Magdalene...but I know also know that Jesus has *forgiven me more* than *St. Mary Magdalene* since He forgave me *in advance* by preventing me from falling" (S. 128).

Abbé André Combes writes that the grace that Thérèse received at her first communion contained "the germ of the whole Thérèsian revolution." [2] The core of the Thérèsian revolution was the recovery of a merciful, loving God in the midst of a land infected by the stern God of Jansenism. Jansenism emphasized the depravity of human nature and its inclination toward sin. It preached a divine justice that was so stern and exacting, that only a few people could be saved. It taught that sacramental absolution did not forgive sins but only declared them forgiven to the person who already possessed the perfect love of God. Likewise, Jansenism held that it was only the unsullied soul, free of all taint of sin, that could approach the communion rail without the fear of committing a sacrilege. Jansenistic piety was excessively rigid, moralistic and rooted in an image of God as a harsh judge of unyielding justice. It taught that the possibility of committing a mortal sin is an ever constant and present danger. These beliefs gave rise to excessive introspection that was the seed bed and breeding ground of scrupulosity.

When Thérèse was making her retreat in preparation for the renewal of her first communion (a year after making her first communion), she was frightened by what Fr. Domin said in his conferences. The titles of his conferences were hell, judgment, mortal sin, the necessity of making a good confession, and sacrilegious communion. "What M. l'Abbé [Domin] told us was frightening," wrote Thérèse in her retreat notes. "He spoke about mortal sin, and he described a soul in the state of sin and how much God hated it" (L. 226).

Thérèse's fear triggered an agonizing attack of scruples that lasted for eighteen months."One would have to pass through this martyrdom to understand it well, and for me to express what I suffered for a *year and a half* would be impossible. All of my most simple thoughts and actions became the cause of trouble for me, and I had relief only when I told them to Marie. This cost me dearly, for I believed I was obliged to tell her the absurd thoughts I had even about her" (S. 129).

Thérèse was not cured of her scrupulosity when this bout with scruples subsided. Rather her tendency towards scrupulosity persisted throughout her life. The stern God of Jansenism that gave rise to Thérèse's scruples, which was in stark contrast to the God of merciful love that Thérèse experienced at the time of her first communion, lurked in the shadows of her mind. "Trust in God had become her special characteristic," testified Pauline. " [But] scruples came to paralyze this impetus, and she was very troubled, too, during her first years in Carmel. This was partly because she had heard it said in some sermons that it was very easy to offend God and to stain one's purity of conscience. This was a real torment to her." [3] Thérèse *believed* in Merciful Love but did not always *feel* God's love.

Several months into her bout with scruples (January, 1886), Thérèse was removed from the boarding school because her father was concerned about Thérèse having a relapse of her illness. Marie testifies: "[Thérèse] was withdrawn from the boarding school about January, 1886. Her sister Céline, who had previously been with her there, had completed her studies in August, 1885. Our little sister returned to the Abbey by herself in October. This isolation, in a house where she had already met with her share of suffering, seemed to endanger her health. And besides, she was suffering from scruples. So father thought it would be better to keep her at home and let her finish her studies there." [4] Recall Thérèse's comment: "The five years I spent in school were the saddest in my life, and if I hadn't had Céline with me, I couldn't have remained there and would have become sick in a month" (S. 81). However, in spite of, or perhaps, because of the social isolation that Thérèse experienced during her school years, she developed a love of reading that nourished her heart as well as her mind.

After withdrawing from the boarding school, Thérèse received instructions from a private tutor (Madame Papinau). It was during this time (October 15, 1886) that Marie entered Carmel. Marie's departure was not as traumatic for Thérèse as Pauline's departure had been; nevertheless, it was wrenching. "[Marie was] the only support of my soul...she was indispensable to me...I told my scruples only to her...I loved her so much I couldn't live without her" (S. 133). After Marie's departure, Thérèse had no one on earth to whom she could confide her scruples; so she prayed to her four siblings in heaven. She asked them to intercede for her. Peace was granted. "[S]oon peace came to inundate my soul with its delightful waves, and I knew then that if I was loved on earth, I was also loved in heaven" (S. 139). The grace of her first communion was revived. "I *felt* that I was *loved*" (S. 121).

### Reflections and Questions.

1. Thérèse tells us that she loved reading "and would have spent [her] life at it." And even though what she read "nourished both [her] heart and [her] mind," she put limits on how much she read; "I was not to go beyond a certain time in my reading, which was the cause of great sacrifices for me as I had to interrupt my reading very often at the most enticing passage." (S. 114). There are two related issues here. With *what* do we feed our minds, and *how much* time do we expend in doing so?

*Questions.* a) We live in a noisy world that clamors for our attention. We are assaulted with a barrage of billboards, flashing neon signs, those annoying "pop up" advertisements on the internet, pesky telemarketers, hackers with handbills and leaflets stuffed under the windshield wipers of our cars. Each year Madison Avenue spends billions of dollars on advertisement based upon the assumption that what they can present to our senses will inculcate desire and change our behavior, namely, to buy their product. But advertisement does more than promote its product; it preaches a philosophy of life. It whispers, "In order to be happy, in order to live the good life, you must have me, use me, taste me, try me, drink me, etc."

And what is true of advertisement is true of almost everything that our modern world presents to our senses. The music we listen to, the books we read, the television programs we watch, all communicate to us a philosophy of life. Plato taught that music shapes our character because it shapes the impulses of the soul. Or as Josep Pieper puts it, "Music may be nothing but a secret philosophizing of the soul." [5] Music philosophizes the soul not by means of concepts but by the emotional impress that it leaves upon us, either for good or for ill. Music will either lighten or darken our mood, soften or harshen our human sensitivities. And what is true of music is also true of what we read and watch on television. For example, what effect do you believe it would have upon you if you watched the Jerry Springer show all day long, every day of the week? How do you think it would influence your vision of life? How do you think it would shape the way you view human nature? Would it nourish or deplete your humanity? Thérèse tells us that what she read *nourished* her heart and her mind. Is this true for you?

b) If Washington Irving had written Rip Van Winkle in our day, he might have opened his story with a man with a long white beard signing off on the internet, with a startled look on his face, as he reads, "You have just spent 20 years online." Many of us have had similar experiences. For example, you log on the internet *just* to read your e-mail when some question of curiosity pops into your mind. "I wonder what ever happened to William "The Refrigerator" Perry who played defensive tackle for the Chicago Bears?" As you spend a few minutes checking out various web sites in order to satisfy this curiosity, another question comes to your mind. "Was it Emily or Charlotte Brontë who wrote *Jane Eyre?* I can never remember which Brontë sister wrote what!" [6] And so on, and so on, and so on. And before you know it, half the morning is shot. "You just spent 97 minutes on line."

Thérèse tells us that it was difficult for her to put a time limit on her reading because it often entailed stopping "at the most enticing passage" (S. 114). How true to life is Thérèse's experience! How difficult it is to stop an activity in which we are engrossed. But perhaps what is more pertinent to us in our over-stimulated, bored culture is setting boundaries to anesthetizing activities. For example, when I find myself "surfing the net," it is usually because I am restless or bored; I don't know what to do with myself, so I indulge in a little diversion. Such mindless activity ("surfing the net" may better be termed as "drifting with the tide" or "aimless wandering," for surfing involves skill and concentration) consumes precious time which could be used for activities that nourish the soul. Our time is limited, and how we spend it is a basic choice in life. What "mindless" activities do I need to limit in order to have time to engage in behaviors that will nourish my soul (doing spiritual reading, communing with nature, sitting in silence, listening to classical music, etc.)?

2. "Fidelity in little things" became a hallmark of Thérèse's spirituality because her realism told her that true love consists of concrete acts of charity. Fidelity in little things is attending to life as we find it and loving the people that God has placed upon our path. As an adolescent, Thérèse had fantasies and great desires to serve God by means of heroic deeds like Joan of Arc but she came to understand that her "own *glory* would not be evident to the eyes of mortals, that it would consist in becoming a great *saint*" (S. 115) through a life of love lived out in the shadows. Thérèse was aware of the temptation to flee from the hard work that love demands by escaping into dreams of glory, of which St. Teresa of Avila writes: "The devil gives us great desires so that we will avoid setting ourselves to the task at hand, serving our Lord in possible things, and instead be content with having desired the impossible."[7]

It is a hard fact to accept that our "own glory" will be enacted under the guise of the ordinary and consist in being faithful in fulfilling the lackluster obligations of our station in life. Yet magnanimity lies within the narrow circumference of the mundane, for fidelity to the daily round requires the fortitude of the long haul. "Faithfulness is consecration in overalls," writes Evelyn Underhill, "It is the steady acceptance and performance of the common duty and immediate task without any reference to personal preferences...Faithfulness means continuing quietly with the job we have been given, in the situation where we have been placed; not yielding to the restless desire for change. It means tending the lamp quietly for God without wondering how much longer it has got to go on."⁸ Faithfulness requires endurance, and endurance is the essence of fortitude says St. Thomas; it is the loving service that holds down the fort, it is the undramatic heroism of the unsung, uncelebrated, unacknowledged, and unrecognized. Such was the existence of Thérèse, whose glory was not evident to the eyes of the world but consisted in practicing the ordinary virtues. Such are our own lives.

*Questions.* How do you see what you do both at home and at work? Do you see your duties (eg. house work, etc) simply as tasks to be done or as the context in which God calls you to the holiness of love? For example, let us say that you are a checkout clerk at a supermarket. Do you define your work as merely ringing up items on the cash register and bagging groceries, or do you see that the real work that God invites you to is being patient and kind to the people you serve? What helps you sustain a faith vision of the eternal significance of what you do in the midst of the mundane? What hinders?

3. Thérèse deeply believed in the truth contained in the old saying "There but for the grace of God go I." "I know without Him, I could have fallen as low as St. Mary Magdalene ...I also know that Jesus has *forgiven me more* than St. Mary Magdalene since He forgave me *in advance* by preventing me from falling" (S. 128). In the opening scene of Dante's *Inferno*, Dante wakes up to the realization that he is lost in a forest of sin and ignorance. He tells us that he has awakened just in the nick of time. In this regard, Dante employs the image of a man who has barely escaped with his life from a shipwreck. "And as one who, with laboring breath/has escaped from the deep to the

shore/turns and looks back at the perilous waters/ my mind, still in flight/ turned back to look once more upon the pass/no mortal being ever left alive." [9] Dante looked back over his life and reflected upon his narrow escape from moral disaster. Similarly, Thérèse was conscious of what her life would have been if God's grace had not prevented her from falling.

*Questions.* Reflect upon the crossroads of your life. Think of how different your life would be, if God had not prevented you from making a disastrous choice. T.S. Eliot writes of "a moment's surrender which an age of prudence can never retract." [10] Think of how close you came to surrendering your will to a deed that could never be undone. And then thank God for his merciful love and know anew: "There but for the grace of God go I."

## Notes

1. O'Mahony, ibid.,173.

2. Abbé André Combes, *The Heart of Saint Thérèse*, trans. a Carmelite nun, (New York: P.J. Kenedy & Sons, 1951), 5.

3. O'Mahony, ibid., 42-3.

4. O'Mahony, ibid.,89.

5. Josep Pieper, *Only the Lover Sings: Art and Contemplation,* (San Francisco: Ignatius Press, 1990), 39.

6. Just to save you a little time, William "The Refrigerator" Perry is the co-owner of a subcontracting company in Aiken, South Carolina, spends much of his spare time fishing and is happier than a little clam. It was Charlotte Brontë who wrote *Jane Eyre*; her sister Emily wrote *Wuthering Heights*.

7. St. Teresa of Avila, "The Interior Castle," in *The Collected*

*Works of St. Teresa of Avila,*vol. 2, trans. Otilio Rodriguez, O.C.D. and Kieran Kavanaugh, O.C.D., (Washington, D.C.: ICS Publications, 1980), VII, 4, 14, 449.

8. Evelyn Underhill, *The Fruits of the Spirit,* compiled by Roger L. Roberts, (Wilton, Conn.: Morehouse-Barlow Co., 1981), 27-28.

9. Dante, *The Inferno,* trans. Robert and Jean Hollander, (New York: Doubleday, 2000), canto 1, 22-27.

10. T. S. Eliot, "The Waste Land," in *Selected Poems,* (New York: Harbrace Paperbound Library, 1964), 66.

# Chapter V

# *AFTER THE GRACE OF CHRISTMAS (1886–1887)*

The Blood of Jesus
Pranzini, my First Child
The Imitation of Christ and Abbé Arminjon
My Desire to Enter Carmel
I Confide in My Father
Uncle's Change of Heart
The Superior's Opposition
The Visit to Bayeux

A lthough God showered His graces upon me, it wasn't because I merited them because I was still very imperfect. I had a great desire, it is true, to practice [44v°] virtue, but I went about it in a strange way. Being the youngest in the family, I wasn't accustomed to doing things for myself. Céline tidied up the room in which we slept, and I myself didn't do any housework whatsoever. After Marie's entrance into Carmel, it sometimes happened that I tried to make up the bed [5] to please God, or else in the evening, when Céline was away, I'd bring in her plants. But as I already said, it was for *God alone* I was doing these things and should not have expected any *thanks* from creatures. Alas, it was just the opposite. If Céline was unfortunate enough not to seem happy or surprised because of these little [10]services, I became unhappy and proved it by my tears.

I was really unbearable because of my extreme touchiness; if I happened to cause anyone I loved some little trouble, even unwittingly, instead of forgetting about it and not *crying*, which made matters worse, I *cried* like a Magdalene and then when [15]I began to cheer up,

I'd begin *to cry again for having cried.* All arguments were useless; I was quite unable to correct this terrible fault. I really don't know how I could entertain the thought of entering Carmel when I was still in the *swaddling clothes of a child!*

God would have to work a little miracle to [20]make me grow up in an instant, and this miracle He performed on that unforgettable Christmas day. On that luminous *night* which sheds such light on the delights of the Holy Trinity, Jesus, the gentle, *little* Child of only one hour, changed the night of my soul into rays of light. On that *night* when He made Himself subject to *weakness* and suffering for love of me, He made me *strong* and courageous, arming me with His weapons. Since that night I have never been defeated in any combat, but rather walked from victory to victory, beginning, so to speak, *"to run as a giant"!*[92] [45r°] The source of my tears was dried up and has since reopened rarely and with great difficulty. This justified what was often said to me: "You cry so much during your childhood, you'll no longer have tears to shed later on!"

It was December 25, 1886, that I received the grace of leaving my childhood, in a [5]word, the grace of my complete conversion. We had come back from Midnight Mass where I had the happiness of receiving the *strong* and *powerful* God. Upon arriving at Les Buissonnets, I used to love to take my shoes from the chimney corner and examine the presents in them; this old custom had given us so much joy in our youth that Céline wanted to continue treating me as a baby since I was the youngest in the family. Papa [10] had always loved to see my happiness and listen to my cries of delight as I drew each surprise from the *magic shoes,* and my dear King's gaiety increased my own happiness very much. However, Jesus desired to show me

---

[92] Psalm 18:6.

that I was to give up the defects of my childhood and so He withdrew its innocent pleasures. He permitted Papa, tired out after the Midnight Mass, to experience annoyance when seeing my shoes at the fireplace, and that he speak [15]those words which pierced my heart: "Well, fortunately, this will be the last year!" I was going upstairs, at the time, to remove my hat, and Céline, knowing how sensitive I was and seeing the tears already glistening in my eyes, wanted to cry too, for she loved me very much and understood my grief. She said, "Oh, Thérèse, don't go downstairs; it would cause you too much grief to look [20]at your slippers right now!" But Thérèse was no longer the same; Jesus had changed her heart! Forcing back my tears, I descended the stairs rapidly; controlling the poundings of my heart, I took my slippers and placed them in front of Papa, and withdrew all the objects joyfully. I had the happy appearance of a Queen. Having regained his own cheerfulness, Papa was laughing; Céline believed it was all a dream! Fortunately, it was a sweet reality; Thérèse had discovered once again the strength of soul which she had lost at the age of four and a half, and she was to preserve it forever!

[45v°] On that *night of light* began the third period of my life, the most beautiful and the most filled with graces from heaven. The work I had been unable to do in ten years was done by Jesus in one instant, contenting himself with my *good will* which was never lacking. I could say to [5]Him like His apostles: "Master, I fished all night and caught nothing."[93] More merciful to me than He was to His disciples, Jesus *took the net Himself,* cast it, and drew it in filled with fish. He made me a fisher of *souls.* I experienced a great desire to work for the conversion of sinners, a desire I hadn't felt so intensely before.

I felt *charity* enter [10] into my soul, and the need to forget myself

---

[93] Luke 5:5.

and to please others; since then I've been happy! One Sunday, look-ing at a picture of Our Lord on the Cross, I was struck by the blood flowing from one of the divine hands. I felt a great pang of sorrow when thinking this blood was falling to the ground without anyone's hastening to gather it up. I was resolved to remain in spirit at the foot of the [15]Cross and to receive the divine dew. I understood I was then to pour it out upon souls. The cry of Jesus on the Cross sounded con-tinually in my heart: *"I thirst!"*[94] These words ignited within me an unknown and very living fire. I wanted to give my Beloved to drink and I felt myself consumed with a thirst for souls. As yet, it was not the [20]souls of priests that attracted me, but those of *great sinners;* I *burned* with the desire to snatch them from the eternal flames.

To awaken my zeal God showed me my desires were pleasing to Him. I heard talk of a great criminal just condemned to death for some horrible crimes;[95] everything pointed to the fact that he would die impenitent. I wanted at all costs to prevent him from falling into hell, and to attain my purpose I employed every means imaginable. Feeling that of myself I could do nothing, I offered [46r°] to God all the infinite merits of Our Lord, the treasures of the Church, and final-ly I begged Céline to have a Mass offered for my intentions. I didn't dare ask this myself for fear of being obliged to say it was for Pranzini, the great criminal. I didn't even want to tell Céline, but she [5]asked me such tender and pressing questions, I confided my secret to her. Far from laughing at me, she asked if she could help convert my sinner. I accepted gratefully, for I would have wished all creatures would unite with me to beg grace for the guilty man.

---

[94] John 19:28.

[95] Henri Pranzini. His case was opened July 9, 1887, and ended with his condemnation to death on July 13. Thérèse became interested in his conversion. Pranzini was executed August 31, 1887.

I felt in the depths of my heart *certain* that our desires would be granted, but to obtain courage [10] to pray for sinners I told God I was sure He would pardon the poor, unfortunate Pranzini; that I'd believe this even if he went to his death without *any signs of repentance* or without *having gone to confession.* I was absolutely confident in the mercy of Jesus. But I was begging Him for a *"sign"* of repentance only for my own simple consolation.

My prayer was [15]answered to the letter! In spite of Papa's prohibition that we read no papers, I didn't think I was disobeying when reading the passages pertaining to Pranzini. The day after his execution I found the newspaper *"La Croix."* I opened it quickly and what did I see? Ah! my tears betrayed my emotion and I was obliged to hide. Pranzini had not gone to confession. [20]He had mounted the scaffold and was preparing to place his head in the formidable opening, when suddenly, seized by an inspiration, he turned, took hold of the *crucifix* the priest was holding out to him and *kissed* the *sacred wounds three times!* Then his soul went to receive the *merciful* sentence of Him who declares that in heaven there will be more joy over one sinner who does penance than over ninety-nine just who have no need of repentance![96]

I had obtained the "sign" I requested, and this sign was a perfect replica of the [46v°] grace Jesus had given me when He attracted me to pray for sinners. Wasn't it before the *wounds of Jesus,* when seeing His divine *blood* flowing, that the thirst for souls had entered my heart? I wished to give them this *immaculate blood* to drink, this blood which was to purify them from their stains, and the lips of my *"first child"* [5]were pressed to the sacred wounds!

What an unspeakably sweet response! After this unique grace

---

[96] Luke 15:7.

my desire to save souls grows each day, and I seemed to hear Jesus say to me what he said to the Samaritan woman: *"Give me to drink!"*[97] It was a true interchange of love: to souls I was giving the *blood of Jesus,* to Jesus I was offering these same souls refreshed by the *divine dew.* [10] I slaked His thirst and the more I gave Him *to drink,* the more the thirst of my poor little soul increased, and it was this ardent thirst He was giving me as the most delightful drink of His love.

God was able in a very short time to extricate me from the very narrow circle in which I was turning without knowing how to come out. When seeing the road He made me [15] travel, my gratitude was great; but I must admit, if the biggest step was taken, there still remained many things for me to leave behind. Freed from its scruples and its excessive sensitiveness, my mind developed.

I had always loved the great and the beautiful, but at this epoch in my life I was taken up with an extreme desire for learning. Not satisfied with the lessons and work [20]my teacher was giving me, I applied myself to some special studies in *history* and *science,* and I did this on my own. The other studies left me indifferent, but these two subjects attracted all my attention; in a few months I acquired more knowledge than during my years of study. Ah! this was really only vanity and affliction of spirit.[98] The chapter in the Imitation which speaks of *knowledge* [99] came frequently to my mind, but I found ways of continuing all the same, telling myself that being at an age for studying, it could not be [47r°] bad to do it. I don't believe I offended God (although I recognize the fact that I spent useless time in it), for I confined myself to a certain number of hours, unwilling to go beyond in order to mortify my intense desire to know things.

---

[97] John 4:7.

[98] Ecclesiastes 2:11.

[99] *The Imitation of Christ* III, 43.

I was at the most dangerous age for young girls, [5] but God did for me what Ezechiel reports in his prophecies:

"Passing by me, Jesus saw that the time had come for me to be *loved,* He entered into a covenant with me and I became *His own.* He spread his mantle over me, he washed me with precious perfumes, He reclothed me in embroidered robes, He gave me priceless necklaces and ornaments. He nourished me with purest flour, with honey and oil in *abundance.* Then I became beautiful in His eyes and He made me a mighty queen."[100]

Yes, Jesus did all this for me. I could take each word and prove it was realized in me, but the graces I already mentioned are sufficient proof. I'm going to speak, therefore, only of the [15] food He provided "in *abundance.*" I was nourished for a long time on the "pure flour" contained in the Imitation of Christ, this being the only book which did me any good, for as yet I had not discovered the treasures hidden in the Gospels.

I knew almost all the chapters of my beloved Imitation by heart. This little book never parted company with me, for in summer I carried it in my pocket, in winter, in my muff. [20] At Aunt's they used to amuse themselves by opening the book at random and telling me to recite the chapter before them. With my new desire for knowledge at the age of fourteen, God found it necessary to join to the *"pure flour"* some *"honey and oil in abundance."* This honey and oil He showed me in Abbé Arminjon's conferences on the end of the present world and the mysteries of the future life.[101] This book had been lent to Papa by my dear Carmelites, and, contrary to my [47v°] custom (I didn't read Papa's books), I asked to read it.

---

[100] See Ezekiel 16:8-13.

[101] Conferences preached at Chambery Cathedral, edited in 1881 under the title *Fin du Monde présent et Mystères de la vie future.*

This reading was one of the greatest graces in my life. I read it by the window of my study, and the impressions I received are too deep to express in human words.

[5]All the great truths of religion, the mysteries of eternity, plunged my soul into a state of joy not of this earth. I experienced already what God reserved for those who love Him (not with the eye but with the heart),[102] and seeing the eternal rewards had no proportion to life's small sacrifices,[103] I wanted to *love, to love* [10] *Jesus with a passion,* giving Him a thousand proofs of my love while it was possible. I copied out several passages on perfect love, on the reception God will give His Elect at the moment *He* becomes their Reward, great and eternal, and I repeated over and over the words of love burning in my heart.

Céline had become the [15]confidante of my thoughts. Ever since Christmas we could understand each other; the distance of age no longer existed because I had grown in both height and grace. Before this epoch I'd often complained at not knowing Céline's secrets, and she told me I was too little, that I'd have to grow "as high as a stool" so that [20] she could have confidence in me. I loved climbing up on that precious stool when I was standing by her side and telling her to speak intimately to me; but all to no avail, a distance separated us still!

Jesus, wanting to have us advance together, formed bonds in our hearts stronger than blood. He made us become *spiritual sisters,* and in us were realized the words of St. John of the Cross' Canticle (speaking to her Spouse, the bride exclaims):

> Following Your footprints
> Maidens run lightly along the way;

---

[102] 1 Corinthians 2:9.

[103] Romans 8:18.

The touch of [48r°] a spark,
The special wine,
Cause flowings in them from the balsam of God.[104]

Yes, it was very *lightly* we followed in Jesus' footprints. The sparks of love He sowed so generously in our souls, and the delicious and strong wine He gave us to drink made all passing [5] things disappear before our eyes, and from our lips came aspirations of love inspired only by Him. How sweet were the conversations we held each evening in the belvédère! With enraptured gaze we beheld the white moon rising quietly behind the tall trees, the silvery rays it was casting upon sleeping nature, the bright stars twinkling in the deep skies, the light breath of the evening breeze [10] making the snowy clouds float easily along; all this raised our souls to heaven, that beautiful heaven whose "obverse side" alone we were able to contemplate.[105]

I don't know if I'm mistaken, but it seems to me the outpourings of our souls were similar to those of St. Monica with her son when, at the port of Ostia, they were lost in ecstasy at the sight of the Creator's marvels! It [15]appears we were receiving graces like those granted to the great saints. As the Imitation says, God communicates Himself at times in the midst of great splendor or *"gently veiled, under shadows and figures."*[106] It was in this way He deigned to manifest Himself to our souls, but how *light* and *transparent* the veil was that hid Jesus from our gaze! Doubt was [20]impossible, faith and hope were unnecessary, and Love made us find on earth the One whom we were seeking. *"Having found us alone, he gave us his kiss, in order that in the*

---

[104] *Spiritual Canticle,* st. 25, *Collected Works,* p. 569.

[105] From a poem of Alfred Besse de Larze (1848–1904), titled *L'envers du Ciel.*

[106] *The Imitation of Christ* III, 43:4.

*future no one could despise us.* "[107]

Graces as great as this were not to be without fruit and it was abundant. The practice of virtue became sweet and natural to us. At the beginning, it is true, my face betrayed the struggle, but little by little this vanished and renunciation was easy, even the first call of grace. Jesus has said: "For to [48v°] him who has will *more be given, and he will have abundance ...* "[108] For a grace received faithfully, He granted me a multitude of others. He gave Himself to me in Holy Communion more frequently than I would have dared hope. I'd taken as a rule of conduct to receive, without missing a single one, [5]the Communions my confessor permitted, allowing him to regulate the number and not asking. At this time in my life, I didn't have the *boldness* I now have, for I'm very sure a soul must tell her confessor the attraction she feels to receive her God. It is not to remain in a golden ciborium that He comes to us *each day* from [10]heaven; it's to find another heaven, infinitely more dear to Him than the first: the heaven of our soul, made to His image, the living temple of the adorable Trinity!

Jesus, aware of the desire and uprightness of my heart, allowed my confessor to tell me to receive Communion during the month of May four times a [15]week; the month having passed, he added a fifth whenever a feast occurred. Sweet were the tears that flowed from my eyes when leaving the confessional. It appeared to be Jesus Himself who desired to give Himself to me, for I went to confession only a few times, and never spoke about my interior sentiments. The way I was [20] walking was so straight, so clear, I needed no other guide but Jesus. I compared directors to faithful mirrors, reflecting Jesus in souls, and I said that for me God was using no intermediary, He was acting directly!

---

[107] Canticle of Canticles 8:1.
[108] Matthew 13:12.

When a gardener carefully tends a fruit he wants to ripen before its time, it's not to leave it hanging on a tree but to set it on his table. It was with such an intention [49r°] that Jesus showered His graces so lavishly upon His little flower, He, who cried out in His mortal life: *"I thank thee, Father, that thou hast hidden these things from the wise and the prudent and revealed them to babes,"*[109] willed to have His mercy shine out in me. Because I was little [5] and weak He lowered Himself to me, and He instructed me secretly in the *things* of His *love.* Ah! had the learned who spent their life in study come to me, undoubtedly they would have been astonished to see a child of fourteen understand perfection's secrets, secrets all their knowledge cannot reveal because to possess them one has to be poor in spirit!

[10] As St. John of the Cross writes in his canticle:

> On that glad night,
> in secret, for no one saw me,
> nor did I look at anything,
> with no other light or guide
> than the one that burned in my heart.
> This guided me
> more surely than the light of noon
> to where he was awaiting me
> — him I knew so well —
> there in a place where no one appeared.[110]

This place was Carmel. Before *"resting in the shadow of him whom I desired,"*[111] I was to pass through many trials, but the [15]divine

---

[109] Matthew 11:25.

[110] *Dark Night,* st. 3 and 4, *Collected Works,* p. 51.

[111] Canticle of Canticles 2:3.

call was so strong that had I been forced to *pass through flames,* I would have done it out of love for Jesus.

I found only *one soul* to encourage me in my vocation, that of my *dear Mother.* My heart found a faithful echo in hers, and without her, perhaps, I would not have reached the blessed shore which received her five years before on its soil permeated with the [20]heavenly dew. Yes, I was separated from you for five years, *dear Mother,* and I believed I'd lost you forever; at the moment of trial your hand pointed out the way I should follow. I needed this help, for my visits to Carmel had become more and more painful, and I was unable to speak of my desire to enter without feeling opposed. Marie, thinking I was too young, did everything possible to prevent my entering; and you, dear Mother, to prove me, sometimes tried to slacken my ardor. [49v°] If I hadn't had a vocation, I would have been stopped from the beginning, so many obstacles did I receive when trying to answer Jesus' call. I didn't want to speak to Céline about my desire to enter so young and this caused me much suffering, for it was difficult for me to hide anything from her.

[5]This suffering, however, didn't last long; soon my dear little sister learned of my determination and, far from turning me away from it, she courageously accepted the sacrifice God was asking of her. To understand how great it was, one would have to know how very close we were. It was, so to speak, the same soul giving us life. For some months we'd [10] enjoyed together the most beautiful life young girls could dream about. Everything around us corresponded with our tastes; we were given the greatest liberty; I would say our life on earth was the *ideal of happiness.*

Hardly had we the time to taste this *ideal of happiness* when it was necessary to turn away from it freely, and my dear Céline did not rebel for one instant. And still it wasn't she [15]whom Jesus was calling first, and she could have complained, for having the same vocation as I, it was her right to leave first! But as in the time of the martyrs, those who remained in prison joyfully gave the kiss of peace to their brothers who were leaving first for combat in the arena, consoling themselves with the thought that perhaps they were reserved for even greater combats, thus *Céline* [20]allowed her Thérèse to leave and she stayed for the glorious and bloody struggle to which Jesus had destined her as the *privileged one of His love!* [112]

Céline became, then, the confidante of my struggles and sufferings, taking the same part as though it were a question of her own vocation. From her I had no fear of opposition. I didn't know what steps to take to announce it to Papa. How should I speak to him about parting from his Queen, he who'd just sacrificed his three eldest? Ah! what interior struggles I went through before [50r°] feeling courageous enough to speak! However, I had to decide. After all, I was going to be fourteen and a half, and six months separated us from the beautiful *night of Christmas,* the day I was determined to enter, at the very hour I'd received "my grace" the year before.

I chose the [5] *feast of Pentecost* as the day to break the news,[113] all day long begging the apostles to pray for me, to inspire me with the right words. Shouldn't they help the timid child who was chosen by God to be the apostle of apostles through her prayers and sacrifices in Carmel? I found the opportunity to speak to my dear little Father only in the afternoon after Vespers. He was seated by the well, [10]contemplating the marvels of nature with his hands joined. The sun whose rays had lost their ardor gilded the high tree tops where little birds were joyfully chanting their evening song. Papa's handsome face had

---

[112] M. Martin's sickness. Céline tended him all through it.

[113] May 29, 1887.

a heavenly expression about it, giving me the feeling that peace flooded his heart. Without saying a word, I sat down by his side, my eyes already wet with tears. He [15]gazed at me tenderly, and taking my head he placed it on his heart, saying: "What's the matter, my little Queen? Tell me." Then rising as though to hide his own emotion, he walked while still holding my head on his heart.

Through my tears, I confided my desire to enter Carmel and soon his tears mingled with mine. He didn't say one word to [20]turn me from my vocation, simply contenting himself with the statement that I was still very young to make such a serious decision. I defended myself so well that, with Papa's simple and direct character, he was soon convinced my desire was God's will, and in his deep faith he cried out that God was giving him a great honor in asking his children from him; we continued our walk for a long time and, encouraged by the kindness with which my incomparable Father received my confidences, [50v°] my heart poured out itself to him.

Papa seemed to be rejoicing with that joy that comes from a sacrifice already made. He spoke just like a saint, and I'd love to recall his words and write them down, but all I preserved of them is a memory too sacred to be expressed. What I do recall, however, [5]is a *symbolic* action my dear King performed, not realizing its full meaning. Going up to a low wall, he pointed to some *little white flowers,* like lilies in miniature, and plucking one of them, he gave it to me, explaining the care with which God brought it into being and preserved it to that very day. While I listened I believed I was hearing my own story, [10]so great was the resemblance between what Jesus had done for the *little flower* and *little Thérèse.* I accepted it as a relic and noticed that, in gathering it, Papa had pulled all its *roots* out without breaking them. It seemed destined to live on in another soil more fertile than the tender moss where it had spent its first days. This was really the same

[15]action Papa had performed a few moments before when he allowed me to climb Mount Carmel and leave the sweet valley which had witnessed my first steps in this life.

I placed the little white flower in my copy of the Imitation at the chapter entitled: "One must love Jesus above all things,"[114] and there it is still, only its stem [20]has broken close to the roots, and God seems to be saying by this that He'll soon break the bonds of His little flower, not allowing her to fade away on this earth!

After receiving Papa's permission, I believed I'd be able to fly to Carmel without any fears, but painful trials were still to prove my vocation. It was with trembling I confided my resolution to Uncle.[115] He showed me great tenderness but did not grant me his permission to leave. He forbade me to [51r°] speak about my vocation to him until I was seventeen. It was contrary to human prudence, he said, to have a child of fifteen enter Carmel. This Carmelite life was, in the eyes of many, a life of mature reflection, and it would be doing a great wrong to the religious life to allow an inexperienced child to embrace it. [5]Everybody would be talking about it, etc., etc. He even said that for him to decide to allow me to leave would require a *miracle*. I saw all reasoning with him was useless and so I left, my heart plunged into the most profound bitterness. My only consolation was prayer. I begged Jesus to perform the *miracle* demanded, since at this price only I'd be able to answer His call.

[10] A long time passed by before I dared speak to him again.[116] It was very difficult for me to go to his home, and he himself seemed to be no longer considering my vocation. I learned later on that my great

---

[114] *The Imitation of Christ* II, 7.

[115] October 8, 1887.

[116] It was only two weeks.

sadness influenced him very much. Before allowing any ray of hope to shine in my soul, God willed to send me a painful martyrdom lasting *three* [15]*days*.[117] Oh! never had I understood so well as during this trial, the sorrow of Mary and Joseph during their three-day search for the divine Child Jesus. I was in a sad desert, or rather my soul was like a fragile boat delivered up to the mercy of the waves and having no pilot. I knew Jesus was there sleeping in my boat, but the night was so black it was impossible to see Him; nothing gave me any light, [20]not a single flash came to break the dark clouds. No doubt, lightning is a dismal light, but at least if the storm had broken out in earnest I would have been able to see Jesus for one passing moment. But it was night! The dark night of the soul! I felt I was all alone in the garden of Gethsemane like Jesus, and I found no consolation on earth or from heaven; God Himself seemed to have abandoned me. Nature seemed to share in my bitter sadness, for during these three days the sun did not [51v°] shine and the rain poured down in torrents. (I have noticed in all the serious circumstances of my life that nature always reflected the image of my soul. On days filled with tears the heavens cried along with me; on days of joy the sun sent forth its joyful rays in profusion and the blue skies were not obscured by a single cloud.)

[5]Finally, on the fourth day, which happened to be a Saturday, the day consecrated to the sweet Queen of heaven, I went to see Uncle. What was my surprise when I saw him looking at me, and, without expressing any desire to speak to him, he had me come into his study! He began by making some gentle reproaches because I appeared to be afraid of him, and then he said[10] it wasn't necessary to beg for a *miracle,* that he had only asked God to give him "a simple change of heart" and that he had been answered. Ah! I was not tempted to beg

---

[117] From Wednesday, October 19, to Saturday, October 22.

for a miracle because *the miracle had been granted;* Uncle was no longer the same. Without making any allusion whatsoever to "human prudence," he told me I was a *little* [15]*flower God wanted to gather,* and he would no longer oppose it!

[27]This definitive response was truly worthy of him. For the third time now, this Christian of another age allowed one of the adopted daughters of his heart to go bury herself far from the world. Aunt, too, was admirable in her tenderness and prudence. I don't remember her saying a single word during my trial that could have increased my sufferings. I understood she pitied [30]her little Thérèse. But when Uncle gave his consent, she too gave hers, but at the same time she showed me in a thousand little ways the great sorrow my departure would be for her. Alas, our dear relatives were far from expecting [52r°] [27]the same sacrifice would be asked of them twice over. But when God stretches out His *hand* to ask, His hand is never *empty,* and His intimate friends can draw from Him the courage and strength they need.

My heart is carrying me far from my subject and so, regretfully, I return to it. After Uncle's response you can easily understand, dear Mother, [51v°cont'd.] [16]how I took the road back to Les Buissonnets with happiness flooding my heart. It was under *"a beautiful* sky, from which all the clouds were dispersed"*! In my soul, too, the night had come to an end. Awakening, Jesus brought back joy, the noise of the waves was abated, and in place of the wind of trial, a light breeze expanded my [20] sail and I believed I'd reach the blessed *shore*, now seemingly so close! It was really very close to my boat, but *more than one storm* was still to arise. Hiding from me the view of the luminous beacon, these storms caused me to fear lest I should be driven far from the shore so ardently desired without any hope of return.

I obtained, then, Uncle's permission and a few days[118] afterward

---

[118] It was actually the day after, Sunday, October 23.

went to see you, dear Mother. I told you of my joy at seeing that my trials were all over. What was my surprise and sadness when you told me that the [52r°] [1]Superior[119] was not giving his consent to my entrance until I was twenty-one. No one had thought of this opposition, and it was the most insurmountable of all. Without giving up hope, however, I went myself with Papa and Céline to pay him a visit, trying to change his mind by showing I really had a Carmelite vocation.

[5]He received us coldly; my *incomparable* little Father joined his insistence to mine but in vain. Nothing would change the Superior's attitude. He told me there wasn't any danger in staying at home, I could lead a Carmelite life there, and if I didn't take the discipline all was not lost, etc., etc. He ended by saying he was only the [10] *Bishop's delegate,* and if the latter wished me to enter Carmel, he himself would have nothing to say.

I left the rectory in *tears,* and fortunately my umbrella was able to hide them as the *rain* was coming down in torrents. Papa was at a loss as to how to console me. He promised to accompany me to Bayeux the moment I expressed my desire to go there since I was determined *to do all within my power,* even saying I would go [15]to the *Holy Father* if the Bishop did not want to allow me to enter at fifteen.

Many things happened before my trip to Bayeux;[120] exteriorly my life appeared to be as usual. I studied, took lessons in drawing from Céline,[121] and my clever teacher recognized in me an aptitude for her art. Above all, I was growing in love for God; [20]I felt within my

---

[119] Father Delatroëtte, ecclesiastical Superior of Lisieux Carmel.

[120] The delay was short, perhaps seven or eight days, and the trip took place October 31.

[121] Céline gave Thérèse lessons in the first semester of 1887; this is evident from a series of exercises dated from February to May.

heart certain aspirations unknown until then, and at times I had veritable transports of love.

One evening, not knowing how to tell Jesus that I loved Him and how much I desired that He be loved and glorified everywhere, I was thinking He would never receive a single act of love from hell; then I said to God that to please Him I would consent to see myself plunged into hell so that He would be *loved* eternally in that place of blasphemy. I realized this could not give Him glory since He desires only our happiness, but when we [52v°] love, we experience the need of saying a thousand foolish things; if I talked in this way, it wasn't because heaven did not excite my desire, but because at this time my heaven was none other than Love, and I felt, as did St. Paul, that nothing could separate us from the Divine Being who so ravished me![122]

[5]Before I left the world, God gave me the consolation of contemplating at close range the *souls of little children.* As I was the youngest in the family, I never had experienced this happiness before. Here are the unfortunate circumstances that made it possible. A poor woman, a relative of our maid, died when still very young and left three very little children; during the woman's illness, we took care of the two [10]little girls; the older one was not yet six. I spent the whole day with them, and it was a great pleasure for me to see with what simplicity they believed everything I said. Holy baptism must implant a very deep seed of the theological virtues in souls since from childhood these virtues are already evident and since the hope of future goods suffices to have them accept sacrifices. When I wanted to see my two little ones reconciled to each other, instead of offering toys and candy to the one who gave in to the other, I spoke to them about the eternal rewards that little Jesus would give in heaven to good little children;

---

[122] Romans 8:39.

the older one, whose reason was beginning to develop, looked at me with eyes that were bright with joy, asking me a thousand charming questions about little Jesus and [20]His beautiful heaven and promising me enthusiastically always to give in to her sister. She said she would never in her life forget what the "big girl" told her; this was what she called me.

Seeing innocent souls at such close range, I understood what a misfortune it was when they were not formed in their early years, when they are soft as wax upon which one can imprint either virtue or vice. I understood, too, what Jesus said: *"But whoever causes one of these little ones to sin, it were better for him to have a great millstone fastened round his neck and to be drowned in the depths of the sea."*[123] [53r°]Ah! how many souls would have reached sanctity had they been well directed!

God has no need for anyone to carry out His work, I know, but just as He allows a clever gardener to raise rare and delicate plants, giving him the necessary knowledge for this while [5]reserving to Himself the care of making them fruitful, so Jesus wills to be helped in His divine cultivation of souls.

What would happen were a clumsy gardener not to graft his bushes properly? If he was ignorant of the nature of each and wished to make roses bloom on peach trees? He'd cause the tree to die, which nevertheless [10]had been good and capable of producing fruit. It's in this way one should know from childhood what God asks of souls and second the action of His graces, without either advancing or holding it back. As little birds learn to *sing* by listening to their parents, [15]so children learn the science of the virtues, the sublime *song* of Divine Love from souls responsible for forming them.

---

[123] Matthew 18:6.

I remember having among my many birds a canary that sang beautifully. I had a little linnet too on which I lavished *"maternal"* cares as I'd adopted it before it was able to enjoy the happiness of freedom. This poor little prisoner had [20]no parents to teach it to sing, but listening to its companion, the canary, rendering its joyful tunes from morning till night, the linnet wanted to imitate it. The undertaking was difficult, and its sweet voice had trouble matching the vibrant voice of its master in music. It was charming, however, to see the poor little thing's efforts, which were eventually crowned with success. His song, though much softer, was absolutely the same as that of the canary.

[53v°] It's you who taught me how to sing, dear Mother. It's your voice that charmed me in my childhood days, and now I have the consolation of hearing it said I resemble you! I know very well I'm far from this, but I trust in spite of my weakness to sing eternally the same Canticle as you do!

[5]Before my entrance into Carmel I had many experiences of life and the miseries of the world. Details such as this would only lead me far astray, and so I'll now take up the account of my vocation once more.

October 31 was the day set for the trip to Bayeux. I left alone with Papa, my heart filled with hope, but also rather scared at the thought of meeting the Bishop. For the first time in my life, I was to make [10]a visit unaccompanied by my sisters and this visit was to a *Bishop!*[124] I had never had any reason to speak unless in answer to questions addressed to me, and now I had to explain the purpose of my visit, to develop the reasons that made me seek entrance into Carmel; in a word, I was to show the firmness of my vocation. Ah! what that

---

[124] Bishop Hugonin (1823–1898), Bishop of Bayeux and Lisieux from 1867.

trip cost me! [15]God had to give me a very special grace to overcome my timidity. It's also very true that *"love never finds impossibilities, because it believes everything is possible, everything is permitted."*[125] It was surely only love of Jesus that could help me surmount these difficulties and the ones that followed, for it pleased Him to have me buy my vocation with very great trials.

[20]Today, when I am enjoying Carmel's solitude *(resting in the shadow of him whom I have so ardently desired),* I find I paid very little for my happiness,[126] and would be ready to bear with even greater trials to acquire it if I still didn't have it!

It *was raining* in torrents when we arrived at Bayeux. Papa, unwilling to have his little Queen enter the Bishop's house with her *beautiful dress* soaking wet, made her get on a bus and brought her to the cathedral. There my miseries began. The Bishop and all the clergy were attending an important funeral. The cathedral was filled with ladies in mourning and, as a consequence, I was stared at by everybody, dressed as I was in a [54r°] bright frock and white hat. I would have much preferred to go out of the church, but this was out of the question because of the rain. To humiliate me more, God permitted that Papa in his fatherly simplicity made me take a front seat in the cathedral. Not wishing to give him [5] any trouble, I executed this with great grace and thus procured this distraction for the good inhabitants of Bayeux, whom I would have preferred never to have known.

Finally, I was able to breathe freely in a small chapel behind the main altar and stayed there a long time praying fervently and waiting for the rain to stop and allow us to leave. When we were leaving, Papa had me admire the beauty of the edifice which appeared [10]much larg-

---

[125] *The Imitation of Christ* III, 5:4.

[126] Canticle of Canticles 2:3.

er when empty, but one single thought occupied my mind and I was able to enjoy nothing. We went directly to Father Révérony's[127] who was aware of our arrival as he himself had set the date of the trip, but he was absent; we had to wander through the streets which appeared *very sad* to me. Finally, we returned close to the Bishop's residence, and Papa brought me into a magnificent [15]hotel where I did not do honors to the excellent cooking. Poor little Father's tenderness for me was incredible! He told me not to be sad, that certainly the Bishop would agree with me. After we had rested, we returned to Father Révérony's; a gentleman arrived at the same time, but the Vicar General politely asked him to wait and [20]had us enter his study first (the poor man had time to be bored for the visit was long).

Father Révérony was very friendly, but I believe the reason for our trip took him by surprise. After looking at me with a smile and asking me a few simple questions, he said: "I am going to introduce you to the Bishop; will you kindly follow me?" Seeing the tears in my eyes, he added: "Ah! I see diamonds; you mustn't show them to the Bishop!" He had us traverse several huge rooms in which [54v°] portraits of bishops were hanging on the walls. When I saw myself in these large rooms, I felt like a poor little ant, and I asked myself what I would dare say to the Bishop.

The Bishop was walking on the balcony with two priests. I saw Father Révérony say a few words to him and return with him to where we were waiting in his study. There, three [5]enormous armchairs were set before the fireplace in which a bright fire was crackling away. When he saw his Excellency enter, Papa knelt down by my side to receive his blessing; the Bishop had Papa take one of the armchairs, and then he sat down facing him. Father Révérony wanted me to take

---

[127] Bishop Hugonin's Vicar General since 1879; he died in 1891.

the one in the middle; I excused myself politely, but he insisted, telling me to show if I knew how to obey. And so I [10] took it without further reflection and was mortified to see him take a chair while I was buried in a huge armchair that could hold four like me comfortably (more comfortably, in fact, for I was far from being so!). I had hoped that Papa would speak; however, he told me to explain the object of our visit to the Bishop. I did so as *eloquently* as possible and his Excellency, accustomed to *eloquence,* [15]did not appear touched by my reasons; in their stead a single word from the Father Superior would have been much better, but I didn't have it and this did not help me in any way.

[27]The Bishop asked me if it had been a long time since I desired to enter Carmel. "Oh! yes, Bishop, a very long time." "Come, now," said Father Révérony with a smile, "you can't say it is fifteen *years* since you've had the desire." Smiling, I said: "That's true, but there aren't too many years to subtract because I wanted to be a religious since the dawn of my reason, and I wanted [30]Carmel as soon as I knew about it. I find all the aspirations of my soul are fulfilled in this Order."

[55r°] I don't know, dear Mother, if these are my exact words. I believe they were expressed more poorly, but they contain the substance.

[54v°cont'd.] [17]The Bishop, believing he'd please Papa, tried to have me stay with him a few more years, and he was very much *surprised* and *edified* at seeing him take my part, interceding for me to obtain [20]permission to fly away at fifteen. And still everything was futile. The Bishop said an interview with the *Superior of Carmel* was indispensable before making his decision. I couldn't possibly have heard anything that would cause me more pain than this because I was aware of his formal opposition. Without taking into account Father Révérony's advice, I did more than *show my diamonds* to the Bishop.

I *gave* him some!

He was very much touched by this and putting his arm around my neck, he placed my head on his shoulder and caressed me as no one, it appears, was [55r°] ever caressed by him before. He told me all was not lost, that he was very happy I was making the trip to Rome to strengthen my vocation, that instead of crying I should rejoice. He added that the following week, before going to Lisieux, he'd speak about me to the pastor of St. James and [5]I would receive an answer from him in Italy. I understood it was useless to make further entreaties, and besides I had nothing to say, having exhausted all the resources of my *eloquence.*

The Bishop brought us out as far as the garden. Papa a*mused him very much* by telling him that in order to appear older I had put up my hair. (This wasn't [10]lost on the Bishop, for he never spoke about "his little daughter" without telling the story of the hair.) Father Révérony wanted to accompany us to the end of the garden, and he told Papa that never had the like been seen before: "A father as eager to give his child to God as this child was to offer herself to Him!"

Papa asked him for a few explanations about the pilgrimage, among them how one [15]must dress to appear before the Holy Father. I still can see him turning around in front of Father Révérony saying: "Am I good enough as I am?" He had told the Bishop that if he didn't allow me to enter Carmel, I was going to ask the Sovereign Pontiff. Papa was very simple in his words and manners, but he was so *handsome,* and he had a [20]natural dignity about him which must have pleased the Bishop, accustomed to see himself surrounded by people who knew all the rules of polite society; but the *King of France and Navarre* in person, along with his *little Queen,* was not one of these.

When in the street again my tears began to flow, not so much because of my sorrow but because of my little Father who had made a useless trip. He had his heart set on sending a telegram to the Carmel announcing a favorable answer from the Bishop and was obliged to [55v°] return without any answer at all. Ah! how painful it was! It seemed my future was ruined forever. The more I approached the goal, the more I saw my affairs all mixed up. My soul was plunged into bitterness but into peace too, for I was seeking God's will.

[5]As soon as we arrived at Lisieux, I went looking for consolation at Carmel, and I found it in your presence, dear Mother. I shall never forget what you suffered on my account. Had I no fear of profaning them when making use of them, I could speak Jesus' words addressed to His apostles, the night of His Passion: "It is you who have been with me in [10]all my trials."[128] My *beloved* sisters also offered me many *sweet consolations.*

---

[128] Luke 22:28.

## *After the Grace of Christmas*
### Background and Context.

Thérèse was overly sensitive. "I was really unbearable because of my extreme touchiness" (S. 151). She had always known this about herself, but as she contemplated entering a religious community, she realized that her touchiness could jeopardize her vocation. "I really don't know how I could entertain the thought of entering Carmel when I was still in the *swaddling clothes of a child"* (S. 152)! Thérèse realized that she had to grow up fast and that God's grace was necessary for this to happen. "God would have to work a little miracle to make me *grow up...*" (S. 152). This miracle happened on Christmas night 1886.

It was the French custom for the baby of the family to have his or her shoes filled with little gifts on Christmas day. This tradition continued in the Martin household until Thérèse was fourteen. When the Martin family returned home from attending midnight mass in 1886, Thérèse's father noticed her shoes near the fireplace and groaned to Céline, "Thérèse ought to have outgrown all this sort of thing, and I hope this will be the last time."[1]

Céline caught Thérèse's eye and realized that she had overheard what had been said. Aware of her hypersensitivity, Céline followed Thérèse upstairs and found her sitting on her bed with her eyes filled with tears. Céline told her not to go downstairs in this state. But Thérèse knew that she "was no longer the same; Jesus had changed her heart!"Thérèse *acted upon* this change: "Forcing back my tears, I descended the stairs rapidly; controlling the poundings of my heart, I took my slippers and placed them in front of Papa, and withdrew all the objects joyfully. I had the happy appearance of a Queen. Having regained his own cheerfulness, Papa was laughing; Céline believed it was all a dream! Fortunately, it was a sweet reality; Thérèse had discovered once again the strength of soul which she had lost at the age of four and a half, and she was to preserve it forever. On that *night of light* began the third period of my life. The work I had been unable to do in ten years was done by Jesus in one instant"(S. 153).

It is important to realize that Thérèse's hypersensitivity did not cease to exist. Rather, God had given her the strength to control it. God "made me *strong* and *courageous,* arming me with His weapons. Since that night I have never been defeated in any combat. The source of my tears was dried up," [and I received] the grace of leaving my childhood, in a word, the grace of my complete conversion" (S. 152).

As the fruits of Thérèse's conversion unfolded, she began to develop in every area of her life. Guy Gaucher writes:

The year of 1887 saw her develop in every way: physical maturity and emotional development went hand in hand. *I was at a dangerous age for young girls.* Her desire to love and be loved was great, and her maternal instinct came to the fore when two orphans were looked after at Les Buissonnets...Her intellectual development was also   great. *Freed from scruples and excessive sensitiveness, my mind developed. I had always loved the great and the beautiful, but in this period of my life I was filled with an ardent desire to learn*...In her attic Thérèse accumulated science and history books. Everything interested her...All her femininity was awakened. [2]

There was also a spiritual awakening in Thérèse at this time; her zeal for souls was deepened as she "felt *charity* enter into [her] soul" (S. 153). The first manifestation of this new born zeal was her praying for the conversion of the murderer Pranzini; Thérèse referred to him as her " first child," whom she continued to pray for all of her life.

Thérèse had a great desire to enter Carmel on the first anniversary of her Christmas conversion (December 25, 1887), but she did not know whether her father would grant her permission to do so. In addition, Thérèse was hesitant to ask because she knew that it would entail a great sacrifice on his part.

Louis had suffered many losses in his life. His wife had died; his two oldest daughters had entered Carmel; his daughter Léonie was due to enter the convent in July, 1887, and on May 1, 1887, he suffered a stroke that paralyzed his entire left side. And now, Thérèse his youngest, whom he doted on, was about to leave him.

Even though Thérèse asked and received her father's permission to enter Carmel on Pentecost Sunday, May 29, 1887, formidable obstacles stood in her way; both her uncle Isidore and Fr. Delatroëtte, the ecclesiastical superior of Lisieux Carmel, were adamantly opposed to her en- trance at such a tender age. Delatroëtte's opposition was both intractable and vitriolic. When Thérèse and her father went to speak to him, "He received us coldly...Nothing could change his attitude"(S. 168), writes Thérèse. Even, Fr. Youf, the chaplain of Lisieux Carmel, was taken back by Delatroëtte's intransigence. [3]

After their unsuccessful interview with Delatroëtte, Thérèse and her father went to Bayeux to talk to the Bishop. The Bishop said neither yes nor no; he said that he would first have to consult with Delatroëtte before making his decision. The chapter ends with Thérèse in Limbo.

### Reflections and Questions.

1. During her first communion retreat, Thérèse came to the sobering realization that she "was still in the *swaddling clothes of a child"* (S. 152)! "In the morning, I found it very nice to see all the students getting up so early and doing the same as they; but I was not yet accustomed to taking care of myself. *Marie* was not there to comb and *curl* my hair, and so I was obliged to go and timidly offer my comb to the mistress in charge of the dressing rooms. She laughed at seeing a big girl of eleven not knowing how to take care of herself....During my retreat I became aware that I was really a child who was fondled and cared for like few other children on earth, especially among those deprived of their mothers" (S. 118).

This realization that she had remained a child began to have its effects upon Thérèse; she tried to do household tasks. "I wasn't accustomed to doing things myself. Céline tidied up the room in which we slept, and I myself didn't do any housework whatsoever. After Marie's entrance into Carmel, it sometimes happened that I tried to make up the bed to please God, or else in the evening, when Céline was away, I'd bring in her plants. [I]t was for *God alone* I was doing these things and should not have expected any *thanks* from creatures. Alas, it was just the opposite. If Céline was unfortunate enough not to seem happy or surprised because of these little services, I became unhappy and proved it by my tears" (S. 151). Thérèse was crestfallen because she was *expecting* Céline to make a big deal out of her small services. Thérèse thought that she was doing her little services for *God alone,* but her emotional reaction when the laudatory response that she expected from Céline was not forthcoming, told her otherwise. This small incident from Thérèse's life provides us with much food for thought.

Have you ever noticed that the world's reactions to your good will, efforts, acts of charity, etc., often do not correspond to your judgment of their worth? Have you ever felt either hurt, angry, or deflated when you were not given what *you* considered *due* recognition? Have you ever shared your hurt feelings with a friend, and he or she responded by saying, "What did you expect?" This is frequently a *rhetorical* question, but it would behoove us to take it as a real question worthy of consideration. What *am* I expecting? How do I imagine, expect, hope, and even need people to respond to my acts of kindness?

Have you ever noticed that the world's response does not cater to your imagination? Do you feel hurt when someone simply says, "Thank you," for a service rendered? Do you often feel deflated by a person's response because your expectation was inflated? To what extent do you feel underappreciated because you over expect?

Pauline's feelings were once hurt because she rendered a service to one of the nuns and did not receive thanks. Thérèse responded. "I assure you, I too experience the feelings you are speaking about. However, I don't allow myself to be trapped by it, for I *expect no reward* at all on earth. I do everything for God, and in this way I can lose nothing" (LC. 42) (italic added). *Experiencing* momentary hurt is one thing, but becoming *trapped* by hurt is another. Is not the hurt that broods and festers more than the result of an unfulfilled *expectation;* is it not often rooted in an unconscious *demand!* Think of it for a moment. Hurt is anger. We feel angry because we believe that someone did not give us our due. We don't feel hurt or slighted because we are not invited to a party but because we *expected* to be invited; we took it for granted. "It is my due; did I not invite her to my party?"

A *quid pro quo* or tit for tat approach to life drains the joy out of giving and is a seed bed for anger and festering resentments. Conversely, we experience the joy of giving when we give freely. Perhaps "God loves a cheerful giver" (2 Cor. 9:7) because the person who gives freely of himself or herself is cheerful. And God wants nothing more than for us to enter into his joy.

In the Jewish tradition, a *mitzvah* is a good deed that is done without expecting anything in return. When we choose to do a *mitzvah,* we experience the truth of the old adage that virtue is its own reward and that every act of love is twice blest; it blesses the one who gives as well as the one who receives.

After Jesus washed the feet of his disciples, he said to them: "What I have given you is an example...*blest* will you be if you put them into practice" (Jn. 13:15,17). *Makarios,* the Greek word that is translated *blest* refers to the happiness that is proper to God alone. It is as if Jesus is telling his disciples, if you want to experience the happiness of God who is Love, then you must love.

*Questions.* When we are self absorbed, we create our own misery; but, when we love freely, we become blest. Thérèse experienced this two-fold truth at the time of her Christmas conversion. "I felt *charity* enter into my soul, and the need to forget myself and to please others; since then I've always been happy...

God was able in a very short time to extricate me from the very narrow circle in which I was turning without knowing how to come out." (S. 156)."How sweet is the way of *love*...it leaves nothing but a humble and profound peace in the depths of the heart" (S. 276). We all know the burden of self absorption and the relief of being freed from our encapsulated ego. Daily life affords many opportunities for selfless giving which is the greatest gift we can give to ourselves. Where do these opportunities exist in your life?

2. When social worker and journalist Jacob Riis, who dedicated his life to eradicating the evils of the slums of New York City, became discouraged, he would meditate on the work of a stonecutter. "When nothing seems to help, I go and look at a stonecutter hammering away at a rock perhaps a hundred times without as much as a crack showing in it. Yet at the hundred and first blow it will split in two, and I know it was not that blow that did it – but all that had gone before." [4] There is a spiritual truth contained in this image. So often our repeated efforts to overcome a fault or failing in ourselves seem futile. Then, one day, we wake up and discover that a change has taken place within us. "The time will come when the Lord will repay [us] all at once," as St. Teresa of Avila puts it. [5]

Thérèse tells us that for ten long years she tried and tried and tried to overcome her oversensitivity but to no avail. Then the "work I had been unable to do in ten years was done by Jesus in one instant, contenting himself with my *good will* which was never lacking" (S. 153). There is a paradoxical truth contained in this statement. Namely, that our efforts are absolutely useless in the process of transformation because that is the work of grace alone; yet, in some mysterious way, our effort is a *necessary* component of growth. Like *The Parable of the Sower,* we are powerless to have the good seed fall upon us, but we can keep the soil of our souls receptive in anticipation of the time of God's visitation.

Perseverance without seeing the results of one's labors is disheartening. In such moments of discouragement we need to believe that if we are doing what we believe is God's will, then in *God's time,* our efforts will bear fruit. But the fruit may not be what we expect, intend, or even imagine, for God's ways are not our ways, and what we often experience as failure, may be to our betterment. Let us take Jacob Riis as an example. Riis may never have seen the stone split in two, that is, he may never have seen the fruits of his labor, but maybe the fruit that was born to him was the deep peace of *not needing to see* it. As T.S. Eliot writes, "And what you thought you came for/Is only a shell, a husk of meaning/From which the purpose breaks only when it is fulfilled/If at all. Either you had no purpose/Or the purpose is beyond the end you figured/And is altered in fulfilment."[6]

*Questions.* How many times have you struggled to overcome a fault in your life but have failed only to wake up one morning to discover that God had removed it? Or have you ever "worked on yourself" in trying to overcome a fault, only to discover that your main fault was that you were taking yourself too seriously? Is there an area of your life in which you have an inordinate need to see the fruit of your labors and become overly discouraged when you don't?

3. In Arthur Miller's play *Death of a Salesman,* Willy

Loman, who is a failure as a traveling salesman is at odds with his son Biff. Biff likes to work with his hands and is happy working as a ranch-hand in the West. But he is restless because he knows that he is a disappointment to his father. Willy has communicated to Biff in many ways that he will never amount to anything unless he is a success in the business world. Biff is torn. He wants to do what makes him happy but he desperately needs his father's approval. The play open as Biff returns home from the West in a state of confusion, which is summed up in a conversation that he has with his brother Happy.

Happy: "But I think if you just got started – I mean – is there any future for you out there?"

Biff: "I tell ya, Hap, I don't know what the future is. I don't know – what I'm *supposed* to want" (Italic added). [7]

Biff is torn between what he wants to do with his life and what his father wants him to do. Biff doesn't know what he is *supposed* to want. Willy wants Biff to become the man that he never was. Willy feels that he is a failure because he never achieved his dream and is hoping that it will be actualized through his son. In Miller's play, we see what happens to a child in this circumstance; he is torn between his wishes and those of his parent.

Louis could have easily placed Thérèse in a similar conflict. When she was contemplating entering Carmel at the age of fifteen, Pauline feared the impact that Thérèse's dream would have upon their father; she feared "the great sorrow which our father would endure for Thérèse was the real ray of sunshine in his life." [8] Thérèse was conscious of the pain that fulfilling her dream would cause her father. She must have been torn. Would she enter Carmel now as she wished, or should she wait until she was twenty-one to avoid causing her father pain? After all, she was the "Benjamin" of the family, her father's youngest on whom he doted. Louis Martin was 63; he was recuperating from a recent stroke and was a man who had been stripped of those he had loved the most. His wife was dead; Pauline and Marie were in the convent, and Léonie would soon follow.

Because Thérèse deeply loved her father and knew that leaving him would cause him great suffering, she was very vulnerable to his wishes. Louis had intimated that Thérèse would *someday* enter a convent; but he was not ready for her to leave him so soon. It must have been very tempting for him to try to persuade Thérèse to postpone her decision. Without expressing it in words, Louis could have very easily communicated to Thérèse how much he needed her. "Thérèse, please wait a little while; I need you right now. Give me some time to recover from my stroke and the shock of your sister's departure." But he did not try to persuade her but only voiced a reservation. "He didn't say one word to turn me from my vocation, simply contenting himself with the statement that I was still very young to make such a serious decision" (S. 164). Even when the Bishop of Bayeux told Thérèse that he shared her father's reservation, Louis did not press his advantage. "The Bishop, believing he'd please Papa, tried to have me stay with him a few more years, and he was very surprised and edified at seeing him take my part" (S. 174).

How easy it would have been for Louis to place Thérèse in a state of confusion as Willy had Biff. Louis could have done this by planting a seed of doubt into Thérèse's mind regarding her motive for entering Carmel *now.* Louis might have said the following:

"Thérèse, I know that you have a great desire to enter Carmel now. But you have just heard the Bishop's reservation about your age. As you know, his opinion is shared by the ecclesiastical superior of Carmel, your uncle Isidore, your sisters Marie and Pauline, and myself. Thérèse, I support your vocation, but maybe God is trying to tell you something. Is it possible that you are going from door to door in search of the answer that *you* want?"

He did not try to persuade her. He supported his daughter's dream because he had made a heart wrenching decision not to cling to her. In a deeply symbolic gesture, he allowed Thérèse her freedom to follow her dream. "Papa seemed to be rejoicing with what comes from a sacrifice already made...[In] a *symbolic* action my dear King...[went] up to a low wall, pointed to some little white flowers...and plucking one of them, he gave it to me explaining the care with which God brought it into being and preserved it to that very day. While I listened I believed that I was hearing my own story...I accepted [the flower] as a relic and noticed that, in gathering it, Papa had pulled all its *roots* without breaking them" (S. 164). Thérèse's identity was shaped by her father's act of handing her over to herself, so to speak. Is it any wonder that she begins her autobiography by referring to herself as *"a little white flower"* (S. 13)? There are many and varied questions that arise from this incident for our consideration.

*Questions.* Have you ever found yourself trying to influence or manipulate a person's choice to fit your need? Have you ever been in a situation where you have had the power to exert undue influence over the life direction of another? If you are a parent, how do you differentiate offering your children advice and guidance from imposing your dreams upon them?

## Notes

1. Ida Görres, *The Hidden Face: A Study of St. Thérèse of Lisieux,* trans. Richard and Clara Winston (New York: Pantheon Books, 1959), 107.

2. Guy Gaucher, *The Story of a Life: St. Thérèse of Lisieux,* trans. Anne Marie Brennan (San Francisco: Harper & Row, 1987), 63-65.

3. In a letter dated October 25, 1887, Pauline writes to her father, "I just talked to M. Youf this moment, and I told him our angel's whole affair. He could not get over Our Father's [Delatroëtte] refusal" (L. 300).

4. David Walker, "The Stonecutter," in *God is a Sea, The Dynamics of Christian Living,* (New York: Alba House, 1977), 63.

5. St.Teresa of Avila, "The Book of Her Life," in *The Collected Works of St. Teresa of Avila,* vol.1, trans. Kieran Kavanaugh, OCD and Otilio Rodgriguez, OCD, Washington, D.C.: ICS Publications, 1987), chapter 11, p.115.

6. T.S. Eliot, "Little Gidding" in *Four Quartets,* (New York: Harcourt, 1971), 50.

7. Arthur Miller, *Death of a Salesman,* (New York: Penguin Books, 1949), Act 1, p. 22.

8. O'Mahony, ibid., 90.

# Chapter VI

# *THE TRIP TO ROME (1887)*

Paris: Notre-Dame des Victoires
Switzerland
Milan, Venice, Bologna, Loreto
The Colosseum
Audience with Leo XIII
Naples, Assisi, Return to France
Three Months of Waiting

T hree days after the trip to Bayeux, I had to make a longer one, that to the Eternal City.[129] Ah! what a trip that was! It taught me more than long years of studies; it showed me the vanity of everything that happens and that *everything is affliction of spirit under the* [15]*sun.*[130] However, I saw some very beautiful things; I contemplated all the marvels of art and religion; above all, I trod the same soil as did the holy apostles, the soil bedewed with the blood of martyrs. And my soul grew through contact with holy things.

I am very happy for having been at Rome, but I understand those worldly persons [20] who thought that Papa had me make the trip in order to change my ideas about the religious life; there was something about it that could shake a vocation less firm. Having never lived among the great of this world, Céline and I found ourselves in the midst of the nobility who almost exclusively made up the pilgrimage.

---

[129] The pilgrimage to Rome was organized by the Coutances diocese to celebrate the golden jubilee of Leo XIII's ordination to the priesthood; the Bayeux diocese was also associated with it.

[130] Ecclesiastes 2:11.

Ah! far from dazzling us, all these titles and these *"de"* appeared to us as nothing but smoke. From a distance, this had sometimes thrown a little powder in my eyes, but close up, I saw that "all that glistens is not gold," and I understood the words [56r°] of the Imitation "Be not solicitous for the shadow of a great name, nor for acquaintance with many, nor for the particular love of individuals."[131]

I understood true greatness is to be found in the soul, not in a name, since as Isaiah says: *"The Lord will call his servants by ANOTHER NAME,"*[132] and [5] St. John says: *"To him that overcomes I will give a white stone, and on the stone a NEW NAME written that no man knows but the one who receives it."*[133] It is in heaven, then, that we shall know our titles of nobility. *Then shall every man have praise from God*[134] and the one who on earth wanted to be the poorest, the most forgotten out of love of Jesus, will be the first, [10] the noblest, and the richest!

The second experience I had relates to priests. Having never lived close to them, I was not able to understand the principal aim of the Reform of Carmel. To pray for sinners attracted me, but to pray for the souls of priests whom I believed to be as pure as crystal seemed puzzling to me!

[15]I understood *my vocation* in *Italy* and that's not going too far in search of such useful knowledge. I lived in the company of many *saintly priests* for a month and I learned that, though their dignity raises them above the angels, they are nevertheless weak and fragile men. If *holy priests,* whom Jesus in His Gospel calls the *"salt* [20] *of the*

---

[131] *The Imitation of Christ* III, 24:2.

[132] Isaiah 65:15.

[133] Revelation 2:17.

[134] 1 Corinthians 4:5.

*earth,"* show in their conduct their extreme need for prayers, what is to be said of those who are tepid? Didn't Jesus say too: *"If the salt loses its savor, wherewith will it be salted?"*[135]

How beautiful is the vocation, O Mother, which has as its aim the *preservation* of the *salt* destined for souls! This is Carmel's vocation since the sole purpose of our prayers and sacrifices is to be the apostle of the *apostles.* We are to pray for them while they are preaching to souls through their words and especially their example. [56vº] I must stop here, for were I to continue I would never come to an end!

I'm going to recount my voyage, dear Mother, with some details; pardon me if I give you too many, for I don't have time to reflect before writing. I'm writing at so many different times because there is little free time, and as a result my recital [5]will perhaps be boring to you. What consoles me is the thought that in heaven I shall speak about the graces I received and will do this in pleasant and charming terms. Nothing will any longer intervene to interrupt our intimate outpourings; at a single glance, you will understand all. Alas, since I must still use the language of the sad earth, I'll try to do it with the [10]simplicity of a child conscious of its mother's love.

The pilgrimage left Paris on November 7, but Papa had taken us there a few days before to visit the Capital. At three o'clock in the morning,[136] I crossed the city of Lisieux which was still wrapped in sleep; many impressions passed through my soul at that moment. I had a feeling I was approaching the unknown, [15]that great things awaited me out there. Papa was very happy; when the train began to move he sang the old refrain, *"Roll, roll, my carriage, here we are on the open road."* We reached Paris in the morning and commenced our

---

[135] Matthew 5:13.

[136] Friday, November 4, 1887.

visit without any delay. Poor little Father tired himself out trying to please us, and very soon we saw all the marvels of the Capital. [20]I myself found *only one* which filled me with delight, *Our Lady of Victories!*

Ah! what I felt kneeling at her feet cannot be expressed. The graces she granted me so moved me that my happiness found expression only in tears, just as on the day of my First Communion. The Blessed Virgin made me feel *it was really herself who smiled on me and brought about my cure.* I understood she was watching over me, that I was her child. I could no longer give her [57r°] any other name but *"Mama,"* as this appeared ever so much more tender than Mother. How fervently I begged her to protect me always, to bring to fruition as quickly as possible my dream of hiding *beneath the shadow of her virginal mantle!* This was one of my first desires as a child. [5]When growing up, I understood it was at Carmel I would truly find the Blessed Virgin's mantle, and toward this fertile Mount I directed all my desires.

I prayed Our Lady of Victories to keep far from me everything that could tarnish my purity; I was fully aware that on a voyage such as [10] this into Italy I could easily meet with things capable of troubling me. I was still unacquainted with evil and so was apprehensive about making its discovery. I had not yet experienced that *to the pure all things are pure,*[137] that the simple and upright soul sees evil in nothing since it resides only in impure hearts, not in inanimate objects.

I also prayed to St. Joseph, asking him to [15]watch over me; ever since my childhood I had a devotion for him that easily merged with my love for the Blessed Virgin. I recited each day the prayer in his honor: "O St. Joseph, Father and Protector of virgins..." And so it was

---

[137] Titus 1:15.

without any fear I undertook the long journey; being so well protected what was there to fear?

[20]After our solemn consecration to the Sacred Heart in the Basilica at Montmartre, we departed from Paris on Monday, at seven in the morning.[138] We very quickly became acquainted with the different people on the pilgrimage. So timid that I usually dared not speak, I was surprised to find myself completely freed from this crippling fault. I was talking freely with the great ladies, the priests, and even the Bishop of Coutances. It seemed to me I had always lived in this milieu. We were, I believe, [57v°] very well loved by everybody and Papa was proud of his two daughters.[139] But if he was proud of us, we too were equally proud of him, for in the whole pilgrimage there was no one as handsome and distinguished as my beloved King. He loved to see himself in Céline's [5]and my company, and when I was separated from him, he called me back to take his arm as we always did at Lisieux. Father Révérony carefully studied all our actions, and I was able to see him do this at a distance. While eating, if I was not opposite him, he would lean over in such a way as to [10] see me and listen to my conversation. He wanted to know me, undoubtedly, to see if I were really capable of becoming a Carmelite. I think he was favorably impressed by his study, for at *journey's end* he seemed well disposed toward me. At Rome he was far from being favorable to me as I will explain later.

---

[138] "The compartments of each car were named after a saint. When we heard ours was named after St. Martin, our father was so happy he went to thank the one in charge. After that he was called M. St. Martin" *(Histoire d'une Ame)*.

[139] "He told me this on his return, adding with a beautiful smile: 'They were the best of all!'" (note of Mother Agnes of Jesus).

Before reaching the "Eternal City," [15]the goal of our pilgrimage, we were given the opportunity of contemplating many marvels. First, there was Switzerland with its mountains whose summits were lost in the clouds, its graceful waterfalls gushing forth in a thousand different ways, its deep valleys literally covered with gigantic ferns and scarlet heather. Ah! Mother, how much good these beauties of nature, poured out *in such profusion,* [20]did my soul. They raised it to heaven which was pleased to scatter such masterpieces on a place of exile destined to last only a day. I hadn't eyes enough to take in everything. Standing by the window I almost lost my breath; I would have liked to be on both sides of the car. When turning to the other side, I beheld land-scapes of enchanting beauty, totally different from those under my immediate gaze.

At times, we were climbing a mountain peak, and at our feet [58r°] were ravines the depths of which our glance could not possibly fathom. They seemed about to engulf us. A little later, we were pass-ing through a ravishing little village with its graceful cottages and its belfry over which floated immaculately white clouds. There was, far-ther on, a huge lake gilded by the [5] sun's last rays, its calm waters blending their azure tints with the fires of the setting sun. All this pre-sented to our enraptured gaze the most poetic and enchanting specta-cle one could possibly imagine. And at the end of the vast horizon, we perceived mountains whose indistinct contours would have escaped us had not their snowy summits made visible by the sun not come [10] to add one more charm to the beautiful lake that thrilled us so.

When I saw all these beauties very profound thoughts came to life in my soul. I seemed to understand already the grandeur of God and the marvels of heaven. The religious life appeared to me *exactly as it is* with its *subjections,* its small sacrifices carried out in the shad-ows. I understood how [15]easy it is to become all wrapped up in self, forgetting entirely the sublime goal of one's calling. I said to myself: When I am a prisoner in Carmel and trials come my way and I have only a tiny bit of the starry heavens to contemplate, I shall remember what my eyes have seen today. This thought will encourage me and I shall easily forget my own little interests, recalling [20] the grandeur and power of God, this God whom I want to love alone. I shall not have the misfortune of snatching after *straws,* now that *"my HEART HAS AN IDEA of what Jesus has reserved for those who love him."*[140]

After considering the power of Almighty God, I had the opportunity of admiring the power He has bestowed on His creatures. The first Italian city we visited was Milan. We examined minutely its white marble cathedral [58v°] in which its statues were so many they could have formed a small population. Céline and I were very brave; we were always the first and were following the Bishop closely in order to see everything pertaining to the relics of the saints and hear the explanations given by the guides. So while the Bishop was offering Mass on the tomb of [5]St. Charles, we were behind the altar with Papa, resting our heads on the tomb enshrining his body which was clothed in its pontifical robes. And it was like this everywhere, except in those places reserved to dignitaries and then we did not follow his Excellency.

We climbed up to the lower pinnacles adorning the roof of the cathedral, and leaving some timid ladies to hide their faces [10]in their hands we followed the braver pilgrims and reached the *top* of the marble belltower. From this vantage point, we had the pleasure of seeing the city of Milan at our feet, its numerous inhabitants milling around like *so many tiny ants.* Descending from our high perch, we [15]commenced a series of driven tours which lasted a whole month. I certainly satisfied my desire forever *to ride* around in comfort!

---

[140] 1 Corinthians 2:9.

Campo Santo attracted us even more than the cathedral. All its
marble statues, seemingly brought to life by the chisel of some great
genius, are placed around the huge cemetery in a sort of haphazard
manner [20]which to me added greatly to their charm. One would
almost be tempted to console these imaginary personages who were
all around us. The expression on the faces is so real, the sorrow so
calm and resigned, one can hardly fail to recognize the thoughts of
immortality which must necessarily have filled the hearts of the artists
creating these masterpieces. One saw a small child scattering flowers
on the grave of its parents; the marble seemed to lose its heaviness as
the delicate petals slipped through the child's fingers and the breeze
scattered them. [59r°] That same breeze appeared to move the light
veils of widows and ribbons adorning the hair of young girls. Papa
was as thrilled as we were. He had been fatigued somewhat in
Switzerland, but now, his customary gaiety returning, he enjoyed the
beautiful sight we were contemplating; his artistic soul was revealed
in the expressions of faith and admiration clearly evident [5]on his
handsome face. An old gentleman (French), who no doubt did not possess as poetic a soul, looked at us critically and said in bad humor, pretending he was sorry he could not share our admiration: "Ah! what
enthusiasts these French people really are!" I believe this poor man
would have been better off to remain at home, for he did not [10]appear
to me to be happy with his trip. He was frequently close to us and
complaints were coming from his mouth constantly: he was unhappy
with the carriages, the hotels, the people, the cities, everything. Papa,
with his habitual kindness, tried to console him by offering him his
place, etc.; he himself felt at home everywhere, being of a temperament directly [15]opposite that of his disobliging neighbor. Ah! what different personages we saw, and what an interesting study the world is
when one is ready to leave it!

At Venice, the scene changed completely; instead of the noise of the great cities one heard in the solitude nothing but the cries of the gondoliers and the murmur of the [20] waves agitated by their oars. Venice was not without its charms, but I found this city sad. The palace of the Doges is splendid, however it too is sad where gold, wood, the most precious statues and paintings of the masters are on display. For a long time now its arches have ceased to resound with the voices of Governors pronouncing the sentence of life or death in the rooms through which we passed. The unfortunate prisoners who were once locked up in these underground cells and [59v°] dungeons have also ceased to suffer. When we were visiting these frightful prisons, I imagined myself living back in the days of the martyrs and would willingly have remained there in order to imitate them! However, we had to pass quickly from there and cross over the "Bridge of Sighs"; it was given this name because of the sighs of consolation heaved by the condemned when they saw themselves [5] freed from the horrors of the underground caverns; they preferred death to these horrors!

After Venice, we went on to Padua where we venerated the tongue of St. Anthony, and then on to Bologna where we saw St. Catherine who retains the imprint of the kiss of the Infant Jesus. I could go into many interesting details about each city and the particular incidents that took place on the [10] trip, but I would never end; I will write only about the principal events.

It was a great joy to leave Bologna since this city had become unbearable to me because of the students who filled it and formed long lines on the streets through which we had the misfortune to go on foot. I disliked it also because of the little incident which happened to me with one of the students.[141] I was indeed happy [15]to be on my way to Loreto.

I am not at all surprised the Blessed Virgin chose this spot to transport her blessed house, for here peace, poverty, and joy reign supreme; everything is primitive and simple. The women have preserved their graceful Italian dress and have not, as in other cities, adopted the *Paris fashions.* Loreto really charmed me!

[20]And what shall I say about the Holy House? Ah! how deep was my emotion when I found myself under the same roof as the Holy Family, contemplating the walls upon which Jesus cast His sacred glance, treading the ground bedewed with the sweat of St. Joseph, under this roof where Mary had carried Jesus in her arms, having carried Him in her virginal womb. I beheld the little room in which the angel had appeared to the Blessed Virgin. I placed my rosary in the little bowl of the Child Jesus. What ravishing memories![142]

[60r°] Our greatest consolation was to receive *Jesus Himself* in His *house* and to be His living temple in the very place He had honored with His presence. As is the custom in Italy, the Blessed Sacrament is reserved on only one altar in the churches, and here alone can one receive [5] Holy Communion. This altar was in the

---

[141] "Céline reported that when they were getting off the train, her Father was separated from them for a moment as he was looking for his baggage. Many students crowded into the station, and one of them took hold of Thérèse, trying to drag her off. Thérèse said: 'But I gave him such a look he soon let go! Besides, Céline had seen what happened and was coming to my rescue'" (note of Mother Agnes).

[142] For an account of the Holy House of Loreto see H.M. Gillett's article, "Loreto," *The New Catholic Encyclopedia,* VIII, pp. 993–94 (translator's note).

Basilica itself where the Holy House is to be found, enclosed like a precious diamond in a white marble casket. This didn't satisfy Céline and me! It was in the *diamond* not in the *casket* that we wanted to receive Holy Communion. Papa with his customary gentleness did like all the rest, but Céline and I [10] went in search of a priest who had accompanied us everywhere and who was just then preparing to say Mass in the Santa Casa by special privilege. He asked for *two small hosts* which he laid alongside the large one on the paten and you can well understand, dear Mother, the joy we *both* experienced at receiving Communion in that blessed house! [15]It was a totally heavenly happiness which words cannot express. And what shall our happiness be when we receive Communion in the eternal abode of the King of heaven? Then we shall see our joy never coming to an end; there will no longer be the sadness of departings, and it will be no longer necessary to have some souvenir, *to dig furtively into the walls* sanctified by His divine presence, [20] for His *home* will be ours for all eternity. He doesn't want to give us His earthly home, but is content to show it to us so as to make us love poverty and the hidden life. What He does reserve for us is His Palace of glory where we shall see Him no longer hidden under the appearance of a child or a white host, but such as He really is, in the brightness of His infinite splendor!

It is about Rome I still have to speak, Rome the goal of [60v°] our voyage, there where I believed I would encounter consolation but where I found the cross! It was night when we arrived and as we were all asleep we were awakened by the shouts of the porters crying: "Rome! Rome!" It was not a dream, I was in Rome![143]

[5]The first day was spent outside the walls and was perhaps the most enjoyable, for the monuments have preserved their stamp of

---

[143] November 13, 1887.

antiquity. In the center of Rome itself one could easily believe one was in Paris, judging by the magnificence of the hotels and stores. This trip through the Roman countryside left an indelible impression upon me. I will not [10] speak of the places we visited, as there are enough guide books describing these fully, but I will speak only of the *principal* impressions I experienced.

One of my sweetest memories was the one that filled me with delight when I saw the Colosseum. I was finally gazing upon that arena where so many martyrs had shed their blood for Jesus. I was already preparing to kneel down and [15]kiss the soil they had made holy, but what a disappointment! The place was nothing but a heap of ruins, and the pilgrims were expected to be satisfied with simply look-ing at these. A barrier prevented them from entering the ruins. No one would be tempted to do so. But was it possible to come all the way to Rome and not go down into the Colosseum? For me it was impossi-ble! I no longer heard [20]the guide's explanations. One thought raced through my mind: get down into the arena! Seeing a workman pass by carrying a stepladder, I was on the verge of asking his advice, and it was good I didn't as he would have considered me a fool. In the Gospel, we read that Mary Magdalene stayed close to the tomb, and *every once in a while* she stooped down to peer inside. She finally saw two angels.[144] Like her, while recognizing the impossibility of seeing my desires fulfilled, I [61r°] continued to look toward the ruins into which I wanted to descend; I didn't see any angels, but I did see *what I was looking for* and I cried to Céline: "Come quick! We can get through!" We crossed the barrier where there was an opening, the fall-en masonry hardly [5]reaching up to the barrier, and we were climbing down over the ruins that rumbled under our feet.

---

[144] John 20:11.

Papa stared at us, surprised at our boldness. He was calling us back, but the two fugitives no longer heard anything. Just as warriors experience an increase in courage in the presence of danger, so our joy increased proportionately to the trouble we met with in attaining the object [10] of our desire. Céline had listened to the guide and remembering that he had pointed out a tiny bit of pavement marked with a cross as the place where the martyrs fought, we began looking for it. We soon found it and threw ourselves on our knees on this sacred soil, and our souls were united in the same prayer. My heart was beating hard when my [15]lips touched the dust stained with the blood of the first Christians. I asked for the grace of being a martyr for Jesus and felt that my prayer was answered! All this was accomplished in a very short time; gathering up a few stones, we returned to the fallen walls and began the dangerous ascent. Papa, seeing us so happy, [20]didn't have the heart to scold us and I could easily see he was proud of our courage. God visibly protected us, for the other pilgrims hadn't noticed our absence. They were farther away, absorbed in the examination of magnificent arches, the guide calling their attention to *"the little CORNICES carrying figures of CUPIDS,"* and so neither he nor the priests knew anything about the joy that inundated our hearts.

The Catacombs, too, left a deep impression on me. They were exactly as [61v°] I had imagined them when reading the lives of the martyrs. After having spent part of the afternoon in them, it seemed to me we were there for only a few moments, so sacred did the atmosphere appear to me. We had to carry off some souvenir from the Catacombs; [5] having allowed the procession to pass on a little, *Céline and Thérèse* slipped down together to the bottom of the ancient tomb of St. Cecilia and took some earth which was sanctified by her presence. Before my trip to Rome I didn't have any special devotion to this saint, but when I visited her house transformed into a church, the site of her martyrdom, when learning [10]that she was proclaimed patroness of music not because of her beautiful voice or her talent for music, but in memory of the *virginal song* she sang to her heavenly Spouse hidden in the depths of her heart, I felt more than devotion for her; it was the real *tenderness of a friend.* She became my saint of predilection, my [15]intimate confidante. Everything in her thrilled me, especially her *abandonment,* her limitless confidence that made her capable of virginizing souls who had never desired any other joys but those of the present life. St. Cecilia is like the bride in the Canticle; in her I see *"a choir in an armed camp."*[145] Her life was nothing else but a [20]melodious song in the midst of the greatest trials, and this does not surprise me because "the Gospel *rested on her heart,"*[146] and in her heart reposed *the Spouse of Virgins!*

The visit to the church of St. Agnes was also very sweet to me; she was a *childhood friend* whom I was visiting in her own home. I spoke a long time to her about the one who carries her name so well, and I exerted all my efforts to get one of the relics of my Mother's angelic patroness and bring it back to her. [62r°] But it was impossible to get any except a small piece of red stone that was detached from a rich mosaic, the origin of which goes back to St. Agnes's time. She must often have gazed upon it. Wasn't it charming that the lovable saint herself should give us what we were looking for and which we were [5]forbidden to take? I've always considered it a delicate attention on her part, a proof, too, of the love with which the sweet St. Agnes looks upon and protects my Mother!

Six days were spent visiting the principal attractions of Rome; it was on the seventh I saw the greatest of them all, namely, Leo XIII. [10]

---

[145] Canticle of Canticles 7:1.

[146] From the Office of the saint.

I had both longed for and dreaded that day! On it depended my vocation. The answer I was supposed to receive from the Bishop hadn't arrived, and besides I learned from one of your letters, *Mother,* that he was no longer favorably disposed toward me. My only plank of salvation was in the permission of the Holy Father, but to obtain it I [15]had to ask for it, I had to *dare speak to the Pope* in front of everybody. This thought made me tremble; what I suffered before the audience only God knows, along with my *dear Céline.* Never shall I forget the part she played in all my trials; it seemed my vocation was hers.

Our mutual love was noticed [20]by the priests on the pilgrimage. One evening, we were in a large gathering and there were not enough chairs. Céline took me on her knees and we looked so lovingly at each other that one of the priests cried out: "How they love one another. Ah! nothing will be able to separate them!" Yes, we loved each other, but our affection was so *pure* and strong the thought of separation did not disturb us. We knew that nothing, not even the ocean, could place any distance between us. Céline was watching my little [62v°] boat approach Carmel's shore, and she was resigned to remain on the stormy sea of the world as long as God willed it. She was sure that she too would approach the same shore which was the object of her desires.

Sunday, November 20, after dressing up according to Vatican [5]regulations, i.e., in black with a lace mantilla as headpiece, and decorated with a large medal of Leo XIII, tied with a blue and white ribbon, we entered the Vatican through the Sovereign Pontiff's chapel. At eight o'clock in the morning our emotion was profound when we saw him enter to celebrate Holy Mass. After blessing the numerous pilgrims [10] gathered round him, he climbed the steps of the altar and showed us through his piety, worthy of the Vicar of Jesus, that he was truly "the *Holy* Father." My heart beat strongly and my prayers were fervent when Jesus descended into the hands of His Pontiff. However,

I was filled with confidence, for the Gospel of the day contained these beautiful words: "Fear not, little [15]flock, for it is your Father's good pleasure to give you the kingdom."[147] No, I did not fear, I hoped the kingdom of Carmel would soon belong to me; I was not thinking then of those other words of Jesus: "And I appoint to you a kingdom even as my Father has appointed to me..."[148] In other words, I reserve crosses and trials for you, and it is thus you will be worthy of possessing this kingdom after [20] which you long; since it was necessary that the Christ suffer and that He enter through it into His glory,[149] if you desire to have a place by His side, then drink the chalice He has drunk![150] This chalice was presented to me by the Holy Father and my tears mingled with the bitter potion I was offered.

After the Mass of thanksgiving, following that of the Holy Father, the audience began. Leo XIII was seated on a large armchair; he was dressed simply [63r°] in a white cassock, with a cape of the same color, and on his head was a little skullcap. Around him were cardinals, archbishops, and bishops, but I saw them only in general, being occupied solely with the Holy Father. We passed in front of him in procession; each pilgrim knelt in turn, kissed [5]the foot and hand of Leo XIII, received his blessing, and two noble guards touched him as a sign to rise (touched the pilgrim, for I explain myself so badly one would think it was the Pope).

Before entering the pontifical apartment, I was really determined *to speak,* but I felt my courage weaken when I saw *Father Révérony* standing by the Holy Father's right side. Almost at the same [10]instant,

---

[147] Luke 12:32.
[148] Luke 22:29.
[149] Luke 24:26.
[150] Matthew 20:21-22.

they told us on the Pope's behalf that *it was forbidden to speak*, as this would prolong the audience too much. I turned toward my dear Céline for advice: "Speak!" she said. A moment later I was at the Holy Father's feet. I kissed his slipper and he presented his hand, but instead of kissing it I joined my own and lifting [15]tear-filled eyes to his face, I cried out: "Most Holy Father, I have a great favor to ask you!"

[24]The Sovereign Pontiff lowered his head toward me in such a way that my face almost touched his, and I saw his *eyes, black and deep,* fixed on me and they seemed to penetrate to the depths of my soul. "Holy Father, in honor of your Jubilee, permit me to enter Carmel at the age of fifteen!"

[16]Emotion undoubtedly made my voice tremble. He turned to Father Révérony who was staring at me with surprise and displeasure and said: "I don't understand very well." Now if God had permitted it, it would have been easy for Father Révérony to obtain what I desired, but it was the cross [20]and not consolation God willed to give me.

"Most Holy Father," answered the Vicar General, "this is *a child* who wants to enter Carmel at the age of fifteen, but the Superiors are considering the matter at the moment." "Well, my child," the Holy Father replied, looking at me kindly, "do what the Superiors tell you!" Resting my hands [63v°] on his knees, I made a final effort, saying in a suppliant voice: "Oh! Holy Father, if you say yes, everybody will agree!" He gazed at me steadily, speaking these words and stressing each syllable: "Go... go... *You will enter if God wills it!"* (His accent [5] had something about it so penetrating and so convincing, it seems to me I still hear it.)

I was encouraged by the Holy Father's kindness and wanted to speak again, but the two guards *touched* me *politely* to make me rise. As this was not enough they took me by the arms and Father Révérony helped them lift me, for I stayed there with joined hands resting on the knees of Leo XIII. [10] It was with *force* they dragged me from his feet. At the moment I was *thus lifted*, the Holy Father placed his hand on my lips, then raised it to bless me. Then my eyes filled with tears and Father Révérony was able to contemplate at least as many *diamonds* as he had seen at Bayeux. The two guards literally carried me to the door and there a [15]third one gave me a medal of Leo XIII.

Céline who followed was a witness to the scene that had just taken place; almost as moved as myself, she still had the courage to ask the Holy Father to bless the Carmel. Father Révérony answered in a displeased tone of voice: "The Carmel is already blessed." The good Holy Father replied gently: "Oh! yes, it [20] is already blessed." Papa had come to the Holy Father's feet before us with the men.[151] Father Révérony had been very charming to him, introducing him as the *father of two Carmelites*. The Sovereign Pontiff, with a sign of particular good will, placed his hand on my dear King's venerable head, seeming to mark it with a *mysterious seal* in the name of Him whose venerable Vicar he is. Ah! now that he is in heaven, this *father of four Carmelites,* it's no longer the Pontiff's hand that rests on his forehead, [64r°] prophesying martyrdom. It's the *hand* of the Spouse of Virgins, the King of Glory, rendering His faithful servant's head resplendent. Forever this adorable hand will rest on this head which He has glorified!

At the termination of the audience, [5]my dear Father was grieved to find me in tears. He did his best to console me but without success. In the bottom of my heart I felt a great peace, since I had done everything in my power to answer what God was asking of me. This *peace,* however, was in the *depths* only; bitterness *filled* my soul, for Jesus

---

[151] Thérèse was wrong here; men came to the audience after the women had passed through.

was silent. [10]He seemed to be absent, nothing served to reveal His presence. That day, too, the sun dared not shine and Italy's beautiful blue skies, covered with dark clouds, never stopped crying with me. Ah! it was all over; my trip no longer held any attraction for me since its purpose had failed. The final words of the Pontiff should have consoled me, for [15]were they not a real prophecy? *In spite of* all obstacles, what *God willed* was really accomplished. *He did not allow* creatures to do what they willed but *what He willed.*

I had offered myself, for some time now, to the Child Jesus as His *little plaything.* I told Him not to use me as a valuable toy children [20]are content to look at but dare not touch, but to use me like a little ball of no value which He could throw on the ground, push with His foot, *pierce,* leave in a corner, or press to His heart if it pleased Him; in a word, I wanted to *amuse little Jesus,* to give Him pleasure; I wanted to give myself up to His *childish whims.* He heard my prayer.

At Rome, Jesus pierced His little plaything; He wanted to see what there was inside it and having seen, content with His discovery, He let His little ball [64v°] fall to the ground and He went off to sleep. What did He do during His gentle sleep and what became of the little abandoned ball? Jesus dreamed *He was still playing* with His toy, leaving it and taking it up in turns, and then having seen it roll quite far He pressed it to His heart, no longer allowing [5]it to ever go far from His little hand.

You understand, dear Mother, how sad the little ball was when seeing itself *on the ground.* Nevertheless, I never ceased hoping against all hope.[152] A few days after the audience with the Holy Father, Papa, having gone to see good Brother Simeon, found Father Révérony there, who was very friendly. [10] Papa chided him gaily for

---

[152] Romans 4:18.

not having aided me in my *difficult undertaking,* then he told his Queen's story to Brother Simeon. The venerable old man listened to his recital with much interest, even took down notes, and said with emotion: "One doesn't see this in Italy!" I believe this interview made a good impression on Father Révérony; afterward he [15]never ceased proving to me that he was *finally* convinced of my vocation.

On the morrow of that memorable day, we had to leave early for Naples and Pompeii. In our honor, Mount Vesuvius made a lot of noise all day long; it allowed, along with its *cannon shots, a thick cloud of smoke to escape.* The traces it has left upon the ruins of Pompeii are [20] frightening and are a manifestation of God's power: *"He looks at the earth and it trembles; he touches the mountains and they are reduced to smoke."*[153]

I would have loved to take a walk all by myself in these ruins, meditating on the fragility of things human, but the number of travelers took away a great part of the charm of the destroyed city. At Naples it was just the opposite. The trip to the monastery of San Martino, placed on top [65r°] a hill dominating the whole city, was made magnificent by the *great number* of carriages drawn by two horses. Unfortunately, the horses took the bit into their own mouths and more than once I was convinced I had seen my last hour. The driver vainly repeated the magic word of Italian drivers: [5] "Appipau! Appipau!"; the horses wanted to turn the carriage upside down. Finally, thanks to our guardian angels we arrived at our magnificent hotel in one piece.

During the course of the whole trip, we were lodged in princely hotels; never had I been surrounded with so much luxury. There's no mistake about it: riches don't bring happiness, for I would have [10] been much happier under a thatched roof with the hope of Carmel in

---

[153] Psalm 103:32.

the offing, than in the midst of these sumptuous dwellings, these marble staircases, and silk tapestries, and all the while bitterness in my heart! Ah! I really felt it: joy isn't found in the material objects surrounding us but in the inner recesses of the soul. One can possess joy in a prison cell as well as in a palace. [15]The proof of this: I am happier in Carmel even in the midst of interior and exterior trials than in the world surrounded by the comforts of life, and even the sweetness of the paternal hearth!

My soul was plunged into sadness and still exteriorly I was the same, for I believed the request I made of the Holy Father was hidden; soon I was to be [20]convinced of the opposite. Having remained alone in the car with Céline (the other pilgrims got off to eat during a short stop), I saw Monsignor Legoux, Vicar General of Coutances, open the door and looking at me with a smile, he said: "Well, how is our little Carmelite?" I understood then that the whole pilgrimage knew my secret; happily no one spoke to me about it, but I saw by their sympathetic way of looking at me that my request had produced no ill [65v°] effect, on the contrary...

I had the opportunity at the little town of Assisi of climbing into Father Révérony's carriage, a favor granted to *no woman* during the whole trip. Here is how I obtained this privilege. After having visited the places made sacred by the virtues of St. Francis and St. Clare, [5]we were ending up in the monastery of St. Agnes, the sister of St. Clare. I had studied the Saint's head at my leisure and was one of the last to leave when I noticed my belt was lost. I *looked* for it in the crowd; a priest had pity on me and helped in the search. After he found it, I saw him depart and I remained alone to *search,* for I had [10] the belt but it was impossible to wear it as the buckle was missing. At last I saw it shining in a corner. Taking it and adjusting it to the belt was the work of an instant, but the work preceding this had taken up much time, and

I was greatly surprised to find myself alone in front of the church. The numerous carriages had all disappeared, with the sole exception of Father Révérony's. [15]What was I to do? Should I run after the carriages no longer in sight and expose myself to the danger of missing the train and thus upsetting my dear Papa, or else ask for a place in Father Révérony's coach? I decided on the latter. With my most gracious manner, trying to appear as little embarrassed as I could though I was greatly embarrassed, I explained my [20]critical situation to him. I put him also in an *embarrassing situation,* for his carriage was filled with the most important *men* of the pilgrimage. There wasn't a single place left, but one good gentleman hastened to descend, made me climb into his place, and humbly took a seat beside the driver. I was like a squirrel caught in a trap and was far from being at ease, surrounded as I was by all these great personages and especially the most *formidable* of all; I was placed directly opposite to him. He was very [66r°] friendly toward me, however, and even interrupted his conversation with the others from time to time to speak to me about Carmel. Before we reached the station, all the *great personages* took their huge [5] purses out to give some money to the driver (already paid). I did the same thing, taking out my very little purse. Father Révérony did not agree with what I drew out from it, some pretty *little* coins, and instead he offered a *large* coin for both of us.

I was by his side, on another occasion, on a bus, and he was even more friendly, promising *to do all he could to have me enter Carmel.* While placing a little balm on my wounds, these [10] little encounters did not prevent my return from being much less agreeable than my going, for I no longer had the hope "of the Holy Father." I found no help at all on earth, which appeared to me as an arid desert without

---

[154] Psalm 62:2.

water.[154] All my hope was in God alone. I had just had the experience that it was much better to have recourse to Him than to his saints.

[15]The sadness of my soul did not hinder me from taking a lively interest in the holy places we were visiting. At Florence, I was happy to contemplate St. Magdalene of Pazzi in the Carmelite choir. They opened the big grille for us. As we did not know we would enjoy this privilege and many wanted to touch their rosaries to the Saint's tomb, I was the [20] only one who could put my hand through the grating which separated us from the tomb. And so everybody was carrying rosaries to me and I was very proud of my office. I always had to find a way of *touching everything.* At the Holy Cross Church in Rome, we were able to venerate several pieces of the true Cross, two thorns, and one of the sacred nails. The nail was enclosed in a magnificent golden reliquary which *did not have a glass covering.* I found a way of placing my *little finger* in [66v°] one of the openings of the reliquary, and could *touch* a nail bathed in the blood of Jesus. Really, I was far too brazen! Happily, God, who knows the depths of our hearts, was aware that my intention was pure and for nothing in the world would I have desired to displease Him. I was acting toward Him like [5] a *child* who believes everything is permitted and looks upon the treasures of its Father as its own.

I still cannot understand why women are so easily excommunicated in Italy, for every minute someone was saying: "Don't enter here! Don't enter there, you will be excommunicated!" Ah! poor women, how they are misunderstood! And yet they love God in [10]much larger numbers than men do and during the Passion of Our Lord, women had more courage than the apostles since they braved the insults of the soldiers and dared to dry the adorable Face of Jesus. It is undoubtedly because of this that He allows misunderstanding to be their lot on earth, since He chose it for Himself. In heaven, He will show that [15]His thoughts are not men's thoughts,[155] for then the *last will be first.*[156] More than once during the trip I hadn't the patience to await heaven to be first. One day when we were visiting a Carmelite monastery, not content with following the pilgrims in the *outer* galleries, I advanced into the *inner* cloisters, when all of a sudden I saw a good old Carmelite friar at a [20]little distance making a sign for me to leave. But instead of going, I approached him and showing him the cloister paintings I made a sign that they were beautiful. He undoubtedly understood by the way I wore my hair and from my youthful appearance that I was only a child, so he smiled at me kindly and left. He saw he was not in the presence of an enemy. Had I been able to speak Italian I would have told him I was a future Carmelite, but because of the builders of the Tower of Babel it was impossible for me.

After visiting Pisa and Genoa once more, we returned to France. On the return trip [67r°] the scenery was magnificent. We travelled at times along the side of the sea and the railroad was so close to it that it seemed the waves were going to come right up to us. This impression was created by a tempest which was in progress. It was evening and the scene became all the more imposing. We passed through fields full of orange trees laden with ripe fruit, [5]green olive trees with their light foliage, and graceful palm trees. It was getting dark and we could see many small seaports lighted up by many lights, while in the skies the first *stars* were beginning to sparkle.

Ah! what poetry flooded my soul at the sight of all these things I was seeing for the first and last time in my life! It was without regret I saw them disappear, for [10] my heart longed for other marvels.[157] It

---

[155] Isaiah 55:8-9.

[156] Matthew 20:16.

[157] "Papa suggested we take a trip to Jerusalem, but in spite of my

had contemplated *earthly beauties* long enough; *those of heaven* were the object of its desires and to win them for *souls* I was willing to become a *prisoner!* But before this prison's doors were to open for me, I was still to suffer and fight. I had a presentiment of this when returning to France, and yet my confidence [15] was so great I didn't stop hoping I'd be allowed to enter on December 25. We had hardly arrived at Lisieux when our first visit was to the Carmel.[158] What an interview that was! We had so many things to talk over after the separation of a month which seemed very long to me and in which I learned more than in several years.

[20]O dear Mother, how wonderful it was to see you once again, to open up to you my poor, little, wounded soul. To you who understood it so well, and to whom a word, a look was sufficient to explain everything! I surrendered myself completely. I had done everything I could, even to speaking to the Holy Father, and I didn't know what I was still supposed to do. You told me to write to the Bishop, reminding him of his promise; I did this immediately in the best way possible, but Uncle found the words too [67v°] simple. He wrote the letter over again and at the moment I was about to mail it, I received a letter from you telling me not to write and to wait for a few days. I instantly obeyed, sure it was the best way to make no mistakes. Finally, ten days before Christmas my letter was on its way! Convinced [5] the answer would not be long in coming, I went every morning after Mass with Papa to the Post Office, believing I would find the permission to take my flight. But each morning brought with it a new disappointment which, nevertheless, didn't shake my faith. I

---

attraction for visiting the places sanctified by Our Lord's passage there, I was tired of earthly pilgrimages" *(Histoire d'une Ame)*.

[158] The pilgrims arrived at Lisieux on December 2 in the afternoon.

begged Jesus to break my bonds; and He broke them, but in a way totally different from what I expected. The beautiful feast of Christmas arrived and Jesus did not awaken. He left His little ball on the ground without so much as casting a glance at it.

My heart was broken when going to Midnight Mass; I was counting so much on assisting at it behind Carmel's grilles! This trial was very great for my faith, but *the One whose heart watches even when he sleeps*[159] made [15]me understand that to those whose faith is like that of a *mustard seed* He grants *miracles* and moves mountains in order to strengthen this faith which is *still small;*[160] but for His *intimate friends,* for His *Mother,* He works no miracles *before having tried their faith.* Did He not allow Lazarus to die even after Martha and Mary told Him he was sick?[161] At the wedding of Cana when [20]the Blessed Virgin asked Jesus to come to the help of the head of the house, didn't He answer her that His hour had not yet come?[162] But after the trial what a reward! The water was changed into wine ... Lazarus was raised from the dead! Thus Jesus acted toward His little Thérèse: after having tried her for a *long time,* He granted all the desires of her heart.

I spent the afternoon of the radiant feast in tears, and I went to see the Carmelites. My surprise was indeed great when they opened the [68r°] grille, and there I saw a radiant little Jesus holding a ball in His hand and on it was written my name. The Carmelites, taking the place of Jesus who was too little to speak, sang a hymn to me which was composed by my dear Mother; each word poured consolation into

---

[159] Canticle of Canticles 5:2.

[160] Matthew 17:19.

[161] John 11:3.

[162] John 2:4.

my soul. Never shall I forget [5]this delicate attention of a maternal heart that always covered me with exquisite tenderness. After thanking all by shedding copious tears, I told them about the surprise Céline gave me when I returned from Midnight Mass. I found in my room, in the center of a charming basin, a little *boat* carrying the *Little* Jesus asleep with a *little* ball at [10]His side, and Céline had written these words on the white sail: "I sleep but my heart watches,"[163] and on the boat itself this one word: "Abandonment!" Ah! though Jesus was not yet speaking to His little fiancée, and though His divine eyes remained closed, He at least revealed Himself to her through souls who understood all the delicacies and the love of His Heart.

[15] On New Year's day, 1888, Jesus again gave me a present of His cross, but this time I was alone in carrying it. It was all the more painful as I did not understand it. A letter from Mother Marie de Gonzague informed me that the Bishop's answer had arrived December 28, feast of the *Holy Innocents,* but that she had not told me as it was decided that my entrance [20] would be delayed until *after Lent.* I was unable to hold back my tears at the thought of such a long wait. This trial had a particular characteristic about it: I saw all my *bonds broken* as far as the world was concerned, but this time it was the holy ark itself which refused entrance to the poor little dove. I really want to believe I must have appeared unreasonable in not accepting my three months' exile joyfully, but I also believe that, without its appearing so, this trial was *very great* and made me *grow* very much in abandonment and in the other virtues.

[68v°] How did those *three months* pass, those months so rich in graces for me? At first the thought came into my mind not to lead a life as well regulated as had been my custom, but soon I understood

---

[163] Canticle of Canticles 5:2.

the value of the time I was being offered. I made a resolution to give myself up more than ever to a [5] *serious* and *mortified* life. When I say mortified, this is not to give the impression that I performed acts of penance. Alas, *I never made any.* Far from resembling beautiful souls who practiced every kind of mortification from their childhood, I had no attraction for this. Undoubtedly this stemmed from my cowardliness, for I could have, like Céline, found a thousand ways [10] of making myself suffer. Instead of this I allowed myself to be wrapped in cotton wool and fattened up like a little bird that needs no penance. My mortifications consisted in breaking my will, always so ready to impose itself on others, in holding back a reply, in rendering little services without any recognition, in not leaning my back against a support when seated, etc., etc. It was through the practice of these *nothings* that I [15]prepared myself to become the fiancée of Jesus, and I cannot express how much this waiting left me with sweet memories. Three months passed by very quickly, and then the moment so ardently desired finally arrived.

# *The Trip to Rome*
## Background and Context.

Thérèse's trip to Rome was the first and only time that she ever stepped foot outside of her native Normandy. The stated purpose of the pilgrimage was to celebrate Pope Leo XIII's golden jubilee of ordination to the priesthood, but its unspoken purpose was to make a political statement. The pilgrims were composed of ultramontane Catholics who supported the monarchy and opposed the French Republic and the anti-clerical forces of the day. Italy's government was deeply anti-clerical, and the pilgrims were harangued at Rome's train station by protesters who shouted, "Down with Leo XIII! Down with the monarchy!" Going to Rome to celebrate the pope's jubilee was like carrying a banner in support of the Church and the papacy. But the pilgrimage was also a social event.

The pilgrimage was an excursion of the rich, a sightseeing tour sprinkled with religious overtones; all the shrines, churches, and holy sites of any note were seen on route to Rome. The group stayed in "princely hotels" (S. 208) and dined in the finest restaurants. "[T] he nobility... almost exclusively made up the pilgrimage," (S. 189) and seventy five of the total one hundred and ninety seven pilgrims were priests.

At three o'clock in the morning, the Martins left their home in Lisieux to board a train bound for Paris. The stillness of the night made Thérèse reflective. "I crossed the city of Lisieux which was still wrapped in sleep; many impressions passed through my soul at that moment. I had a feeling I was approaching the unknown, that great things awaited me out there" (S. 191). The great things that awaited Thérèse were not to be found in shrines or museums but in an inner healing and new found realizations.

For example, the high point of Thérèse's two-day stay in Paris was neither her visit to the Louvre, the Bastille, the Royal Palace, the Arc de Triomphe or other tourist sites, but a visit to an obscure church – Our Lady of Victories. It was in this church, four years earlier, when Thérèse was bedridden in Lisieux with her mysterious illness, that a novena of masses had been said to obtain a cure for her. While the novena was being said, Thérèse was cured. In light of this fact, it is understandable that Thérèse would want to visit Our Lady of Victories in order to render due thanks for her cure. But there was another reason why Thérèse wanted to visit this shrine.

When Thérèse was cured, Marie asked her about her cure. Thérèse told Marie that she had seen the Blessed Virgin smile at her. After Thérèse shared this with Marie, Thérèse felt that she had betrayed a "secret" (S. 98). This "betrayal" filled her with a deep sense of guilt for the next four years. "[F]or the next four years... I was unable to look upon myself without a feeling of *profound horror.* I was not to find my happiness again until I was kneeling at the feet of Our Lady of Victories" (S. 98-97). When Thérèse knelt before Our Lady of Victories, her feeling of horror vanished as she experienced the intimacy of Mary's maternal presence. This intimacy was so profound that the deep emotional healing that ensued from it was as miraculous as her cure." I understood she was watching over me, that I was *her* child. I could no longer give her any other name but *'Mama'* "(S. 192).

Thérèse came to other realizations on the pilgrimage as she saw the world of the rich up close for the first time. She was not impressed by their snobbish superficiality. "Ah!, far from dazzling us, all these titles and these *"de"* appeared to us as nothing but smoke. From a distance, this had sometimes thrown a little powder in my eyes, but close up I saw that "all that glistens is not gold" "(S. 190). In contrast to the haughty ostentatiousness of the rich, Thérèse saw true nobility of spirit manifested in the "habitual kindness" of her father, who patiently related to a malcontent, who complained constantly. Likewise, Thérèse's eyes were opened to the worldliness of priests who hobnobbed with the wealthy. From a distance they appeared to her to be "as pure as crystal," but up close, she saw them as "weak and fragile men" (S. 190).

Thérèse's main purpose for going to Rome was to obtain permission from Pope Leo XIII to enter Carmel at the age of fifteen, but all she received from him was an exhortation to obedience and faith: "Well, my child...do what the Superiors tell you!...Go...go...*You will enter if God wills it"* (S. 205). Bitterness filled her soul, but Thérèse was also at peace with herself because she knew that she had done everything God had asked her to do.

When the Martins arrived back in Lisieux, they went almost immediately to Carmel only to discover that Fr. Delatroëtte was as obstinate as ever in his opposition to Thérèse's request to enter Carmel on Christmas day. But on New Year's day, Thérèse received news from Mother Gonzague that the bishop had given her permission to allow Thérèse to enter immediately. All seemed well. But now the opposition came from *within* Carmel. Thérèse's sister Pauline had second thoughts. She feared that the Lenten fast would be too stressful for Thérèse and persuaded Mother Gonzague to postpone Thérèse's entrance for three months. [1]

This infuriated Louis Martin. He came to Carmel and "pointed his finger, saying, 'She (Pauline) is always the same; she says something, then she takes it back.' Oh! He was angry..."[2] Thérèse was also upset about the postponement, but she did not put her life on hold, rather she continued to lead "a life as well regulated as had been [her] custom," and in the process, came to learn "the value of time" (S. 216).

## Reflections and Questions .

1. In spite of Thérèse's shyness and the fact that the majority of the pilgrims were from the upper echelon of French society, Thérèse found herself able to enter into conversation with them. "We very quickly became acquainted with the different people on the pilgrimage. So timid that I usually dared not to speak, I was surprised to find myself completely freed from this crippling fault" (S. 193). This "fault" may best be seen as an expression of Thérèse's personality change that took place as a result of her mother's death. "[M]y happy disposition completely changed after Mama's death. I, once so full of life, became timid and retiring... [and] could not bear the company of strangers" (S. 49). We may attribute the overcoming of this "fault" to her Christmas conversion. Nevertheless, we should not conclude that this newfound freedom made it *easy* for Thérèse to enter into conversation with strangers, for the effects of the deep wounds of our childhood are never completely eradicated. Thérèse discovered that her crippling anxiety to talk to strangers had disappeared, but her choice to enter into conversation with them still required effort on her part.

*Questions.* Some of us are like Thérèse; we do not feel at ease in a group of strangers, and when we find ourselves in such a gathering, our natural tendency is to remain silent and let everyone else do the talking. However, there are times when God calls us to step out of the circle of our shyness or reserve and speak a truth that needs to be heard. Conversely, some of us have the tendency to take over or dominate a conversation and find it difficult to be quiet and to listen. Whatever the case may be, like Thérèse, God often asks us to "step out of character" for the sake of others. If you are a shy person, can you think of times when God asked you to overcome your natural timidity for the sake others? Conversely, if your ego tends to fill a room at social gatherings, can you remember a time that God whispered in your ear to remain silent for the sake of others?

2. Bernard MacLaverty's "The Beginnings of Sin," is a story of the shattering of innocence. Colum, a fatherless boy from a poor Irish family, so idolizes Father Lynch that he is unable to see that he is a frail human being. When Miss Grant, the parish housekeeper had to announce to the early morning congregation, with increasing regularity, that "Father Lynch was ill and that there would be no Mass that day," it never even crossed Colum's mind to doubt that Fr. Lynch was ill.[3] However, "Colum [ who often served Fr. Lynch's Mass] always wondered why Father Lynch was so nervous saying his morning Mass. He had served for others and they didn't tremble like that." Colum's innocence and idealization of Fr. Lynch lead him to interpret the trembling in the best light." Perhaps it was because [Fr. Lynch] was holier than [other priests], that they weren't as much in awe of the Blessed Sacrament as he was."[4]

Colum looked up to Father Lynch as the father he didn't have, and to make Fr. Lynch proud of him, he worked tirelessly to sell raffle tickets for the parish building fund. One night, after selling forty-two books of tickets, Colum ran excitedly to the rectory to tell Father Lynch. Father Lynch was drunk. He staggered toward Colum, tripped and lunged forward; his hand caught the side of Colum's face, knocked off his glasses, and shattered them on the floor. Colum left the rectory in a state of fear and confusion. He told his mother that he had broken his glasses when he slipped on the ice.

The next morning, when Colum entered the sacristy, he was surprised to see that Fr. Lynch was already there. After Mass, Father Lynch sat down and talked to Colum about the previous night.

Father Lynch put his hand in his pocket and gave Colum some folded pound notes.

"Did you mention it to your mother?"

"What?"

"How they were broken?"

"No."

"Are you sure? To anyone?"

Colum nodded that he hadn't. He was turning to get out the door. The priest raised his voice, trying to keep him there.

"I knew your father well, Colum," he shouted, "You remind me of him a lot." The altar-boy ran, slamming the door after him. He heard an empty wooden coat-hanger rattle on the hardboard panel of the door and it rattled in his mind until he reached the bottom of the hill. There he stopped running. He unfolded the wad of pound notes still in his hand and counted one-two-three-four of them with growing disbelief." [5]

Colum's disbelief was the blasting and shattering of innocence. Embarrassment, disillusionment, bewilderment, fear,
shame, a sense of betrayal were all crumpled up in a bribe of
secrecy in a fist full of one pound notes. What is shattered when
innocence is betrayed at a tender age is hard to put into words.
One's universe is shaken because belief in the existence of
goodness that is strong and loving is called into question. The
loss of innocence is a fearful grief; it is the loss of a person
whom we trusted, believed in, and looked up to; it is the lone-
someness that asks "whom can I go to now; whom can I trust; is
there anyone who can understand my hopes and fears?"

What makes the shattering of innocence in youth so devastating is youth's inability to understand evil and process one's
feelings. But even to sophisticated, worldly-wise adults, the
betrayal of innocence is still a heavy blow to bear. Psychiatrist
Peter Rutter relates how devastated he was when he learned that
his trusted and revered mentor was having sexual relations with
his clients. To Rutter, his mentor represented all the best qualities of teacher and healer, a role model to be emulated. For a long
time, Rutter denied the rumors about his mentor because "I still
needed to protect my image of the 'good father'" [6]

At the age of fifteen, Thérèse's image of the "good father"
was shattered. On her trip to Rome, Thérèse, who had always
held priests in veneration and regarded them "as pure as crystal,"
saw them for what they were – "weak and fragile men...[who]
show in their conduct their extreme need for prayers" (S. 190).
This rude awakening neither scandalized nor dissuaded Thérèse
from her vocation; rather, it answered a question that had always
puzzled her: "Why did Carmel have a special mission to pray for
priests?" Now she knew – they *needed* prayers! Thus, Thérèse

could write: "I understood *my vocation* in *Italy"* (S. 190).

*Questions.* How do we react when an icon is shattered? Do
we lose faith in the human race? Do we become cynical or sus-
picious of goodness? Or like Thérèse, when we realize that our
heroes and heroines are mere mortals, can we accept them as
fellow human beings who need our prayers?

3.  In John Cheever's short story *Goodbye, My Brother,* four
siblings and their spouses spend a week together at a seaside cot-
tage, where the protagonist becomes increasing irritated at his
brother Lawrence's negativity. Lawrence constantly complains
and criticizes everything and everyone. In a moment of rage, the
protagonist  picks up a branch and strikes Lawrence on the back
of the head. Lawrence gets up, packs his bag, and goes home
enraged and resentful. The story ends with the protagonist shaking his head and thinking to himself. "Oh, what can you do with
a man like that? What can you do? How can you dissuade his eye
in a crowd from seeking out the cheek with acne, the infirm hand;
how can you teach him to respond to the estimable greatness of
the race, the harsh surface beauty of life; how can you put his finger for him on the obdurate truths before which fear and horror
are powerless?" [7]
     At the end of the story we sympathize with the protagonist;
yet, he is just as blind and obdurate as his brother Lawrence, for
he tells us indirectly that his anger that culminated in violence
has been a life long pattern. "I realized that our dislikes are as
deeply ingrained as our better passions, and I remember that
once, twenty-five years ago, when I hit Lawrence on the head
with a rock, he had picked himself up and gone directly to our

father to complain." [8]

After a lifetime of conflict with his brother, he is still asking the same question, "Oh, what can you do with a man like that?" He is trapped in his futile response to Lawrence because he lacks the wisdom to accept the things he cannot change. So, what do you do with a man like Lawrence? Thérèse offers us one approach.

On the train to Rome, there was a man similar to Lawrence. His "complaints were coming from his mouth constantly; he was unhappy with the carriages, the hotels, the people, the cities, everything" (S.196). What good would it have done to say to the man, "Stop your griping, you're making everyone miserable?" In doing so, one would quickly become sucked into a row. Sometimes the best, the most prudent, the most charitable thing that we can do is to give these people a wide berth. But when we *have to* deal with such people, we need to give up the futile goal of trying to talk them out of their negativity (or to beat it out of them, as the protagonist of Cheever's story tried to do with his brother Lawrence), and simply love them as best we can, without expecting them to change. This is what Thérèse's father did. "Papa, with his habitual kindness, tried to console him by offering him his place, etc.; he himself felt at home everywhere, being of a temperament directly opposite that of his disobliging neighbor" (S. 196).

Louis Martin remained at home with himself because he did not lose himself by losing his composure. He *responded* in love instead of *reacting* in rage. His kindness did not *transform* the man but it prevented Louis from being *deformed*. As the old adage cautions – be careful in choosing your enemies, for you will become a lot like them. At times, God calls us to be prophets, to confront and challenge the behavior of others; at other times, God calls us to be peacemakers, to accept people as they are. The later case, is neither giving up nor giving in, but letting go. It is the first step in accepting the things we cannot change.

There is a story of a man who tried every conceivable method to rid his lawn of dandelions, but failed. In desperation, he wrote to the Department of Agriculture. He gave an exhaustive list of the methods he had tried and asked what else he could do. He received the following reply. "Dear Sir, We have read your letter with great interest and have reviewed your various methods. We suggest that you learn to love your dandelions."

*Questions.* What people are the "dandelions" in your life, that is, the people that God is asking you to love *as they are?* Or, are you like Lawrence in Cheever's story or the malcontent on the train to Rome – a person who complains about everything?

## Notes

1. Another factor that may have pressured Mother Gonzague to postpone Thérèse's entrance date was Fr.Delatroëtte's opposition. Postponing Thérèse's entrance date may have been an attempt to placate his anger.

2. This is the testimony of Marie Martin (Sr.Marie of the Sacred Heart), quoted from *Thérèse of Lisieux* by Patricia O'Connor, (Huntington: Our Sunday Visitor, Inc., 1983), 48.

3. Bernard MacLaverty, "The Beginnings of Sin," in *Substance of Things Hoped For: Fiction and Faith Outstanding Modern Short Stories,* ed. John B. Breslin,

S.J., (New York: Doubleday, 1987), 3.

4. Ibid., 6.

5. Ibid., 12.

6. Peter Rutter, M.D., *Sex in the Forbidden Zone: When Men in Power-Therapists, Doctors, Clergy, Teachers, and Others-Betray Women's Trust,* (New York: Fawcett Crest, 1989), 11.

7. John Cheever, "Goodby, My Brother," in *The Stories of John Cheever,* (New York: Ballantine Books, 1978), 23.

8. Ibid., 3.

# Chapter VII

# *THE FIRST YEARS IN CARMEL (1888–1890)*

Confession to Father Pichon
Thérèse and Her Superiors
The Holy Face
Reception of the Habit
Illness of Her Father
Little Virtues

T he day chosen for my entrance into Carmel was April 9, 1888, the same day the community was celebrating the feast of the Annunciation, transferred because of Lent. The evening before, the whole [20] family gathered round the table where I was to sit for the last time. Ah! how heartrending these family reunions can really be! When you would like to see yourself forgotten, the most tender caresses and words are showered upon you, making the sacrifice of separation felt all the more.

Papa was not saying very much, but his gaze was fixed upon me lovingly. Aunt cried from time to time and Uncle paid me many affectionate compliments. Jeanne and Marie gave me all sorts of little attentions, especially Marie, who, [69r°] taking me aside, asked pardon for the troubles she thought she caused me. My dear little Léonie, who had returned from the Visitation a few months previously,[164] kissed and embraced me often. There is only Céline, about whom I have not spoken, but you can well imagine, dear Mother, how we spent that last night [5] together.

---

[164] Léonie entered the Visitation at Caen, July 16, 1887; left January 6, 1888.

On the morning of the great day, casting a last look upon Les Buissonnets, that beautiful cradle of my childhood which I was never to see again, I left on my dear King's arm to climb Mount Carmel. As on the evening before, the whole family was reunited to hear Holy Mass and receive Communion. As soon as Jesus [10] descended into the hearts of my relatives, I heard nothing around me but sobs. I was the only one who didn't shed any tears, but my heart was beating *so violently* it seemed impossible to walk when they signaled for me to come to the enclosure door. I advanced, however, asking myself whether I was going to die because of the [15] beating of my heart! Ah! what a moment that was! One would have to experience it to know what it is.

My emotion was not noticed exteriorly. After embracing all the members of the family, I knelt down before my matchless Father for his blessing, and to give it to me he placed [20] *himself on his knees* and blessed me, tears flowing down his cheeks. It was a spectacle to make the angels smile, this spectacle of an old man presenting his child, still in the springtime of life, to the Lord! A few moments later, the doors of the holy ark closed upon me, and there I was received by the *dear Sisters* who embraced me. They had acted as mothers to me and I was going to take them as models for my actions from now on. My desires were at last accomplished; my soul experienced a *PEACE* so sweet, so deep, it would be impossible [69v°] to express it. For seven years and a half that inner peace has remained my lot, and has not abandoned me in the midst of the greatest trials.

I was led, as are all postulants, to the choir immediately after my entrance into the cloister. The choir was in darkness because the Blessed Sacrament was exposed[165] and what struck me [5]first were the

---

[165] The choir was in semi-darkness to prevent people seeing the Carmelite nuns in choir where the grating was open because of the exposition of the Blessed Sacrament.

eyes of our holy Mother Geneviève[166] which were fixed on me. I remained kneeling for a moment at her feet, thanking God for the grace He gave me of knowing a saint, and then I followed Mother Marie de Gonzague[167] into the different places of the community. Everything thrilled me; I felt as though I was transported into a desert; our little [10] cell, above all, filled me with joy. But the joy I was experiencing was *calm,* the lightest breeze did not undulate the quiet waters upon which my little boat was floating and no cloud darkened my blue heaven. Ah! I was fully recompensed for all my trials. With what deep joy I repeated those words: "I am here forever and ever!"

[15]This happiness was not passing. It didn't take its flight with "the illusions of the first days." *Illusions,* God gave me the grace *not to have* A SINGLE ONE when entering Carmel. I found the religious life to be *exactly* as I had imagined it, no sacrifice astonished me and yet, as you know, dear Mother, my first steps met with more thorns than roses! Yes, [20] suffering opened wide its arms to me and I threw myself into them with love. I had declared at the feet of Jesus–Victim, in the examination preceding my Profession, what I had come to Carmel for: "I came to save souls and especially to pray for priests." When one wishes to attain a goal, one must use the means; Jesus made me understand that it was through suffering that He wanted to give me souls, and

---

[166] Mother Geneviève of St. Teresa (1805–1891) was professed at the Poitiers Carmel and sent as Foundress and Subprioress of the Lisieux Carmel in 1838. She held office as Prioress for some years.

[167] Mother Marie de Gonzague (1834–1904) entered Lisieux Carmel in 1860 and was elected for first time as Prioress in 1874. Thérèse had her as Superior all through her religious life except for the years 1893–1896 when her sister Pauline (Mother Agnes of Jesus) was Prioress.

my attraction for suffering grew in proportion to its increase. This was my way for five years; exteriorly [70r°] nothing revealed my suffering, which was all the more painful since I alone was aware of it. Ah! what a surprise we shall have at the end of the world when we shall read the story of souls! There will be those who will be surprised when they see the way through which my soul was guided!

[5]This is so true that, a few months after I entered, Father Pichon, having come for the Profession of Sister Marie of the Sacred Heart,[168] was surprised to see what God was doing in my soul. He told me that he was watching me at prayer in the choir one evening, and that he believed my fervor was childish and my way was very sweet. My interview with the good Father was a great consolation to me, but it was [10] veiled in tears because I experienced much difficulty in confiding in him. I made a general confession, something I had never made before, and at its termination he spoke the most consoling words I ever heard in my life: *"In the presence of God, the Blessed Virgin, and all the Saints, I DECLARE THAT YOU HAVE NEVER COMMITTED A MORTAL SIN."*[15]Then he added: "Thank God for what He has done for you; had He abandoned you, instead of being a little angel, you would have become a little demon." I had no difficulty in believing it; I felt how weak and imperfect I was and gratitude flooded my soul. I had such a great fear of soiling my baptismal robe that such an assurance, coming [20]from the mouth of a director such as St. Teresa desired, i.e., one combining *knowledge and virtue,*[169] it seemed to me to be coming from the mouth of Jesus Himself. The good priest also spoke these words which are engraved in my heart: "My child, may Our Lord always be your Superior and your Novice Master."

---

[168] Sister Marie made her Profession on May 22, 1888.

[169] St. Teresa of Avila, *Way of Perfection*, ch. 6.

He was this in fact, and He was also "my Director." I don't mean by this that I closed my soul to my Superiors; far from it, for I tried always to be an [70v°] *open book* to them. However, our Mother Prioress, frequently ill, had little time to spend with me. I know that she loved me very much and said everything good about me that was possible, nevertheless, God permitted that she was VERY SEVERE *without her even being aware of it.* I was unable to meet her without having to kiss the floor,[170] and it was the same thing on [5]those rare occasions when she gave me spiritual direction. What an inestimable grace! How *visibly* God was acting within her who took His place! What would have become of me if I had been the "pet" of the community as some of the Sisters believed? Perhaps, instead of seeing Our Lord in

---

[170] This was customary when a religious was corrected for a fault. Histoire d'une Ame adds: "Once, I remember having left a cobweb in the cloister; she said to me before the whole community: 'We can easily see that our cloisters are swept by a child of fifteen! Go and take that cobweb away and be more careful in the future.' What pained me most was not to know how I was to correct my faults, for example, my slowness, my want of thoroughness in the offices. One day, I said to myself that no doubt Mother Prioress wanted me to work during free time; this I ordinarily gave to prayer. And so I plied my needle without looking up. As I wanted to be faithful and act solely for Jesus, no one ever knew about it. During my postulancy, our Novice Mistress sent me each afternoon to weed the garden at 4:30. This cost me much since I was almost sure to meet Mother Marie de Gonzague. Once she said: 'Really, this child does nothing at all! What sort of novice has to take a walk every day?' She acted this way in everything concerning me. O Mother, how I thank God for having given me so firm and precious an education!"

my Superiors, I would have looked upon them as [10]ordinary persons only and my heart, so well guarded while I was in the world, would have become humanly attached in the cloister. Happily I was preserved from this misfortune. I loved Mother Prioress *very much,* but it was a pure affection which raised me to the Bridegroom of my soul.

Our Novice Mistress[171] was *really a saint,* the finished product of the first [15]Carmelites. I was with her all day long since she taught me how to work. Her kindness toward me was limitless and still my soul did not expand under her direction. It was only with great effort that I was able to take direction, for I had never become accustomed to speaking about my soul and I didn't know how to express what was going on within it. One good old Mother[172] understood one day what I was experiencing, and [20] she said laughingly during recreation: "My child, it seems to me you don't have very much to tell your Superiors." "Why do you say that, Mother?" "Because your soul is extremely *simple,* but when you will be perfect, you will be even *more simple;* the closer one approaches to God, the simpler one becomes." The good Mother was right; however, the difficulty I had in revealing my soul, while coming from my simplicity, was a veritable trial; I recognize it now, for I express my thoughts [71r°] with great ease without ceasing to be simple.

I have said that Jesus was "my Director." Upon entering Carmel, I met one who was to serve me in this capacity, but hardly had I been numbered among his children when he left for exile.[173] Thus [5]I

---

[171] Sister Marie of the Angels (1845–1924) was Mistress in 1886.

[172] Sister Fébronie was then Subprioress; Thérèse assisted her in her last moments (note of Mother Agnes of Jesus).

[173] Father Pichon was sent to Canada as preacher. He left Le Havre, November 3, 1888.

came to know him only to be deprived of him. Reduced to receiving one letter a year from him to my twelve, my heart quickly turned to the Director of directors, and it was He who taught me that science hidden from the wise and prudent and revealed to *little ones.*[174]

[10]The little flower transplanted to Mount Carmel was to expand under the shadow of the cross. The tears and blood of Jesus were to be her dew, and her Sun was His adorable Face veiled with tears. Until my coming to Carmel, I had never fathomed the depths of the treasures hidden in the Holy Face.[175] It was through you, dear Mother, that I learned to know these treasures. Just as formerly [15]you had preceded us into Carmel, so also you were first to enter deeply into the mysteries of love hidden in the Face of our Spouse. You called me and I understood. I understood what *real glory* was. He whose Kingdom is not of this world[176] showed me that true wisdom consists in "desiring to be unknown and counted as nothing,"[177] in "placing one's [20]joy in the contempt of self."[178] Ah! I desired that, like the Face of Jesus, "my face be truly hidden, that no one on earth would know me."[179] I thirst-

---

[174] Matthew 11:25.

[175] Devotion to the Holy Face sprang up in the 19th century, following certain revelations made to Sister Marie of St. Pierre in the Tours Carmel. Thérèse was introduced to the devotion by Sister Agnes of Jesus. She studied it in a very personal way, using the texts of the prophet Isaiah. She did this principally at the time of her father's illness. She signed her name for the first time as "Sister Thérèse of the Child Jesus and the Holy Face" the day she received the habit, January 10, 1889.

[176] John 18:36.

[177] *The Imitation of Christ* I, 2:3.

[178] *The Imitation of Christ* III, 49:7.

[179] Isaiah 53:3.

ed after suffering and I longed to be forgotten.

How merciful is the way God has guided me. Never has He given me the desire for anything which He has not given me, and even His bitter chalice seemed delightful to me.

After those beautiful festivities of the month of May, namely, the Profession and taking of the Veil [71v°] of our dear Marie, the *oldest* in the family being crowned on her wedding day by the *youngest,* we had to be visited by trial. The preceding year, in May, Papa was seized with a paralytic stroke in the limbs and we were greatly disturbed. But [5]the strong character of my dear King soon took control and our fears disappeared. However, more than once during the trip to Rome we noticed that he easily grew tired and wasn't as cheerful as usual. What I noticed especially was the progress he was making in perfection. He had succeeded, like St. Francis de Sales, [10] in overcoming his natural impetuosity to such an extent that he appeared to have the most gentle nature in the world.[180] The things of earth seemed hard-

------

[180] "Allow me, Mother, to cite in this regard an example of his virtue. During the pilgrimage, the days and nights on the train were long for the pilgrims. We saw them playing card games which, at times, became rather noisy. One day, they asked Céline and me to join them, but we refused, giving as our excuse that we knew little about the game. Unlike them, we found the time none too long for enjoying the magnificent panoramas that spread out before us. They were annoyed and our dear Papa came to our defense, suggesting that as pilgrims we could pray a little more. Forgetting the respect due to white hairs, one of them exclaimed: 'Fortunately, Pharisees are rare!' Papa did not answer and appeared even pleased. He found a chance later to shake this man's hand, accompanying his action with a kind word, giving the impression the insult was not heard or at least forgotten. You know,

ly to touch him, he easily surmounted contradictions, and God was *flooding* him with *consolations*. During his daily visits to the Blessed Sacrament his eyes were often filled with tears and his [15]face breathed forth a heavenly beatitude. When Léonie left the Visitation, he was not disturbed and made no reproaches to God for not having answered the prayers he offered up to obtain his daughter's vocation. It was even with joy that he left to go and bring her home.

Here is the faith with which Papa accepted the separation of his little Queen, announcing [20] it to his friends in these words: "My dear Friends, Thérèse, my little Queen, entered Carmel yesterday! Only God could demand such a sacrifice. Don't sympathize with me, for my heart is overflowing with joy."

It was time that such a faithful servant receive the reward of his works, and it was right that his wages resemble those which God gave to the King of heaven, His only Son. Papa had just made a donation to God of an *altar,*[181] and it was he who was chosen as victim to be offered with the Lamb without spot.[182] [72r°] You are aware, dear Mother, of our bitter sufferings during the month of June, and espe-

------

Mother, this habit of pardoning didn't date from that day. According to Mama's testimony and that of others who knew him, never did he speak an unkind word" *(Histoire d'une Ame).*

[181] The main altar of St. Peter's church at Lisieux.

[182] "O Mother, do you remember the day and the visit when he said to us: 'Children, I returned from Alençon where I received in Notre-Dame church such great graces, such consolations that I made this prayer: My God, it is too much! yes, I am too happy, it isn't possible to go to heaven this way. I want to suffer something for you! I offer myself...' the word victim died on his lips; he didn't dare pronounce it before us, but we had understood" *(Histoire d'une Ame).*

cially June 24, 1888.[183] These memories are too deeply engraved in the bottom of our hearts to require any mention in writing. O Mother! how we suffered! And this was still only the *beginning* of[5]the trial.

The time for my reception of the Habit had arrived. I was accepted by the conventual chapter, but how could we dream of any kind of ceremony? Already they were talking of giving me the Habit without my going outside the cloister,[184] and then they decided to wait. Against all expectation, our dear Father recovered from his second attack, and the Bishop set the ceremony for January 10.[10] The wait had been long, but what a beautiful celebration it was!

Nothing was missing, not even the *snow!* I don't know if I've already told you how much I love snow? When I was small, its whiteness filled me with delight, and one of the greatest pleasures I had was taking a walk under the light snowflakes. Where did this love of snow come from? Perhaps it was because I was [15]*a little winter flower,* and the first adornment with which my eyes beheld nature clothed was its white mantle. I had always wished that on the day I received the Habit, nature would be adorned in white just like me. The evening before, I was gazing at the gray skies from which a fine rain was falling every now and again, and the temperature was so mild [20] I could no longer hope for any snow. The following morning the skies hadn't changed.[185]

---

[183] Saturday, June 23, 1888, M. Martin disappeared without notifying anyone. Céline and M. Guérin found him at Le Havre, June 27.

[184] The day the postulant receives the Habit, she goes outside the cloister dressed in wedding clothes. There she takes part in an exterior ceremony in the presence of her family.

[185] "I gave up my childish desire then which was not realizable and went out of the monastery. Papa was waiting for me at the cloister door. Advancing toward me, eyes filled with tears, he crushed me to

The celebration, however, was wonderful. The most beautiful, the most attractive flower of all was my dear King; never had he looked so handsome, so *dignified.* Everybody admired him. This was really his day of *triumph* and it was to be his last celebration on this earth. He had now given *all* his children to God, for Céline, too, had confided her vocation to him. He had *wept tears of joy,* and had gone with her to thank Him who "bestowed such honor on him by taking all his children."[186]

[72v°] At the termination of the ceremony the Bishop intoned the Te Deum. One of the priests remarked to him that this hymn of *thanksgiving* was usually sung only at Professions, but, once begun, it was continued to the end. And indeed it was fitting that the feast be thus completed [5] since in it were united all the others.

After embracing my dear King for the last time, I entered the cloister once more, and the first thing that struck my eye was the statue of "the little Jesus" smiling at me from the midst of flowers and lights. Immediately afterward, my glance was drawn to the snow, the monastery garden was white like me! [10]What thoughtfulness on the part of Jesus! Anticipating the desires of His fiancée, He gave her snow. Snow! What mortal bridegroom, no matter how powerful he

---

his heart, crying out: 'Ah! here is my little Queen!' Then he gave me his arm, and we both made our solemn entrance into the chapel" *(Histoire d'une Ame).*

[186] " 'Come, let us go together to the Blessed Sacrament to thank the Lord for the graces He bestowed on our family, and for the honor He gave me of choosing His spouses in my home. Yes, if I possessed anything better, I would hasten to offer it to Him.' This better thing was himself! And the Lord received him as a victim of holocaust, trying him like gold in a furnace and finding him worthy" *(Histoire d'une Ame;* Wisdom 3:6).

may be, could make snow fall from heaven to charm his beloved? Perhaps people wondered and asked themselves this question. What is certain, though, is that many considered the snow on my [15]Clothing Day as a little miracle and the whole town was astonished. Some found I had a strange taste, loving snow!

Well, so much the better! This accentuated even more the *incomprehensible condescension* of the Spouse of virgins, of Him who loves *Lilies white as SNOW!*

The Bishop came into the cloister after the ceremony and was [20]very kind to me.[187] I believe he was very proud I had succeeded and told everyone I was *"his* little girl." He was always kind to me on his return trips to the Carmel. I remember especially his visit on the occasion of our Father St. John of the Cross's Centenary. He took my head in his hands and gave me a thousand caresses; never was I so honored! At the same time, God reminded me of the caresses [73r°] He will bestow on me in the presence of the angels and saints, and now He was giving me only a faint image of this. The consolation I experienced at this thought was very great indeed!

January 10, as I have just said, was my [5]King's day of triumph. I compare it to the entry of Jesus into Jerusalem on the day of the palms. Like that of our Divine Master, Papa's glory of *a day* was followed by a painful passion and this passion was not his alone. Just as the sufferings of Jesus pierced His Mother's heart with a sword of sorrow, so our hearts experienced the sufferings of the one we cherished [10]most tenderly on earth. I recall that in the month of June, 1888, at the moment of our first trials, I said: "I am suffering very much, but I

---

[187] "He recounted the story of my visit to Bayeux to all the priests, and also my trip to Rome. He didn't forget the way I had put up my hair to appear older than fifteen" *(Histoire d'une Ame).*

feel I can still bear greater trials." I was not thinking then of the ones reserved for me. I didn't know that on February 12, a month after my reception of the Habit, our dear Father would drink [15]the *most bitter* and *most humiliating* of all chalices.[188]

Ah! that day, I didn't say I was able to suffer more! Words cannot express our anguish, and I'm not going to attempt to describe it. One day, in heaven, we shall love talking to one another about our *glorious* trials; don't we already feel happy for having suffered them? [20]Yes, Papa's three years of martyrdom appear to me as the most lovable, the most fruitful of my life; I wouldn't exchange them for all the ecstasies and revelations of the saints. My heart overflows with gratitude when I think of this inestimable *treasure* that must cause a holy jealousy to the angels of the heavenly court.

My desire for suffering was answered, and yet my attraction for it did not diminish. My soul soon shared in the sufferings of my [73v°] heart. Spiritual aridity was my daily bread and, deprived of all consolation, I was still the happiest of creatures since all my desires had been satisfied.

O dear Mother! how sweet our great trial was since [5] from our hearts came only sighs of love and gratitude! We were no longer walking in the way of perfection, we were flying, all five of us. The two poor little exiles of Caen,[189] while still in the world, were no longer of it. Ah! what marvels the trial worked in my dear Céline's soul! All the letters she wrote at this epoch are filled with resignation and [10]love. And who could express the visits we had together? Ah! far from sep-

---

[188] February 12, 1889, M. Martin had to leave Lisieux to enter a mental institution, the Bon Sauveur at Caen.

[189] Léonie and Céline boarded at the orphanage of St. Vincent de Paul, close to the Bon Sauveur, to be near their Father.

arating us, Carmel's grilles united our souls more strongly; we had the same thoughts, the same desires, the same *love for Jesus* and *for souls.* When Céline and Thérèse were speaking together, never did a word concerning the things of the earth mingle in their conversations which were already [15]in the heavens. As formerly in the *belvédère,* they dreamed about things of *eternity.* To enjoy this endless happiness as soon as possible, they chose as their lot here on earth both *suffering* and *contempt.*[190]

Thus flowed by the time of my espousals. It was a very long time indeed for poor little Thérèse! Our Mother Prioress told me, at the end of my year, [20]not to even think of making Profession, that the Father Superior would reject my request. I was to wait for another eight months. I found it difficult, at first, to accept this great sacrifice, but soon light shone in my soul. I was meditating on the *Foundations of the Spiritual Life* by Father Surin at the time. One day, during my prayer, I understood that my intense desire to make Profession was mixed with a great self-love. Since I had *given* myself to Jesus to please and console Him, [74r°] I had no right to oblige Him to do *my will* instead of His own. I understood, too, that a fiancée should be adorned for her wedding day, and I myself was doing absolutely nothing about this. Then I said to Jesus:

"O my God! I don't ask you to make Profession. *I will wait* [5]*as long as you desire,* but what I don't want is to be the cause of my sep-

---

[190] This is a reference to one of the sayings of St. John of the Cross. Our Lord asked St. John what he wanted in return for a service rendered, and John's reply was: "Lord, what I want You to give me is trials to suffer for You, to be despised and esteemed as of little worth." Crisógono de Jesús, O.C.D., The Life of St. John of the Cross, trans. Kathleen Pond (New York: Harper, 1958), p. 268.

aration from You through my fault. I will take great care, therefore, to make a beautiful dress enriched with priceless stones, and when You find it sufficiently adorned, I am certain all the creatures in the world will not prevent You from coming down to me to unite me to Yourself forever, O my Beloved!"

[10] I had already received, since my taking of the Habit, abundant lights on religious perfection, principally with regard to the Vow of Poverty. During my postulancy, I was content to have nice things for my use and to have everything necessary for me at my disposal. *"My Director"*[191] bore this patiently, for He doesn't like pointing everything out[15]at once to souls. He generally gives His light little by little.

(At the beginning of my spiritual life when I was thirteen or fourteen, I used to ask myself what I would have to strive for later on because I believed it was quite impossible for me to understand perfection better. I learned very quickly since then that the more one advances, the more one sees the goal is still far off. And now I am simply[20]resigned to see myself always imperfect and in this I find my joy.)

But let us return to the lessons *"My Director"* gave me. One evening, after Compline, I was looking in vain for our lamp on the shelves reserved for this purpose. It was during the time of Great Silence and so it was impossible to complain to anyone about my loss. I understood that a Sister, believing she was taking her lamp, picked up ours which I really needed. Instead of feeling annoyed at being thus deprived of it, I was really happy, feeling that Poverty consists in being deprived not only of agreeable things but [74v°] of indispensable things too. And so in this *exterior darkness,* I was interiorly illumined!

I was taken up, at this time, with a real attraction for objects that were both very ugly and the least convenient. So it was with joy that

---

[191] Thérèse's "Director" was Jesus (see p. 150).

I saw myself deprived of a pretty *little jug* in our cell and supplied with another large one, [5]*all chipped.* I was exerting much effort, too, at not excusing myself, which was very difficult for me, especially with our Novice Mistress from whom I didn't want to hide anything. Here was my first victory, not too great but it cost me a whole lot. A little vase set behind a window was broken, and our Mistress, thinking it was my fault, [10]showed it to me and told me to be more careful in future. Without a word, I kissed the floor, promising to be more careful in the future. Because of my lack of virtue these little practices cost me very much and I had to console myself with the thought that at the Last Judgment everything would be revealed. I noticed this: when one performs her duty, never excusing herself, no one [15]knows it; on the contrary, imperfections appear immediately.

I applied myself to practicing little virtues, not having the capability of practicing the great. For instance, I loved to fold up the mantles forgotten by the Sisters, and to render them all sorts of little services. Love for mortification was given me, and this love was all the [20]greater because I was allowed nothing by way of satisfying it. The only little mortification I was doing while still in the world, which consisted in not leaning my back against any support while seated, was forbidden me because of my inclination to stoop. Alas! my ardor for penances would not have lasted long had the Superiors allowed them. The penances they did allow me consisted in mortifying my self-love, which did me much more good than corporeal penances.

[75r°] The refectory, which I was given charge of immediately after I received the Habit, furnished me, on more than one occasion, with the chance of putting my self-love in its proper place, i.e., under my feet. It's true, I had the great consolation of having the same task as you, dear Mother, and of being able to study [5]your virtues at close range, but this closeness was the source of great suffering. I did not feel, as *formerly,* free to say everything to you, for there was the Rule to observe. I was unable to confide in you; after all, I was in *Carmel* and no longer at *Les Buissonnets* under the *paternal roof!*

The Blessed Virgin, nevertheless, was helping me prepare the dress of my soul; [10] as soon as this dress was completed all the obstacles went away by themselves. The Bishop sent me the permission I had sought, the community voted to receive me, and my Profession was fixed for *September 8, 1890.*

Everything I have just written in so few words would require many detailed pages, but these pages will never be read on this earth. Very soon, [15] dear Mother, I shall speak to you about everything in our *paternal home,* in that beautiful heaven toward which the sighs of our hearts rise!

My wedding dress was finally ready. It had been enriched by some old jewels given me by my Bridegroom, but this didn't satisfy His liberality. He wanted to give me a *new* diamond containing numberless rays. [20] Papa's trial, with all its sad circumstances, made up the *old* jewels, and the *new* one was a trial, small in appearance, but one that caused me to suffer intensely.

For some time now, our poor little Father was somewhat better. He was allowed to go out in a carriage, and there was question of his taking a trip by train to see us. *Céline* naturally thought that the best day to choose would be the day of my receiving the Veil. She wrote: "In order not to fatigue him too much, I will not have him[75v°]assist at the whole ceremony. I will bring him in at the end and lead him quietly to the grille where Thérèse will receive his blessing."

Ah! I recognized here the thoughtfulness of my dear Céline, and it's really true that "love never sees anything as [5]impossible, for it believes everything is possible and everything is permitted."[192] *Human*

---

[192] *The Imitation of Christ* III, 5:4.

*prudence,* on the other hand, trembles at each step and doesn't dare to set down its foot, so to speak, and so God willed to try me and He made use of it as a docile instrument. On the day of my wedding I was really an orphan, no longer having a Father on this earth and being able to look [10] to heaven with confidence, saying in all truth: "Our Father who art in Heaven..."

# The First Years in Carmel
## Background and Context.

On April 9, 1888 "casting a last look upon Les Buissonnets, that beautiful cradle of [her] childhood which [she] was never to see again," Thérèse left home and entered Lisieux Carmel. It was a deeply emotional day for Thérèse. The sadness of leaving her family behind, coupled with the joy and excitation of being received into "the holy ark" (S. 230) make her heart beat *"so violently* it seemed impossible to walk when they signaled [Thérèse] to come to the enclosure door" (S. 230).

When Thérèse crossed the threshold, Fr. Delatroëtte said caustically, "Well! Reverend Mothers, you can sing a Te Deum! As the bishop's delegate I give you this fifteen-year-old child whose entrance you have wished for. I hope she does not disappoint your hopes, but I remind you that if she does you alone will bear responsibility."[1] Twenty years later, Thérèse's relatives remembered with indignation, this biting remark. We do not know if Thérèse overheard what was said, for she only records the joyful memories of that day. She tells us that her soul "experienced a *PEACE* so sweet, so deep...[that for] seven years and a half that inner peace [had] not abandoned [her] in the midst of the greatest trials" (S. 230).

The first trial that Thérèse encountered in Carmel was the makeup of the community. Between Thérèse and the majority of the nuns, "[t]here were such differences in temperament, social background and everyday behavior!"[2] The majority of the nuns were ill-educated peasant women who lacked the social refinements and mental endowments common to the culture in which Thérèse was reared. Thérèse found their "lack of judgment, good manners and touchiness" (S. 389) difficult to endure. In short, we might say, that Thérèse, who was raised in an upper middle class bourgeois culture, now found herself living in a "blue collar" neighborhood.

The contrast between Thérèse's upbringing (both socially and personally) and that of the majority of the nuns was clearly evident in the area of work. Having been raised in the leisure class, "the grand lady," as Thérèse was called by one of the nuns, lacked domestic skills and was unaccustomed to doing simple household tasks. Thérèse was very slow and awkward when it came to sewing and sweeping a corridor, the two main tasks to which she was assigned as a postulant. Sr. Saint Vincent de Paul, who nicknamed Thérèse, "the big nanny goat," because of her slowness when it came to manual labor, told Thérèse's novice mistress that Thérèse would never be of use to the community. Once, when Thérèse entered the laundry room, Sr. Saint Vincent de Paul said, "Here she comes! She certainly is in no hurry! When is she going to get to work?" Thérèse did not fire back with a cutting quip (of which she was very capable, for she had a quick wit), but simply smiled. In spite of her patience, Thérèse felt the smart of the barbs, jabs and cutting remarks that came her way. "We don't have any enemies in Carmel, but there are feelings" (S. 349). But negative feelings were not the only emotions that proved to be a trial for Thérèse when she entered Carmel.

On entering Carmel, Thérèse was reunited with the two women who had mothered her as a child (Pauline and Marie). Even though Thérèse resisted their attempts to mother her, she found it difficult to do so because her desire to be mothered was very strong. "I didn't come to Carmel to live with my sisters but to answer Jesus's call. Ah! I really felt in advance that this living with one's own sisters had to be the cause of continual suffering when one wishes to grant nothing to one's natural inclinations"(S. 338). Her desire to receive maternal succoring was also transferred to the mother prioress. "I remember when I was still a postulant that I had such violent temptations to satisfy myself and to find a few crumbs of pleasure that I was obliged to walk rapidly by your [Mother Gonzague's] door and to cling firmly to the banister of the staircase in order not to turn back. There came into my mind a crowd of permissions to seek; in a word, dear Mother, I found a thousand reasons for pleasing myself " (S. 378).

In short, Thérèse's entrance into Carmel required that she "leave home" in two ways. First, she had to learn how to live with people who had come from a different background than she had; second, she had to resist the temptation to reestablish old familiar roles with mother figures, namely her older siblings and Mother Gonzague."What would have become of me if I had become the 'pet' of the community, as some of the Sisters believed" (S. 233)? But as painful as Thérèse's struggle was not to become the baby of the community, it was nothing in comparison to what she had to endure regarding her father's illness.

On June 23, two months after Thérèse entered Carmel, her beloved father suddenly disappeared  from Les Buissonnets and was found four days later in Le Havre with the fixed idea  that he wanted to live as a hermit. Louis Martin's mental confusion was the result of physical and emotional factors; he was suffering from arteriosclerosis and a kidney infection, and he was mourning the loss of his children. Thérèse had entered Carmel on April 9, Céline had informed her father on June 15 of her desire to do the same, and Léonie had made plans to reenter the Visitation convent at Caen. "Oh, my children are abandoning me," sobbed Louis.[3]

As time went on, Louis' mental condition became so unstable that it became questionable whether or not he would be able to attend Thérèse's clothing ceremony (January 10, 1889). He did, and Thérèse called this day "his day of *triumph*," (S. 239) but the triumph was short lived. Within a fortnight, Louis became delusional. He heard the sounds of battles and screams of slaughter and began to carry a revolver in order to defend his family. When he was finally disarmed by his brother-in-law Isidore Guérin, Louis was institutionalized in Bon Sauveur mental asylum in Caen on February 12, 1889. This trial was almost more than Thérèse could bear. "I recall that in the month of June 1888, at the moment of our first trials [the time of Louis' flight to Le Havre], I said: 'I am suffering very much, but I feel I can still bear greater trials.' I was not thinking then of the ones reserved for me. I didn't know that on February 12, a month after my reception of the Habit, our dear Father would drink the *most bitter* and *most humiliating* of all chalices" (S. 241). Louis stayed in Bon Sauveur for the next three years.

Thérèse was due to make her final vows in January, 1890, but the date was postponed until September because Mother Gonzague felt that if Thérèse requested that she make her vows in January, Fr. Delatroëtte's would oppose the request. The nine month's wait was difficult but purifying for Thérèse, for in the process of waiting, she realized how much self-will was contained in making her vows according to her own timetable. In September, Thérèse made her final commitment. She hoped that her father would be able to attend; that hope was never realized.

On May 10, 1892, Isidore Guérin traveled to Caen and brought Louis back to Lisieux for a visit. It was the last time that

Thérèse ever saw her father. It was a heartrending encounter for Thérèse. Louis, once so handsome and dignified, was now gaunt and his faculties were diminished. He was almost mute; when he spoke, he did so only in phrases, "My little queen," etc. As he left in tears, Louis pointed upwards and said, *"Au ciel!"* ("In heaven!"). Heaven, was the first word that Thérèse had ever read (S. 51), and it was the last word that she ever heard her father speak.

**Reflections and Questions.**

We kissed at the barrier; and passing through
She left me, and moment by moment got
Smaller and smaller, until to my view
She was but a spot;
A wee white spot of muslin fluff
That down the diminishing platform bore
Through hustling crowds of gentle and tough
To the carriage door.
Under the lamplight's fitful glowers,
Behind dark groups from far and near,
Whose interests were apart from ours,
She would disappear,
Then show again, till I ceased to see
That flexible form, that nebulous white;
And she who was more than my life to me
Had vanished quite...[4]

This scene is repeated countless times each day at airports, railway stations, bus terminals, and ocean piers. But no two partings are the same, for no two intimacies are identical. Yet every human heart that beats knows the truth of Emily

Dickinson's words; "Parting is all we know of heaven and all we need of hell." [5]

Thérèse knew the hell of parting at a tender age." [C]asting a last look upon Les Buissonnets, that beautiful cradle of my childhood, which I was never to see again, I left my dear King's arms" (S. 230). In addition to the pain that is part and parcel of every parting, there were two factors that increased the pain of Thérèse's separation from her family. The first was that there was a certain finality about her parting – "casting a *last* look...*never to see again*"(S. 230). It is one thing to say *Adieu,* knowing that a separation is temporary; it is a far different reality to say *farewell forever.* There was a certain forevermore quality that attended upon Thérèse's departure. While it is true that Thérèse would be able to see her family after she entered Carmel, the thousand and one ways of being and doing that bound them together, were gone forever. The experience of Thérèse's loss was similar to that of the death of a loved one. We do not know how much we are connected to people whom we deeply love until they are taken from us. This is because they are so much a part of our lives, so linked to every memory triggered by the senses, that everything around us is a reminder of that person's absence. "But O for the touch of a vanish'd hand/And the sound of a voice that is still!/...But the tender grace of a day that is dead/ Will never come back to me." [6]

The second factor that added pain to Thérèse's departure was that it was the result of *her choice.* Thérèse could have stayed home with her father for the rest of his life, or at least until she was twenty-one, as had been recommended to her, but she chose not to. In consequence, Thérèse had to bear a suffer-ing almost too heavy to bear. Namely, watching someone you deeply love, suffer, knowing that you are the cause of the suffering and that you could have prevented it. The town gossip that seeped through the cloister walls was that Louis had lost his mind because his daughters, most particularly his youngest, had abandoned him in his old age. Had not Louis exclaimed, "Oh, my children are abandoning me!"[7] This vicious rumor was tactlessly talked about by the nuns in Thérèse's presence.

Place yourself in Thérèse's situation. You have made a decision to do God's will, which will entail leaving your elderly father, knowing full well that your choice will cause him to suffer greatly. Two months after your departure, you receive news from home that your father has become disorientated. You hear rumors that it was your choice to leave home that was the catalyst of his breakdown. Finally, you are a scrupulous person who is prone to rumination and self doubt. Imagine the guilt that you would feel, and the second guessing as you call into question the choice that you have made. So, what do you do? What is God's will for you in this situation? There are no easy answers to this question. But let us presume that in spite of your doubts, you believe that God wants you to stay where you are. In such a situation, there is a two-fold suffering that you are called to bear. First, holding fast to a choice that is besieged by a barrage of doubts. Second, like Mary at the foot of the Cross, you have to watch someone you love suffer and feel helpless to do anything about it.

*Questions.* What choices in your life entail these kinds of sufferings?

2. "Peace is my farewell to you, my peace is my gift to you.

I do not give it as the world gives peace" (Jn. 14: 27). Jesus said these words on the most anxious night of his life, the night before he died. The peace that Jesus is referring to is a peace that can coexist with pain and anxiety; it is the peace of soul that ensues upon doing the right thing, or knowing that you have done your best or have not left anything undone. It is the peace of a clear conscience.

Thérèse writes of this peace, regarding her first years in Carmel: "For seven years and a half that inner peace has remained my lot...in the midst of the greatest trials" (S. 230). Also, when Thérèse was devastated because she had not received permission to enter Carmel from Leo XIII, she retained this peace of soul. "In the bottom of my heart I felt a great peace, since I had done everything in my power to answer what God was asking of me. This *peace,* however, was in the *depths* only; bitterness *filled* my soul, for Jesus was silent" (S. 206). In addition, on the day that Thérèse received the veil (September 24, 1890), and her father was unable to attend the ceremony, Thérèse still was able to retain the peace of God. "[E]verything was sadness and bitterness. And still *peace,* always *peace,* reigned at the bottom of the chalice" (S. 262). The basis of Thérèse's peace was that she accepted suffering as a part of God's will. "I see very clearly that it's God's will that he not be here...Today's trial is a difficult sorrow to understand... [but] let us accept with a good heart the thorn that Jesus is offering us" (L. 684). The three long years that Thérèse's father was confined to the mental asylum in Caen were the most painful of her life; yet, she could write that they were "the most fruitful of my life" (S. 241), for she was given the grace to see all things as a part of God's mysterious design.

*Questions.* Think of times in your life when you made a painful decision to do the will of God and felt the strength of God's peace. Conversely, there is a false peace that "brings perpetual war" writes St.Teresa.[8] It is the temporary relief that we experience in the short run, that follows in the wake of a choice that *avoids* doing God's will, but which in the long run, leaves a queasy feeling in the pits of our stomachs because we know that we are living in an uneasy alliance with our conscience. Have you ever found yourself in this state of soul?

3. One morning, several years ago, I was sitting at my desk working on a retreat conference, when I heard a knock at my door. It was one of my Carmelite brothers who needed a ride to the airport. I said, "Yes," to his request but was tense until I was able to get back to my desk. I remember saying to myself, "Well, that shoots the morning." As I heard myself saying these familiar words, I was struck by their strangeness. Why would an act of charity shoot my morning? Isn't growing in love what life is all about? Yes, but the purpose of life often gets in the way of my agenda!

Langston Hughes' question, "What happens to a dream deferred?" may be personalized as "What do you do when your plans are frustrated? What do you do when your life is put on hold?" How do you interpret interruptions in your life? Henri Nouwen once told the story of a research professor who was always complaining about interruptions *in* his work, until one day he came to the realization that interruptions *were* his work.

Have you ever felt that your life was put on hold? The next time that you feel this way, ask yourself this question, "Whose life am I living now, if not my own?" Even though *our plans* are often frustrated by unseen roadblocks and *our agendas* laid waste by a world that hasn't yet come to consciousness of the supreme importance of the designs that we have upon our day, it is impossible for *our life* to be put on hold, for whatever is happening in the moment is our life. As John Lennon puts it, "Life is what is happening to you as you're making other plans."

Thérèse's plans were often frustrated. The dates of her entrance into Carmel, her reception of the habit and her profession, were all postponed. One of the dangers in such situations is that we can subtly disengage from life or slacken our efforts to do God's will, until our *real* life begins. Thérèse experienced this temptation when her entrance date into Carmel was postponed. "How did those *three months* pass, those months so rich in graces for me? At first the thought came into my mind not to lead a life as well regulated as had been my custom" (S. 215). But then Thérèse realized the importance of the present moment. "[B]ut soon I understood the value of the time I was being offered. I made a resolution to give myself up more than ever to a *serious* and *mortified* life....My mortifications consisted in breaking my will, always so ready to impose itself on others, in holding back a reply, in rendering little services without any recognition, in not leaning my back against a support when seated, etc., etc...I cannot express how much this waiting left me with sweet memories" (S. 215-216).

*Questions.* During the various times when Thérèse's plans were frustrated, she did not put her life on hold, but rather embraced these interruptions as opportunities to grow in virtue. In your daily life, where are you faced with similar opportunities?

## Notes

1. Guy Gaucher, ibid., 87.

2. Ibid., 93.

3. Ibid., 104.

4. Thomas Hardy, "On the Departure Platform," in *Thomas Hardy: The Complete Poems,* ed. James Gibson, (New York: Palgrave, 2001), 221.

5. Emily Dickinson, "My life closed twice before its close" #1732 in *The Complete Poems of Emily Dickinson,* (Boston: Little Brown and Company, 1960), 702.

6. Alfred Lord Tennyson, "Break, Break, Break," in *Poems of Tennyson,* (Boston: Houghton Mifflin Company, 1958), 84.

7. There was also a vicious rumor that Louis Martin lost his mind because he had contracted syphilis as the result of an immoral lifestyle. This rumor, coupled with the shame of Louis being in a mental institution, made him a source of embarrassment in Lisieux Carmel. Pauline writes: "Silence settled more and more around the venerated name of him whom we loved. In the Community where, until then, it had enjoyed a kind of prestige, if we pronounced it, this was in a whisper as though it were the name of a man almost in disgrace" (L. 701).

8. St. Teresa of Avila, "Meditations on the Song of Songs," in *The Collected Works of St. Teresa of Avila, Vol.2.,* trans. Kieran Kavanaugh O.C.D. & Otilio Rodriguez O.C.D., (Washington, D.C.: ICS Publications, 1980), 222.

# Chapter VIII

## *PROFESSION AND OFFERING TO MERCIFUL LOVE (1890–1895)*

Reception of the Veil
Mother Geneviève and St. Thérèse
Influenza Epidemic
Retreat of Father Alexis
Mother Agnes as Prioress
Papa's Death
Céline's Entrance into Carmel
End of Manuscript A

I should have spoken to you about the retreat preceding my Profession,[193] dear Mother, before speaking about the trial I have mentioned; it was far from bringing me any consolations since the most absolute aridity and almost total abandonment were my lot. Jesus was sleeping as usual in my little [15]boat; ah! I see very well how rarely souls allow Him to sleep peacefully within them. Jesus is so fatigued with always having to take the initiative and to attend to others that He hastens to take advantage of the repose I offer to Him. He will undoubtedly awaken before my great eternal retreat, but instead of being troubled about it this only gives me extreme pleasure.

[20] Really, I am far from being a saint, and what I have just said is proof of this; instead of rejoicing, for example, at my aridity, I should attribute it to my little fervor and lack of fidelity; I should be desolate for having slept (for seven years) during my hours of prayer and my *thanksgivings* after Holy Communion; well, I am not desolate. I remember that *little children* are as pleasing to their parents when

---

[193] This retreat began on August 28, 1890.

they are asleep as well as when they are wide awake; I remember, too, that when they perform operations, doctors [76r°] put their patients to sleep. Finally, I remember that: *"The Lord knows our weakness, that he is mindful that we are but dust and ashes."*[194]

Just as all those that followed it, my Profession retreat was one of great aridity. God [5]showed me clearly, however, without my perceiving it, the way to please Him and to practice the most sublime virtues. I have frequently noticed that Jesus doesn't want me to lay up *provisions;* He nourishes me at each moment with a totally new food; I find it within me without my knowing how it is there. I believe [10]it is Jesus Himself hidden in the depths of my poor little heart: He is giving me the grace of acting within me, making me think of all He desires me to do at the present moment.

A few days before my profession, I had the happiness of receiving the Sovereign Pontiff's blessing. I had requested it through [15]good Brother Simeon for both Papa and myself, and it was a great consolation to be able to return to my dear little Father the grace he obtained for me when taking me with him to Rome.

The *beautiful day* of my wedding finally arrived.[195] It was without a single cloud; however, the preceding evening a storm arose within my soul the like of which I'd [20]never seen before. Not a single doubt concerning my vocation had ever entered my mind until then, and it evidently was necessary that I experience this trial. In the evening, while making the Way of the Cross after Matins, my vocation appeared to me as a *dream,* a chimera. I found life in Carmel to be very beautiful, but the devil inspired me with the assurance that it wasn't for me and that I was misleading my Superiors by advancing on this way to which I wasn't called. The darkness was so great that I

---

[194] Psalm 102:14.

[195] Monday, September 8, 1890.

could see and [76v°] understand one thing only: I didn't have a vocation. Ah! how can I possibly describe the anguish in my soul? It appeared to me (and this is an absurdity which shows it was a temptation from the devil) that if I were to tell my Novice Mistress about these fears, she would prevent me from pronouncing my Vows. [5]And still I wanted to do God's will and return to the world rather than remain in Carmel and do my own will. I made the Mistress come out of the choir and, filled with confusion, I told her the state of my soul. Fortunately, she saw things much clearer than I did, and she completely reassured me. The act of humility I had just performed put the devil to flight since he had [10] perhaps thought that I would not dare admit my temptation. My doubts left me completely as soon as I finished speaking; nevertheless, to make my act of humility even more perfect, I still wished to confide my strange temptation to our Mother Prioress, who simply laughed at me.

In the morning of September 8, I felt as though I were flooded with a river of peace, [15]and it was in this peace "which surpasses all understanding"[196] that I pronounced my Holy Vows. My union with Jesus was effected not in the midst of thunder and lightning, that is, in extraordinary graces, but in the bosom of a light breeze similar to the one our Father St. Elijah heard on the Mount.[197] What graces I begged for on that day! [20] I really felt I was the Queen and so I profited from my title by delivering captives, by obtaining favors from the *King* for His ungrateful subjects, finally, I wanted to deliver all the souls from purgatory and convert all sinners. I prayed very much for my *Mother,* my dear Sisters, my whole family, but especially for my poor Father, who was so tried and so saintly. I offered myself to Jesus in order to accomplish His will perfectly in me without creatures ever being able

[196] Philippians 4:7.

[197] 1 Kings 19:12-13.

to place any obstacle in the way.[198]

[77r°] This beautiful day passed by just as do the saddest since the most radiant day has a tomorrow; it was without sadness, however, that I placed my crown at the Blessed Virgin's feet. I felt that time could not take away my happiness. Mary's nativity! What a beautiful feast on which [5] to become the spouse of Jesus! It was the *little* Blessed Virgin, one day old, who was presenting her *little* flower to the *little* Jesus. Everything was little that day except the graces and the peace I received, and the peaceful joy I experienced in the evening when gazing at the stars shining in the firmament and thinking that *soon* this beautiful heaven would open up to my ravished eyes, and I would be able to unite myself [10] to my Spouse in the bosom of eternal happiness.

The ceremony of my reception of the Veil took place on the 24th of September and the day was veiled in tears. Papa was not there to bless his Queen; Father Pichon was in Canada; the Bishop, who was supposed to come and dine with Uncle, did not come at all since he was sick. In a word, everything [15]was sadness and bitterness. And still *peace,* always *peace*, reigned at the bottom of the chalice. That day, too, Jesus permitted that I was unable to hold back my tears and these were misunderstood. In fact, I had been able to bear up under much greater crosses without crying; however, this was because I was helped by powerful graces. Jesus left me to my own [20]resources on the 24th and I soon showed how little these resources really were.

Jeanne's wedding[199] took place eight days after I received the Veil. It would be impossible, dear Mother, for me to tell you how

---

[198] Between folios 76 and 77 of the manuscripts there is a letter that Thérèse had on her heart on the day of her Profession. See page 275.
[199] Jeanne Guérin, who was Thérèse's cousin, married Doctor Francis La Néele, October 1, 1890.

much I learned from her example concerning the delicate attentions a bride can bestow upon her bridegroom. I listened eagerly to what she was saying so that I would learn all I could since I didn't want to do less for my beloved Jesus than Jeanne did for her Francis; true, he was a perfect creature, but he was still only a *creature!*

[77v°] I even went so far as to amuse myself to composing a letter of invitation which was comparable to Jeanne's own letter, and this is how it was written:

Letter of Invitation to the Wedding of Sister Thérèse
of the Child Jesus and the Holy Face.

[5]God Almighty, Creator of Heaven and Earth, Sovereign Ruler of the Universe, and the Most Glorious Virgin Mary, Queen of the Heavenly Court, announce to you the Spiritual Espousals [10]of Their August Son, Jesus, King of kings, and Lord of lords, with little Thérèse Martin, now Princess and Lady of His Kingdoms of the Holy Childhood and the Passion, assigned to her in dowry by her Divine Spouse, [15]from which Kingdoms she holds her titles of nobility—of the Child Jesus and the Holy Face.

Monsieur Louis Martin, Proprietor and Master of the Domains of Suffering and Humiliation and Madame Martin, Princess and [20]Lady of Honor of the Heavenly Court, wish to have you take part in the Marriage of their Daughter, Thérèse, with Jesus, the Word of God, the Second Person of the Adorable [25]Trinity, Who through the operation of the Holy Spirit was made Man and Son of Mary, Queen of Heaven..

Being unable to invite you to the Nuptial Blessing which was given on Mount Carmel, September 8, 1890, [30](the heavenly court alone was admitted), you are nevertheless asked to be present at the Return from the Wedding which will take place Tomorrow, the Day of Eternity, on which day Jesus, Son of God, will come on the

Clouds of Heaven in the splendor of His Majesty, to judge the Living and the Dead.

The hour being as yet uncertain, you are invited to hold yourselves in readiness and to watch.

[78r°] And now, dear Mother, what more is there to say? Ah! I thought I was finished, but I haven't said anything to you as yet concerning my good fortune at knowing our holy Mother Geneviève. This certainly was a priceless gift; God, who had given me so many graces, [5]willed that I should live with a *saint*. Not one that was inimitable, but one who was made holy by the practice of the hidden virtues, the ordinary virtues. On more than one occasion I received great consolations from her, but especially on one Sunday in particular.

Coming to pay her a visit as was my custom, I found two other Sisters with Mother Geneviève; I looked at her with a smile and was preparing to [10]leave since three Sisters are not permitted with a patient,[200] but she said with an inspired look on her countenance: "Wait, my little child, I'm going to say just a little word to you; every time you come you ask for a spiritual bouquet. Well, today, I will give you this one: Serve God with *peace* and *joy;* [15]remember, my child, *Our God is a God of peace.'*[201] After thanking her very simply, I left but was moved to the point of tears and was convinced that God had revealed the state of my soul to her. That day I had been severely tried even to the verge of sadness; I was in such a night that I no longer knew whether God loved me. You can readily understand, dear Mother, the joy [20]and consolation I then experienced!

The following Sunday, I wanted to know what revelation Mother

[200] "This was the custom of the monastery regarding the visiting of the sick: no more than two at a time" (note of Mother Agnes of Jesus).
[201] 1 Corinthians 14:33.

Geneviève had received; she assured me she had received *none* at all, and then my admiration was greater still when I saw the degree to which Jesus was living within her and making her act and speak. Ah! that type of sanctity seems the *truest* and the *most holy* to me, and it is the type that I desire because in it one meets with no deceptions.

[78v°] On the day of my Profession I was also very much consoled to learn from Mother Geneviève's own mouth that she had passed through the same trial as I did before pronouncing her Vows. You recall, dear Mother, the consolation we received from her at the time of our *great* sorrows. [5]Finally, the memory which Mother Geneviève left in my heart is a sacred memory. The day of her departure for heaven,[202] I was particularly touched; it was the first time I had assisted at a death and really the spectacle was ravishing. I was placed at the foot of the dying saint's bed, and witnessed her slightest movements. [10] During the two hours I spent there, it seemed to me that my soul should have been filled with fervor; however, a sort of insensibility took control of me. But at the *moment itself* of our saintly Mother Geneviève's birth in heaven, my interior disposition changed and in the twinkling of an eye I experienced an inexpressible joy and fervor; it was as though [15]Mother Geneviève had imparted to me a little of the happiness she was enjoying, for I was convinced she went straight to heaven. While she was still living, I said to her one day: "Mother, you will not go to purgatory!" She answered gently: "I hope not." Ah! surely, God does not disappoint a trust so filled with humility; the many favors we have received [20]since are a proof of this.

After Mother's death, each of the Sisters hastened to claim some relic, and you know the one I have the happiness of possessing. During her last agony, I had noticed a single *tear* glistening like a dia-

---

[202] She died on December 5, 1891.

mond on her eyelash, *and this tear, the last she was to shed on earth,* never fell; I saw it still glistening there when she was laid out in the choir. So when evening came, unseen by anyone, I made bold to approach her and with a little piece of linen I took the *saint's tear as a relic.* Since then I have carried it in the little [79r°] container which holds my Vows.

I attach no importance to dreams; besides, I have rarely had any meaningful dreams, even wondering why it is that I think of God all day long and yet am so little occupied with Him in my [5]sleeping hours. I dream usually about such things as woods, flowers, streams, and the sea; I see beautiful children almost all the time; I catch butterflies and birds the like of which I've never seen before. You can see, dear Mother, that though my dreams are rather fanciful, they are never mystical. One night after Mother Geneviève's death, I had a very consoling dream: I[10] dreamed she was making her last will and testament, giving each of the Sisters something which she possessed. When my turn finally came, I thought I would get nothing as there was really nothing left to give; however, she said: "To you I leave my *heart.*" She repeated this three times with great emphasis.

Influenza broke out in the [15] monastery one month after Mother Geneviève's death. Two Sisters and myself were the only ones left on our feet. Never could I describe all the things I witnessed, what life appeared to be like, and everything that happened.

My nineteenth birthday was celebrated with a death,[203] and this was soon followed by two other deaths. At this time I was all alone in the sacristy because the first in charge was seriously ill;[204] I was the

---

[203] Sister St. Joseph died on January 2, 1892; she was the oldest member of the community.

[204] Sister St. Stanislaus (1824–1914).

one who had to prepare for the burials, open [20] the choir grilles for Mass, etc. God gave me very many graces making me strong at this time, and now I ask myself how I could have done all I did without experiencing fear. Death reigned supreme. The ones who were most ill were taken care of by those who could scarcely drag themselves around. As soon as a Sister breathed her last, we were obliged to leave her alone. One morning upon arising I had a presentiment that Sister Magdalene was dead; the dormitory was in darkness, and no one was coming out of the cells. I decided [79v°] to enter Sister Magdalene's cell since the door was wide open. I saw her fully dressed and lying across her bed. I didn't have the least bit of fear. When I saw that she didn't have a blessed candle, I went to fetch one for her, along with a wreath of roses.

The night Mother Subprioress died[205] I was all alone with the infirmarian. [5]It's impossible to imagine the sad state of the community at this time; the ones who were up and about can give some idea of the conditions, but in the midst of this abandonment I felt that God was watching over us. It was without effort that the dying passed on to a better life, and immediately after their death an expression of joy and peace covered their faces and gave the impression almost that they were [10] only asleep. Surely this was true because, after the image of this world has passed away, they will awaken to enjoy eternally the delights reserved for the Elect.

All through the time the community was undergoing this trial, I had the unspeakable consolation of receiving Holy Communion *every day*. Ah! this was [15]sweet indeed! Jesus spoiled me for a long time, much longer than He did His faithful spouses, for He permitted me *to receive Him* while the rest didn't have this same happiness. I was very

---

[205] Sister Fébronie died January 4, 1892.

fortunate, too, to touch the sacred vessels and to prepare the little linen cloths destined to come in contact with Jesus. I felt that I should be very fervent and recalled frequently these words spoken to a holy deacon: "You are to be holy, you [20]who carry the vessels of the Lord."[206]

I can't say that I frequently received consolations when making my thanksgivings after Mass; perhaps it is the time when I receive the least. However, I find this very understandable since I have offered myself to Jesus not as one desirous of her own consolation in His visit but simply to please Him who is giving Himself to me. When I am preparing for Holy Communion, I picture my soul as a piece of land and I beg the Blessed Virgin to remove from it *any rubbish* that would prevent it [80r°] from being *free;* then I ask her to set up a huge tent worthy of *heaven,* adorning it with *her own* jewelry; finally, I invite all the angels and saints to come and conduct a magnificent concert there. It seems to me that when Jesus descends into my heart He is content to find Himself so well received and I, too, [5]am content. All this, however, does not prevent both distractions and sleepiness from visiting me, but at the end of the thanksgiving when I see that I've made it so badly I make a resolution to be thankful all through the rest of the day. You see, dear Mother, that I am far from being on the way of fear; I always find a way [10] to be happy and to profit from my miseries; no doubt this does not displease Jesus since He seems to encourage me on this road. Contrary to my usual state of mind, one day I was a little disturbed when going to Communion; it seemed to me that God was not satisfied with me and I said to myself: Ah! if I receive only *half a host* today, this will cause [15]me great sorrow, and I shall believe that Jesus comes regretfully into my heart. I approached, and oh, what joy! For the first time in my life I saw the priest take *two hosts* which

---

[206] Isaiah 52:11; liturgy of the ordination of a deacon.

were well separated from each other and place them on my tongue! You can understand my joy and the sweet tears of consolation I shed when beholding a mercy so great!

[20] The year that followed my Profession, that is, two months before Mother Geneviève's death, I received great graces during my retreat.[207] Ordinarily, the retreats that are preached are more painful to me than the ones I make alone, but this year it was otherwise. I had made a preparatory novena with great fervor, in spite of the inner sentiment I had, for it seemed to me that the preacher would not be able to understand me since he was supposed to do good to great sinners but not [80v°] to religious souls. God wanted to show me that He was the Director of my soul, and so He made use of this Father specifically, who was appreciated only by me in the community. At the time I was having great interior trials of all kinds, even to the point of asking myself whether heaven really existed. I felt [5] disposed to say nothing of my interior dispositions since I didn't know how to express them, but I had hardly entered the confessional when I felt my soul expand. After speaking only a few words, *I was understood* in a marvelous way and my soul was like a book in which this priest read better than I did myself. [10]He launched me full sail upon the waves of *confidence and love* which so strongly attracted me, but upon which I dared not advance. He told me that *my faults caused God no pain, and that holding as he did God's place,* he was telling me *in His name* that God was very much pleased with me.

Oh! how happy I was to hear those consoling words! Never had

---

[207] This retreat was preached by Father Alexis Prou (1844–1914), a Franciscan recollect from Caen; he was Superior of the house of St. Lazaire. The retreat was conducted from the 8th to the 15th of October, 1891.

I [15]heard that our faults *could not cause God any pain,* and this assurance filled me with joy, helping me to bear patiently with life's exile. I felt at the bottom of my heart that this was really so, for God is more tender than a mother, and were you not, dear Mother, always ready to pardon the little [20]offenses I committed against you involuntarily? How often I experienced this! No word of reproach touched me as much as did one of your caresses. My nature was such that fear made me recoil; with *love* not only did I advance, I actually *flew.*

O Mother, it was especially since the blessed day of your election[208] that I have flown in the ways of love. On that day Pauline became my living Jesus.

[81r°] I had the happiness of contemplating for a long time the *marvels Jesus* is working by means of my dear Mother. I see that *suffering alone* gives birth to souls, and more than ever before these sublime words of Jesus unveil their depths to me: *"Amen, amen, I say to you, unless the grain of [15]wheat falls into the ground and dies, it remains alone; but if it dies, it will bring forth much fruit."*[209] What an abundant harvest you have reaped! You have sown in tears, but soon you will see the result of your works, and you will return filled with joy, carrying sheaves in your arms.[210] O Mother, among these ripe sheaves is hidden the little [10]*white flower;* however, in heaven she will have a voice with which to sing of your *gentleness and your virtues* which she sees you practice every day in the darkness and the silence of life's exile!

Yes, for the past two years I have understood very well the mysteries hidden from me until then. God showed me the same

---

[208] Sister Agnes of Jesus was elected Prioress on February 20, 1893.
[209] John 12:24.
[210] Psalm 125:5-6.

mercy He showed to King [15]Solomon. He has not willed that I have one single desire which is not fulfilled, not only my desires for perfection but those too whose vanity I *have understood* without having experienced it.

As I have always looked upon you, dear Mother, as my *ideal,* I desired to be like you in everything; when I saw you do beautiful paintings and [20] delightful poems, I said to myself: How happy I would be if I were able to paint and to know how to express my thoughts in verse and thus do good to souls. I would not have wanted *to ask* for these natural gifts and my desires remained *hidden away* at the bottom of my *heart. Jesus hidden* also in this poor little heart was pleased to show it that *everything is vanity and affliction of spirit under the sun.*[211] To the great astonishment of the Sisters I was told to paint, and God permitted that I profit by the lessons my dear Mother gave me. He willed also[81v°] that I write poems and compose little pieces that were considered beautiful. And just as Solomon, when he *considered all the works of his hands in which he had placed so much useless toil, saw that all is vanity and affliction of spirit,* in the same way I recognized from EXPERIENCE that happiness consists in [5]hiding oneself, in remaining ignorant of created things. I understood that without *love* all works are nothing, even the most dazzling, such as raising the dead to life and converting peoples.

Instead of doing me any harm, of making me vain, the gifts which God showered upon me (without my having asked for them) drew me to *Him;* and [10]I saw that He alone was *unchangeable,* that He alone could fulfill my immense desires.

There are other desires of another kind that Jesus was pleased to grant me, childish desires similar to the snow at my reception of

---

[211] Ecclesiastes 2:11.

the Habit.

You know, dear Mother, how much I love flowers; when making myself a [15]prisoner at the age of fifteen, I gave up forever the pleasure of running through fields decked out in their springtime treasures. Well, never in my life did I possess so many flowers as after my entrance into Carmel. It is the custom for fiancés to often give their fiancées bouquets and Jesus didn't forget it. He sent me in great abundance sheaves of cornflowers, huge daisies, poppies, etc., all the flowers that [20] delighted me the most. There was even a little flower called corncockle that I had never found since our stay at Lisieux; I wanted very much to see it again, that flower of *my childhood* which I had picked in the fields of Alençon. And at Carmel it came to smile at me again and show me that in the smallest things as well as the greatest, God gives the hundredfold in this life to those souls who leave everything for love of Him.[212]

But the most intimate of my desires, the greatest of them all, which I thought would never [82r°] be realized, was my dear Céline's entrance into the same Carmel as ours. This *dream* appeared to be improbable: to live under the same roof, to share the joys and pains of the companion of my childhood; I had made my sacrifice complete by confiding to Jesus my dear sister's future, [5]resolved to see her leave for the other side of the world if necessary. The only thing I couldn't accept was her not being the spouse of Jesus, for since I loved her as much as I loved myself it was impossible for me to see her give her heart to a mortal being. I had already suffered very much when knowing she was exposed to dangers in the world which were unknown to me. Since my entrance into Carmel, I can say that my affection [10] for

---

[212] Matthew 19:29.

Céline was a mother's love rather than a sister's. When she was to attend a party[213] one day, the very thought of it caused me so much pain that I begged God to *prevent her from dancing,* and (contrary to my custom) I even shed a torrent of tears. Jesus deigned to answer me. He permitted that His little fiancée *be unable to dance* that evening (even though she was not[115]embarrassed to dance gracefully when it was necessary). She was invited to dance and was unable to refuse the invitation, but her partner found out he was totally powerless to make her dance; to his great confusion he was condemned simply *to walking* in order to conduct her to her place, and then he made his escape and did not reappear for the whole evening. This incident, unique in its kind, made me grow in confidence and love for the One [20]who set *His seal* upon my forehead and had imprinted it at the same time upon that of my dear Céline.

Last year, July 29, God broke the bonds of His incomparable servant[214] and called him to his eternal reward; at the same time He broke those which still held His dear fiancée in the world because she had accomplished her mission. Having been given the office of *representing us* all with our Father whom we so tenderly loved, she had accomplished this mission just like an angel. And angels don't remain

---

[213] This incident took place at the wedding of Henri Maudelonde, the nephew of M. and Mme. Guérin, April 20, 1892.

[214] "During the two years preceding Papa's death, Uncle kept him in his own home, taking care of him in his old age. We were able to see him only once during the whole course of his illness because he was so weak. Ah! what a visit that was! You recall it, Mother! When he was leaving and we were saying good by, he lifted his eyes to heaven and remained that way a long time and had only one word with which to express his thoughts: 'In heaven!'" *(Histoire d'une Ame).*

[82v°] on earth once they've fulfilled God's will, for they return immediately to Him, and this is why they're represented with wings. Our angel also spread her white wings; she was ready to fly *far away* to find Jesus, but He made her fly *close by*. He was content with simply accepting the great sacrifice [5]which was very painful for little Thérèse. Her Céline had kept a secret hidden from her for *two full years*.[215] Ah, how Céline herself had suffered because of this! Finally, from heaven my dear King, who never liked stragglers when he was still with us on earth, hastened to arrange Céline's muddled affairs, and she joined us on September 14!

[10]When the difficulties seemed insurmountable one day, I said to Jesus during my act of thanksgiving: "You know, my God, how much I want to know whether Papa went *straight to heaven;* I am not asking You to speak to me, but give me a sign. If Sister A. of J.[216] consents to Céline's entrance or places no obstacle to it, this will be an answer that Papa went *straight to You.*" This Sister, [15]as you are aware, dear Mother, found we were already too many with three, and she didn't want another of our family to be admitted. But God who holds the hearts of His creatures in His hand, inclining them to do His will, changed this Sister's dispositions. The first one to meet me after my thanksgiving was Sister Aimée, and she called me over to her with a friendly smile and told me to come up with her to [20]your cell. She spoke to me about Céline and there were tears in her eyes. Ah! how many things I have to thank Jesus for; He answers all my requests!

And now I have no other desire except *to love* Jesus unto folly. My childish desires have all flown away. I still love to adorn the Infant

---

[215] Thérèse is referring to a missionary project in Canada that Father Pichon, S.J. had suggested to Céline.

[216] Sister Aimée of Jesus of the Heart of Mary (1851–1930).

Jesus' altar with flowers, but ever since He has given me the *Flower* I desired, my *dear Céline,* I desire no other; she is the one I [83r°] offer Him as my most delightful bouquet.

Neither do I desire any longer suffering or death, and still I love them both; it is *love* alone that attracts me, however. I desired them for a long time; I possessed suffering and believed I had touched the shores of heaven, [5]that the little flower would be gathered in the springtime of her life. Now, abandonment alone guides me. I have no other compass! I can no longer ask for anything with fervor except the accomplishment of God's will in my soul without any creature being able to set obstacles in the way. I can speak these words of the Spiritual Canticle of St. John of the Cross:

> [10] In the inner wine cellar
> I drank of my Beloved, and, when I went abroad
> through all this valley
> I no longer knew anything,
> and lost the herd that I was following.
>
> Now I occupy my soul
> and all my energy in his service;
> I no longer tend the herd,
> nor have I any other work
> now that my every act is LOVE.[217]

Or rather:

> After[15]I have known it
> LOVE works so in me
> that whether things go well or badly

---

[217] *Spiritual Canticle,* st. 26 and 28, Collected Works, p. 78.

love turns them to one sweetness
transforming the soul in ITSELF.[218]

How sweet is the way of love, dear Mother. True, one can fall
or commit infidelities, but, knowing *how to draw profit from everything,* love quickly consumes everything that can be displeasing to
[20]Jesus; it leaves nothing but a humble and profound peace in the
depths of the heart.

Ah! how many lights have I not drawn from the works of our
holy Father, St. John of the Cross! At the ages of seventeen and eighteen I had no other spiritual nourishment; later on, however, all books
left me in aridity and I'm still in that state. If I open a book composed
by a spiritual author (even the most beautiful, the most touching
book), I feel my heart contract immediately and I read without understanding, so to speak. Or if I do understand, my mind comes to a
standstill without the capacity of meditating. In this helplessness,
Holy Scripture and the [83v°] Imitation come to my aid; in them I discover a solid and very *pure* nourishment. But it is especially the
*Gospels* that sustain me during my hours of prayer, for in them I find
what is necessary for my poor little soul. I am constantly discovering
in them new lights, hidden and mysterious meanings.

[5] I understand and I know from experience that: *"The kingdom
of God is within you."*[219] Jesus has no need of books or doctors to
instruct souls; He, the Doctor of doctors, teaches without the noise of
words.[220] Never have I heard Him speak, but I feel that He is within
me at each moment; He is guiding and inspiring me with what I must
say and do. I find just [10] when I need them certain lights that I had not

---

[218] "Without support yet with support," st. 3, *Collected Works,* p. 70.
[219] Luke 17:21.
[220] *The Imitation of Christ* III, 43:3.

seen until then, and it isn't most frequently during my hours of prayer that these are most abundant but rather in the midst of my daily occupations.

O my dear Mother! after so many graces can I not sing with the Psalmist: *"How GOOD is the Lord, his MERCY endures forever!"*[221] [15]It seems to me that if all creatures had received the same graces I received, God would be feared by none but would be loved to the point of folly; and through *love,* not through fear, no one would ever consent to cause Him any pain. I understand, however, that all souls cannot be the same, that it is necessary there be different types in order to honor[20]each of God's perfections in a particular way. To me He has granted His *infinite* Mercy, and *through it* I contemplate and adore the other divine perfections! All of these perfections appear to be resplendent *with love;* even His Justice (and perhaps this even more so than the others) seems to me clothed in *love.* What a sweet joy it is to think that God is *Just,* i.e., that He takes into account our weakness, that He is perfectly aware of our fragile nature. What should I fear then? Ah! must not the infinitely just God, who deigns [84r°] to pardon the faults of the prodigal son with so much kindness, be just also toward me who "am with Him always"?[222]

This year, June 9, the feast of the Holy Trinity, I received the grace to understand more than ever before how much Jesus desires to be loved.[223]

[5]I was thinking about the souls who offer themselves as victims of God's Justice in order to turn away the punishments reserved to sinners, drawing them upon themselves. This offering seemed great and

---

[221] Psalm 117:1.

[222] Luke 15:31.

[223] Act of Oblation to Divine Mercy, page 276.

very generous to me, but I was far from feeling attracted to making it. From the depths of my heart, I cried out:

"O my God! Will Your Justice alone find souls willing to immolate themselves as victims? Does not Your [10]*Merciful Love* need them too? On every side this love is unknown, rejected; those hearts upon whom You would lavish it turn to creatures, seeking happiness from them with their miserable affection; they do this instead of throwing themselves into Your arms and of accepting Your infinite *Love*. O my God! Is Your disdained Love going to remain closed up within Your Heart? It seems to me that if You were [15]to find souls offering themselves as victims of holocaust to Your Love, You would consume them rapidly; it seems to me, too, that You would be happy not to hold back the waves of infinite tenderness within You. If Your Justice loves to release itself, this Justice *which extends only over the earth,* how much more does Your Merciful Love desire to *set souls on fire* since Your Mercy *reaches* [20] *to the heavens.*[224] O my Jesus, let me be this happy victim; consume Your holocaust with the fire of Your Divine Love!"

You permitted me, dear Mother, to offer myself in this way to God, and you know the rivers or rather the oceans of graces that flooded my soul. Ah! since the happy day, it seems to me that *Love* penetrates and surrounds me, that at each moment this *Merciful Love* renews me, purifying my soul and leaving no trace of sin within it, and [84v°] I need have no fear of purgatory. I know that of myself I would not merit even to enter that place of expiation since only holy souls can have entrance there, but I also know that the Fire of Love is more sanctifying than is the fire of purgatory. I know that Jesus cannot desire [5] useless sufferings for us, and that He would not inspire the longings I feel unless He wanted to grant them.

---

[224] Psalm 35:6.

Oh! how sweet is the way of Love! How I want to apply myself to doing the will of God always with the greatest self-surrender!

Here, dear Mother, is all I can tell you about the life of[10] your little Thérèse; you know better than I do what she is and what Jesus has done for her. You will forgive me for having abridged my religious life so much.

How will this "story of a little white flower" come to an end? Perhaps the little flower will be plucked in her youthful freshness or else transplanted to other shores.[225] [15]I don't know, but what I am certain about is that God's Mercy will accompany her always, that it will never cease blessing the dear Mother who offered her to Jesus; she will rejoice eternally at being one of the flowers of her crown. And with this dear Mother she will sing eternally the new canticle of Love.

---

[225] This is a reference to the possible departure for the missions. The Carmel of Saigon, founded by Lisieux, was asking for members for a foundation at Hanoi.

## *Profession and Offering to Merciful Love*

### Background and Context.

On August 28, 1890, Thérèse began a private retreat in preparation for her solemn profession. Like the retreat that she had made the previous year and those that she would make in subsequent years, this retreat was devoid of any spiritual consolation. Her prayer was arid and she felt abandoned.

Thérèse dreaded making retreats ever since her first communion retreat, which had triggered an attack of scruples. Retreats awakened painful memories in Thérèse and revived in her the fear of another attack of scruples. [1] This fear was fed by many of the sermons that Thérèse heard in Carmel.[2] Pauline testifies: "[S]cruples came to paralyze this impetus (trust in God), and she was very troubled, too, during her first years in Carmel. This was partly because she had heard it said in some sermons that it was very easy to offend God and to stain one's purity of conscience." [3] This is exactly what Thérèse was told by Abbé Domin during her first communion retreat.

Thérèse's fear of a reoccurrence of an attack of scruples was not an empty one, for on the eve of her profession, she began to have obsessive doubts regarding her vocation. "Not a single doubt concerning my vocation had ever entered my mind until then...[The evening before my profession] my vocation appeared to me as a *dream*, a chimera...The darkness was so great that I could see and understand one thing only; I didn't have a vocation" (S. 260-261).

Thérèse made her profession on September 8th, but she was still searching to find her path to God. The spirituality of the community, infected by Jansenism, stressed appeasing the justice of a wrathful God by means of physical penances. Thérèse was not attracted by this stark spirituality. Thérèse's God was a humane God. One example that shows that Thérèse's God was a loving God rather than a wrathful God was her lack of fear and guilt over her habit of falling asleep during prayer. She writes that she did not feel " desolate" about falling asleep during prayer because she "remembers that *little children* are as pleasing to their parents when they are asleep as well as when they are wide awake" (S. 259).

Thérèse believed in a loving God. She knew that her path to God was *not* the path of physical penances. But what her path would be, was still uncertain to her. She discovered her path when she was so depressed that she "no longer knew whether God loved [her]"(S. 264). One day when Thérèse visited Mother Geneviève in the infirmary, she found two nuns with her. Thérèse excused herself. However, as she was leaving, Mother Geneviève said to her, "Serve God with peace and joy; remember my child, Our God is a God of peace" (S. 264). These words were such healing balm to Thérèse's beleaguered soul that she was convinced that Mother Geneviève had received a special revelation from God. It was in Mother Geneviève that Thérèse discovered a spirituality by which "one was made holy by the practice of the hidden virtues, the ordinary virtues..that type of sanctity seems the *truest* and the *most holy* to me" (S. 265).

A year after Thérèse's profession, the community made its annual retreat (October 8-15, 1891) conducted by Fr. Alexis Prou. The retreat was a time of darkness for Thérèse. "I was having great interior trials of all kinds, even to the point of asking myself whether heaven really existed" (S. 269). But just as Mother Geneviève was an unexpected ray of light that pierced

Thérèse's darkness the year before, so too was Fr. Alexis.

The community did not expect much from Fr. Alexis, who was assigned at the last moment to conduct the retreat, when his provincial Fr. Bénigene de Janville, who was slated to give it, had to cancel. Fr. Alexis had no experience giving retreats to religious; his ministry in the main was to large crowds of lay people in factories. At first, Thérèse, like the rest of the community, felt that Fr. Alexis was a bad fit. "I had made a preparatory novena with great fervor, in spite of the inner sentiment I had, for it seemed to me that the preacher would not be able to understand me since he was supposed to do good to great sinners but not to religious souls" (S. 269).

In the light of this sentiment, coupled with her difficulty of expressing the trials that she was experiencing, Thérèse was "disposed to say nothing of [her] interior dispositions," (S.269) to Fr. Alexis. Translated into the vernacular, Thérèse's feeling about sharing her interior trials with Fr. Alexis was, "Why even try; he won't be able to understand me anyway."

"[B]ut I had hardly entered the confessional when I felt my soul expand. After speaking only a few words I was *understood* in a marvelous way...He launched me full sail upon the waves of *confidence and love* which so strongly attracted me...he told me that *my faults caused God no pain*...This assurance filled me with joy. My nature was such that fear made me recoil; with love not only did I advance, I actually flew" (S. 270).

This account of Thérèse being freed from the crippling fear of scruples and being launched upon the waves of love was a great grace for her, but it can give us the erroneous impression that from this point on, Thérèse never had any further problems with scrupulosity. This was not the case. For example, nearly two years after this retreat, Thérèse became so scrupulous that she doubted that she was forgiven *after* going to confession. In a letter dated January 20, 1893, Fr. Almire Pichon writes the following to Thérèse in this regard: "Dear Child of my soul, listen to what I am about to tell you in the name and on the part of our Lord: No, no, you have not committed any mortal sins. I swear it. No, we cannot sin gravely without knowing it. No, after absolution, we must not doubt about our state of grace. To your Mother St. Teresa, who was praying one day for souls, who were deluding themselves, Our Lord answered: "My daughter, no one is lost without knowing it perfectly." Banish, then, your worries. God wills it, and I command it. Take my word for it: Never, never, never, have you committed a mortal sin" (L. 767). [4]

In January, 1892, influenza ravaged the community. It claimed the lives of three nuns and confined most of the others to bed. Only three nuns were left on their feet; Thérèse was one of them. She rose to the occasion by nursing the sick and preparing the dead for burial. She impressed and edified the community with her maturity and tireless dedication in the face of a difficult situation. The little girl with golden ringlets in her hair who was always taken care of, now took charge. Even Fr. Delatroëtte was swayed in his estimation of Thérèse. "She shows great promise to this community."

After being devastated by influenza, the community received new life into its midst in the person of a Céline Martin, but not without opposition. Fr. Delatroëtte questioned whether the entrance of a fourth Martin girl was advisable or even permissible. [5] Sr. Aimée was adamant in her opposition and voted against Céline's entrance. She felt that Céline would increase the influence of the "Martin clan," as she called them. In addition,

Sr. Aimée, being of a practical bent of mind, felt that Céline, an "artist," would be of little use to the community.[6] But in the end, Sr. Aimée relented and Céline was received into the community on September 14, 1894.

Céline entered when her sister Pauline (Mother Agnes) was prioress, having been elected to that position on February 20, 1893. Mother Gonzague was the novice mistress and Thérèse the assistant novice mistress. Céline was assigned to Thérèse's guidance, which proved to be a task for both of them. While Céline was good-hearted and eager to learn, her independent spirit, impetuosity, and perfectionism made her a tall order for Thérèse, a salad "well seasoned with vinegar and spices" (S. 389) as Thérèse referred to her. Even Céline recognized these traits in herself: "I was far too eager about my assignments, and I seemed to be pushed by an irresistible drive to carry them out, meticulously, to an exaggerated stage of perfection. Consequently, whenever I did not achieve this, I experienced a sense of frustration."[7]

## Reflections and Questions.

1. Retreats made Thérèse vulnerable to attacks of scruples because they revived emotionally laden memories of the retreat that had triggered her first attack of scruples. A similar dynamic is true in our own lives. Whenever we experience something in the present that resembles a traumatic event from our past, old memories and their attending feelings are reactivated. And like Thérèse, whenever we are in the vice grip of deeply seated fears and insecurities, we need someone who can help us to calm our anxieties, to quell our insecurities, and to put things in perspective for us. And like Thérèse, we need to be told the same things,

over and over and over again.

*Questions.* Who are the loving, patient, understanding people in your life whom you go to in your hour of need? Conversely, who are the people whom God asks you to minister to in like manner?

2. Thérèse did not expect that Fr. Alexis would be able to help her with her trials, for as she wrote, "it seemed to me that the preacher would not be able to understand me since he was supposed to do good to great sinners but not to religious souls" (S. 269). Thérèse was wrong. The person whom Thérèse thought would not be able to help her proved to be one of the greatest graces of her life.

*Questions.* How often in your life has God used the most unlikely person to minister to you in your hour of need? How often has a chance encounter or a parenthetical remark proved to be the means by which God's providence has changed your life?

3. St. Teresa of Avila exhorted her nuns to speak to God in prayer "as with a father, or a brother, or a lord, or as with a spouse; sometimes in one way, at other times in another; He will teach you what you must do in order to please Him"[8] We see Teresa's advice manifested in the opening paragraphs of chapter eight of *Story of a Soul,* where Thérèse writes of two ways by which she related to God. The first is that of Jesus sleeping in the bow of a boat. The second is that of a loving parent who understands his or her child's frailties. It is instructive to notice *when* Thérèse used each image.

a) *Jesus asleep.* When Thérèse was in a state of aridity and felt abandoned by God, she imaged Jesus being asleep in her presence. This image helped Thérèse to bear her desolation because it took her mind off herself and focused it on God. "[S]ince the most absolute aridity and almost total abandonment were my lot, Jesus was sleeping as usual in my little boat; ah! I see very well how rarely souls allow Him to sleep peacefully within them. Jesus is so fatigued with always having to take the initiative and to attend to others that he hastens to take advantage of the repose *I offer to Him* "(S. 259) (italic added).

Let us apply this image to ourselves. Place yourself in a boat with the person whom you love the most, as Thérèse did. You are in the middle of the ocean; it is night; you are lonely and your beloved is fast asleep. You want to wake him in order to relieve your loneliness but decide to let him sleep because he is exhausted. As you gaze at his loving face, your loneliness is transfigured; you are still lonely but something has changed. Mysteriously, your self-pity has vanished; it has been purged away by love. As St. Teresa writes: "Oh, how everything that is suffered with love is healed again!"[9]

b) *God as a Loving Parent.* Thérèse used the image of God as a loving parent to counteract her tendency toward discouragement. "I should be desolate for having slept (for seven years) during my hours of prayer and my *thanksgiving* after Holy Communion; well, I am not desolate. I remember that *little children* are as pleasing to their parents when they are asleep as well as when they are wide awake" (S. 259-260).

In the monastery, we Carmelite friars often use a phrase to describe our hours of mental prayer– "mental sleep." The phrase refers to the common experience of falling asleep during meditation. Even though I find it very comforting to know that I have something in common with Thérèse, what I really want to share with her is not that I *fall asleep* during prayer but what she said to God when she *woke up.*

When we wake up from our "mental sleep" a barrage of castigating words directed toward ourselves and a litany of remorse offered up to God are not helpful. In fact, they are downright harmful. They focus our minds on ourselves and paint in our imaginations an image of an over-sensitive God, who stands upon his dignity and takes offense where no offense is given. Would you be angry at a small child who fell asleep on your lap in church? Rather, wouldn't you be more inclined to look down lovingly on such a tender sight? This is how Thérèse imagined that God looked down upon her during her "mental sleep." "I remember that little children are as pleasing to their parents when they are asleep as well as when they are wide awake." In the light of this truth, would it not be more appropriate to say to God as you're waking up from your "mental sleep," "O, thank you God for the nap, I really needed it."

Both images – Jesus asleep in the bow of the boat and God as a parent who gazes down lovingly upon his child–have this in common; they take our minds off ourselves and help us to focus them on God.

*Questions.* Do you use different images of God during prayer? Why do you use them? How do they function in prayer? Regarding her habit of falling asleep during prayer, Thérèse transformed false guilt into gratitude. Are there areas in your life (besides falling asleep during prayer) where you can do the same?

## Notes

1. Guy Gaucher writes, "Abbé Domin's retreats had had such a strong effect on her that she always dreaded retreats, whether private or preached." *The Story of a Life,* ibid., 97.

2. Lisieux's chaplain, Abbé Youf was also very scrupulous. Once, after going to him for confession, one of the nuns went in tears to Mother Gonzague and said, "Mother, the chaplain told me that I already have one foot in hell and if I continue in my ways I will soon have my second one there." Mother Gonzague smiled and said, "Don't be concerned, I already have both feet there!"

3. O'Mahony, ibid., 42-3.

4. In an earlier letter dated October 4, 1889, Fr. Pichon wrote the following to Thérèse: "I forbid you in the name of God to call into question your being in the state of grace. The devil is laughing heartily at you. I protest against this ugly mistrust. Believe obstinately that God loves you" (L. 585).

5. In a letter dated July 22, 1579, St. Teresa of Avila wrote the following to Mother Mary of St. Joseph in Seville Carmel: "The youngest cannot possibly be received at present, both on account of her age and because *it is not well to have three sisters of one family in any convent, much less in ours, in which the communities are limited*" (italic added). *The Letters of Saint Teresa, vol. III,* trans. Benedictines of Stanbrook, (London: Thomas Baker, 1922) 256.

6. Sr. Aimée's opposition to Céline's entrance may be viewed in part as another example of a clash of cultures. Sr. Aimée, who came from peasant stock, was irritated by the "bourgeois" ways of the Martins. Her practical bent, which once voiced opposition to plant rose trees in the cloister quadran-

gle because she felt that planting potatoes would be more use-ful, was in opposition Céline's artistic nature. "Carmel does not need artists," she adamantly proclaimed, "it has far greater need of good infirmarians and laundresses!"

Céline, by contrast, was highly educated. She was a vora-cious reader with a wide range of interests including Plato, religious and literary authors, and the scientific journals of her day. She was an accomplished artist and photographer; she had professional training in both areas.

7. Geneviève of the Holy Face (Céline Martin), *A memoir of my sister St. Thérèse,* trans. Carmelite Sisters of New York, (New York: P.J. Kenedy & Sons, 1959), 100. Thérèse's coun-sel to Céline was as follows: "You have not come to Carmel merely to turn out a mountain of work or even, strictly speak-ing to become an *indefatigable* worker. Are you unduly con-cerned at the present moment as to what is happening in other Carmelite Monasteries, and whether the nuns there are busy or not? Does their work interfere with your prayer and medi-tation? Well, in the same way you should become detached from your daily occupations, conscientiously devoting to them the time prescribed but with perfect freedom of heart." ibid., 100.

8. St. Teresa of Avila, "The Way of Perfection," in *The Collected Works of St. Teresa of Avila,* vol. 2, trans. Otilio Rodriguez, O.C.D. and Kieran Kavanaugh, O.C.D. (Wash-ington, D.C.: ICS Publications, 1980), chapter 28, par. 3, p. 141.

9. Ibid., chapter 16, par. 7, p. 96.

# LETTER TO

# SISTER MARIE OF THE SACRED HEART

## Manuscript B

# Chapter IX

# *MY VOCATION IS LOVE (1896)*

The Secrets of Jesus
Venerable Mother Anne of Jesus
All Vocations
Strewing Flowers
The Little Bird
The Divine Eagle
End of Manuscript B

[1r°]                    J.M.J.T.
Jesus +

O my dear Sister! you ask me to give you a souvenir of my re-treat,[226] one which will probably be my last.[227] Since Mother Prioress[228] permits it, it will be a joy for me to come and speak with you who are [5] doubly my Sister, with you who lent me your voice promising in my name that I wished to serve Jesus only. This child, dear little godmother, whom you offered to the Lord and who speaks to you this evening, is one who loves you as a child loves its mother. [10] Only in heaven will you understand the gratitude that overflows my heart. O my dear Sister, you wish to hear about the secrets Jesus confides to your little sister; however, I realize He confides these secrets

---

[226] Thérèse is answering a written request from Sister Marie of the Sacred Heart, September 13, 1896. This first section was written after the second, which was done on September 8.

[227] Good Friday, 1896, Thérèse had her first hemoptysis.

[228] Mother Marie de Gonzague, Prioress again since March 21, 1896.

293

to you too, for you are the one who taught me how to gather the divine instructions. Nevertheless, I am going to stammer some words even though I [15]feel it is quite impossible for the human tongue to express things that the human heart can hardly understand.

Do not believe I am swimming in consolations; oh, no, my consolation is to have none on earth. Without showing Himself, without making His voice heard, Jesus teaches me in secret; it is [20]not by means of books, for I do not understand what I am reading. Sometimes a word comes to console me, such as this one which I received at the end of prayer (after having remained in silence and aridity): "*Here is the teacher whom I am giving you; he will teach you everything that you must do. I want to make you read in the book of life, wherein is contained the* [20] *science of LOVE.* "[229] The science of Love, ah, yes, this word resounds sweetly in the ear of my soul, and I desire only this science. *Having given all my riches for it,* I esteem it as *having given nothing* as did the bride in the sacred Canticles.[230] I understand so well that it is only love that makes us acceptable to God, [30]that this love is the only good I ambition. Jesus deigned to show me the road that leads to this Divine Furnace, and this road is the *surrender* of the little child who sleeps without fear in its Father's arms. "Whoever is a *little one,* let him come to me."[231] So speaks the Holy Spirit through the mouth of Solomon. This same Spirit of Love [35]also says: "*For to him that is little, mercy will be shown.* "[232] The Prophet Isaiah reveals in His name that on the last day: "*God shall feed his*

---

[229] Words of Our Lord to St. Margaret Mary, found in the *Little Breviary of the Sacred Heart,* a book in the Lisieux Carmel.

[230] Canticle of Canticles 8:7.

[231] Proverbs 9:4.

[232] Wisdom 6:7.

*flock like a shepherd; he shall gather together the lambs with his arm, and shall take them up in his bosom.'*[233] As though these promises were not sufficient, this same prophet whose gaze was already plunged into the [40]eternal depths cried out in the Lord's name: *"As one whom a mother caresses, so will I comfort you; you shall be carried at the breasts and upon the knees they will caress you.'*[234]

After having listened to words such as these, dear godmother, there is nothing to do but to be silent and to weep with gratitude [1v°] and love. Ah! if all weak and imperfect souls felt what the least of souls feels, that is, the soul of your little Thérèse, not one would despair of reaching the summit of the mount of love. Jesus does not demand [5]great actions from us but simply *surrender* and *gratitude.* Has He not said: *"I will not take the he-goats from out your flocks, for all the beasts of the forest are mine, the cattle on the hills and the oxen. I know all the fowls of the air. If I were hungry, I would not* [10] *tell you, for the world is mine, and the fullness thereof. Shall I eat the flesh of bulls or shall I drink the blood of goats?* OFFER TO GOD THE SACRIFICES OF PRAISE AND THANKSGIVING.*"*[235]

See, then, all that Jesus lays claim to from us; He has no need of our works but only of our *love,* for the same God who [15]declares He *has no need to tell us when He is hungry* did not fear *to beg* for a little water from the Samaritan woman. He was thirsty. But when He said: *"Give me to drink,'*[236] it was the *love* of His poor creature the Creator of the universe was seeking. He was thirsty for love. Ah! I feel it more than ever before, Jesus is *parched,* for [20]He meets only the

---

[233] Isaiah 40:11.

[234] Isaiah 66:12-13.

[235] Psalm 49:9-14.

[236] John 4:7.

ungrateful and indifferent among His disciples in the world, and among *His own disciples,* alas, He finds few hearts who surrender to Him without reservations, who understand the real tenderness of His infinite Love.

How fortunate we are, dear Sister, to understand the [25] intimate secrets of our Spouse. Ah! if you wished to write all you know about these secrets, we would have beautiful pages to read, but I know you prefer to keep *"the King's secrets"* in the bottom of your heart. And yet you say to me, *"it is honorable to publish the works of the Most High."*[237] I find you are very right [30]to maintain silence, and it is only to please you that I write these lines. I feel how powerless I am to express in human language the secrets of heaven, and after writing page upon page I find that I have not yet begun. There are so many different horizons, so many nuances of [35]infinite variety that only the palette of the Celestial Painter will be able to furnish me after the night of this life with the colors capable of depicting the marvels He reveals to the eye of my soul.

You asked me, dear Sister, to write to you *my dream* and "my little doctrine" as you call it. I did this in [40]these following pages, but so poorly it seems to me you will not understand it. Perhaps you will find my expressions exaggerated. Ah! pardon me, this will have to be put down to my poor style, for I assure you there is *no exaggeration* in my *little soul.* Within it all is calm and at rest.

[45]When writing these words, I shall address them to Jesus since this makes it easier for me to express my thoughts, but it does not prevent them from being very poorly expressed!

---

[237] Tobit 12:7.

[2r°]                    J.M.J.T.

                                September 8, 1896

(To my dear Sister Marie of the Sacred Heart)

O Jesus, my Beloved, who could express the tenderness and sweetness with which You are guiding my soul! It pleases You to cause the rays of Your grace to shine through even in the midst of the darkest storm! Jesus, the storm was raging very strongly in my [5]soul ever since the beautiful feast of Your victory, the radiant feast of Easter; one Saturday in the month of May,[238] thinking of the mysterious dreams which are granted at times to certain souls, I said of myself that these dreams must be a very sweet consolation, and yet I wasn't asking for such a consolation. In the evening, considering the clouds which were covering her heaven, my little soul [10] said again within herself that these beautiful dreams were not for her. And then she fell asleep in the midst of the storm. The next day was May 10, the second SUNDAY of Mary's month, and perhaps the anniversary of the day when the Blessed Virgin deigned to smile upon her little flower.[239]

At the first glimmerings of dawn I was (in a dream) in a [15]kind of gallery and there were several other persons, but they were at a distance. Our Mother was alone near me. Suddenly, without seeing how they had entered, I saw three Carmelites dressed in their mantles and long veils. It appeared to me they were coming for our Mother, but what I did understand clearly was that they [20]came from heaven. In the depths of my heart I cried out: "Oh! how happy I would be if I

---

[238] May 9, 1896.

[239] It was on the second Sunday in May that the Virgin smiled on Thérèse in 1883, but that year the second Sunday was May 13.

could see the face of one of these Carmelites!" Then, as though my prayer were heard by her, the tallest of the saints advanced toward me; immediately I fell to my knees. Oh! what happiness! the Carmelite *raised her veil or rather she raised it and covered me with it.* [25] Without the least hesitation, I recognized *Venerable Anne of Jesus,*[240] Foundress of Carmel in France. Her face was beautiful but with an immaterial beauty. No ray escaped from it and still, in spite of the veil which covered us both, I saw this heavenly face suffused with an unspeakably gentle light, a light [30]it didn't receive from without but was produced from within.

I cannot express the joy of my soul since these things are experienced but cannot be put into words. Several months have passed since this sweet dream, and yet the memory it has left in my soul has lost nothing of its freshness and heavenly charms. [35]I still see Venerable Mother's glance and smile which was FILLED with LOVE. I believe I can still feel the caresses she gave me at this time.

Seeing myself so tenderly loved, I dared to pronounce these words: "O Mother! I beg you, tell me whether God will leave me for a long time on earth. Will He come soon [40]to get me?" Smiling tenderly, the saint whispered: *"Yes, soon, soon, I promise you."* I added: "Mother, tell me further if God is not asking something [2v°] more of me than my poor little actions and desires. Is He content with me?" The saint's face took on an expression *incomparably more tender* than the first time she spoke to me. Her look and her caresses were the

---

[240] Anne de Lobera (1545–1621) was born in Spain. In 1570 she entered St. Joseph's Convent in Avila, the first monastery of the reformed Carmel. She became counsellor and companion of St. Teresa of Avila. She obtained the Spiritual Canticle from St. John of the Cross, and she founded the Teresian Carmel in France and Flanders.

sweetest of answers. However, she [5] said to me: "God asks no other thing from you. He is content, very content!" After again embracing me with more love than the tenderest of mothers has ever given to her child, I saw her leave. My heart was filled with joy, and then I remembered my Sisters, and I wanted [10] to ask her some favors for them, but alas, I awoke!

O Jesus, the storm was no longer raging, heaven was calm and serene. I *believed, I felt* there was a *heaven* and that this *heaven* is peopled with souls who actually love me, who consider me their child. This impression remains in my heart, and [15] this all the more because I was, up until then, *absolutely indifferent to Venerable Mother Anne of Jesus.* I never invoked her in prayer and the thought of her never came to my mind except when I heard others speak of her, which was seldom. And when I understood to what a degree *she loved me,* how *indifferent* I had been toward her, my [20]heart was filled with love and gratitude, not only for the Saint who had visited me but for all the blessed inhabitants of heaven.

O my Beloved! this grace was only the prelude to the greatest graces You wished to bestow upon me. [25]Allow me, my only Love, to recall them to You today, *today* which is the sixth anniversary of *our union.* Ah! my Jesus, pardon me if I am unreasonable in wishing to express my desires and longings which reach even unto infinity. Pardon me and heal my soul by giving her what she longs for so much!

[30]To be Your *Spouse,* to be a *Carmelite,* and by my union with You to be the *Mother* of souls, should not this suffice me? And yet it is not so. No doubt, these three privileges sum up my true *vocation: Carmelite, Spouse, Mother,* and yet I feel within me other *vocations.* I feel the *vocation* of the WARRIOR, [35]THE PRIEST, THE APOSTLE, THE DOCTOR, THE MARTYR. Finally, I feel the need and the desire of carrying out the most heroic deeds for *You, O Jesus.* I feel

within my soul the courage of the *Crusader,* the *Papal Guard,* and I would want to die on the field of battle in defense of the Church.

[40]I feel in me the *vocation of* the PRIEST. With what love, O Jesus, I would carry You in my hands when, at my voice, You would come down from heaven. And with what love would I give You to souls! But alas! while desiring to be a *Priest,* I admire and envy the humility of St. Francis of Assisi and I feel the *vocation* of [45]imitating him in refusing the sublime dignity of the *Priesthood.*

O Jesus, my Love, my Life, how can I combine these contrasts? [3r°] How can I realize the desires of my poor *little soul?*

Ah! in spite of my littleness, I would like to enlighten souls as did the *Prophets* and the *Doctors.* I have the *vocation of the Apostle.* I would like to travel over the whole earth to preach Your Name and to plant Your glorious Cross [5]on infidel soil. But *O my Beloved,* one mission alone would not be sufficient for me, I would want to preach the Gospel on all the five continents simultaneously and even to the most remote isles. I would be a missionary, not for a few years only [10] but from the beginning of creation until the consummation of the ages. But above all, O my Beloved Savior, I would shed my blood for You even to the very last drop.

*Martyrdom* was the dream of my youth and this dream [15]has grown with me within Carmel's cloisters. But here again, I feel that my dream is a folly, for I cannot confine myself to desiring *one kind* of martyrdom. To satisfy me I need *all.* Like You, my Adorable Spouse, I would be scourged and crucified. [20]I would die flayed like St. Bartholomew. I would be plunged into boiling oil like St. John; I would undergo all the tortures inflicted upon the martyrs. With St. Agnes and St. Cecilia, I would present my neck to the sword, and like Joan of Arc, my dear sister, [25]I would whisper at the stake Your Name, O JESUS. When thinking of the torments which will be the lot of

Christians at the time of Anti-Christ, I feel my heart leap with joy and I would that these torments be reserved for me.[241] Jesus, Jesus, if I wanted to write all my desires, I would have to borrow Your *Book* [30] *of Life*,[242] for in it are reported all the actions of all the saints, and I would accomplish all of them for You.

O my Jesus! what is your answer to all my follies? Is there a soul more *little,* more powerless than mine? Nevertheless even because of my weakness, it has pleased You, O Lord, to [35]grant my *little childish desires* and You desire, today, to grant other desires that are *greater* than the universe.

During my meditation, my desires caused me a veritable martyrdom, and I opened the Epistles of St. Paul to find some kind of answer. Chapters 12 and 13 of the First Epistle to the Corinthians fell [40]under my eyes. I read there, in the first of these chapters, that *all* cannot be apostles, prophets, doctors, etc., that the Church is composed of different members, and that the eye cannot be the hand at *one and the same time.*[243] The answer was clear, but it did not fulfill my desires and gave me no peace. But just as Mary Magdalene [45] found what she was seeking by always stooping down [3v°] and looking into the empty tomb, so I, abasing myself to the very depths of my nothingness, raised myself so high that I was able to attain my end.[244] Without becoming discouraged, I continued my reading, and this sentence consoled me: *"Yet strive after THE* [5]*BETTER GIFTS, and I*

---

[241] Abbé Arminjon, *Fin du Monde présent et Mystères de la vie future* (Lyon: Lescuyer & Fils, 1964), second conference, pp. 73–74.

[242] Revelation 20:12.

[243] 1 Corinthians 12:29, 21.

[244] Allusion to the poem of St. John of the Cross: "I went out seeking love," *Collected Works,* pp. 56-57.

*point out to you a yet more excellent way.* "[245] And the Apostle explains how all *the most PERFECT gifts* are nothing without *LOVE. That Charity is the EXCELLENT WAY that leads most surely to God.*

I finally had rest. Considering the mystical body [10]of the Church, I had not recognized myself in any of the members described by St. Paul, or rather I desired to see myself in them *all. Charity* gave me the key to my *vocation.* I understood that if the Church had a body composed of different members, the most necessary and most noble of all could not be lacking [15]to it, and so I understood that the Church *had a Heart and that this Heart* was *BURNING WITH LOVE. I understood it was Love alone* that made the Church's members act, that if *Love* ever became extinct, apostles would not preach the Gospel and martyrs would not shed their blood. I understood that [20]LOVE COMPRISED ALL VOCATIONS, THAT LOVE WAS EVERYTHING, THAT IT EMBRACED ALL TIMES AND PLACES.... IN A WORD, THAT IT WAS ETERNAL!

Then, in the excess of my delirious joy, I cried out: O Jesus, my Love .... my vocation, at last I [25]have found it.... MY VOCATION IS LOVE!

Yes, I have found my place in the Church and it is You, O my God, who have given me this place; in the heart of the Church, my Mother, I shall be *Love.* Thus I shall be everything, and thus my dream will be realized.

[30]Why speak of a delirious joy? No, this expression is not exact, for it was rather the calm and serene peace of the navigator perceiving the beacon which must lead him to the port.... O luminous Beacon of love, I know how to reach You, I have found the secret of possessing Your flame.

---

[245] 1 Corinthians 12:31; 13:1.

[35]I am only a child, powerless and weak, and yet it is my weakness that gives me the boldness of offering myself as *VICTIM of Your Love, O Jesus!* In times past, victims, pure and spotless, were the only ones accepted by the Strong and Powerful God. To satisfy Divine *Justice,* perfect victims were necessary, [40]but the *law of Love* has succeeded to the law of fear, and *Love* has chosen me as a holocaust, me, a weak and imperfect creature. Is not this choice worthy of *Love?* Yes, in order that Love be fully satisfied, it is necessary that It lower Itself, and that It lower Itself to nothingness [45]and transform this nothingness into *fire.*

[4r°] O Jesus, I know it, love is repaid by love alone,[246] and so I searched and I found the way to solace my heart by giving you Love for Love. "Make use of the riches which render one unjust in order to make friends who will receive you into [5] everlasting dwellings."[247] Behold, Lord, the counsel You give Your disciples after having told them that "The children of this world, in relation to their own generation, are more prudent than are the children of the light."[248] A child of light, I understood that *my desires of being everything,* of embracing all vocations, were the riches that [10] would be able to render me unjust, so I made use of them *to make friends.* Remembering the prayer of Elisha to his Father Elijah when he dared to ask him for HIS DOUBLE SPIRIT,[249] I presented myself before the angels and saints and I said to them: "I am the smallest of creatures; I know my misery

---

[246] St. John of the Cross, *Spiritual Canticle,* stanza 9, no. 7, *Collected Works,* p. 506. St. Thérèse inscribed these words on her coat of arms, January 1896.

[247] Luke 16:9.

[248] Luke 16:8.

[249] 2 Kings 2:9.

[15]and my feebleness, but I know also how much noble and generous hearts love to do good. I beg you then, O Blessed Inhabitants of heaven, I beg you to ADOPT ME AS YOUR CHILD. *To you alone will be the glory* which you will make me merit, but deign to answer my prayer. It is bold, I know; [20]however, I dare to ask you to obtain for me YOUR TWOFOLD LOVE."

Jesus, I cannot fathom the depths of my request; I would be afraid to find myself overwhelmed under the weight of my bold desires. My excuse is that I am a *child,* and children do not reflect on the meaning of their words; however, their parents, once they are placed [25]upon a throne and possess immense treasures, do not hesitate to satisfy the desires of the *little ones* whom they love as much as they love themselves. To please them they do foolish things, even going to the extent of *becoming weak* for them. Well, I am the *Child of the Church* and the Church is a Queen since she is Your Spouse, O divine King of kings. [30]The heart of a child does not seek riches and glory (even the glory of heaven). She understands that this glory belongs by right to her brothers, the angels and saints. Her own glory will be the reflected glory which shines on her Mother's forehead. What this child asks for is Love. She knows only one [35]thing: to love You, O Jesus. Astounding works are forbidden to her; she cannot preach the Gospel, shed her blood; but what does it matter since her brothers work in her stead and she, *a little child,* stays very close to the *throne* of the King and Queen. She *loves* in her brothers' place while they do the fighting. But how will she prove her *love* since [40] *love* is proved by works? Well, the little child *will strew flowers,* she will perfume the royal throne with their *sweet scents,* and she will sing in her silvery tones the canticle of *Love.*

Yes, my Beloved, this is how my life will be consumed. I have no other means of proving my love for you other than that of strewing flowers, [45]that is, not allowing one little sacrifice to escape, not one look, [4v°] one word, profiting by all the smallest things and doing them through love. I desire to suffer for love and even to rejoice through love; and in this way I shall strew flowers before Your throne. I shall not come upon one without *unpetalling* it for You. While I am [5]strewing my flowers, I shall sing, for could one cry while doing such a joyous action? I shall sing even when I must gather my flowers in the midst of thorns, and my song will be all the more melodious in proportion to the length and sharpness of the thorns.

O Jesus, of what use will my flowers be to You? Ah! I know [10]very well that this fragrant shower, these fragile, worthless petals, these songs of love from the littlest of hearts will charm You. Yes, these nothings will please You. They will bring a smile to the Church Triumphant. She will gather up my flowers unpetalled *through love* and have them pass through Your own divine hands, O Jesus. And this Church in heaven, desirous of playing with [15]her little child, will cast these flowers, which are now infinitely valuable because of Your divine touch, upon the Church Suffering in order to extinguish its flames and upon the Church Militant in order to gain the victory for it!

O my Jesus! I love You! I love the Church, my Mother! I [20]recall that *"the smallest act of* PURE LOVE *is of more value to her than all other works together."*[250] But is PURE LOVE in my heart? Are my measureless desires only but a dream, a folly? Ah! if this be so, Jesus, then enlighten me, for You know I am seeking only the truth. [25] If my desires are rash, then make them disappear, for these desires are the greatest martyrdom to me. However, I feel, O Jesus, that after having aspired to the most lofty heights of Love, if one day I am not

---

[250] St. John of the Cross, Spiritual Canticle, stanza 29, no. 2, Collected Works, p. 587.

to attain them, I feel that I shall have tasted *more sweetness in my martyrdom and my folly* than I [30]shall taste in the bosom of the *joy of the Fatherland,* unless You take away the memory of these earthly hopes through a miracle. Allow me, then, during my exile, the delights of love. Allow me to taste the sweet bitterness of my martyrdom.

Jesus, O Jesus, if the *desire of loving You* is so delightful, what [35] will it be to possess and enjoy this Love?

How can a soul as imperfect as mine aspire to the possession of the plenitude of *Love?* O Jesus, *my first and only Friend,* You whom *I love* UNIQUELY, explain this mystery to me! Why do You not reserve these [40] great aspirations for great souls, for the *Eagles* that soar in the heights?

I look upon myself as a *weak little bird,* with only a light down as covering. I am not an eagle, but I have only an eagle's EYES AND HEART. In spite of my extreme littleness I still dare to gaze upon the [45] Divine Sun, the Sun of Love, and my heart feels within it all [5r°] the aspirations of an *Eagle.*

The little bird wills *to fly* toward the bright Sun that attracts its eye, imitating its brothers, the eagles, whom it sees climbing up toward the Divine Furnace of the Holy Trinity. But alas! the only thing it can do is [5]*raise its little wings*; to fly is not within its *little* power!

What then will become of it? Will it die of sorrow at seeing itself so weak? Oh no! the little bird will not even be troubled. With bold surrender, it wishes to remain gazing upon its Divine Sun. Nothing will frighten it, neither wind nor rain, and if dark [10]clouds come and hide the Star of Love, the little bird will not change its place because it knows that beyond the clouds its bright Sun still shines on and that its brightness is not eclipsed for a single instant.

At times the little bird's heart is assailed by the storm, and it seems it should believe in the existence of no other thing except the clouds surrounding it; [15]this is the moment of *perfect joy* for the *poor little weak creature.* And what joy it experiences when remaining there just the same! and gazing at the Invisible Light which remains hidden from its faith!

O Jesus, up until the present moment I can understand Your love for the little bird because it has not strayed far from You. But I know and so do You that very often the imperfect little creature, [20]while remaining in its place (that is, under the Sun's rays), allows itself to be somewhat distracted from its sole occupation. It picks up a piece of grain on the right or on the left; it chases after a little worm; then coming upon a little pool of water, it wets its feathers still hardly formed. It sees an attractive flower and its little mind is occupied with [25]this flower. In a word, being unable to soar like the eagles, the poor little bird is taken up with the trifles of earth.

And yet after all these misdeeds, instead of going and hiding away in a corner, to weep over its misery and to die of sorrow, the little bird turns toward its beloved Sun, presenting its wet wings to its beneficent rays. [30]It cries like a swallow and in its sweet song it recounts in detail all its infidelities, thinking in the boldness of its full trust that it will acquire in even greater fullness the love of *Him* who came to call not the just but sinners.[251] And even if the Adorable Star remains deaf to the plaintive chirping of the little creature, even if it [35]remains hidden, well, the little one will remain wet, accepting its numbness from the cold and rejoicing in its suffering which it knows it deserves.

O Jesus, Your *little bird* is happy to be *weak and little.* What would become of it if it were big? Never would it have the boldness to appear in Your presence, *to fall asleep* in front of You. [40]Yes, this is

---

[251] Matthew 9:11.

still one of the weaknesses of the little bird: when it wants to fix its gaze upon the Divine Sun, and when the clouds prevent it from seeing a single ray of that Sun, in spite of itself, its little eyes close, its little head is hidden beneath its wing, and the poor little thing falls asleep, believing all the time that it is fixing its gaze upon its Dear Star. When it awakens, it doesn't feel desolate; its little heart is at peace and it [45]begins once again its work of *love*. It calls upon the angels and saints who rise like eagles before the consuming Fire, and since this is the object of the little bird's desire [5v°] the eagles take pity on it, protecting and defending it, and putting to flight at the same time the vultures who want to devour it. These vultures are the demons whom the little bird doesn't fear, for it is not destined to be their prey but the prey of the *Eagle* whom it contemplates in the [5]center of the Sun of Love.

O Divine Word! You are the Adored Eagle whom I love and who alone *attracts me!* Coming into this land of exile, You willed to suffer and to die in order *to draw* souls to the bosom of the Eternal Fire of the Blessed Trinity. Ascending once again to the Inaccessible Light, henceforth Your abode, You remain [10] still in this "valley of tears," hidden beneath the appearances of a white host. Eternal Eagle, You desire to nourish me with Your divine substance and yet I am but a poor little thing who would return to nothingness if Your divine glance did not give me life from one moment to the next.

O Jesus, allow me in my boundless gratitude to say to You that Your *love reaches* [15] *unto folly.* In the presence of this folly, how can You not desire that my heart leap toward You? How can my confidence, then, have any limits? Ah! the saints have committed their *follies* for You, and they have done great things because they are eagles.

Jesus, I am too little to perform great actions, [20]and my own *folly* is this: to trust that Your Love will accept me as a victim. My *folly* consists in begging the eagles, my brothers, to obtain for me the favor of flying toward the Sun of Love with the *Divine Eagle's own wings!*[252]

As long as You desire it, O my Beloved, Your little bird [25]will remain without strength and without wings and will always stay with its gaze fixed upon You. It wants to be *fascinated* by Your divine glance. It wants to become the *prey* of Your Love. One day I hope that You, the Adorable Eagle, will come to fetch me, Your little bird; and ascending with it to the Furnace of Love, You will plunge it for all eternity into the burning [30]Abyss of this Love to which it has offered itself as victim.

O Jesus! why can't I tell all *little souls* how unspeakable is Your condescension? I feel that if You found a soul weaker and littler than mine, which is impossible, You [35]would be pleased to grant it still greater favors, provided it abandoned itself with total confidence to Your Infinite Mercy. But why do I desire to communicate Your secrets of Love, O Jesus, for was it not You alone who taught them to me, and can You not reveal them to others? Yes, I know it, and I beg You [40]to do it. I beg You to cast Your Divine Glance upon a great number of *little* souls. I beg You to choose a legion of *little* Victims worthy of Your LOVE!

*The very little Sister Thérèse of the Child Jesus*
*and the Holy Face, unworthy Carmelite religious.*

---

[252] Deuteronomy 32:11.

## *My Vocation is Love*
### Background and Context.

In the Spring of 1894, Thérèse began suffering from a persistent sore throat, a nagging cough, frequent fevers, and occasional chest pains. These early signs of Thérèse's tuberculosis were not taken any more seriously than the early symptoms of Zélie's breast cancer. Two years later, in April, 1896, Thérèse suffered her first hemoptysis (spitting up of blood), a definite indication that she had contracted tuberculosis. In spite of this alarming symptom, Doctor de Cornière, the monastery's official physician, refused to accept that Thérèse had tuberculosis and remained adamant in his opinion for the next two years. In July, 1896, after a cursory examination by Doctor de Cornière, Thérèse wrote the following to her aunt Céline: "Doctor de Cornière to whom I had the *distinguished honor* of being presented yesterday in the speakroom ...after having honored me with a look, declared that I looked well" (L. 969)! And even as late as July, 1897, three months before Thérèse's death, he still insisted that she did not have tuberculosis. "It is not tuberculosis but rather an accident which has caused serious lung congestion."[1]

Pauline wanted Thérèse to be examined by Dr. Francis La Néele, the husband of her cousin Jeanne Guérin, but Mother Gonzague, who was a personal friend of Doctor de Cornière, dissuaded her. Even though Pauline was the current prioress (up until March, 1896, when Mother Gonzague was reelected), Pauline found it difficult to assert her authority in the face of Mother Gonzague's wishes. "Yes it was Mother Marie de Gonzague who worked for my election, but she would only be hurt if I exercised too much authority. How I suffered and wept uring those three years!"

Many in the community accepted the doctor's diagnosis and believed that rest and the proper treatment would restore Thérèse to health. One of the reasons this belief could be maintained for so long was that Thérèse continued to work with the novices, was able to attend community functions, and hid her suffering from the community. But in the final months of her life, all of this changed. Thérèse stopped going to choir in April, 1897, ceased attending community recreation the following month, and by June, no longer took her meals in the refectory.

As the tuberculosis was taking its toll, Thérèse was finding it increasingly more difficult to put up a good front. During one of the last times she attended community recreation, she sat next to Sister Marie of the Trinity and said to her, "I have come near you so that you can *guard* me. I feel that I have not the strength to carry on a conversation. Look as if you are talking to me so that others won't come to speak to me. I do feel so sick, but I don't want to tell Mother Agnes yet, she would worry so much!"[2]

On August, 15, Thérèse began to experience great difficulty breathing. The next day, Mother Gonzague gave Pauline permission to contact Dr. Francis La Néele; Dr. de Cornière was away on vacation. After examining Thérèse, he wrote his findings. "The right lung is completely lost, filled with tubercles in the process of softening. The lower part of the left lung is affected." [3] After the examination, Dr. La Néele spoke harshly to Mother Gonzague. In consequence, Mother Gonzague "created a scene, lost her patience and rallied out against the whole [Martin] family, including the patient, but Thérèse remained calm," testified Pauline. [4]

It has been falsely alleged that one of the ways that Mother Gonzague rallied against Thérèse was by refusing permission to administer morphine to Thérèse in her final agony. Céline says otherwise; it was not out of cruelty or revenge that Mother Gonzague refused to allow morphine to be given to Thérèse but because "sedatives were prohibited as a disgrace."[5] Likewise, even though "[Thérèse] was involved in some rather painful scenes caused by poor Mother Marie de Gonzague [during Thérèse final illness]," it should not be concluded that there was anything vindictive in Mother Gonzague's behavior, but rather that her behavior was an expression of her "unstable and eccentric temperament," testified Céline. [6]

By the end of the month, Thérèse's intestines were gangrenous and she began to suffocate. The pain was so intense that Thérèse asked that all poisonous medicines be placed out of her reach for the fear that she would take her own life. Pauline testified: "She asked that we not leave poisonous medicines for external use within her reach and advised us never to leave them near patients suffering the same tortures, always for the same reason, the pain 'is enough to make one lose one's reason,' and, no longer knowing what one is doing, one could easily take one's life" (LC. 162-3). "Yes! What a grace it is to have faith," said Thérèse, "If I had not had any faith, I would have committed suicide without an instant's hesitation" (LC. 196).

In these final months of Thérèse's life, there was no longer any question of either her diagnosis or prognosis; she had contracted tuberculosis and would die very soon. This was no surprise to Thérèse, for in April, 1895, a whole year prior to her first hemoptysis, Thérèse confided to Sr. Thérèse of St. Augustine, "I shall die soon," (L. 897). And on May 10, the following year, Thérèse had a dream in which Blessed Ann of Jesus told Thérèse that she would die very soon; the dream confirmed what she had known for a long time. Thérèse confided this presentiment of her death to her sister Marie. It is within this context, that Marie asked Thérèse, while Thérèse was making her personal retreat (September 7-18, 1896) to jot down a summary of her "little way of confidence and love."[7] Thérèse submitted to Marie's request; it resulted in what would become chapter nine (Manuscript B) of *Story of a Soul.*

Contained within this chapter are two important passages: first, Thérèse's account of having discovered that love is the principle of unity that reconciled all of the various ways that she desired to show her love for God ("my vocation is love," S. 299-302); second, Thérèse's story of "the little bird" (S. 306-309) which is one of her best explanations of "the little way."

**Reflections and Questions.**

1. After Marie read what Thérèse had written in her retreat notes, Marie experienced "a certain feeling of sadness" (L. 997) for she did not recognize in herself the same burning desires of love that were evident in her sister. In response to Marie's discouragement, Thérèse wrote the following: "How can you ask me if it is possible for you to love God as I love Him...If you had understood the story of my little bird, you would not have asked me this question. My desires of martyrdom *are nothing;* they are not what gives me the unlimited confidence that I feel in my heart. They are, to tell the truth, the spiritual riches that *render one unjust,* when one rests in them with complacence and when one believes they are *something great*...These desires are a *consolation,* it is a grace of *privilege.* Recall those words of Father: "The martyrs suffered with joy, and the King of Martyrs suffered with sadness." Dear Sister, how can you say after this that my

desires are the sign of my love? ...Oh, dear Sister, I beg you, understand your little girl, understand that to love Jesus...the weaker one is without desires or virtues, the more suited one is for the workings of this consuming and transforming Love" (L. 998-9).

Like Marie, we can erroneously believe that our desires and fervor are the measure of our love for God; this is an example of judging our spiritual life with an emotional yardstick. Thérèse tells us that the opposite is true, namely, that our love for God is proved when we *act* in a loving manner without the support of *affect*. In this regard, Thérèse writes to Céline: "What a grace when, in the morning, we feel no courage, no strength to practice virtue; it is the moment to put the axe to the root of the tree...we can dip into diamonds and what a profit at the end of the day... In one act of love, even *unfelt* love, all is repaired, and Jesus smiles" (L. 467). It is as if Thérèse is saying to Céline, " On those days when you get up in the morning and you don't feel like praying or don't have the energy to love your neighbor, isn't it wonderful to know that these are the times that you can truly *prove* your love  for God, because it is precisely at these times that your love arises from your will alone without the support of emotion."

*Questions.* What Thérèse calls *unfelt* love is an invitation for us to look at situations in our lives from a spiritual perspective. For example, think of a person in your life whom you don't like. How do you regard your feelings toward this person? Do you consider your feelings an obstacle to love? Do you feel guilty because you believe that you should not feel this way? Or like Thérèse, can you view your feelings  as an *opportunity* to prove your love for God?

2. When Thérèse began meditating upon 1 Corinthians, 12, she found herself in *none* of the various vocations that St. Paul enumerates. "God has set up in the church first apostles, second prophets, third teachers, etc..." (1 Cor.12: 28), but as she read chapter 13, she found herself in *all* of them; this made her exclaim, "Then, in the excess of my delirious joy, I cried out: O Jesus, my love...my *vocation*, at last I have found it...MY VOCATION IS LOVE" (S. 302)!

What exactly did Thérèse find? Some contend that it was her "little way." But had Thérèse not found her "little way" years before during her encounter with Mother Geneviève? "God...willed that I live with a saint....[O]ne that was made holy by the practice of the hidden virtues, the ordinary virtues....Ah! That type of sanctity seems the truest and the *most holy* to me, and the type that I desire because in it one meets with no deceptions" (S. 265). It is futile to try to pinpoint the *exact moment* when Thérèse discovered her "little way" because her spirituality evolved over time; it would be better to say that toward the end of 1896, when Thérèse was meditating upon 1 Corinthians, 13, that God enlightened her regarding a two-fold dilemma.

The first part of the dilemma was this; Thérèse believed that God does not inspire unrealizable desires. This conflicted with her powerlessness to fulfill the various desires that God had planted in her heart. "I feel the *vocation* of the WARRIOR, THE PRIEST, THE APOSTLE, THE DOCTOR, THE MARTYR" (S. 299). This dilemma was resolved when Thérèse realized that love was both the root of all of her desires and the bond that connects all the members of the Mystical Body of

Christ. In consequence, whenever Thérèse loved, she *contributed to* and *participated in* all the works of the entire body. "If one member suffers all the members suffer with it; if one member is honored, all the members share its joy" (1 Cor.12: 26-7). "I shall be *Love*. Thus I shall be everything, and thus my dream will be realized" (S. 302). In short, when we abide in love, we abide in God and in one another.

The second part of Thérèse's dilemma is similar to the first. Thérèse desired to perform *extraordinary* deeds for God. "I feel the need and the desire of carrying out the most heroic deeds for *You, O Jesus,"* (S. 299) but Thérèse realized that she was "too little to perform great actions" (S. 308). Her solution was the realization that "Jesus does not demand great actions from us but simply surrender and gratitude... He has no need of our works but only of our *love*" (S. 295).

Thus, what makes a deed extraordinary, is not the deed itself, but the *love* that is contained in the deed, and Thérèse knew that all of her deeds, no matter how small, were done in love. "I have no other means of proving my love for you other than that of strewing flowers, that is, not allowing one little sacrifice to escape, not one look, one word, profiting by all the smallest things and doing them through love" (S. 304-305).

Thus, it is because Thérèse's *little sacrifices* were true deeds of love that they were *extraordinary* deeds. It is easy for us to miss the magnitude of this statement because love has been reduced to an emotion or trivialized to "being nice." But love is neither of these watery realities; it is the deepest reality of life, for God is love. Thus when we love with the love of charity, our actions are the actions of God. St. John of the Cross writes that each action of a soul in union with God "is more meritorious and valuable than all the deeds a person may have performed in the whole of life without this transformation, however great they may have been... [because] all the acts of the soul are divine, since both the movement of these acts and their execution stem from God."⁸ It is this mystical reality that is behind Thérèse's words "I shall be *Love*" (S. 302).

*Questions.* The same is true for us. Whenever we act with the love of charity, God loves through us and is made manifest in this world. Have you ever considered your "strewing of flowers," your daily acts of charity, from this perspective?

3. " 'I have frequently noticed,' Thérèse confided to me, [wrote Céline], 'that after I have committed a fault, even a slight one, my soul experiences a certain sadness or uneasiness for some little time. Then I tell myself, 'Now little one, this is the price you must pay for your fault, and so I patiently bear with the trial until the little debt is paid.' According to Thérèse's understanding of the virtue of hope, that was the extent of satisfaction required by Divine Justice for those who are humble and who abandon themselves to God in love. She could not believe such souls would have to go to Purgatory. She thought, rather, that at the moment of death their Father in heaven, because of their confidence, would kindle in their souls as they realized their misery an attitude of perfect contrition, and that in this way their entire debt should be cancelled."⁹

In short, Thérèse is saying, that by patiently bearing the pain that follows in the wake of committing some fault or failing, we are confiding ourselves to the mercy of God and it is by the mercy of God alone that we are purified. Thérèse gives us an example of how we are to confide ourselves to the mercy of God in her image of the *"weak little bird,"* who after committing "misdeeds, instead of going and hiding away in a corner, to weep over its misery and to die of sorrow...turns towards its beloved Sun, presenting its wet wings to its beneficent rays... recounts in detail all its infidelities, thinking in boldness of its full trust that it will acquire in even greater fullness the love of Him who came to call not the just but sinners" (S. 307).

What Thérèse is proposing is more difficult than it seems, for when we are filled with guilt and a sense of our own wretchedness, it is hard to believe in the mercy of God, for guilt tends to project upon the face of God a stern grimace. Our sins do not alter God's merciful love toward us; they simply make it more difficult for us to believe in it.

Julian of Norwich writes that there is no wrath in God. "God is that goodness which cannot be angry, for God is nothing but goodness." Commenting upon this passage, Robert Llewelyn writes: "God's face of compassionate love is always turned towards us, and if what we see in God is wrath, that is because of a corruption within ourselves which we have projected on to God, for our tendency is always to make God in our own image... Moreover we are not to be surprised, nor depressed, nor discouraged by occasions of falling, for what at least is certain is that we can never fall outside of God's love. Our falling, Julian might well have said, is not so much a falling into sin as a falling into the arms of God's mercy." [10]

In Francis Thompson's poem *The Hound of Heaven,* Thompson images God as a vicious hound that is pursuing him, but at the end of the poem when God finally corners him, Thompson realizes that he has been mistaken. What he interpreted as the menacing shadow of God's wrath is revealed as the refreshing shade of God's mercy; what he thought was God's hand poised to strike him was in truth God's hand reaching out to caress him. "Is my gloom, after all, Shade of His hand, out-stretched caressingly?" [11]

Our sins can make us feel that we are beyond the reach of God's mercy. Thérèse believed just the opposite. "I feel [that] even though I had on my conscience all the sins that can be committed, I would go, my heart broken with sorrow, and throw myself into Jesus' arms, for I know how much He loves the prodigal child who returns to Him" (S. 404).

The prodigal son returned home to his father's house not for any noble motive but because he was hungry and down on his luck. Nevertheless, his father welcomed him home with open arms, without reproach. This is the image of God that Jesus reveals to us and we are invited to believe. But how difficult it is to believe in God's mercy when we have squandered our inheritance and feel that we no longer deserve to be called God's child. How difficult it is at these times not to give in to the temptation to run away and hide "in a corner, to weep over [one's] misery and to die of sorrow"(S. 307). What strength it takes to be like the little weak bird and present the wet wings of our soul to the Sun of God's mercy.

*Questions.* Think of times when you have felt that your sins have put you beyond the reach of God's mercy. During these times, what has helped you to believe in God's merciful love?

## *Notes*

1. Quoted from *The Passion of Thérèse of Lisieux* by Guy Gacher, trans. Sr. Marie Brennan, OCD, (New York: Crossroads, 1989), 81.

2. Ibid., 73.

3. Ibid., 86.

4. Ibid., 111.

5. Quoted from *In Search of St. Thérèse* by Patricia O"Connor, (Collegeville: Liturgical Press, 1987), 169. Mother Gonzague's decision to withhold painkillers from Thérèse should not be viewed as a masochistic act but rather as an expression of the spirituality of the times. Abbé André Combes writes: "The apostolic doctrine of the French Carmel is contained fully in the notion by which a Carmelite nun is put in the place of a sinner, acting as a substitute...to appease the justice of God by willingly accepting the punishments due to sinners. When this plan was taken literally, the fidelity of the nun to her calling was judged according to the intensity of her spiritual and bodily mortifications. Spiritual mortifications not readily admitting of measurement, much insistence was laid upon corporeal austerities. This was the ideal in favor at the Carmel of Lisieux under the government of Mère Marie de Gonzague. The cross of iron and the whip of nettles were held in high honor." André Combes, *St. Thérèse and Her Mission,* trans. Alastair Guinan (New York: P.J. Kenedy & Sons, 1955), 134-5. It is also worth noting that in her final illness (cancer of the mouth) Mother Gonzague refused painkillers. She died on December 17, 1904.

6. O'Mahony, ibid., 159 & 119. An example of Mother Gonzague's jealously that was exhibited during Thérèse's

final illness is recounted by Pauline. "On several occasions Thérèse was made to feel her jealousy which flared up because the novices often went to the infirmary. Just a few days before [Thérèse] died, Mother Marie de Gonzague spoke to her coldly and made her visits so brief that Thérèse asked one of the novices, 'Do you know what I have done to upset Mother?' 'I know,' replied the novice, 'I did not wish to tell you lest I caused you pain. Our Mother has noticed that I love you very much and that I am very happy when I can come and see you and she said to me: If I had known of your close ties with Sister Thérèse of the Child Jesus and how she suffices for you in everything, I would not have worried about you.' Sister Thérèse of the Child Jesus replied simply to the novice: 'Ah! That's the reason. Thank you.'" Guy Gaucher, ibid., 111.

7. O'Mahony, ibid., 92. On September 13, 1896, Marie wrote the following to Thérèse: "I am writing not because I have something to tell you but to get something from you, from you who are so close to God, from you who are His little privileged spouse to whom He confides His secrets... The secrets of Jesus to Thérèse are sweet, and I would like to hear about them once again. Write me a short note. This is perhaps your last retreat..."(L. 991).

8. St. John of the Cross, "The Living Flame of Love," in *The Collected Works of St. John of the Cross,* trans. Kieran Kavanaugh, O.C.D. and Otilio Rodriguez, O.C.D. (Washington, D.C.: ICS Publications, 1991), stanza 1, 642. Thérèse quotes a similar passage from *The Spiritual Canticle* (stanza 29, no. 2) of St. John of the Cross and connects it to the divine activity of a soul in union. "I recall that *'the smallest*

*act of PURE LOVE is of more value to her than all other works together'* " (S. 305). Thérèse quotes this passage in conjunction with her acts of love– "strewing flowers" (S. 305).

9. Geneviève of the Holy Face (Céline Martin), *A Memoir of my sister St. Thérèse,* trans. Carmelite Sisters of New York (New York: P. J. Kenedy & Sons, 1959), 61-62. Conrad De Meester writes, "Toward the end of her life, she [Thérèse] was speaking of purgatory; here is her reaction preserved in a letter from Marie of the Eucharist to M. Guérin. 'Oh! How you grieve me! You do a great injury to God in believing you're going to purgatory. When we love, we can't go there.' So Thérèse's thought on human guilt is that love and confidence which she possessed, and consequently its productive power, is still for many only an ideal. Thérèse did not arrive at this point in a single day; she had to transverse a long 'little way.' But as those who follow her penetrate into her way, they open themselves up to the 'abysses' of divine mercy" (LT. 247, 1132). *The Power of Confidence: Genesis and Structure of the "Way of Spiritual Childhood" of St. Thérèse of Lisieux,* trans. Susan Conroy, (New York: Alba House, 1998), 348.

10. Robert Llewelyn, *All Shall Be Well: The Spirituality of Julian of Norwich for Today,* (New York: Paulist Press, 1982), 20-22.

11. Francis Thompson, "The Hound of Heaven" in *Complete Poetical Works of Francis Thompson,* (New York: Boni and Lightright, Inc, 1913), 93.

*Manuscript Addressed to*

## *MOTHER MARIE DE GONZAGUE*

*Manuscript C*

# Chapter X

# *THE TRIAL OF FAITH*
# *(1896–1897)*

Thérèse and Her Prioress
The Divine Elevator
The First Hemoptysis
The Table of Sinners
The Call to the Foreign Missions
What Is Charity?

[1r°]                    J.M.J.T.
June 1987

Y ou have told me, my dear Mother,[253] of your desire that I finish *singing* with you the *Mercies of the Lord.*[254] I began this sweet song with your dear daughter, Agnes of Jesus, who was the mother entrusted by God with guiding me in the days of my childhood. It was [5] with her that I had to sing of the graces granted to the Blessed Virgin's *little flower* when she was in the springtime of her life. And it is with you that I am to sing of the happiness of this little flower now that the timid glimmerings of the dawn have given way to the burning heat of noon. Yes, dear Mother, I shall try to express, in [10]answer to your wishes,[255] the sentiments of my soul, my gratitude to God and to

---

[253] Mother Marie de Gonzague, elected Prioress March 21, 1896, succeeding Mother Agnes of Jesus.

[254] Psalm 88:2.

[255] June 3, 1897, at the suggestion of Mother Agnes of Jesus, Mother Marie de Gonzague ordered Thérèse to continue writing her memories.

you, who represent Him visibly to me, for was it not into your maternal hands that I delivered myself entirely to Him? O Mother, do you remember that day?[256] Yes, I know your heart could not forget it. [15]As for me, I must await heaven because I cannot find here on earth words capable of expressing what took place in my heart on that beautiful day.

There is another day, my beloved Mother, when my soul was united with yours even more, if that were possible, and that was the day you were entrusted once again with the burden of Superior. On that day, dear Mother, [20]you sowed in tears, but you will be filled with joy in heaven [1v°] when you see yourself entrusted with precious sheaves.[257] O Mother, pardon my childish simplicity. I feel you will allow me to speak to you without considering what is allowed a young religious to say to her Prioress. Perhaps, at times, I shall not keep within the limits [5]prescribed for subjects, but, dear Mother, I make bold to say it, this is your own fault. I am acting with you as a child because you do not act with me as a Prioress but a Mother.

Ah! dear Mother, I know very well that it is really God who is speaking to me through you. Many of the Sisters think that you [10]spoiled me, that since my entrance into the holy ark, I have received from you nothing but caresses and compliments. Nevertheless it was not so. You will see, dear Mother, in the copybook containing my childhood memories, what I think of the *strong* and maternal education I received from you. From the bottom of my heart [15]I want to thank you for not sparing me. Jesus knew very well that His little flower stood in need of the living waters of humiliation, for she was too weak to take root without this kind of help, and it was through you, dear Mother, that this blessing was given to me.

---

[256] The day of her Profession, September 8, 1890.
[257] Psalm 125:5-6.

For a year and a half now, Jesus has willed to change the manner of [20]making His little flower grow. He has no doubt found her sufficiently *watered,* for now it is the *sun* that aids her growth. Jesus wants to give her nothing but His smile and this He does through you, dear Mother. This gentle sun, far from causing the little flower to wilt, [2r°] makes her progress in a marvelous manner. She preserves, in the bottom of her calyx, the precious drops of dew she had received, and these serve to remind her always how little and weak she is. All creatures can bow toward her, admire her, and shower their praises upon her. I don't [5]know why this is, but none of this could add one single drop of false joy to the true joy she experiences in her heart. Here she sees herself as she really is in God's eyes: a poor little thing, nothing at all.

I say I do not know why, but isn't it because she was preserved from the water of praise all the time [10]her little calyx was not sufficiently filled with the dew of humiliation? Now there is no longer any danger; on the contrary, the little flower finds the dew with which she was filled so delightful that she would be very careful not to exchange it for the insipid water of praise.

I don't want to speak, dear Mother, about the love and [15]confidence you are giving me; but do not believe the heart of your child is insensible to these. It is only that I feel I have nothing to fear now. In fact, I can rejoice in them, referring to God whatever good there is in me since He has willed to place it there. If He pleases to make me appear better [20] than I am, this is none of my affair since He is free to act as He likes.

O Mother, how different are the ways through which the Lord leads souls! In the life of the saints, we find many of them who didn't want to leave anything of themselves behind [2v°] after their death, not the smallest souvenir, not the least bit of writing. On the contrary, there are others, like our holy Mother St. Teresa, who have enriched

the Church with their lofty revelations, having no fears of revealing
the secrets of the King[258] in order that they may make Him [5]more
loved and known by souls. Which of these two types of saints is more
pleasing to God? It seems to me, Mother, they are equally pleasing to
Him, since all of them followed the inspiration of the Holy Spirit and
since the Lord has said: *"Tell the just man ALL is well."*[259] Yes, all is
well when one seeks only the will [10]of Jesus, and it is because of this
that I, a poor little flower, obey Jesus when trying to please my
beloved Mother.

　　You know, Mother, I have always wanted to be a saint. Alas! I
have always noticed that when I compared myself to the saints, there
is between them and me the same difference that exists between [15]a
mountain whose summit is lost in the clouds and the obscure grain of
sand trampled underfoot by passers-by. Instead of becoming discouraged, I said to myself: God cannot inspire unrealizable desires. I can,
then, in spite of my littleness, aspire to holiness. It is impossible for me
to grow up, and so I must bear with myself such [20]as I am with all my
imperfections. But I want to seek out a means of going to heaven by a
little way, a way that is very straight, very short, and totally new.

　　We are living now in an age of inventions, and we no longer
have to take the trouble of climbing [3r°] stairs, for, in the homes of
the rich, an elevator has replaced these very successfully. I wanted to
find an elevator which would raise me to Jesus, for I am too small to
climb the rough stairway of perfection. I searched, then, in the
Scriptures for some sign of this [5]elevator, the object of my desires,
and I read these words coming from the mouth of Eternal Wisdom:
*"Whoever is a LITTLE ONE, let him come to me."*[260] And so I suc-

---

[258] Tobit 12:7.

[259] Isaiah 3:10.

[260] Proverbs 9:4.

ceeded. I felt I had found what I was looking for. But wanting to know, O my God, what You would do to *the very little one* who answered Your call, I continued my search and this is what [10]I discovered: *"As one whom a mother caresses, so will I comfort you; you shall be carried at the breasts, and upon the knees they shall caress you."*[261] Ah! never did words more tender and more melodious come to give joy to my soul. The elevator which must raise me to heaven is Your arms, O Jesus! And for this I had no need [15]to grow up, but rather I had to remain *little* and become this more and more.

O my God, You surpassed all my expectation. I want only to sing to Your mercies. "You have taught me from my youth, O God, and until now I will declare Your wonderful works. And until old age and gray hairs, O God, forsake me not."[262] What will this old age [20]be for me? It seems this could be right now, for two thousand years are not more in the Lord's eyes than are twenty years, than even a single day.[263]

Ah! don't think, dear Mother, that your child wants to leave you; don't think she feels it is a [3v°] greater grace to die at the dawn of the day rather than at its close. What she esteems and what she desires only is *to please* Jesus. Now that He seems to be approaching her in order to draw her into the place of His glory, your child is filled with joy. For a long time she has [5]understood that God needs no one (much less her) to do good on earth. Pardon me, Mother, if I make you sad because I really want only to give you joy. Do you believe that though your prayers are really not heard on earth, though Jesus separates the child [10] from its mother for a *few days,* that these prayers will be answered in heaven?

---

[261] Isaiah 66:13, 12.

[262] Psalm 70:17-18.

[263] Psalm 89:4.

Your desire, I know, is that I carry out at your side a very sweet and easy mission;[264] but shall I not be able to finish it from the heights of heaven? You said to me, just as Jesus one day said to St. Peter: *"Feed my lambs."*[265] I was [15]astonished, and I told you that *I was too little;* I begged you *to feed your lambs yourself,* and to keep me and *have me feed* with them. And you, dear Mother, responding a *little* to my just request, retained the little lambs with the sheep;[266] but you ordered me to go often and pasture them in the shade, [20]pointing out the best and most nourishing herbs, showing them the bright flowers they must not touch except to trample them under their feet.

You didn't fear, dear Mother, that I would lead your little lambs astray. My lack of experience and my [4r°] youthfulness did not frighten you in the least. Perhaps you remembered that often the Lord is pleased to grant wisdom to the little ones, and that one day, in a transport of joy, He blessed His *Father* for having hidden His secrets from the wise and prudent and for revealing them to the *little ones.*[267]

Mother, you [5]know yourself that those souls are rare who don't measure the divine power according to their own narrow minds; people want exceptions everywhere on earth, but God alone hasn't the right to make any exceptions! For a very long time, I have known that this way of measuring experience according to years is practiced among human beings. For instance, [10] the holy King David has sung

---

[264] Thérèse was helping Mother Marie with the training of the novices ever since the latter's election on March 21, 1896.

[265] John 21:15.

[266] Mother Marie de Gonzague combined the offices of Prioress and Novice Mistress. The "little lambs" were the novices; the "sheep," the professed religious.

[267] Matthew 11:25.

to the Lord: *"I am YOUNG and despised."*[268] And in the same Psalm 118, he does not hesitate to add: *"I have had understanding above old men, because I have sought your will. Your word is a lamp to my feet. I am prepared to carry out your commandments and I am* [15]*TROU-BLED ABOUT NOTHING."*[269]

You did not hesitate, dear Mother, to tell me one day that God was enlightening my soul and that He was giving me even the experience of *years.* O Mother! I am *too little* to have any vanity now, I am *too little* to compose beautiful [20]sentences in order to have you believe that I have a lot of humility. I prefer to agree very simply that the Almighty has done great things in the soul of His divine Mother's child, and the greatest thing is to have shown her her *littleness,* her impotence.

[4v°] Dear Mother, you know well that God has deigned to make me pass through many types of trials. I have suffered very much since I was on earth, but, if in my childhood I suffered with sadness, it is no longer [5]in this way that I suffer. It is with joy and peace. I am truly happy to suffer. O Mother, you must know all the secrets of my soul in order not to smile when you read these lines, for is there a soul less tried than my own if one judges by appearances? Ah! if the trial I am suffering for a year [10] now[270] appeared to the eyes of anyone, what astonishment would be felt!

Dear Mother, you know about this trial; I am going to speak to you about it, however, for I consider it as a great grace I received during your office as Prioress.

God granted me, last year, the consolation of observing [15]the

---

[268] Psalm 118:141.

[269] Psalm 118:100, 105, 60.

[270] Her temptation against faith, which lasted from Easter 1896.

fast during Lent in all its rigor. Never had I felt so strong, and this strength remained with me until Easter. On Good Friday, however, Jesus wished to give me the hope of going to see Him soon in heaven. Oh! how sweet this memory really is! After remaining at the Tomb[271] until midnight, I returned to our [20]cell, but I had scarcely laid my head upon the pillow when I felt something like a bubbling stream mounting to my lips. I didn't know what it was, but I thought that perhaps I was going to die and my soul was flooded [5r°] with joy. However, as our lamp was extinguished, I told myself I would have to wait until the morning to be certain of my good fortune, for it seemed to me that it was blood I had coughed up. The morning was not long in coming; upon awakening, I thought [5]immediately of the joyful thing that I had to learn, and so I went over to the window. I was able to see that I was not mistaken. Ah! my soul was filled with a great consolation; I was interiorly persuaded that Jesus, on the anniversary of His own death, wanted to have me hear His first call. *It was like a sweet and [10]distant murmur that announced the Bridegroom's arrival.*[272]

It was with great fervor that I assisted at Prime and the Chapter of Pardons.[273] I was in a rush to see my turn come in order to be able, when asking pardon from you, to confide my hope and my happiness to you, dear Mother; however, I added that I was not suffering [15]in the least (which was true) and I begged you, Mother, to give me nothing special. In fact, I had the consolation of spending Good Friday just as

---

[271] The Altar of Reposition. The Carmelite Nuns remained all night in prayer before the Blessed Sacrament.

[272] T*he Imitation of Christ* III, 47.

[273] On Good Friday the Prioress customarily gave the community an exhortation to greater charity; then each begged pardon from her Sisters.

I desired. Never did Carmel's austerities appear so delightful to me; the hope of going to heaven soon transported me with joy. When the evening of that blessed day [20] arrived, I had to go to my rest; but just as on the preceding night, good Jesus gave me the same sign that my entrance into eternal life was not far off.

At this time I was enjoying such a living faith, such a clear *faith,* that the thought of heaven made up all my happiness, and I was [5v°] unable to believe there were really impious people who had no faith. I believed they were actually speaking against their own inner convictions when they denied the existence of heaven, that beautiful heaven where God Himself wanted to be their Eternal Reward. During those very joyful days of the Easter season, Jesus made me feel that [5] there were really souls who have no faith, and who, through the abuse of grace, lost this precious treasure, the source of the only real and pure joys. He permitted my soul to be invaded by the thickest darkness, and that the thought of heaven, up until then so sweet to me, be no longer anything but the cause of struggle and torment. This trial was to [10]last not a few days or a few weeks, it was not to be extinguished until the hour set by God Himself and this hour has not yet come. I would like to be able to express what I feel, but alas! I believe this is impossible. One would have to travel through this dark tunnel to understand its darkness. I will try to explain it [15]by a comparison.

I imagine I was born in a country that is covered in thick fog. I never had the experience of contemplating the joyful appearance of nature flooded and transformed by the brilliance of the sun. It is true that from childhood I heard people speak of these marvels, and I know the country I am living in [20]is not really my true fatherland, and there is another I must long for without ceasing. This is not simply a story invented by someone living in the sad country where I am, but it is a reality, for the King of the Fatherland of the bright sun actually came and lived for thirty-three [6r°] years in the land of darkness. Alas! the darkness did not understand that this Divine King was the Light of the world.[274]

Your child, however, O Lord, has understood Your divine light, and she begs pardon for her brothers. She is resigned to eat the bread of sorrow as long as [5]You desire it; she does not wish to rise up from this table filled with bitterness at which poor sinners are eating until the day set by You. Can she not say in her name and in the name of her brothers, *"Have pity on us, O Lord, for we are poor sinners!"*[275] Oh! Lord, [10] send us away justified. May all those who were not enlightened by the bright flame of faith one day see it shine. O Jesus! if it is needful that the table soiled by them be purified by a soul who loves You, then I desire to eat this bread of trial at this table until it pleases You to [15]bring me into Your bright Kingdom. The only grace I ask of You is that I never offend You!

What I am writing, dear Mother, has no continuity; my little story which resembled a fairy tale is all of a sudden changed into a prayer, and I don't know what interest you [20]could possibly have in reading all these confused and poorly expressed ideas. Well, dear Mother, I am not writing to produce a literary work, but only through obedience, and if I cause you any boredom, then at least you will see that your little child has given proof of her good will. I am going [6v°] to continue my little comparison where I left off.

I was saying that the certainty of going away one day far from the sad and dark country had been given me from the day of my childhood. I did not believe this only [5] because I heard it from persons much more knowledgeable than I, but I felt in the bottom of my heart

---

[274] John 1:5, 9.
[275] Luke 18:13.

real longings for this most beautiful country. Just as the genius of Christopher Columbus gave him a presentiment of a new world when nobody had even thought of such a thing; so also I felt that [10] another land would one day serve me as a permanent dwelling place. Then suddenly the fog that surrounds me becomes more dense; it penetrates my soul and envelops it in such a way that it is impossible to discover within it the sweet image of my Fatherland; everything has disappeared! When I want to rest my [15]heart fatigued by the darkness that surrounds it by the memory of the luminous country after which I aspire, my torment redoubles; it seems to me that the darkness, borrowing the voice of sinners, says mockingly to me: "You are dreaming about the light, about a fatherland embalmed in the sweetest perfumes; you are dreaming about the *eternal* possession of the [20]Creator of all these marvels; you believe that one day you will walk out of this fog that surrounds you! Advance, advance; rejoice in death which will give you not what you hope for but a night still more profound, the night of nothingness."

[7r°] Dear Mother, the image I wanted to give you of the darkness that obscures my soul is as imperfect as a sketch is to the model; however, I don't want to write any longer about it; I fear I might blaspheme; I fear even that I have already said too much.

[5]Ah! may Jesus pardon me if I have caused Him any pain, but He knows very well that while I do not have *the joy of faith,* I am trying to carry out its works at least. I believe I have made more acts of faith in this past year than all through my whole life. At each new occasion of combat, when my enemies provoke me, I [10] conduct myself bravely. Knowing it is cowardly to enter into a duel, I turn my back on my adversaries without deigning to look them in the face; but I run toward my Jesus. I tell Him I am ready to shed my blood to the last drop to profess my faith in the existence of *heaven.* I tell Him, too,

I am happy not to enjoy this [15]beautiful heaven on this earth so that He will open it for all eternity to poor unbelievers. Also, in spite of this trial which has taken away *all my joy,* I can nevertheless cry out: *"You have given me DELIGHT, O Lord, in ALL your doings."*[276] For is there a *joy* greater than that of suffering out of love for You? The more interior the suffering is and [20]the less apparent to the eyes of creatures, the more it rejoices You, O my God! But if my suffering was really unknown to You, which is impossible, I would still be happy to have it, if through it I could prevent or make reparation for one single sin against *faith.*

[7v°] My dear Mother, I may perhaps appear to you to be exaggerating my trial. In fact, if you are judging according to the sentiments I express in my little poems composed this year, I must appear to you as a soul filled with consolations and one for whom the [5]veil of faith is almost torn aside; and yet it is no longer a veil for me, it is a wall which reaches right up to the heavens and covers the starry firmament. When I sing of the happiness of heaven and of the eternal possession of God, I feel no joy in this, for I sing simply what I WANT TO BELIEVE. [10]It is true that at times a very small ray of the sun comes to illumine my darkness, and then the trial ceases for *an instant,* but afterward the memory of this ray, instead of causing me joy, makes my darkness even more dense.

Never have I felt before this, dear Mother, how [15]sweet and merciful the Lord really is, for He did not send me this trial until the moment I was capable of bearing it. A little earlier I believe it would have plunged me into a state of discouragement. Now it is taking away everything that could be a natural satisfaction in my desire [20]for heaven. Dear Mother, it seems to me now that nothing could prevent me

---

[276] Psalm 91:5.

from flying away, for I no longer have any great desires except that of loving to the point of dying of love. June 9.[277]

[8r°] I am totally surprised, dear Mother, when I see what I wrote yesterday. What scribbling! My hand was trembling so much that I found it impossible to continue and I even regret having tried to write. I hope that today [5] I will write more legibly, for I am no longer in bed but in a pretty little white armchair.

I feel that everything I said has no continuity to it, but I feel, too, the necessity of telling you my present feelings before speaking to you about the past. Perhaps later on [10]I will have completely forgotten about them. I wish first of all to tell you how much I am touched by all your maternal attention. Ah! believe it, Mother, the heart of your child is filled with gratitude, and never will she forget what she owes you.

Mother, what touches me above all else is the novena [15]you are making at Our Lady of Victories,[278] I mean the Masses you are having offered up to obtain my cure. I feel all these spiritual treasures do great good to my soul; at the commencement of the novena I told you the Blessed Virgin would have to cure me or carry me off to heaven because I [20] find it very sad for you and the community to have to take care of a young sick religious. But now I would want to be sick all my life if this pleases God, and I even consent to my life being very long; the only favor [8v°] I desire is that it be broken through love.

Oh! no, I do not have any fears of a long life and I do not refuse the fight, for the Lord is the Rock to which I am raised. *"He teaches my hands to fight, and my fingers to make war. He is my protector, and*

---

[277] The date, June 9, is written in pencil at the bottom of the page of her manuscript. It commemorates the second anniversary of her Act of Oblation to Merciful Love, June 9, 1895.

[278] The novena began June 5, 1897.

*I have hoped [5] in him!"*[279] I never did ask God for the favor of dying young, but I have always hoped this would be His will for me. Frequently God is satisfied with the desire of working for His glory, and you know my desires have been great, dear Mother. You are aware, too, that Jesus has offered me more than one bitter chalice which He [10] removed from my lips before I drank it, but not before making me taste its bitterness. The holy King David was right, dear Mother, when he sang: *"How sweet and pleasant it is for brothers to live together in unity."*[280] It is true, I felt this very often, but on this earth this [15]unity must take place in the midst of sacrifices. I didn't come to Carmel to live with my sisters but to answer Jesus' call. Ah! I really felt in advance that this living with one's own sisters had to be the cause of continual suffering when one wishes to grant nothing to one's natural inclinations.

[20]How can anyone say it is more perfect to separate oneself from one's blood relatives? Has anyone ever found fault with brothers who were fighting on the same field of battle? Are brothers blamed when they fight together for the martyr's palm? Undoubtedly, as some have [9r°] rightly judged, they are a source of encouragement to one another, but still the martyrdom of each becomes the martyrdom of all. And it is the same in the religious life, which has been called a daily martyrdom by theologians. When the human heart gives itself to God, it loses nothing of its innate tenderness; in fact, this tenderness [5]grows when it becomes more pure and more divine.

I love you, dear Mother, with this tenderness, and I love my sisters too. I am happy to fight *as a family* for the glory of heaven's King. However, I am prepared to fight on another battlefield if the Divine

---

[279] Psalm 143:1-2.

[280] Psalm 132:1.

General [10] expresses His desire that I do so. A command would not be necessary, only a look, a simple sign.

Since my entrance into the blessed ark, I have always thought that if Jesus did not bring me swiftly to heaven, my lot would be the same as that of Noah's little dove: the Lord would open the window of the ark one day, telling me [15]to fly very far, very far, toward infidel shores, carrying with me the little olive branch. Dear Mother, this thought has matured my soul, making me soar higher than all created things. I understood that even in Carmel there could still be separations, and that only in heaven will the union [20]be complete and eternal; so I wanted my soul to dwell in the heavens, and that it look upon the things of earth only from a distance. I accepted not only exile for myself among an unknown people, but also, and this was *far more bitter* for me, I accepted exile [9v°] for my sisters. Never shall I forget August 2, 1896; that day was precisely the day of the missionaries' departure,[281] and there was serious consideration of the departure of Mother Agnes of Jesus. Ah! I would not have desired to make any move to prevent her [5] leaving; I felt, however, a great sadness in my heart, for I found that her very sensitive and delicate soul was not made to live in the midst of souls who could not understand her; a thousand other thoughts crowded into my mind, and Jesus was silent; He was giving no commands to the storm. [10] I said to Him: My God, I accept everything out of love for You: if You will it, I really want to suffer even to the point of dying of grief. Jesus was content with this acceptance. However, a few months after this, they spoke of the departure of Sister Geneviève and Sister Marie of the Trinity. Then this was another kind of suffering, very intimate, very [15]deep; I imagined all

---

[281] August 2, 1896, Father Roulland, the Saint's spiritual brother, left from Marseilles for China, accompanied by two other missionaries.

the trials, the disappointment they would suffer, and my heaven was covered with clouds; calm and peace remained only in the depths of my heart.

Dear Mother, your own prudence was able to discover God's will and in His name you forbade your novices to [20]think of leaving the cradle of their religious childhood; but you understood their aspirations since you had asked in your own youthful days to go to Saigon. It is thus that the desires of Mothers find an echo in the soul [10r°] of their children. O dear Mother, your apostolic desire finds a faithful echo in my own soul, as you know; but let me confide why I desired and still desire, if the Blessed Virgin cures me, to leave the delightful oasis where I have lived so [5] happily under your motherly care, and to go into a foreign land.

Dear Mother, as you told me, a very special vocation is necessary to live in foreign Carmels. Many believe they are called to this, but it isn't so. You told me, too, that I had this vocation and only my poor health stood in the way. I know very well [10]this obstacle would disappear if God were calling me to the missions, and so I live without any unrest. If I have to leave my dear Carmel some day it would not be without pain, for Jesus has not given me an indifferent heart. And precisely because my heart is capable of suffering I want it to give Jesus everything [15]possible. *Here,* dear Mother, I live without any burdens from the cares of this miserable earth, and have only to accomplish the sweet and easy mission you have confided to me. *Here,* I receive your motherly attention and do not feel the pinch of poverty since I never lack anything. But *here,* above all, I am loved by you and all [20]the Sisters, and this affection is very sweet to me. This is why I dream of a monastery where I shall be unknown, where I would suffer from poverty, the lack of affection, and finally, the exile of the heart.

Ah! it is not with any intention of rendering services to the Carmel which [10v°] would receive me that I would leave everything dear to me. I would do everything that depended on me, but I know my incapacity, and I know that in doing my very best I would not succeed in doing well, having, as I just [5]said, no knowledge of the things of earth. My one purpose, then, would be to accomplish the will of God, to sacrifice myself for Him in the way that would please Him.

I really feel that I would have no disappointment, for when one expects pure and unmixed suffering, the smallest [10]joy becomes an unhoped-for surprise. And you know, Mother, that suffering itself becomes the greatest of joys when one seeks it as the most precious of treasures.

Oh, no! it is not with the intention of enjoying the fruit of my labors that I would want to leave; and if my purpose were that, I would not [15]feel this sweet peace which floods me and would actually suffer at not being able to realize my vocation for the foreign missions. For a long time I have not belonged to myself since I delivered myself totally to Jesus, and He is therefore free to do with me as He pleases. He has given me the attraction for a complete exile and He has made me *understand*[20]*all the sufferings* I would meet with, asking me if I would want to drink this chalice to the dregs; I wanted to seize this cup immediately when Jesus presented it, but He withdrew His hand and made me understand that my resignation alone was pleasing to Him.

[11r°] O Mother, what anxieties the Vow of Obedience frees us from! How happy are simple religious! Their only compass being their Superiors' will, they are always sure of being on the right road; they have nothing to fear from [5]being mistaken even when it seems that their Superiors are wrong. But when they cease to look upon the infallible compass, when they stray from the way it indicates under the pretext of doing God's will, unclear at times even to His representatives, then they wander into [10] arid paths where the water of grace is soon lacking.

Dear Mother, you are the compass Jesus has given me as a sure guide to the eternal shore. How sweet it is to fix my eyes upon you and thus accomplish the will of the Lord! Since the time He permitted me to suffer [15] temptations against the *faith,* He has greatly increased the *spirit of faith* in my heart, which helps me to see in you not only a loving Mother but also Jesus living in your soul and communicating His will to me through you. I know very well, dear Mother, you are treating me as a [20] feeble soul, a spoiled child, and as a consequence I have no trouble in carrying the burden of obedience. But because of what I feel in my heart, I would not change my attitude toward you, nor would my love decrease if it [11v°] pleased you to treat me severely. I would see once more that it was the will of Jesus that you were acting in this way for the greater good of my soul.

This year, dear Mother, God has given me the [5] grace to understand what charity is; I understood it before, it is true, but in an imperfect way. I had never fathomed the meaning of these words of Jesus: *"The second commandment is LIKE the first: You shall love your neighbor as yourself."*[282] I applied myself especially to loving God, [10]and it is in loving Him that I understood my love was not to be expressed only in words, for: *"It is not those who say: 'Lord, Lord!' who will enter the kingdom of heaven, but those who do the will of my Father in heaven."*[283] Jesus has revealed this will several times or [15]I should say on almost every page of His Gospel. But at the Last Supper, when He knew the hearts of His disciples were burning with a more ardent love for Him who had just given Himself to them in the

---

[282] Matthew 22:39.

[283] Matthew 7:21.

unspeakable mystery of His Eucharist, this sweet Savior wished to give them a *new commandment*. He said to them with [20] inexpressible tenderness: *"A new commandment I give you that you love one another: THAT AS I HAVE LOVED YOU, YOU ALSO LOVE ONE ANOTHER. By this will all men know that you are my disciples,* if you have love for one another."[284]

[12r°] How did Jesus love His disciples and why did He love them? Ah! it was not their natural qualities that could have attracted Him, since there was between Him and them an infinite distance. He was knowledge, Eternal Wisdom, while they were poor ignorant fishermen filled with [5]earthly thoughts. And still Jesus called them his *friends, His brothers.*[285] He desires to see them reign with Him in the kingdom of His Father, and to open that kingdom to them He wills to die on the cross, for He said: *"Greater love than this no man has than that he lay down his life for his friends."*[286]

[10] Dear Mother, when meditating upon these words of Jesus, I understood how imperfect was my love for my Sisters. I saw I didn't love them as God loves them. Ah! I understand now that charity consists in bearing with the faults of others, in not being surprised at their weakness, [15]in being edified by the smallest acts of virtue we see them practice. But I understood above all that charity must not remain hidden in the bottom of the heart. Jesus has said: *"No one lights a lamp and puts it under a bushel basket, but upon the lampstand, so as to give light to ALL in the house."*[287] It seems to me that [20]this lamp represents charity which must enlighten and rejoice not only those who

---

[284] John 13:34-35.

[285] John 15:15.

[286] John 15:13.

[287] Matthew 5:15.

are dearest to us but "ALL *who are in the house"* without distinction.

When the Lord commanded His people to love their neighbor [12v°] as themselves,[288] He had not as yet come upon the earth. Knowing the extent to which each one loved himself, He was not able to ask of His creatures a greater love than this for one's neighbor. But when Jesus gave His Apostles a [5]new commandment, HIS OWN COMMANDMENT,[289] as He calls it later on, it is no longer a question of loving one's neighbor as oneself but of loving him as *He, Jesus, has loved him,* and will love him to the consummation of the ages.

Ah! Lord, I know you don't command the [10] impossible. You know better than I do my weakness and imperfection; You know very well that never would I be able to love my Sisters as You love them, unless *You,* O my Jesus, *loved them in me.* It is because You wanted to give me this grace that You made Your new commandment. Oh! how I [15]love this new commandment since it gives me the assurance that Your Will is *to love in me* all those You command me to love!

Yes, I feel it, when I am charitable, it is Jesus alone who is acting in me, and the more united I am to Him, the more also do I love my Sisters. When I wish to increase this love in me, and when [20]especially the devil tries to place before the eyes of my soul the faults of such and such a Sister who is less attractive to me, I hasten to search out her virtues, her good intentions; I tell myself that even if I did see her fall once, she could easily have won a great [13r°] number of victories which she is hiding through humility, and that even what appears to me as a fault can very easily be an act of virtue because of her intention. I have no trouble in convincing myself of this truth because of a little experience I had which [5] showed me we must never judge.

---

[288] Leviticus 19:18.

[289] John 15:12.

During recreation the portress rang twice; the large workman's gate had to be opened to bring in some trees for the crib. Recreation was not too gay because you were not there, dear Mother, and I thought that if they sent me to serve as third party[290] I would be [10] happy; at exactly that moment Mother Subprioress told me to go and serve in this capacity, or else the Sister who was at my side. Immediately I began to untie our apron but slowly in order that my companion untie hers before me, for I thought of giving her the pleasure of serving as third party. The Sister who was replacing the Procuratrix [15]was looking at us, and seeing me get up last, she said: "Ah! I thought as much, that you were not going to gain this pearl for your crown, you were going too slowly."

Certainly, the whole community believed I had acted through selfishness, and I cannot say how much good such a small thing [20]did to my soul, making me indulgent toward the weaknesses of others. This incident prevents me from being vain when I am judged favorably because I say to myself: Since one can take my little acts of virtue for imperfections, one can also be [13v°] mistaken in taking for virtue what is nothing but imperfection. Then I say with St. Paul: *"To me it is a very small thing to be judged by you, or by any human tribunal, but neither do I judge myself. He who judges me is THE LORD."*[291]

[5]In order that this judgment be favorable or rather that I be not judged at all, I want to be charitable in my thoughts toward others at all times, for Jesus has said: *"Judge not, and you shall not be judged."*[292]

Mother, when reading what I have just written, you could

---

[290] The religious who accompanied the Procuratrix when laborers had to work in the monastery.

[291] 1 Corinthians 4:3-4.

[292] Luke 6:37.

believe that the practice of charity is not difficult for me. It is true;
[10]for several months now I no longer have to struggle to practice this
beautiful virtue. I don't mean by this that I no longer have any faults;
ah! I am too imperfect for that. But I mean that I don't have any trouble in rising when I have fallen because in a certain combat I won a
great victory; and the [15]heavenly militia now comes to my aid since it
cannot bear seeing me defeated after having seen me victorious in the
glorious battle I am going to try to describe.

There is in the Community a Sister who has the faculty of displeasing me in everything, in her ways, her words, her character,
everything [20]seems *very disagreeable* to me. And still, she is a holy
religious who must be very pleasing to God. Not wishing to give in to
the natural antipathy I was experiencing, I told myself that charity
must not consist in feelings but in works; then [14r°] I set myself to
doing for this Sister what I would do for the person I loved the most.
Each time I met her I prayed to God for her, offering Him all her
virtues and merits. I felt this was pleasing to Jesus, for there is no artist
[5]who doesn't love to receive praise for his works, and Jesus, the Artist
of souls, is happy when we don't stop at the exterior, but, penetrating
into the inner sanctuary where He chooses to dwell, we admire its
beauty. I wasn't content simply with praying very much for this Sister
who gave me so many struggles, but I took care to render her all the
services possible, [10] and when I was tempted to answer her back in a
disagreeable manner, I was content with giving her my most friendly
smile, and with changing the subject of the conversation, for the
Imitation says: *"It is better to leave each one in his own opinion than
to enter into arguments."* [293]

Frequently, when I was at recreation (I mean during [15]the work

---

[293] *The Imitation of Christ* III, 44:1.

periods) and had occasion to work with this Sister, I used to run away like a deserter whenever my struggles became too violent. As she was absolutely unaware of my feelings for her, never did she suspect the motives for my conduct and she remained convinced that her character was very pleasing to me. One day at recreation she [20]asked in almost these words: "Would you tell me, Sister Thérèse of the Child Jesus, what attracts you so much toward me; every time you look at me, I see you smile?" Ah! what attracted me was Jesus hidden in the depths of her soul; Jesus who makes sweet what is most bitter.[294] I answered that I was smiling because I was happy to see her (it is understood that I [25]did not add that this was from a spiritual standpoint).

[14v°] Dear Mother, I have already told you that my last means of not being defeated in combats is desertion; I was already using this means during my novitiate, and it always succeeded perfectly with me. I wish, Mother, to give you an example which [5]I believe will make you smile. During one of your bronchial attacks, I came to your cell very quietly one morning to return the keys of the Communion grating since I was sacristan. I wasn't too displeased at having this opportunity to see you; I was very much pleased, but I didn't dare to show it. A Sister, [10] animated with a holy zeal, and one who loved me very much, believed I was going to awaken you when she saw me entering your quarters; she wanted to take the keys from me. I was too stubborn to give them to her and to cede *my rights.* As politely as I could, I told her that it was *my duty* to return [15]the keys. I understand now that it would have been more perfect to cede to this Sister, young, it is true, but still older than I. I did not understand it at the time, and as I wanted absolutely to enter in spite of the fact that she was pushing the door to prevent me, very soon the thing we feared most hap-

---

[294] *The Imitation of Christ* III, 5:3.

pened: the racket [20]we were making made you open your eyes. Then, Mother, everything tumbled upon me. The poor Sister whom I had resisted began to deliver a whole discourse, the gist of which was: It's Sister Thérèse of the Child Jesus who made the noise; my God, how disagreeable she is, etc. [15r°] I, who felt just the contrary, had a great desire to defend myself. Happily, there came a bright idea into my mind, and I told myself that if I began to justify myself I would not be able to retain my peace of soul. I felt, too, that I did not have enough [5]virtue to permit myself to be accused without saying a word. My last plank of salvation was in flight. No sooner thought than done. I left without fuss, allowing the Sister to continue her discourse which resembled the imprecations of Camillus against the city of Rome. My heart was beating so rapidly that it was impossible for me to go far, and I sat down on the [10] stairs in order to savor the fruits of my victory. There was no bravery there, Mother; however, I believe it was much better for me not to expose myself to combat when there was certain defeat facing me.

Alas! when I think of the time of my novitiate I see how imperfect I was. I made so much fuss over such little [15]things that it makes me laugh now. Ah! how good the Lord is in having matured my soul, and in having given it wings. All the nets of the hunters would not be able to frighten me, for: *"... the net is spread in vain before the eyes of them that have wings."*[295] Later on, no doubt, the time in which I am now will appear filled with imperfections, but [20]now I am astonished at nothing. I am not disturbed at seeing myself *weakness* itself. On the contrary, it is in my weakness that I glory,[296] and I expect each day to discover new imperfections in myself. Remembering that *"charity*

---

[295] Proverbs 1:17.

[296] 2 Corinthians 12:5.

*covers a multitude of* [15v°] *sins,* "[297] I draw from this rich mine that Jesus has opened up before me.

The Lord, in the Gospel, explains in what *His new commandment* consists. He says in St. Matthew: *"You have heard that it was said, 'You shall love your neighbor and hate your enemy.' But I*[5] *say to you, love your enemies ... pray for those who persecute you.* "[298] No doubt, we don't have any enemies in Carmel, but there are feelings. One feels attracted to this Sister, whereas with regard to another, one would make a long detour in order to avoid meeting her. And so, without even knowing it, she becomes the subject of persecution. [10] Well, Jesus is telling me that it is this Sister who must be loved, she must be prayed for even though her conduct would lead me to believe that she doesn't love me: *"If you love those who love you, what reward will you have? For even sinners love those who love them.* " [299] St. Luke, VI. And it isn't enough to love; we must prove it. We are naturally [15]happy to offer a gift to a friend; we love especially to give surprises; however; this is not charity, for sinners do this too. Here is what Jesus teaches me also: *"Give to EVERYONE who asks of you, and from HIM WHO TAKES AWAY your goods, ask no return.* "[300] Giving to all those who ask is less sweet than offering [20]oneself by the movement of one's own heart; again, when they ask for something politely, it doesn't cost so much to give, but if, unfortunately, they don't use very delicate words, the soul is immediately up in arms if she is not well founded in charity. She finds a thousand reasons to refuse [16r°] what is asked of her, and it is only after having convinced the asker of

---

[297] Proverbs 10:12.

[298] Matthew 5:43-44.

[299] Luke 6:32.

[300] Luke 6:30.

her tactlessness that she will finally give what is asked, and then only *as a favor;* or else she will render a light service which could have been done in one-twentieth of the time that was spent in setting forth her[5] imaginary rights.

Although it is difficult to give to one who asks, it is even more so *to allow one to take what belongs to you, without asking it back.* O Mother, I say it is difficult; I should have said that this *seems* difficult, for *the yoke of the Lord is sweet and light.*[301] When one accepts it, one feels its sweetness immediately, and cries out with the Psalmist: [10] *"I have run the way of your commandments when you enlarged my heart."*[302] It is only charity that can expand my heart. O Jesus, since this sweet flame consumes it, I run with joy in the way of *Your NEW commandment.* I want to run in it until that blessed day when, joining the virginal procession, I[15]shall be able to follow You in the heavenly courts, singing Your NEW *canticle*[303] which must be Love.

I was saying: Jesus does not want me to lay claim to what belongs to me; and this should seem easy and natural to me since *nothing is mine.* I have renounced the goods of this earth through the Vow of Poverty, and[20]so I haven't the right to complain when one takes a thing that is not mine. On the contrary, I should rejoice when it happens that I feel the pinch of poverty. Formerly, it seemed to me that I was attached to nothing, but ever since I understood the words of Jesus, I see on occasions that [16v°] I am very imperfect. For example, in my work of painting there is nothing that belongs to me, I know. But if, when I am preparing for some work, I find that the brushes and the paints are in disorder, if a rule or a penknife has dis-

---

[301] Matthew 11:30.

[302] Psalm 118:32.

[303] Revelation 14:3.

appeared, patience is very close to [5]abandoning me and I must take my courage in both hands in order to reclaim the missing object without bitterness. We really have to ask for indispensable things, but when we do it with humility, we are not failing in the commandment of Jesus; on the contrary, we are acting like the poor who extend their hand [10] to receive what is necessary for them; if they are rebuked they are not surprised, as no one owes them anything.

Ah! what peace floods the soul when she rises above natural feelings. No, there is no joy comparable to that which the truly poor in spirit experience. If such a one asks for something with [15]detachment, and if this thing is not only refused but one tries to take away what one already has, the poor in spirit follow Jesus' counsel: *"If anyone take away your coat, let go your cloak also."*[304]

To give up one's cloak is, it seems to me, renouncing one's [20]ultimate rights; it is considering oneself as the servant and the slave of others. When one has left his cloak, it is much easier to walk, to run, and Jesus adds: *"And whoever forces you to go one mile, go two more with him."*[305] Thus [17r°] it is not enough to give *to everyone who asks;*[306] I must even anticipate their desires, appear to be very much obliged and honored to render service, and if anyone takes something which is for my use, I must not appear to be sorry about this but happy at being *relieved* of it. [5] Dear Mother, I am very far from practicing what I understand, and still the desire alone I have of doing it gives me peace.

I feel that I have explained myself poorly, even more so than on the other days. I made a *kind of discourse* on charity which must have tired you when you were reading it. Pardon me, dear Mother, and

---

[304] Matthew 5:40.
[305] Matthew 5:41.
[306] Luke 6:30.

[10]remember that at this very moment the infirmarians practice in my regard what I have just written; they don't hesitate to take two thousand paces when twenty would suffice.[307] So I have been able to contemplate charity in action! Undoubtedly my soul is embalmed with it; as far as my mind is concerned I admit it is paralyzed in the presence of such devotedness, and my pen has [15]lost its lightness. In order for me to translate my thoughts, I have to be *like the solitary sparrow,*[308] and this is rarely my lot. When I begin to take up my pen, behold a Sister who passes by, a pitchfork on her shoulder. She believes she will distract me with a little idle chatter: hay, ducks, [20]hens, visits of the doctor, everything is discussed; to tell the truth, this doesn't last a long time, but there is *more than one good charitable Sister,* and all of a sudden another hay worker throws flowers on my lap, perhaps believing these will inspire me with poetic thoughts. I am not looking [17v°] for them at the moment and would prefer to see the flowers remain swaying on their stems. Finally, fatigued by opening and shutting this famous copybook, I open a book (which doesn't want to stay open) and say resolutely that I shall copy out some thoughts from the psalms and the Gospels for [5]the feast of Our Mother.[309] It's very true that I am not sparing in these quotes.

Dear Mother, I would amuse you, I believe, when telling you about all my adventures in the groves of Carmel; I don't know if I have been able to write ten lines without being disturbed; this should not make me laugh nor amuse me; however, for the love of [10]God and my Sisters (so charitable toward me) I take care to appear happy and

---

[307] She is writing in the garden in a wheelchair (note of Mother Agnes).

[308] Psalm 101:8.

[309] Mother Marie de Gonzague's feast was on June 21, feast of St. Aloysius Gonzaga.

especially *to be so.* For example, here is a hay worker who is just leaving me after having said very compassionately: "Poor little Sister, it must tire you out writing like that all day long." "Don't worry," I answer, "I appear to be writing very much, [15]but really I am writing almost nothing." "Very good!" she says, "but just the same, I am very happy we are doing the haying since this always distracts you a little." In fact, it is such a great distraction for me (without taking into account the infirmarians' visits) that I am not telling any lies when I say that I am writing practically nothing.

[20]Fortunately, I don't easily get discouraged and to prove it, I am going to finish explaining what Jesus makes me understand concerning charity. I have spoken to you only about external charity; now I would like to confide to you what I understand about [18r°] purely spiritual charity. I am very sure that I won't be long in mixing the one with the other, but, since I am speaking to you, it will not be difficult for you to grasp my thought and to unravel your child's skein.

[5]It is not always possible in Carmel to practice the words of the Gospel according to the letter. One is obliged at times to refuse a service because of one's duties; but when charity has buried its roots deeply within the soul, it shows itself externally. There is such a delightful way of refusing what cannot be given that the refusal gives as much [10]pleasure as the gift itself. It is true that one hesitates less to claim a service from a Sister who is always disposed to oblige but Jesus has said: *"...and from him who would borrow of you, do not turn away."*[310] Thus under the pretext that one would be forced to refuse, one must not stay away from the Sisters who are always in the habit of asking for help. Neither should one [15]be obliging in order to *appear* so or in the hope that another time the Sister whom one obliges will

---

[310] Matthew 5:42.

return the service in her turn, for Our Lord says again: *"And if you lend to those from whom you hope to receive in return, what merit have you? For even sinners lend to sinners that they may get back as much in return. But do good, and lend, NOT HOPING FOR* [20] *ANYTHING IN RETURN, and your reward shall be great."* [311]

Oh, yes! the reward is great, even on this earth; in this way it is only the first step that costs anything. To lend without *hoping for anything* appears difficult to nature; one would prefer to give, for a thing given [18v°] no longer belongs to one. When one comes to you and says in a very convincing way: "Sister, I need your help for a few hours, but don't worry, I have Mother's permission and I *will return* the time you are giving me because I know how rushed you are." [5]Truly, when one knows very well that never will the time one *lends* ever be returned, one would prefer to say: "I give it to you." This would satisfy self-love, for giving is a more generous act than lending, and then we make the Sister feel we don't depend on her services. Ah! how contrary [10]are the teachings of Jesus to the feelings of nature! Without the help of His grace it would be impossible not only to put them into practice but to even understand them.

---

[311] Luke 6:34-35.

## *The Trial of Faith*
### Background and Context.

One night, four months before Thérèse died, Pauline could not sleep; there was something that she needed to tell the prioress and it couldn't wait. "Towards midnight on 2 June, 1897, four months before Sister Thérèse's death, I went to Mother Prioress's room and said: 'Mother, I cannot sleep until I tell you a certain secret. While I was prioress, Sister Thérèse wrote some memoirs of her childhood. She did so out of obedience to please me. The other day I read them through again and they are very charming but... [they] hardly say anything about her life as a nun. Now, if you were to order her to do so, she could write something more serious.'"[1] The next day, Mother Gonzague commanded Thérèse to write about her experiences in Carmel; the result was chapters ten and eleven (Manuscript C) of *Story of a Soul.*

It was the worst of times for Thérèse to write. "She set to work, and wrote as it came to her...It was quite disorderly, however, because of her illness and the interruptions caused by the constant coming and going of the infirmarians and the novices, these latter taking as much advantage as they could of her last days with them. So much so that one day she said to me: 'I don't know what I'm writing...I am writing about charity, but I have not been able to do it as well as I should have liked to; in fact, I couldn't have done it worse if I'd tried.' She stopped writing at the beginning of July 1897. She was so weak that she had to use a pencil for the last page." [2] Chapter ten deals with several aspects of Thérèse's spiritual life but focuses on her trial of faith and charity.

*a) Thérèse's Trial of Faith.* A month after Thérèse made her last private retreat (the retreat during which she wrote a summary of her "little way" for her sister Marie), the community's retreat took place (October 8-15, 1896).[3] During this retreat, Thérèse confided to the retreat master Fr. Godefroy Madeleine that she had been experiencing doubts in faith for the past six months; he advised Thérèse to always carry a copy of the Creed on her person and place her hand on it whenever these doubts arose in her mind. Thérèse followed this advice and wrote out the Creed in her own blood.

Thérèse's trial of faith began on Easter Sunday, April 6, 1896, two days after her first hemoptysis. Doubts of all kinds began to plague her. "I do not believe in eternal life. It seems to me that after this mortal life, there is nothing any more." "Last evening, I was seized with a veritable anguish and my darkness increased. [A] voice said to me. 'Are you sure of being loved by God? Did he come and tell you?' "[4] "[I]t seems to me that the darkness, borrowing the voice of sinners, says mockingly to me: 'You are dreaming about the light, about a fatherland embalmed in the sweetest perfumes; you are dreaming about the *eternal* possession of the Creator of all these marvels; you believe that one day you will walk out of this fog which surrounds you! Advance, advance; rejoice in death which will give you not what you hope for but a night still more profound, the night of nothingness" (S. 335). "I want to do good after my death, but I will not be able to do so! It will be as it was for Mother Geneviève: We expected to see her work in miracles, and complete silence fell over her tomb "(LC. 257-8). "Frightful thoughts obsess me!...It's the reasoning of the worst materialists which is imposed upon my mind "(LC. 257). "[Science is] unceasingly making new advances, science will explain everything naturally; we shall have the absolute reason for everything that exists and that still remains a problem" (LC. 257). In short, Thérèse's doubts were expressive of the scientific age in which she lived, an age in which that which could not be verified by experimentation or empirical evidence was called into question, an age in which metaphysics and the claims of religion were scoffed at, an age of skepticism and suspicion of all that laid claim to the supernatural.

Thérèse was knowledgeable of history and science, the two great subjects of her day. "I applied myself to some special studies in *history and science,* and I did this on my own. The other studies left me indifferent, but these two studies attracted all my attention; in a few months I acquired more knowledge than during my years of study" (S. 156).Thérèse thought about what her contemporaries were saying about life after death and wondered if what they said was true. As a reflective child, Thérèse spend long periods of times thinking about the ultimate questions of existence. "I *thought*...I think about God, about life, about ETERNITY...I think" (S. 117).

Thérèse *believed* in the promise of eternal life but she had her *doubts.* And these doubts were not peculiar to her trial of faith that occurred at the end of her life. "At that time I was having great interior trials of all kinds, even to the point of asking myself whether heaven really existed" (S. 269). The time was 1891, five years prior to the onset of her trial of faith.

Thérèse shared the obdurate doubts and anxieties of her contemporaries and in the process grew in understanding and compassion for the agnostics and atheists of her age, whom she referred to as "her brothers" (S. 334) and once referred to Nietzsche as her " sick little brother."She also entered into the darkness of people who freely rejected the light, "who, through the abuse of grace, lost this precious treasure, the source of the only real and pure joys" (S. 333).

While we do not know the exact nature of Thérèse's trial of faith, suffice it to say, that while Therese was growing in *the virtue of faith,* she was devoid of the *consolation of faith.* "I do not have the joy of faith, I am trying to carry out its works at least" (S. 335).

*b) Charity.* There are three fundamental truths about charity that Thérèse addresses in this chapter. The first is that charity is a not a feeling but a choice. "I told myself that charity must not consist in feelings but in works" (S. 346). The second is that it is very difficult to be charitable to people whom we don't like, people whom we have a "natural antipathy"(S. 346) toward, to use Thérèse phrase. Third, it is precisely in loving those to whom we have a natural aversion, that our love becomes divine because such love requires that we love with the charity of Jesus himself. Thérèse writes of two nuns whom she had a natural aversion toward but whom she choose to love with the love of Jesus – Sr. Marie of St. Joseph and Sr. Teresa of St. Augustine.

*Sr. Marie of St. Joseph.* During the darkest days of Thérèse's life, when her body was being consumed by tuberculosis and her soul was submerged in a dark night of faith, she *volunteered* to work in the linen closet with Sr. Marie of St. Joseph, a women with a depressive temperament who was prone to such outbursts of anger that none of the nuns would work with her. In due course, Sr. Marie lived on the fringe of the community.[5]

Thérèse worked with Sr. Marie from March, 1896 to May,

1897. In June, 1897, Thérèse wrote the following: "This year...God has given me the grace to understand what charity is; I understood it before, it is true, but in an imperfect way... I understood how imperfect was my love for my Sisters. I saw that I didn't love them as God loves them. Ah! I understand now that charity consists in bearing with the faults of others...I understood...that charity must not remain hidden in the bottom of the heart [but is a lamp that is placed upon the lampstand] *so as to give light to ALL in the house...*All *in the house"* without distinction" (S. 343-344).

Thérèse once compared Sr. Marie to "an old clock that has to be rewound every quarter of an hour,"[6] and said that if she "had an infirmity such as hers and so defective a spirit...[she] would despair."[7] Even for Thérèse, Sr. Marie was a difficult person to love.

*Sr. Teresa of St. Augustine.* If we reflect upon our experience, we will find that there are certain people to whom we have a natural aversion – an aversion that is so irrational that it defies explanation. "[God's] hand is so gentle!...But creatures!... Those who surround me are very good, but there is something, I don't know what, that repels me! ...I cannot give you any explanation" (L. 499-500).[8] Sr. Teresa of St. Augustine was such a person. She had a rigid personality that reminded Thérèse of a "potted lily." "There is in the Community a Sister who has the faculty of displeasing me in everything, in her ways, her words, her character, everything seems *very disagreeable* to me" (S. 346).Thérèse *felt* a natural antipathy toward Sr. Teresa of St. Augustine, but this did not prevent Thérèse from acting in love. "I told myself that charity must not consist in feelings but in works; then I set myself to doing for this Sister what I would do for the person I loved the most" (S. 346). So well did Thérèse mask her feelings, that it was only years after Thérèse's death that Sr. Teresa of St. Augustine came to the sobering realization that she was the person whom Thérèse wrote about in *Story of a Soul*.

*c) Drawing Profit From Everything.* Thérèse wrote that God granted her the grace "to draw profit from everything" (L. 795). We see this in an incident where Thérèse was rash judged as being unwilling to help another nun bring the community Christmas tree through the garden gate (S. 345). When Thérèse was rash judged, she did not become resentful, but rather she became more "indulgent toward the weaknesses of others" (S. 345).

*d) Perspective.* One of the graces that interrelated with Thérèse's ability to draw profit from every situation was her ability to see the "little things" of life in perspective. "Alas! when I think of the time of novitiate I see how imperfect I was. I made so much fuss over such little things that it makes me laugh now" (S. 348). Thérèse, even got to the point in her spiritual development where she was able to laugh at being misjudged. "When we're misunderstood and judged unfavorably, what good does it do to defend or explain ourselves? Let the matter drop and say nothing. It's so much better to say nothing and allow others to judge us as they please!...O blessed silence that gives so much peace to souls" (LC. 36)!

## Reflections and Questions.

1. Thérèse was elated on Good Friday morning, 1896, when

she discovered that she had spit up blood during the night. "I was going to die and my soul was flooded with joy...the hope of going to heaven soon transported me with joy" (S. 332). The joy that she would soon be in heaven so filled Thérèse's heart and mind that she could not even imagine that anyone did not believe in the existence of heaven. "At this time I was enjoying such a living faith, such a clear *faith*, that the thought of heaven made up all my happiness, and I was unable to believe there were really impious people who had no faith. I believed they were actually speaking against their own inner convictions when they denied the existence of heaven" (S. 333).This statement seems to contradict the doubts Thérèse had during her 1891 retreat. "At that time I was having great interior trials of all kinds, even to the point of asking myself whether heaven really existed" (S. 269).

But there is no contradiction here. Thérèse is simply saying that her *joy at the moment* when she thought that she would soon be going to heaven was so intense that it pushed out of her mind the memory of all of her previous doubts. Thérèse's experience is similar to our own; when we feel on top of the world, it is as if past miseries never happened. Conversely, when we are extremely anxious, worried, or depressed, we feel that our life has come to an end. In short, our perception of reality is greatly impacted by our emotions, and our emotions, in turn, color our perception of life.

Also, Therese's experience of one day being transported by joy at the prospect that she will soon be in heaven and the next day being thrown down into the deepest doubts is a reflection of the mercurial nature of our moods. One moment, we feel peaceful and think that life is good, and then, without warning, a half conscious thought crosses our mind like a cloud that blots out the sun, and for the rest of the day we feel anxious and we know not why. It may have happened as your driving to work one morning. You are feeling relaxed, but as you turn the dial of your radio in an attempt to find some music, you hear that there has been a terrorist attack on an American embassy abroad. You don't get the details of what happened because you quickly change the station, but just the thought that there has been a terrorist attack sends a cold shiver through your body, as your deepest insecurities are triggered. And for the rest of the day, even though you are not consciously thinking about what happened, you feel vaguely apprehensive about something that you cannot name.

Our changing feelings and shifting moods are a part of life, and we all know the impact that they exert upon our will; there are days when we feel we can conquer the world, and there are days when it takes all the courage we can muster to crawl out of bed. As St. Teresa puts it, "At times I think I have great courage and that I wouldn't turn from anything of service to God; and when put to the test, I do have this courage for some things. Another day will come in which I won't find the courage in me to kill even an ant for God if in doing so I'd meet with any opposition." [9] What we see in chapter ten of *Story of a Soul* is one of the main reasons why Therese became a saint; she continued in her struggle to do God's will in the midst of emotional desolation.

In *The Screwtape Letters* by C.S. Lewis, Screwtape writes to his nephew Wormwood about the spiritual reality of a soul that continues to strive to do God's will in the midst of darkness. "Do not be deceived, Wormwood. Our cause is never more in

danger than when a human, no longer desiring, but still intend-
ing, to do our Enemy's [God's] will, looks round upon a universe
from which every trace of Him seems to have vanished, and asks
why he has been forsaken, and still obeys."[10] In short, our feelings are not the best judge of our spiritual condition, for often
when we feel that our faith is the weakest it is actually the
strongest. "I do not have the *joy of faith,* I am trying to carrying
out its works at least." (S. 335)

*Questions.* When in your life have you felt devoid of the
joy of faith yet experienced God's strength that en-abled you to
do his will?

2." In A.D. 627 the monk Paulinus visited King Edwin in
northern England to persuade him to accept Christianity. He hes-
itated and decided to summon his advisers. At the meeting one
of them stood up and said: 'Your majesty, when you sit at table
with your lords and vassals, in the winter when the fire burns
warm and bright on the hearth and the storm is howling outside,
bringing the snow and the rain, it happens of a sudden that a little bird flies into the hall. It comes in at one door and flies out
through the other. For the few moments that it is inside the hall,
it does not feel the cold, but as soon as it leaves your sight, it
returns to the dark of winter. It seems to me that the life of man
is much the same. We do not know what went before and we do
not know what follows. If the new doctrine can speak to us surely of these things, it is well for us to follow it.'"[11]
    The question of death hems life in on all sides. Is there any-
thing beyond the grave, beyond the outer darkness of the castle
walls? And if death is the termination of life, does life have any

ultimate meaning? We may never have to endure a trial of faith as intense as the one that Thérèse experienced; nevertheless, we all know the periodic doubts that attend upon issues of faith and the meaning of life. These doubts arise especially during times of sickness or when the drudgery of the daily grind seeps into every corner of our soul. "Tomorrow and tomorrow and tomorrow/ Creeps in this petty pace from day to day/To the last syllable of recorded time..." At such times, like Thérèse, our prayer and worship feel empty and dry. "When I sing of the happiness of heaven and of the eternal possession of God, I feel no joy in this, for I sing simply what I WANT TO BELIEVE" (S. 336).

But Thérèse knew that belief is not a matter of *feeling* but of *choice;* she knew that she could not rid herself of the darkness, so she accepted it. "She is resigned to eat the bread of sorrow as long as You desire it; she does not wish to rise up from this table filled with bitterness at which poor sinners are eating until the day set by You" (S. 334). Thérèse accepted her darkness for the sake of others. "May all those who were not enlightened by the bright flame of faith one day see it shine. O Jesus! if it is needful that the table soiled by them be purified by a soul who loves You, then I desire to eat this bread of trial at this table until it pleases You to bring them into Your bright Kingdom" (S. 334). Here we are confronted with the mystery of our participation in the work of redemption. *How* uniting ourselves to Jesus on the Cross makes our suffering redemptive for others is indeed a mystery of our faith, but the fact that it *does* is one of the great consolations of our faith, for what makes suffering unbearable is the belief that it has no purpose.

*Questions.* Our faith proclaims that if we offer our suffering to God in faith, it has eternal value. Do you ever feel that what you do in life has no lasting value? What helps you retain your faith vision that every act of love that you do has eternal significance?

3. One evening during community recreation, one of the nuns needed assistance in bringing a Christmas tree through the convent gate. The subprioress said that either Thérèse or the sister sitting next to her could go. Thérèse wanted to leave this "not too gay" (S. 345) recreation, but she noticed that the sister sitting next to her had a greater need to depart. In consequence, Thérèse deliberately took her time in untying her apron in order to give the other sister the opportunity to get up first and assist the extern. When the nun who had asked for assistance noticed Thérèse's behavior, she interpreted it as reluctance to help. "Ah! I thought as much, that you were not going to gain this pearl for your crown, you were going too slowly." As a result of this remark, "the whole community believed I had acted through selfishness" (S. 345).

This was a painful experience for Thérèse to bear, but it bore good fruit. It taught her how easy it is to misjudge the motives of others and to misconstrue even the best and purest motives of our neighbor. This incident also made Thérèse "indulgent toward the weaknesses of others," and "charitable in [her] thoughts toward others at all times" (S. 345).

If we interpret Thérèse's words about being "indulgent toward the weaknesses of others" within its original context, then Thérèse is saying that we should not be too harsh in our judgments even toward those who misjudge us, for it is a common weakness of human nature. Thérèse's words may be applied to any situation in life where we tend to be harsh in our judgments regarding the weaknesses of others.

*Questions.* In the literature of the Desert we find the following story. "Some elders came to see Abba Poimen to ask him, 'if we see some brothers dozing in the congregation, do you want us to reprove them so that they stay awake?' He said to them, 'For my part, when I see a brother dozing, I lay his head on my lap and let him rest.'" [12] Where in your life is God asking you to gently lay on the lap of your thoughts the weaknesses of your neighbor?

4. Toward the end of Dante's *Paradiso,* Beatrice and Dante are about to ascend into the realm of God, but in order for Dante to endure the beatific vision, his eyes need to be purified. To accomplish this task, Beatrice directs Dante to look back upon his journey and gaze down upon the earth. "My eyes went back through the seven spheres below,/and I saw this globe, so small, so lost in space,/I had to smile at such a sorry show/ I saw that dusty little threshing ground that makes us ravenous for our mad sins." [13] And as Dante looks down upon the earth and smiles at all the vain pursuits that drive us mad and the daily squabbles that keep us stirred up in constant agitation, he begins to ascend into heaven with Beatrice.

Perhaps one of the truths that Dante is trying to convey to us in this passage is that we can only ascend into the joy of God when we *lighten up;* when we can look down and smile upon our foolishness. Chesterton once said that the devil cannot laugh at himself and that he fell from heaven because of his *gravity* and that angels can fly because they *take themselves lightly.*

Dante's image mirrors Thérèse's experience. As she looked back over her life from the distance of years, she could laugh at herself for having made mountains out of molehills. "Alas! when I think of the time of novitiate I see how imperfect I was. I made so much fuss over such little things that it makes me laugh now" (S. 348).

*Questions.* Is there anyone of us who cannot identify with this? What are the things in the present that you are making a big fuss over, which in the *future* you will look back upon and laugh? What can you do to *lighten up* and start laughing *now?*

5. When Elizabeth Dickens, the mother of Charles Dickens, read her son's novel *Nicholas Nickleby,* she couldn't believe that it was possible that anyone could be so silly, scatterbrained, and garrulous as Mrs Nickleby. Little did Mrs. Dickens realize that her son had based the character of Mrs. Nickleby upon herself. Such was the case with Sr. Teresa of St. Augustine. Even after she read *Story of a Soul,* she did not recognize herself as the nun whom Thérèse had a natural antipathy toward. She remained in this state of blindness most of her life. It was only a month before she died on June 9, 1929 that she learned the truth – she was the nun toward whom Thérèse had felt a natural antipathy.

*Questions.* All of us are blind. Have you ever had an experience similar to that of Sr. Teresa of St. Augustine when she became aware of how her behavior was affecting others? If so, even though the self knowledge that you gained from the revelation was painful was it ultimately beneficial to your personal growth?

## Notes

1. O'Mahony, ibid., 34.
2. Ibid., 34-5.
3. Godefroy Madelaine O. Praem preached the annual retreat of Lisieux Carmel in 1890, 1892 and 1896. He was very instrumental in editing and publishing *Story of a Soul.* A month after Thérèse died, Mother Gonzague asked Madelaine if he would read over the autobiographical writings of Thérèse and give his opinion of them. Madelaine was impressed by what he had read and was convinced that the manuscript should be published. He obtained permission for its publication from the Bishop of Bayeux (Flavien Hugonin, the same bishop who had received Thérèse and her father in 1887 and who had presided at the reception of her habit in 1889) but only after he convinced the bishop that the manuscript was not the product of "the female imagination." "What happened was this," testified Madelaine, "When the bishop heard of a manuscript by Sister Thérèse, his first reaction was one of distrust of the female imagination. But I was able to assure him in all conscience that I had studied the matter carefully and that I had been forced, ...to recognize that this whole manuscript bore evident marks of the Spirit of God, and that I had been unable to find any doctrinal error in it. On the strength of this testimony, the bishop granted his *imprimatur."* (O'Mahony, 273-4).
4. Emmanuel Renault, O.C.D., "Thérèse in the Night of Faith," in *Saint Thérèse of Lisieux: Her Life, Times, and Teaching,* ed. Conrad De Meester, O.C.D. (Wash-ington, D.C.: ICS Publications, 1997), 22&78.
5. Shortly before Thérèse died, Sr. Marie of St. Joseph placed

a violet on the window sill next to Thérèse's bed as a sign of her love. The day after Thérèse died, Sr. Marie smelled the scent of violets in her room. As she remembered the violet that she had placed on Thérèse's window sill two weeks before, she realized that the scent was a gift from Thérèse. In 1909, when she was fifty-five years old, after spending twenty-eight years in religious life, Sr. Marie of St. Joseph left Lisieux Carmel because her mental condition had deteriorated. She died in 1936 at the age of seventy eight after wandering aimlessly throughout the whole of France. However, she kept in touch with Lisieux Carmel. In 1929, she wrote the following to Pauline (Mother Agnes). "The work of sanctification which my beloved Thérèse began so lovingly in me before she died still continues. And I can say in all sincerity that 'my house is at rest.' And I live now in complete abandonment. As long as I love Jesus, and He and Thérèse are pleased, nothing else matters to me."

When Sr.Marie left Lisieux Carmel, there was something that she did not leave behind – the poem that Thérèse had written for her *(The Eternal Canticle Sung Even in Exile)*. In the years that followed her departure, the word *Exile* proved to have symbolic significance far beyond what Thérèse had ever intended. I like to think that during her wanderings, the poem was like manna in the desert for Sr.Marie, that it was one of the means through which Thérèse's love continued to be Sr. Marie's daily bread. But beyond the sacrament of the poem, Thérèse's interceding presence continued to be with Sr. Marie until her death in 1936, at the age of 78.

6. O'Mahony, ibid., 94.
7. Ibid., 51.

8. The nun to whom Thérèse is referring in this letter is Sr. Saint Vincent de Paul. She was of a practical nature and had no patience for Thérèse who was very clumsy and slow in doing any type of manual labor. Sr. Saint Vincent de Paul nicknamed Thérèse "the big clumsy goat" and often gave voice to her feelings: "Look at her; she is in no hurry; when will she ever start the washing; she's good for nothing." Once, after Thérèse was fitted for a pair of sandals by Sr. St. Vincent de Paul, Thérèse wrote to Pauline. "This morning, I had trouble with Sister St. Vincent de Paul; I went away with a heavy heart"(L. 503). But in spite of Sr. Vincent de Paul's gruffness, she had a good heart, edified the community by long hours before the Blessed Sacrament, and did not hesitate to give voice to the extraordinary virtue that she saw in Thérèse.

9. St.Teresa of Avila, "The Way of Perfection" in *The Collected Works of St. Teresa of Avila,* vol. 2, trans. Otilio Rodriguez, O.C.D. and Kieran Kavanaugh, O.C.D. (Washington, D.C.: ICS Publications, 1980), chapter 38, 187.

10. C. S. Lewis, *The Screwtape Letters,* (New York: The Macmillian Company, 1961), Letter 8, 39.

11. The story of Paulinus is found in Bede's *The Ecclesiastical History of the English People* quoted here from *A New Catechism: Catholic Faith for Adults with Supplement,* trans. Kevin Smyth (New York: Seabury Press, 1969), 3.

12. Oliver Clément, *The Roots of Christian Mysticism,* trans. Theodore Berkeley, O.C.S.O. and Jeremy Hum-merstone, (Hyde Park, N.Y.: New City Press, 1995), 147-8.

13. Dante, *The Paradiso,* trans. John Ciardi, (New York: New

American Library, 1970), canto 22, lines 133-35 & 152-3, pp. 250-251.

# Chapter XI

# *THOSE WHOM YOU HAVE GIVEN ME (1896–1897)*

Novices and Spiritual Brothers
God's Instruments
The Little Brush
Power of Prayer and Sacrifice
Sister St. Pierre
Two Missionaries
"Draw me, we shall run"
End of Manuscript C

J esus granted your child, dear Mother, the grace of penetrating into the mysterious depths of charity. If she could express what she understands, you would hear a [15] heavenly melody; but, unfortunately, I can have you listen to nothing but the stammerings of a little child. Unless the words of Jesus were serving me as a support, I would be tempted to ask your permission to lay aside my pen. But, no, I must continue through obedience what I have begun through obedience.

[20] Dear Mother, I was writing yesterday that since earthly goods do not belong to me, I should find no difficulty in never reclaiming them when they are sometimes taken away from me. The goods of heaven don't belong to me either; they are *lent* to me by God, who can [19r°] withdraw them without my having a right to complain. However, the goods which come directly from God, inspirations of the mind and heart, profound thoughts, all this forms a richness to which we are attached as to a proper good which no one has a [5] right to touch. For example, if on a free day I tell a Sister about some light received during prayer and shortly afterward this same Sister, speak-

ing to another, tells her what I confided to her as though it were her own thought, it seems as though she were taking what does not belong to her. Or else if during recreation one Sister whispers [10] to her companion something that is very witty and to the point, if her companion repeats it aloud without making known its source, this appears again as a theft from the owner who doesn't claim it, but would like to do so and will seize the first opportunity to make it known that her thoughts have been borrowed.

[15]Mother, I would not be able to explain these sad sentiments of nature if I had not felt them in my own heart, and I would like to entertain the sweet illusion that they visited only my heart, but you commanded me to listen to the temptations of your dear little novices. I learned very much when carrying out the mission you [20] entrusted to me; above all I was forced to practice what I was teaching to others. And so now I can say that Jesus has given me the grace of not being any more attached to the goods of the mind and heart than to those of earth. If it happens that I think or say something [19v°] that is pleasing to my Sisters, I find it very natural that they take it as a good that belongs to them. This thought belongs to the Holy Spirit and not to me since St. Paul says we cannot, without the Spirit of Love, give the name of *"Father"* to our Father in [5]heaven.[312] He is therefore free to use me to give a good thought to a soul; and if I think this inspiration belongs to me, I would be like "the donkey carrying the relics"[313] who believed the reverence paid to the saints was being directed to him.

I do not hold in contempt beautiful thoughts which nourish the soul and [10] unite it with God; but for a long time I have understood that we must not depend on them and even make perfection consist in

---

[312] Romans 8:15.

[313] La Fontaine, Fables, Book 5, 14.

receiving many spiritual lights. The most beautiful thoughts are nothing without good works. It is true that others can draw profit from them if they humble themselves and show their gratitude to God for [15]permitting them to share in the banquet of a soul whom He is pleased to enrich with His graces. But if this soul takes delight in her *beautiful thoughts* and says the prayer of the Pharisee, she is like a person dying of hunger at a well-filled table where all his guests are enjoying abundant food and [20]at times cast a look of envy upon the person possessing so many good things. Ah! how true it is that God alone knows human hearts and that creatures are terribly narrow in their thoughts! When they see a soul more enlightened than others, immediately [20r°] they conclude that Jesus loves them less than this soul, and that they cannot be called to the same perfection. Since when has the Lord *no longer the right* to make use of one of His creatures to dispense necessary nourishment to souls whom He loves? The Lord, even at the [5]time of the Pharaohs, had this right, for in Scripture He says to this monarch: *"And therefore have I raised you, that I may show* MY POWER *in you, and my name may be spoken of throughout all the earth."*[314] Century has followed on century since the Most High has spoken those words, and since then His conduct has undergone no [10] change, for He is always using His creatures as instruments to carry on His work in souls.

If a piece of canvas painted on by an artist could think and speak, it certainly would not complain at being constantly touched and retouched by the *brush,* and would not envy the lot of that instrument, [15]for it would realize it was not to the brush but to the artist using it that it owed the beauty with which it was clothed. The brush, too, would not be able to boast of the masterpiece produced with it, as it

---

[314] Exodus 9:16.

knows that artists are not at a loss; they play with difficulties, and are pleased to choose at times weak and defective instruments.

[20] My dear Mother, I am a little brush that Jesus has chosen in order to paint His own image in the souls you entrusted to my care. An artist doesn't use only one brush, but needs at least two; the first is the more useful and with it he applies the general tints [20v°] and covers the canvas entirely in a very short time; the other, the smaller one, he uses for details.

Mother, you are the precious brush that the hand of Jesus lovingly holds when He wishes to do a *great*[5] *work* in the souls of your children, and I am the *very small brush* He deigns to use afterward for the smallest details. The first time Jesus used His little brush was around December 8, 1892. I always recall this epoch as a time of graces, and I am going to confide[10] these memories to you, dear Mother.

At the age of fifteen, when I had the happiness of entering Carmel, I found a companion in the novitiate[315] who had preceded me by several months; she was my senior in age by eight years, but her childlike character made one forget the difference in years, and very soon, Mother, [15]you had the joy of seeing your two little postulants understanding each other marvelously and becoming inseparable companions. In order to foster this growing affection which should bring forth fruit, you permitted us to hold little spiritual conferences together from time to time. My dear little companion charmed me by her innocence and her [20] frank disposition, but she surprised me when I saw how much her affection for you differed from my own. Besides, there were many things in her conduct toward the Sisters that I would have liked to see her change. At this time, God made me [21r°] under-

---

[315] Sister Martha of Jesus entered the novitiate December 23, 1887, as a lay sister.

stand that there are souls for whom His mercy never tires of waiting and to whom He grants His light only by degrees; so I was careful not to advance His hour and waited patiently till it pleased Jesus to have this hour come.

[5]Reflecting one day on the permission you had granted us of conversing together as our Holy Constitutions say for the purpose *"of inciting one another to a greater love of our Spouse,"* I was thinking regretfully that our conversations were not attaining their desired purpose. God made me feel that the moment had come and I [10] must no longer fear to speak out or else end these interviews which resembled those of two worldly friends. This was on a Saturday; the next day, during my thanksgiving, I begged God to place sweet and convincing words in my mouth, or rather that He speak through me. Jesus answered my prayer; He permitted that the result [15]totally surpass my expectation, for: *"Those who turn their eyes toward him shall be enlightened."* Ps. XXXIII.[316] And again: *"To the upright of heart a light has risen in the darkness."*[317] The first statement is addressed to me; the second, to my companion who was truly upright of heart.

[20]The hour we decided on for coming together arrived; the poor little Sister, casting a look at me, saw immediately that I was no longer the same; she sat down beside me, blushing, and I, placing her head upon my heart, told her with tears in my [21v°] voice *everything I was thinking about her,* but I did this with such tender expressions and showed her such a great affection that very soon her tears were mingled with mine. She acknowledged with great humility that what I was saying was true, and she promised to commence a new [5]life, asking me as a favor always to let her know her faults. When the time came

---

[316] Psalm 33:6.

[317] Psalm 111:4.

for us to separate, our affection had become totally spiritual with nothing human in it. And in us was realized this passage from Scripture: *"A brother who is helped by a brother is like a strong city."*[318]

[10] What Jesus effected with His little brush would have been very soon erased had He not acted through you, dear Mother, to accomplish His work in the soul He wanted for Himself. The trial seemed very bitter to my poor companion, but your own firmness triumphed. I was able to console [15]her whom you had given me as a sister among the rest and to explain in what love really consisted. I pointed out to her that it was *herself* she was loving, not you. I told her, too, how I loved you and the sacrifices I was obliged to make at the commencement of my religious life in order not to become attached to you in a [20] physical way as a dog is attached to its master. Love is nourished only by sacrifices, and the more a soul refuses natural satisfactions, the stronger and more disinterested becomes her tenderness.

I remember when I was still a postulant that I had such violent [22r°] temptations to satisfy myself and to find a few crumbs of pleasure that I was obliged to walk rapidly by your door[319] and to cling firmly to the banister of the staircase in order not to turn back. There came into my mind a crowd of permissions to seek; in a word, [5] dear Mother, I found a thousand reasons for pleasing my nature. How happy I am now for having deprived myself from the very beginning of my religious life! I already enjoy the reward promised to those who fight courageously. I no longer feel the necessity of refusing all [10]human consolations, for my soul is strengthened by Him whom I wanted to love uniquely. I can see with joy that in loving Him the heart

---

[318] Proverbs 18:19.

[319] The door to the Prioress's office. It was the first cell at the entrance to the dormitory. Thérèse's cell was three doors down.

expands and can give to those who are dear to it incomparably more tenderness than if it had concentrated upon one egotistical and unfruitful love.

[15]I have recalled to you, dear Mother, the first work Jesus and you saw fit to accomplish through me. This was the prelude of those which were to be confided to me. When I was given the office of entering into the sanctuary of souls,[320] I saw immediately that the task was beyond my strength. I threw myself into the arms of [20]God as a little child and, hiding my face in His hair, I said: "Lord, I am too little to nourish Your children; if You wish to give through me what is suitable for each, fill my little hand and without leaving Your arms or turning my head, [22v°] I shall give Your treasures to the soul who will come and ask for nourishment. If she finds it according to her taste, I shall know it is not to me but to You she owes it; on the contrary, if she complains and finds bitter what I present, my peace [5]will not be disturbed, and I shall try to convince her this nourishment comes from You and be very careful not to seek any other for her."

Mother, from the moment I understood that it was impossible for me to do anything by myself, the task you imposed upon me no longer appeared difficult. I felt that the only thing necessary [10] was to unite myself more and more to Jesus and that *"all things will be given to you besides."*[321] In fact, never was my hope mistaken, for God saw fit

---

[320] From 1893 to 1896, Thérèse watched over her companions in the novitiate as "senior" and "angel" (this term designates the religious charged with helping a postulant to adapt to conventual life), especially after the entrance of Sr. Marie of the Trinity (June 16, 1894) and Sr. Geneviève (September 14, 1894). From March, 1896, she became Novice Mistress without the title.

[321] Matthew 6:33.

to fill my little hand as many times as it was necessary for nourishing the soul of my Sisters. I admit, dear Mother, that if I had [15]depended in the least on my own strength, I would very soon have had to give up. *From a distance* it appears all roses *to do good to souls,* making them love God more and molding them according to one's personal views and ideas. *At close range* it is totally the contrary, the roses disappear; one feels that to do [20]good is as impossible without God's help as to make the sun shine at night. One feels it is absolutely necessary to forget one's likings, one's personal conceptions, and to guide souls along the road which Jesus has traced out for them without trying to make them walk [23r°] one's own way. But this is still not the most difficult thing; what cost me more than anything else was to observe the faults and lightest imperfections and to wage a war to the death on these. I was going to say: unhappily for me! (but this would be cowardly), and [5] so I say: happily for my Sisters, since the time I took my place in the arms of Jesus, I am like the watchman observing the enemy from the highest turret of a strong castle. Nothing escapes my eyes; I am frequently astonished at seeing so clearly, and I find the Prophet Jonah very excusable when taking to flight rather than announcing the ruin of Niniveh. [10]I would prefer a thousand times to receive reproofs than to give them to others; however, I feel it is necessary that this be a suffering for me, for, when we act according to nature, it is impossible for the soul being corrected to understand her faults; she sees only one thing: the Sister charged with directing me is angry, and all the blame is put on me [15] who am filled with the best intentions.

I know very well that your little lambs find me severe. If they were to read these lines, they would say that it doesn't seem to be the least bit difficult for me to be running after them, to be speaking severely to them when showing them that their beautiful fleece is soiled, or to be bringing them some [20] light tuft of wool which they allowed to be torn by the thorns along the way. The little lambs can say what they please; in the depths of their hearts they feel that I love them with a real love, that never will I imitate *"the hireling who sees the wolf coming and leaves the sheep and* [23v°] *takes to flight."*[322] I am prepared to lay down my life for them, but my affection is so pure that I don't want them to know it. With the grace of Jesus never have I tried to attract their hearts to me; I understood that my mission was to lead them [5] to God and to make them understand that here on earth you are, Mother, the visible Jesus whom they must love and respect.

I told you, dear Mother, that I had learned very much when I was teaching others. I saw first of all that all souls have very much the same struggles to fight, but they differ so much from each other in other aspects that [10] I have no trouble in understanding what Father Pichon was saying: *"There are really more differences among souls than there are among faces."* It is impossible to act with all in the same manner. With certain souls, I feel I must make myself little, not fearing to humble myself by admitting my own struggles and [15]defects; seeing I have the same weaknesses as they, my little Sisters in their turn admit their faults and rejoice because I understand them *through experience*. With others, on the contrary, I have seen that to do them any good I must be very firm and never go back on a decision once it is made. To abase oneself would not [20]then be humility but weakness. God has given me the grace not to fear the battle; I must do my duty at all costs. I have heard the following on more than one occasion: "If you want to get anything out of me, you will have to win me with sweetness; [24r°] force will get you nothing." I myself know that nobody is a good judge in his own case, and that a child, whom a

---

[322] John 10:12.

doctor wants to perform a painful operation upon, will not fail to utter loud cries and to say that the remedy is worse than the sickness; however, when he is cured a [5]few days later, he is very happy at being able to play and run. It is exactly the same for souls; soon they recognize that a little bit of bitterness is at times preferable to sugar and they don't fear to admit it.

Sometimes I can't help smiling interiorly when I witness the change that takes place from one day to the next; it is like [10] magic almost. A Sister will come and say to me: "You were right yesterday when you were severe; at first, I rebelled, but after I recalled everything, I saw that you were very right. Listen. When I was leaving you, I was thinking I had enough and I said to myself: I am going to find Mother Prioress and tell her that I will go no more with Sister Thérèse of the Child Jesus. But I [15]felt it was the devil who inspired this thought in me, and then it seemed that you were praying for me. I remained calm and the light began to shine, but now you must enlighten me further. This is the reason I came." We quickly begin to talk the matter over; I am very happy to be able to follow the inclination of my heart and [20]not serve up a bitter dish. Yes, but I notice quickly that I must not advance too far, one *word* could destroy the beautiful edifice constructed in tears. If unfortunately I say one word which seems to soften what I said the evening before, I see my little Sister [24v°] taking advantage of the situation; then I say a little prayer interiorly and truth always wins out. Ah! it is prayer, it is sacrifice which give me all my strength; these are the invincible weapons which Jesus has given me. They can touch [5]souls much better than words, as I have very frequently experienced. There is one among them all which made a sweet and profound impression upon me.

It was during Lent, and I was occupied then with the one and only novice[323] who was here and whose angel I was. She came looking for me one morning, her face radiant with joy, and said: "Ah! if you only knew [10] what I dreamt last night. I was with my sister and wanted to detach her from all the vanities she loves so much. To do this I was explaining this stanza of *Vivre d'Amour* ["Living on Love"]:

> Loving you, Jesus, is such a fruitful loss!...
> All my perfumes are yours forever.

"I had a feeling that my words penetrated her soul and I was carried away with joy. [15] This morning when I awoke I thought that God perhaps willed that I give Him this soul. May I write her after Lent to tell her about my dream and tell her that Jesus wants her entirely for Himself?"

Without giving it much thought, I told her she could try to do this, but first she must ask permission from Mother Prioress. [20]As Lent was still far from coming to a close, you were very much surprised, dear Mother, at the request which appeared too premature; and certainly inspired by God, you answered it was not through letters

---

[323] "Sister Marie of the Trinity who received the Habit two months before Sister Geneviève. At this time, there were really four novices in the novitiate and Mother Marie de Gonzague was Novice Mistress, and our little Saint was occupied with these also but not in the same way. That is, not as openly as she was with Sister Marie of the Trinity who had been confided to her especially in order to study her more closely because she had come from another Carmel" (note of Mother Agnes). This incident took place probably in Lent, 1895. Thérèse had just composed the poem *Vivre d'Amour* on February 26, 1895. The quotation is from stanza 13.

Carmelites [25r°] must save souls but through *prayer.*

When I learned of your decision I understood at once it was that of Jesus, and I said to Sister Marie of the Trinity: "We must get to work; let's pray very much. What a joy if we [5]are answered *at the end of Lent!"* Oh! infinite mercy of the Lord, who really wants to answer the prayer of His little children. *At the end of Lent* one more soul was consecrated to Jesus. It was a real miracle, a miracle obtained by the fervor of a humble novice!

How great is the power of *Prayer!* One could call it a [10] Queen who has at each instant free access to the King and who is able to obtain whatever she asks. To be heard it is not necessary to read from a book some beautiful formula composed for the occasion. If this were the case, alas, I would have to be pitied! Outside the *Divine Office* which I am very unworthy to recite, I do not have the courage to force myself to search out *beautiful* prayers in books. There are so many of them it really gives me a headache! and each prayer is more *beautiful* than the others. I cannot recite them all and not knowing which to choose, I do like children who do not know how to read, I say very simply to [20]God what I wish to say, without composing beautiful sentences, and He always understands me. For me, prayer is an aspiration of the heart, it is a simple glance directed to heaven, it is a cry of gratitude and love in the midst of trial as well as joy; finally, it is something [25v°] great, supernatural, which expands my soul and unites me to Jesus.

However, I would not want you to believe, dear Mother, that I recite without devotion the prayers said in common in the choir or the hermitages. On the contrary, I love [5]very much these prayers in common, for Jesus has promised *to be in the midst of those who gather together in His name.*[324] I feel then that the fervor of my Sisters makes

---

[324] Matthew 18:20.

up for my lack of fervor; but when alone (I am ashamed to admit it) the recitation of the rosary is more difficult for me than the wearing of an instrument of penance. I feel I [10] have said this so poorly! I force myself in vain to meditate on the mysteries of the rosary; I don't succeed in fixing my mind on them. For a long time I was desolate about this lack of devotion that astonished me, for I love the Blessed Virgin so much that it should be easy for me to recite in her honor prayers which are so pleasing to her. Now I am [15]less desolate; I think that the Queen of heaven, since she is *my MOTHER,* must see my good will and she is satisfied with it.

Sometimes when my mind is in such a great aridity that it is impossible to draw forth one single thought to unite me with God, I *very slowly* recite an "Our Father" and then [20] the angelic salutation; then these prayers give me great delight; they nourish my soul much more than if I had recited them precipitately a hundred times.

The Blessed Virgin shows me she is not displeased with [26r°] me, for she never fails to protect me as soon as I invoke her. If some disturbance overtakes me, some embarrassment, I turn very quickly to her and as the most tender of Mothers she always takes care of my interests. How many times, when speaking to the [5] novices, has it happened that I invoked her and felt the benefits of her motherly protection!

Often the novices say to me: "You have an answer for everything; I believed I would embarrass you this time. Where do you go to get everything you say?" There are those who are simple enough to believe I can read [10] their soul because it has happened that I anticipated them by saying what they were thinking. One night, one of my companions[325] made a resolution to hide something from me which

---

[325] Sister Martha of Jesus testified to this.

was causing her much suffering. I met her in the morning and there was joy in her face when she was speaking to me. Without responding to what she was saying, I said to her with [15]great conviction: "You are sad about something." If I had made the moon fall at her feet, she could not have looked at me with greater surprise. Her astonishment was so great that it even took hold of me, and for an instant I was seized with a supernatural fright. I was really sure I didn't have the gift of reading souls, and this surprised me all the more [20] because I had been so right. I felt that God was very close, and that, without realizing it, I had spoken words, as does a child, which came not from me but from Him.

Dear Mother, you understand that everything is permitted to the novices; [26v°] that they must be able to say what they think, the good and the bad. This is all the easier with me because they don't owe me the respect one renders a Novice Mistress. I cannot say that Jesus makes me [5]walk the way of humiliations exteriorly. He is content to humble me in the depths of my soul; in the eyes of creatures I succeed in everything. I travel the road of honors insofar as this is possible in religion. I understand that it is not for my sake but for that of others that I must walk [10] this road that appears so dangerous. In fact, if I were to pass in the eyes of the community for a religious filled with faults, incapable, without understanding or judgment, it would be impossible for you, Mother, to have me help you. This is why God has cast a veil over all my interior and [15]exterior faults. At times, this veil draws upon me certain compliments from the novices; I feel that they don't do this through flattery but that it is the expression of their naive sentiments. Truly, this does not inspire vanity in me, for there is always present to my mind the remembrance of what I am. However, sometimes there [20]comes to me a great desire to hear something else besides praises. You know, dear Mother, that I prefer vinegar to sugar;

my soul, too, is tired of too sweet a nourishment, and Jesus permits someone to serve it a good little salad, [27r°] well seasoned with vinegar and spices, nothing is missing except the oil which gives it added flavor. This good little salad is served up to me by the novices at a time when I least expect it. God lifts the veil which hides my imperfections, and then my [5]dear little Sisters, seeing me just as I am, no longer find me according to their taste. With a simplicity which delights me, they tell me all the struggles I give them, what displeases them in me; finally, they are under no restraint any more than if they were talking about another person, for they know they give me [10] pleasure when acting in this way. Ah! truly, it is more than pleasure, it is a delightful banquet which fills my soul with joy. I cannot explain how a thing which is so displeasing to nature can cause such a great happiness; if I had not experienced it, I could not believe it. One day when I particularly [15]desired to be humiliated, a novice[326] took it upon herself to satisfy me and she did it so well that I was immediately reminded of Shimei cursing David.[327] I said to myself: Yes, it is the Lord who has commanded her to say all these things to me. And my soul enjoyed the bitter food served up to it in such abundance.

[20]This is the way God sees fit to take care of me. He cannot always be giving me the strengthening bread of exterior humiliation, but from time to time He allows *me to be fed the crumbs which fall from the table OF HIS CHILDREN.*[328] Ah! how great is His mercy; I shall be able to [27v°] sing of it only in heaven.

Dear Mother, since it is with you that I am trying to begin to sing about this infinite mercy here on earth, I must tell you about a great

---

[326] This was her own sister, Céline (Sister Geneviève).

[327] 2 Samuel 16:10.

[328] Mark 7:28.

benefit I drew from the mission you [5] confided to me. Formerly, when I saw a Sister doing something which displeased me and appeared to be against the Rule, I said to myself: Ah! if I could only tell her what I think and show her she is wrong, how much good this would do me! Ever since I have practiced a little the trade of correcting, I assure you, dear Mother, that I have entirely changed my attitude. When [10] it happens that I see a Sister perform an action which appears imperfect to me, I heave a sigh of relief and say: How fortunate! this is not a novice; I am not obliged to correct her. I then very quickly take care to excuse the Sister and to give her the good intentions she undoubtedly has.

Ah! Mother, ever since I got sick, the cares [15]you bestowed on me taught me a great deal about charity. No remedy appeared too expensive to you, and when it did not succeed you tried another thing without tiring. When I was going to recreation, what attention you paid in order to shelter me from drafts! Finally, if I wanted to tell all, I would never end.

[20] When thinking over all these things, I told myself that I should be as compassionate toward the spiritual infirmities of my Sisters as you are, dear Mother, when caring for me with so much love.

I have noticed (and this is very natural) that the most saintly Sisters are the [28r°] most loved. We seek their company; we render them services without their asking; finally, these souls so capable of bearing with the lack of respect and consideration of others see themselves surrounded with everyone's affection. We may apply to them these words of our Father St. John of the Cross: "All goods [5]were given to me when I no longer sought them through self-love."[329]

On the other hand, imperfect souls are not sought out. No doubt

---

[329] This maxim appears in the "Sketch of Mount Carmel" drawn by St. John of the Cross, Collected Works, pp. 110-111.

we remain within the limits of religious politeness in their regard, but we generally avoid them, fearing lest we say something which isn't too amiable. When I speak of imperfect souls, I don't want to [10]speak of spiritual imperfections since the most holy souls will be perfect only in heaven; but I want to speak of a lack of judgment, good manners, touchiness in certain characters; all these things which don't make life very agreeable. I know very well that these moral infirmities are chronic, that there is no hope of a cure, but I also know that my Mother [15]would not cease to take care of me, to try to console me, if I remained sick all my life. This is the conclusion I draw from this: I must seek out in recreation, on free days, the company of Sisters who are the least agreeable to me in order to carry out with regard to these wounded souls the office of the good Samaritan. A word, an amiable smile, often suffice to make a sad soul bloom; but it is [20]not principally to attain this end that I wish to practice charity, for I know I would soon become discouraged: a word I shall say with the best intention will perhaps be interpreted wrongly. Also, not to waste my time, I want to be friendly with everybody [28v°] (and especially with the least amiable Sisters) to give joy to Jesus and respond to the counsel He gives in the Gospel in almost these words:

*"When you give a dinner or a supper do not invite your friends, or your brethren, or your relatives, or your rich neighbors, lest perhaps they also invite you in return, and* [5]*a recompense be made to you. But when you give a feast, invite the poor, the crippled, the lame, the blind; and blessed shall you be, because they have nothing to repay you with,*[330] *and your Father who sees in secret will reward you."*[331]

What banquet could a Carmelite offer her Sisters except a spiri-

---

[330] Luke 14:12-14.

[331] Matthew 6:4.

tual banquet of loving and joyful charity? As far as [10] I am concerned, I know no other and I want to imitate St. Paul who *rejoiced with those who rejoice;*[332] it is true he wept with the afflicted and tears must sometimes appear in the feast I wish to serve, but I shall always try *to change these tears into joy,*[333] since the Lord *loves* [15]*a cheerful giver.*[334]

I remember an act of charity God inspired me to perform while I was still a novice. It was only a very small thing, but *our Father who sees in secret* and who looks more upon the intention than upon the greatness of the act *has already* rewarded me without my having to wait for the next life. [20] It was at the time Sister St. Pierre was still going to the choir and the refectory. She was placed in front of me during evening prayer. At ten minutes to six a Sister had to get up and lead her to the refectory, for the infirmarians had too many patients and were unable [29r°] to attend to her. It cost me very much to offer myself for this little service because I knew it was not easy to please Sister St. Pierre. She was suffering very much and she did not like it when her helpers were changed. However, I did not want to lose such a [5] beautiful opportunity for exercising charity, remembering the words of Jesus: *"Whatever you do to the least of my brothers, you do to me."*[335] I offered myself very humbly to lead her, and it was with a great deal of trouble that I succeeded in having my services accepted! I finally set to work and had so much good will that I succeeded perfectly.

[10] Each evening when I saw Sister St. Pierre shake her hourglass I knew this meant: Let's go! It is incredible how difficult it was for me

---

[332] Romans 12:15.

[333] John 16:20.

[334] 2 Corinthians 9:7.

[335] Matthew 25:40.

to get up, especially at the beginning; however, I did it immediately, and then a ritual was set in motion. I had to remove and carry her little bench in a certain way, above all I was not to hurry, and then [15] the walk took place. It was a question of following the poor invalid by holding her cincture; I did this with as much gentleness as possible. But if by mistake she took a false step, immediately it appeared to her that I was holding her incorrectly and that she was about to fall. "Ah! my God! You are going too fast; I'm going to break something." If I tried to go more [20]slowly: "Well, come on! I don't feel your hand; you've let me go and I'm going to fall! Ah! I was right when I said you were too young to help me."

Finally, we reached the refectory without mishap; and here other difficulties arose. I had to seat Sister St. Pierre and I had to act skillfully in order [29v°] not to hurt her; then I had to turn back her sleeves (again in a certain way), and afterward I was free to leave. With her poor crippled hands she was trying to manage with her bread as well as she could. I soon noticed this, and, each evening, I did not leave her until after I had rendered [5]her this little service. As she had not asked for this, she was very much touched by my attention, and it was by this means that I gained her entire good graces, and this especially (I learned this later) because, after cutting her bread for her, I gave her my most beautiful smile before leaving her all alone.

[10] Dear Mother, perhaps you are surprised that I write about this little act of charity, performed so long ago. Ah! if I have done so, it is because I feel I must sing of the Lord's mercies because of it. He deigned to leave its memory with me as a perfume which helps me in the practice of charity. I recall [15]at times certain details which are like a springtime breeze for my soul. Here is one which comes to my memory: One winter night I was carrying out my little duty as usual; it was cold, it was night. Suddenly, I heard off in the distance the harmonious

sound of a musical instrument. I then pictured a well-lighted drawing room, [20]brilliantly gilded, filled with elegantly dressed young ladies conversing together and conferring upon each other all sorts of compliments and other worldly remarks. Then my glance fell upon the poor invalid whom I was supporting. Instead of the beautiful strains of music I heard only her occasional complaints, and instead of the rich gildings [30r°] I saw only the bricks of our austere cloister, hardly visible in the faintly glimmering light. I cannot express in words what happened in my soul; what I know is that the Lord illumined it with rays of *truth* which so surpassed the dark brilliance of earthly feasts that I could not [5]believe my happiness. Ah! I would not have exchanged the ten minutes employed in carrying out my humbleoffice of charity to enjoy a thousand years of worldly feasts. If already in suffering and in combat one can enjoy a moment of happiness that surpasses all the joys of this earth, and this when simply considering that God has withdrawn us from this world, what will this happiness be in heaven when one shall see [10] in the midst of eternal joy and everlasting repose the incomparable grace the Lord gave us when He chose us *to dwell in His house,*[336] heaven's real portal?

It wasn't always in such transports of joy that I practiced charity, but at the beginning of my religious life Jesus wanted to [15] have me experience how sweet it is to see Him in the souls of His brides. When I was guiding Sister St. Pierre, I did it with so much love that I could not possibly have done better had I been guiding Jesus Himself. The practice of charity, as I have said, dear Mother, was not always so sweet for me, and to prove it to you [20] I am going to recount certain little struggles which will certainly make you smile. For a long time at evening meditation, I was placed in front of a Sister who had a strange

---

[336] Psalm 22:6.

habit and I think many lights because she rarely used a book during meditation. This is what I [30v°] noticed: as soon as this Sister arrived, she began making a strange little noise which resembled the noise one would make when rubbing two shells, one against the other. I was the only one to notice it because I had extremely sensitive hearing (too [5]much so at times). Mother, it would be impossible for me to tell you how much this little noise wearied me. I had a great desire to turn my head and stare at the culprit who was very certainly unaware of her "click." This would be the only way of enlightening her. However, in the bottom of my heart I felt it was much better to suffer this out of love for [10] God and not to cause the Sister any pain. I remained calm, therefore, and tried to unite myself to God and to forget the little noise. Everything was useless. I felt the perspiration inundate me, and I was obliged simply to make a prayer of suffering; however, while suffering, I searched for a way of doing it [15] without annoyance and with peace and joy, at least in the interior of my soul. I tried to love the little noise which was so displeasing; instead of trying not to hear it (impossible), I paid close attention so as to hear it well, as though it were a delightful concert, and my prayer (which was not the *Prayer of Quiet*) was spent in [20]offering this concert to Jesus.

Another time, I was in the laundry doing the washing in front of a Sister who was throwing dirty water into my face every time she lifted the handkerchiefs to her bench; my first reaction was to draw back and [31r°] wipe my face to show the Sister who was sprinkling me that she would do me a favor to be more careful. But I immediately thought I would be very foolish to refuse these treasures which were being given to me so generously, and I took care not to show my struggle. I put forth all my efforts [5]to desire receiving very much of this dirty water, and was so successful that in the end I had really taken a liking to this kind of aspersion, and I promised myself to return another time to this nice place where one received so many treasures.

My dear Mother, you can see that I am a *very little soul* and that I can offer God only *very little things*. It often happens [10] that I allow these little sacrifices which give such peace to the soul to slip by; this does not discourage me, for I put up with having a little less peace and I try to be more vigilant on another occasion.

Ah! the Lord is so good to me that it is quite impossible for me to fear Him. He has always given me what I desire or rather He [15]has made me desire what He wants to give me; thus a short time before my trial against the faith began, I was saying to myself: Really, I have no great exterior trials and for me to have interior ones God would have to change my way. I do not believe He will do this, and still I cannot always live in repose as I am now; what means, then, will Jesus find [20]to try me? The answer was not long in coming, and it showed me that the One whom I love is not at a loss as to the means He uses. Without changing my way He sent me the trial which was to mingle a salutary bitterness with all my joys. It is not only when He wishes to try me [31v°] that Jesus makes me feel and desire trials. For a very long time, I had a desire which appeared totally unrealizable to me, that of having *a brother as a priest*. I often thought that had my little brothers not flown away to heaven, I would have had the happiness of seeing them mount the altar; [5]but since God chose to make little angels of them, I could not hope to see my dream realized. And yet, not only did Jesus grant me the favor I desired, but He united me in the bonds of the spirit to *two* of His apostles, who became my brothers. I wish to [10] recount in detail, dear Mother, how Jesus answered my desire and even surpassed it, since I wanted only *one* priest as brother to remember me each day at the holy altar.

It was our Holy Mother St. Teresa who sent me my first little brother[337] as a feastday gift in 1895. I was in the laundry, very much occupied by [15]my work, when Mother Agnes of Jesus took me aside and read a letter she had just received. It was from a young seminarian, inspired, he said, by St. Teresa of Avila. He was asking for a Sister who would devote herself especially to the salvation of his soul and aid him through her prayers and sacrifices when he was a missionary so that he [20] could save many souls. He promised to remember the one who would become his sister at the Holy Sacrifice each day after he was ordained. Mother Agnes of Jesus told me she wanted me to become the sister of this future missionary.

[32r°] Mother, it would be impossible for me to express my happiness. My desire, answered in this unexpected way, gave birth in my heart to a joy which I can describe only as that of a child. I would really have to go back to my childhood days to recapture once more the memory of joys so great that the soul [5] is too little to contain them, and not for years had I experienced this kind of happiness. I felt my soul was renewed; it was as if someone had struck for the first time musical strings left forgotten until then.

I understood fully the obligation I was imposing upon myself and I set to work [10]by trying to redouble my fervor. I must admit that at first I had no consolations for stimulating my zeal. After writing one charming letter filled with noble aspirations in which he thanked Mother Agnes of Jesus, my little brother gave no further sign of life until the following July, except that in November he sent a notice

---

[337] Father Maurice Barthélemy-Bellière (1874–1907), an orphan, was at this time a seminarian of the diocese of Bayeux and candidate for the foreign missions. He left for Algiers, where he was to enter the novitiate of the White Fathers, on September 29, 1897, the day before St. Thérèse's death.

[15]saying he had entered the military service. Dear Mother, it was to you that God reserved the completion of the work already begun. No doubt it is through prayer and sacrifice that we can help missionaries, but when it pleases Jesus to join two souls for His glory, He permits them to communicate their [20]thoughts from time to time in order to incite each other to love God more. However, the *express permission* of authority is necessary for this, for it seems to me that this correspondence would do more harm than good, if not to the missionary, then at least to the Carmelite because of her type of life [32v°] which tends to too much self-reflection. Instead of uniting her to God, this exchange of letters (even at long intervals) would occupy her mind, and imagining herself to be doing great marvels, she would be simply procuring useless distraction for herself under the cover of zeal. [5]As for me, it is exactly the same with this matter as with all others, and I feel that if my letters are to do any good they must be written under obedience, and that I should feel repugnance rather than pleasure in writing them. For example, when I interview a novice, I try to do this as a mortification and I refrain from asking questions simply to satisfy my curiosity. If she [10] begins to tell me something interesting and then passes on to something which bores me, without finishing what she was saying, I am very careful not to remind her of the subject she set aside, for it seems to me we can do no good when we seek ourself.

Dear Mother, I notice I shall never correct myself, [15]for here I am once again far from my subject, with all my dissertations; I beg you to excuse me, and permit me to begin on another occasion as I cannot do otherwise. You act like God Himself who does not weary of hearing me even when I tell Him simply my pains and joys as if He did [20]not know them. You, too, dear Mother, you have known for a long time what I am thinking and all the unimportant events of my life; I cannot, then, teach you anything new. I can hardly help laughing when I think of how I scrupulously write down so many things [33r°] you know as well as I. Well, Mother, I am obeying you and if at present you find no interest in reading these pages, perhaps they will distract you in the future and serve to rekindle your fire, and so I will not have lost my time. But I am only joking by speaking [5] like a child; do not believe, Mother, I am trying to discover what use my poor work can have; since I am doing it under obedience, it is enough for me, and if you were to burn it before my eyes without having read it, it would cause me no pain.

It is time to resume the story of my brothers who [10] now hold such a large place in my life. Last year at the end of the month of May,[338] I remember how you called me one day before we went to the refectory. My heart was beating very fast when I entered your cell, dear Mother; I was wondering what you could have to tell me since this was the very first time you called me in this way. After [15]having told me to be seated, you asked me: "Will you take charge of the spiritual interests of a missionary who is to be ordained and leave very soon?"[339] And then, Mother, you read this young priest's letter in order that I might know exactly what he was asking. My first sentiment was one of joy which was immediately replaced by fear. I [20] explained, dear Mother, that having already offered my poor merits for one future apostle, I believed I could not do it for the intentions of another, and that, besides, there were many Sisters better than I who would be able to answer his request. All my objections were useless. You [33v°] told me that one could have several brothers. Then I asked you whether

---

[338] Saturday, May 30, 1896.

[339] Father Adolphe Roulland (1870–1934) was a seminarian at the Foreign Mission Society in Paris. He was ordained June 28, 1896, and left for China August 2, 1896.

obedience could double my merits. You answered that it could, and
you told me several things which made me see that I had to accept a
new brother without any scruples. In the bottom of my heart, Mother,
I was thinking the same way as you, and since *"the zeal of a Carmelite
embraces the whole world,"*[340] I hope with the grace of God to be use-
ful to more than *two*[5] missionaries and I could not forget to pray for
all without casting aside simple priests whose mission at times is as
difficult to carry out as that of apostles preaching to the infidels.
Finally, I want to be a daughter of the Church[341] as our holy Mother St.
Teresa was and to pray for the Holy Father's intentions which I know
embrace [10] the whole universe. This is the general purpose of my life,
but all this would not have prevented me from praying and uniting
myself in a special way to the works of my dear little angels if they
had become priests. Well, then! this is how I am spiritually united to
the apostles whom Jesus has given me as brothers: all that I have, each
of them has, and I know very well that [15]God is too good to make
divisions; He is so rich He can give without any measure everything I
ask Him.... But do not think, Mother, I am going to lose time in a long
enumeration.

꠸   Since I have two brothers and my little Sisters, the novices, if I
wanted to ask for each soul what each one needed and go into detail
about it, the days [20]would not be long enough and I fear I would forget something important. For simple souls there must be no compli-
cated ways; as I am of their number, one morning during my thanksgiving, Jesus gave me a simple means of accomplishing my mission.

He made me [34r°] understand these words of the Canticle of

---

[340] Quote from *The Sacred Banquet of the Ideal of the Perfect
Carmelite,* a retreat composed by M. Jeanne-Marguerite, O.C.D.

[341] "I am a daughter of the Church," St. Teresa said on her deathbed.

Canticles: *"DRAW ME, WE SHALL RUN after you in the odor of your ointments."*[342] O Jesus, it is not even necessary to say: *"When drawing me, draw the souls whom I love!"* This simple statement: "Draw me" suffices; I understand, Lord, that when a soul allows herself to be captivated [5]by *the odor of your ointments,* she cannot run alone, all the souls whom she loves follow in her train; this is done without constraint, without effort, it is a natural consequence of her attraction for You. Just as a torrent, throwing itself with impetuosity into the ocean, drags after it everything it encounters in its passage, in the same way, [10] O Jesus, the soul who plunges into the shoreless ocean of Your Love, draws with her all the treasures she possesses. Lord, You know it, I have no other treasures than the souls it has pleased You to unite to mine; it is You who entrusted these treasures to me, and so I dare to borrow the words You addressed to the heavenly Father, the last night which saw You on [15]our earth as a traveler and a mortal. Jesus, I do not know when my exile will be ended; more than one night will still see me singing Your Mercies in this exile, but for me will finally come the last night, and then I want to be able to say to You, O my God:

*"I have glorified you on earth; I have finished the work you gave me to do. And now do you, Father, glorify me with yourself, with the glory I had with you before the world existed.*

*"I have manifested your name to those whom you* [20] *have given me out of the world. They were yours, and you have given them to me, and they have kept your word. Now they have learned that whatever you have given me is from you; because the words you have given me, I have given to them. And they have received them, and have known of a truth that I came from you, and they have believed that you sent me.*

*"I pray for them, not for the world do I pray, but for those whom*

---

[342] Canticle of Canticles 1:3.

*you have given me, because they are yours; and all things that are*
*mine are yours, and yours are mine; and I am glorified in them.* [34v°]
*And I am no longer in the world, and I am coming to you. Holy Father,*
*keep in your name those whom you have given to me.*

"*But now I am coming to you; and these things I speak in the*
*world, in order that they may have joy made full in themselves. I have*
*given them your word; and the world has hated them, because they are*
*not of the world, even as I am not of the world. I do not* [5] *pray that*
*you take them out of the world, but that you keep them from evil. They*
*are not of the world, even as I am not of the world.*

"*Yet not for these only do I pray, but for those who through their*
*word are to believe in me.*

"*Father, I will that where I am, these also whom you have given*
*me* [10] *may be with me, that they may see my glory which you have*
*given me, because you loved me from the foundation of the world. And*
*I have made known your name to them, and will make it known, that*
*the love with which you loved me may be in them, and I in them.*"[343]

Yes, Lord, this is what I would like to repeat after You before flying into Your arms. Perhaps this is boldness? No, for a long time You
permitted me to be bold with You. You have said to me as the [15]father
of the prodigal son said to his older son: "EVERYTHING *that is mine*
*is yours.*"[344] Your words, O Jesus, are mine, then, and I can make use
of them to draw upon the souls united to me the favors of the heavenly Father. But, Lord, when I say: "I will that where I am, these also
whom you have given me may be with me," I do not mean that [20]these
cannot attain a higher glory than the one You will be pleased to give
me, but I simply ask that we all be one day united in Your beautiful

---

[343] John 17:4 ff.
[344] Luke 15:31.

heaven. You know, O my God, I have never desired anything but to love You, and I am ambitious for no other glory. [35r°] Your Love has gone before me, and it has grown with me, and now it is an abyss whose depths I cannot fathom. Love attracts love, and, my Jesus, my love leaps toward Yours; it would like to fill the abyss which attracts it, but alas! it is not even like a [5]drop of dew lost in the ocean! For me to love You as You love me, I would have to borrow Your own Love, and then only would I be at rest. O my Jesus, it is perhaps an illusion but it seems to me that You cannot fill a soul with more love than the love with which You have filled mine; it is for this reason that I dare to [10] ask You *"to love those whom you have given me with the love with which you loved me."*[345] One day, in heaven if I discover You love them more than me, I shall rejoice at this, recognizing that these souls merit Your Love much more than I do; but here on earth, I cannot conceive a greater immensity of love than the one which it has pleased You [15]to give me freely, *without any merit of my part.*

My dear Mother, I finally return to you; I am very much surprised at what I have just written, for I had no intention of doing so. Since it is written it must remain, but before returning to the story of my brothers, I want to tell you, Mother, that I do not apply to them but [20]to my little Sisters the first words borrowed from the Gospel: *"I have given them the words that you have given to me,"*[346] etc., for I do not believe myself capable of instructing missionaries; happily, I am not as yet proud enough for that! I would not have been capable either [35v°] of giving my Sisters a few counsels, if you, Mother, who represent God to me, had not given me the grace for this.

On the other hand, it is about your spiritual sons who are my

---

[345] John 17:23.

[346] John 17:8.

brothers that I was thinking when I wrote these words of Jesus and those that follow: *"I do not* [5] *pray that you will take them out of the world ... I pray also for those who will believe in you because of their word."*[347] How could I not pray for the souls whom they will save in their distant mission through suffering and preaching?

Mother, I think it is necessary to give a few [10] more explanations on the passage in the Canticle of Canticles: *"Draw me, we shall run,"* for what I wanted to say appears to me little understood. *"No man can come after me, unless the FATHER who sent me draw him,"* Jesus has said.[348] Again, through beautiful parables, and often even without using this means so well known to the people, He teaches us that it is enough to knock and it will be opened, to seek [15]in order to find, and to hold out one's hand humbly to receive what is asked for.[349] He also says that everything we ask the *Father in His name,* He will grant it.[350] No doubt, it is because of this teaching that the Holy Spirit, before Jesus' birth, dictated this prophetic prayer: *"Draw me, we shall run."*

[20]What is it then to ask to be *"Drawn"* if not to be united in an intimate way to the object which captivates our heart? If fire and iron had the use of reason, and if the latter said to the other: "Draw me," would it not prove that it desires to be identified with the fire in such a way that the fire penetrate [36r°] and drink it up with its burning substance and seem to become one with it? Dear Mother, this is my prayer. I ask Jesus to draw me into the flames of His love, to unite me so closely to Him that He live and act in me. I feel that the more the fire of love [5] burns within my heart, the more I shall say: *"Draw me,"* the more also the souls who will approach me (poor little piece of iron,

---

[347] John 17:15, 20.

[348] John 6:44.

[349] Matthew 7:8.

[350] John 16:23.

useless if I withdraw from the divine furnace), the more these souls *will run swiftly in the odor of the ointments of their Beloved,* for a soul that is burning with love cannot remain inactive. No doubt, she will remain at [10] Jesus' feet as did Mary Magdalene, and she will listen to His sweet and burning words. Appearing to do nothing, she will give much more than Martha who torments herself with many things[351] and wants her sister to imitate her. It is not Martha's works that Jesus finds fault with; His divine Mother submitted humbly to these works all through her life since she had to prepare the meals of the Holy Family. [15]It is only the *restlessness* of [352] His ardent hostess that He willed to correct.

All the saints have understood this, and more especially those who filled the world with the light of the Gospel teachings. Was it not in prayer that St. Paul, St. Augustine, St. John of the Cross, St. Thomas Aquinas, St. Francis, St. Dominic, and so many other famous [20]Friends of God have drawn out this divine science which delights the greatest geniuses? A scholar has said: *"Give me a lever and a fulcrum and I will lift the world."* What Archimedes was not able to obtain, for his request was not directed by God and was only made from a material viewpoint, the saints have obtained [36v°] in all its fullness. The Almighty has given them as *fulcrum: HIMSELF ALONE;* as *lever:* PRAYER which burns with a fire of love. And it is in this way that they have *lifted the world*; it is in this way that the saints still militant lift it, and [5]that, until the end of time, the saints to come will lift it.

---

[351] Luke 10:41.

[352] From this word on the text is written in pencil. On July 8, 1897, Thérèse was taken down to the infirmary. She wrote a few more lines, but her weakness was such that she could not complete her manuscript.

Dear Mother, now I would like to tell you what I understand by the *odor of the ointments* of the Beloved. Since Jesus has reascended into heaven, I can follow Him only in the traces He has left; [10] but how luminous these traces are! how perfumed! I have only to cast a glance in the Gospels and immediately I breathe in the perfumes of Jesus' life, and I know on which side to run. I don't hasten to the first place but to the last; rather than advance like the Pharisee, [15]I repeat, filled with confidence, the publican's humble prayer. Most of all I imitate the conduct of Magdalene; her astonishing or rather her loving audacity which charms the Heart of Jesus also attracts my own. Yes, I feel it; even though I had on my conscience all the sins that can be committed, I would go, my heart broken with sorrow, and throw myself into Jesus' arms, for I [20]know how much He loves the prodigal child who returns to Him.[353] It is not because God, in His anticipating Mercy, has preserved my soul from mortal sin that I go to Him [37r°] with confidence and love....

---

[353] "No, there is no one who could frighten me, for I know too well what to believe concerning His Mercy and His Love. I know that this whole multitude of sins would be lost in the twinkling of an eye like a drop of water cast into a burning furnace. In the lives of the desert fathers, it is told how one of them converted a public sinner whose evil deeds were the scandal of the whole country. Touched by grace, the sinful woman followed the Saint into the desert to perform a rigorous penance. On the first night of the journey, before even reaching the place of her retreat, the vehemence of her love and sorrow broke the ties binding her to earth, and at the same moment the holy man saw her soul carried by angels to God's bosom. This is a striking illustration of what I want to say, but the reality itself is beyond the power of words to express" (*Histoire d'une Ame*).

# *Those Whom You Have Given Me*
## Background and Context.

St. Teresa of Avila writes that we should practice poverty of spirit in all things but "most of all in thought."[1] In the opening pages of this final chapter of *Story of a Soul*, we see this deep interior detachment manifested in Thérèse. When another sister passed off Thérèse's spiritual insights as her own, Thérèse said nothing because "Jesus has given me the grace of not being any more attached to the goods of the mind and heart than to those of the earth" (S. 374). The reason Thérèse was able to be detached from her spiritual insights is that she possessed the knowledge that her insights could only nourish her soul if she were detached from them.

One of the fruits of detachment is not having one's behavior determined by the fear of what other people think of us. We see this detachment manifested in Thérèse's confrontation with Sr. Martha (S. 376-378) and her dealings with the novices who often found Thérèse "severe" (S. 380) because she never glossed over the truth, regardless of the cost involved. As Pauline testified, "[Thérèse] was not afraid of being hurt; she corrected fearlessly, whatever the cost to herself...She never tried to be popular with [the novices]... She let the novices say whatever they liked against her."[2]

*Thérèse's Last Days.* At the beginning of July, Thérèse was moved from her cell to the infirmary that was situated on the ground floor of the monastery. Thérèse was so weak that she could no longer hold a pen, so she used a small pencil to write her last letter and the concluding words of *Story of a Soul.*

Thérèse's last letter, dated August 10, 1897, was to

Maurice Bellière, a young seminarian, who had written to Lisieux Carmel in October 1875 requesting that one of the nuns pray that he would persevere in his vocation. Thérèse was assigned to be his "spiritual brother." Over the next for two years, Thérèse's correspondence provided Bellière with counsel and encouragement.[3]

Thérèse's last letter to Bellière is a testament to her belief in the mercy of God. She writes to her disheartened, dispirited brother, who fears that once she is in heaven, she will not be able to look upon him with the same tenderness and mercy with which she had regarded him on earth because then she will be sharing in the justice of God. "I am now already to leave; I have received my passport for heaven... I received *Viaticum* for my *long* journey!...Little Brother, we do not understand heaven in the same way. It seems to you that sharing in the justice, in the holiness of God, I would be unable to as on earth excuse your faults. Are you forgetting, then, that I shall be sharing also in the *infinite mercy* of the Lord? I believe the Blessed have great compassion on our miseries, they remember, being weak and mortal like us, they committed the same faults, sustained the same combats, and their fraternal tenderness becomes greater than it was when they were on earth, and for this reason, they never cease protecting us and praying for us" (L.1173).

It is on this same note of trusting in the infinite mercy of God that Thérèse ends *Story of a Soul.* "Yes, I feel; even though I had on my conscience all the sins that can be committed, I would go, my heart broken with sorrow, and throw myself into Jesus' arms, for I know how much He loves the prodigal child who returns to Him. It is not because God, in His anticipating

Mercy, has preserved my soul from mortal sin that I go to Him with confidence and love..."(S. 404). The manuscript ends in mid-sentence as if Thérèse were saying, there is nothing more that can be said.

How fitting it is that Thérèse's last letter and the last words of her manuscript echo her childlike trust in God's mercy and love. In the opening pages of *Story of a Soul,* Thérèse told us that "Perfection consists in doing His will, in being what He wills us to be"(S. 15). What God wills us to be, is what we are–his children.

## Reflections and Questions.

1. In *The Sketch of Mount Carmel,* St John of the Cross drew two roads that do not lead to the summit of the Mount (union with God). One path is entitled *The Goods of Earth,* which consists of different categories of earthly objects that a soul can become attached to–possessions, joy, knowledge, consolation, rest. The other path entitled *The Goods of Heaven,* consists of various spiritual gifts that a soul can become attached to–glory, joy, knowledge, consolation, rest.

It is John's teaching that all of the goods of earth and heaven are meant to help us on the way to salvation, but they can become obstacles if we relate to them with possessiveness. This is true even of the most spiritual gifts. For example, John tells us that God will often shower a soul with sensible consolations in prayer for the sake of weaning it away from the things of the world. Thus, a consoling experience of God's presence can be beneficial to our spiritual growth, but if a person becomes attached to consolation, then it becomes an obstacle on the path, for the person begins to seek *a consoling expe-*

*rience* and ceases to seek the God who granted the experience; the person is more concerned with receiving a *gift* than serving the *giver* of the gift. As John writes, "Some [people] let themselves be encumbered by the very consolations and favors God bestows on them for the sake of advancing, and they advance not at all."[4]

Thérèse begins chapter eleven with her thoughts on our relationship to the spiritual good of knowledge, "...the goods which come directly from God, inspirations of the mind and heart, profound thoughts..."(S. 373). Thérèse writes that God has given her the grace not to lay claim to spiritual insights that have been granted to her. This grace allowed Thérèse to remain silent when another sister acted "as a thief" by passing off Thérèse's insights as her own.

Put yourself in Thérèse's situation. One day you tell a person a profound insight that you received in prayer. Six months later, you read an article written by this person that contains your insight, and you are not even mentioned in a footnote. How do you feel? Enraged? Betrayed? Hurt? So what should you do in this situation? Should you confront the person about the "theft?" Perhaps, but only if you have discerned that God is asking you to do so. Or maybe God is offering you the grace to be silent for the sake of transformation? Maybe your outrage has nothing to do with the "theft." Maybe it has everything to do with your sense of ownership and your need to be recognized as an insightful person.

The Hindu saint Baba Hari Daas, who had not spoken a single word for over thirty years because of a vow of silence, was once asked what was the most difficult thing about keeping his vow. He said that it was the impulse to intervene in a conversation for the sake of dispelling ignorance. But over time, as his compulsion subsided, it became clear to him that his desire to intervene was rooted in vanity, in his desire to impress others with his wisdom and to be the center of attention. Over time, the clamour of his ego subsided, and his soul experienc- ed profound peace and tranquillity. This is the same tranquillity of spirit that Thérèse received: "the grace of not being any more attached to the goods of the mind and heart than to those of earth" (S. 374).

*Questions.* We can never achieve true peace of mind and heart without quieting the clamour and tumult of our ego. So often, the issues that we are so quick to defend or take offense at too readily are indicative of either a  wounded or inflated ego. The things that drive us crazy about people and the issues that make us see red consume an enormous amount of psychic energy and keep us in a state of constant turmoil and agitation. Choosing to remain silent when we are bristling inside is an important step on the path to peace. The more that something galls us, the greater the peace that will ensue when it is put to rest. There is much wisdom contained in the advice, "Give it a rest," which is often said to us by  family or friends when we are harping upon an issue. Is there something in your life that you need to *"give a rest?"*

2. "I do not hold in contempt beautiful thoughts which nourish the soul and unite it with God; but for a long time I have understood that we must not depend on them and even make perfection consist in receiving many spiritual lights. The most *beautiful thoughts* are nothing without good works. It is

true that others can draw profit from them if they humble themselves and show their gratitude to God for permitting them to share in the banquet of a soul whom He is pleased to enrich with His graces. But if this soul takes delight in her beautiful thoughts and says the prayer of the Pharisee, she is like a person dying of hunger at a well-filled table where all his guests are enjoying abundant food and at times cast a look of envy upon the person possessing so many good things" (S. 375).

In the above passage, Thérèse touches upon a basic law of the spiritual life that goes far beyond the specific example of which she writes, namely, that whenever we feed our ego, we starve our spirit in the process, for it is only the love of God, not the approval and applause of the world, that can nourish our spirits. We might compare the consequences of trying to impress people with our spiritual "wisdom" to ingesting coffee into our system. The immediate effect of drinking coffee is feeling stimulated, but since caffeine depletes our body of B vitamins, we become malnourished in the process, and when the stimulation wears off, we feel drained.

*Questions.* Thérèse's tragic image of a person who is dying of hunger at the very table that he or she has set out before others is akin to the fate of King Midas who almost starved to death because he obtained his wish that everything he touch be turned into gold. Have you ever fulfilled your desire of being the center of attention and felt spiritually empty afterwards?

3. As St. Paul was departing from Ephesus, he said to the Christian community gathered, "I know that as I speak these

words that none of you among whom I went about preaching the kingdom will ever see my face again. Therefore I solemnly declare this day that I take no blame for no man's conscience, I have never shrunk from announcing to you God's design in its entirety" (Acts. 20, 25-27).

It is a sobering, if not frightening fact, that to one degree or another we bear responsibility for the consciences of others, that it is a duty in charity to speak unpopular truths and confront people about their wayward behaviour when God calls us to do so. So often, however, when God calls us to admonish or reprove our neighbour, we shrink back in fear and find refuge in silence.

As novice mistress, Thérèse knew this fear first hand, for she was often called upon to correct a novice about her behavior. She found this difficult because she feared that her novices might judge her to be too severe. Nevertheless, she did not allow her fear to stand in the way of doing her duty. [5] "Nothing escapes my eyes... I would prefer a thousand times to receive reproofs than to give them to others; however, I feel it is necessary that this be a suffering for me, for... I know very well that your little lambs find me severe...[but] in the depths of their hearts they feel that I love them with a real love, that I never will imitate '*the hireling who sees the wolf coming and leaves the sheep and takes to flight*'" (S. 380-381). Is it not true for most of us that we prefer to receive a correction rather than to give one? And does not the fear of what others think make us hesitate to administer a correction? Regardless of our fear, God sometimes calls us to love by speaking to someone about their behavior. "Speak the truth in love," is the guiding principle of fraternal correction. St.Thomas Aquinas writes of fraternal correction under the aegis of charity, which should be administered with prudence, gentleness and discernment. We see these qualities manifested in Thérèse's admonition to Sr. Martha.

Sr. Martha was eight years Thérèse's senior and entered Carmel at the age of twenty-two, four months prior to Thérèse's entrance. Her parents had died when she was young, and she was shuttled around from orphanage to orphanage throughout her childhood and adolescence. In consequence of a lack of parental bonding that resulted from her childhood deprivation, Sr. Martha was emotionally unstable and tended to form intense and erratic relationships. She developed a love/hate relationship with Thérèse; one moment she would serve Thérèse leftovers from the kitchen that no one else would eat, and the next moment she would invite Thérèse to warm herself by the kitchen stove. She both loved and envied Thérèse; she requested to remain in the novitiate in order to benefit from Thérèse's tutelage but was often sarcastic to Thérèse when she offered advice. Sr. Marie's maternal deprivation also sheds light on why she formed an excessive attachment to Mother Gonzague "as a dog is attached to its master" (S. 378). In this chapter (S. 376-378) Thérèse writes of the time that she confronted Sr. Martha about her relationship with Mother Gonzague.

Thérèse, knowing that Sr.Martha was a moody person and one "whom [God] grants His light only by degrees...waited patiently,"(S. 377) for the right moment to speak to her. How difficult it is to wait in such a situation. Personally, when I know that God is asking me to confront someone about his behavior, I am tempted to rush in and do my duty because I cannot stand the anxiety of waiting. But when we "advance the hour"(S. 377), the person whom we are confronting may be less amenable and persuadable to what is being said.

When Thérèse realized that the designated hour had come, she knew that she "must no longer fear to speak out" (S. 377). And Thérèse had good reason to fear, for Pauline told her that if Mother Gonzague ever got wind of what she had said to Sr. Martha, she risked being sent away to another monastery. "Yes I know," said Thérèse. "But since I'm now sure that it's my duty to speak, I cannot let the possible consequences deter me."[6]

And when Thérèse finally did speak to Sr. Martha, she did so in a gentle and non-judgmental manner. "I begged God to place sweet and convincing words in my mouth...and placing her head upon my heart, told her with tears in my voice *everything I was thinking about her,* but I did this with such tender expressions and showed her such a great affection that very soon her tears were mingled with mine" (S. 377). In this incident with Sr. Martha we see Thérèse's *courage* in speaking the truth, her *patience* in waiting for the opportune moment and her *gentleness* in expressing her concern.

There is much to reflect upon here. For Thérèse, fraternal correction was always an act of love. May it be the same with us, for there is always the danger that we can use truth as a blunt instrument, under the guise of "tough love." Honesty and telling the truth are not synonymous; truth is a statement of fact, but honesty is a virtue guided by love. We need to examine our motives before we speak. We need to be sure that we are not using truth in the service of evil. As William Blake writes, "A truth that's told with bad intent/ Beats all the lies you can invent."[7]

    *Questions.* St. Gregory the Great writes that "The word of reproach is the key that unlocks a door because reproach reveals a fault of which the evildoer is often unaware."[8] Do you hold such a key in your hand, and is God asking you to use it for the sake of your neighbor? Conversely, is there someone whom you are strongly tempted to reprove for a wrong reason?[9]

    4. "How great is the power of *Prayer*" (S. 384). One night, two months before she died, Thérèse recounted to Pauline the following incident that underlines the efficacy and apostolic nature of prayer. "Sr. Marie of the Eucharist wanted to light the candles for a procession; she had no matches; however, seeing the little lamp which was burning in the front of the relics [which was in the infirmary where Thérèse was lying], she approached it. Alas, it was half out; there remained only a feeble glimmer on its blackened wick. She succeeded in lighting her candle from it, and with this candle, she lighted those of the whole community. It was, there- fore, the half-extinguished little lamp which had produced all these beautiful flames which, in their turn, could produce an infinity of others and even light the whole universe. Nevertheless, it would always be the little lamp which would be the first cause of all of this light... It is the same with the Communion of Saints. Very often, without our knowing it, the graces and lights that we receive are due to a hidden soul, for God wills that the saints communicate grace to each other through prayer with great love...How often have I thought that I may owe all the graces I've received to the prayers of a person who begged them from God for me, and whom I shall only know in heaven. Yes, a very little spark will

be capable of giving birth to great lights in the Church, like the Doctors and Martyrs, who will undoubtedly be higher in heaven than the spark...In heaven, we shall not meet with indifferent glances, because all the elect will discover that they owe to each other the graces that merited the crown for them" (LC. 99-100).

What an awesome power we possess in prayer as members of the Mystical Body of Christ, even though our prayer be as frail and feeble as a half-extinguished little lamp, even though we are not conscious of the effects that it has upon others. The author of *The Cloud of Unknowing* writes, "Your fellow men are marvellously enriched by [prayer], even if you may not fully understand how; the souls in purgatory are touched, for their suffering is eased by the effects of this work; and, of course, your own spirit is purified and strengthened by this contemplative work more than by all others put together."[10]

As King Arthur lay dying and breathing his last, he turned to his faithful knight Bedivere and bid him pray for his soul.

If thou shouldst never see my face again
Pray for my soul. More things are wrought by prayer
Than this world dreams of. Wherefore, let thy voice
Rise like a fountain for me night and day.
For what are men better than sheep or goats
That nourish a blind life within the brain,
If, knowing God, they lift not hands of prayer
Both for themselves and those who call them friend? [11]

My dear friends, since this is the end of our study guide, I do not wish to close this reflection with a question, as has been our custom, but with a request. As we go our separate ways, let us pray for one another with the belief that prayer is an act of love and that it is love and love alone that helps us on our journey home to God. *Oremus pro invicem*

Marc Foley O.C.D.
November 15, 2003
Commemoration of All Carmelite Souls

## Notes

1. St.Teresa of Avila, "The Way of Perfection," ibid., chapter 3, 8, p. 46.

2. O'Mahony, ibid., 31-32.

3. For an excellent treatment of the correspondence between Thérèse and Bellière see *Maurice and Thérèse: The Story of a Love* by Patrick Ahern.

4. St. John of the Cross, "The Ascent of Mount Carmel" in *The Collected Works of St. John of the Cross*, trans. Kieran Kavanaugh, O.C.D. and Otilio Rodriguez, O.C.D. (Washington, D.C.: ICS Publications, 1991), Prologue, 117.

5. In regard to Thérèse's dealing with her novices, Céline writes, "She assures us that whenever truth was in the balance she feared nothing and would in fact go out to meet the enemy. She gave proof of this one day shortly before her death when, burning with fever and suffering from a tuberculous throat which seemed to be on fire, she summoned up all her strength and vigour in order to admonish a novice who was at fault. Later she said to me, 'You see, I must die with my weapons in hand–and in my mouth'" Geneviève of the Holy Face (Céline Martin), *A Memoir of my sister St.*

*Thérèse*, trans. Carmelite Sisters of New York (New York: P.J. Kenedy & sons, 1959), 5.

6. Quoted from *The Little Way* by Bernard Bro, trans. Alan Neamne, Westminister, Md.: Christian Classics, 1980), 34.

7. William Blake, "Auguries of Innocence," in *The Complete Poems of William Blake*, ed. Alicia Astriker, (New York: Penguin Books, 1988), 508.

8. St. Gregory the Great, *The Pastoral Guide*, part 2, chapter 6. Quoted from *The Liturgy of the Hours, Volume IV*, (New York: Catholic Book Publishing Co., 1975), 343.

9. In *The City of God*, St. Augustine writes the following reasons why we should not engage in fraternal correction. "It is not self interest, but the discretion of charity that makes us spare evil-doers, not rebuking and chiding them on the spot, but waiting to find a more favorable occasion; or again because we fear that it will only make them worse, or cause them to hinder or oppress others who are weak and need instruction in a life of goodness and piety, even to the extent of turning them away from the faith" (Bk. 1, 9).

10. *The Cloud of Unknowing and The Book of Privy Counseling*, ed. William Johnson (Garden City: Doubleday, 1973), 99.

11. Alfred Lord Tennyson, "The Passing of Arthur," in *Idylls of the King*, (New York: Washington Square Press, 1965), lines 414-419, 305.

\*\*\*\*\*\*\*\*\*\*\*\*\*\*\*\*\*\*\*\*\*\*\*\*\*\*\*\*\*\*\*\*\*\*\*\*\*\*\*\*\*\*\*\*\*

In gratitude to my friend Sandra Gettings for her generous assistance and editorial skills that made this book possible

# EPILOGUE

The concluding words of the manuscript are *"...through confidence and love."* Here the pencil which has replaced the clumsy pen falls from Thérèse's hands. The manuscript shows evidence of wavy lines and illustrates the strong will of Thérèse who cannot finish her work. She gives up and still has three months to live.

While reading over these pages that are filled with wisdom and peace, the reader would find it hard to believe that Thérèse has been seriously ill for several weeks. There are scarcely any allusions to the medical care she was receiving; without the notes taken down by Mother Agnes of Jesus while at her sister's bedside, we would have no details concerning the sickness, the last agony, and the death of Sister Thérèse of the Child Jesus and the Holy Face. Thanks to her notes and those of other witnesses, we can follow Thérèse's final hours step by step.

When Thérèse finally gave up writing her manuscript, she was already a few days in the infirmary which was on the ground floor. She had been seriously ill for some months, but she was not declared officially sick until the end of Lent. Up until that time, she was only gradually relieved of her daily duties and permitted to stay away from the choral recitation of the Divine Office and from the periods of recreation in common. In the month of June, 1897, her sole duties were to rest in her cell, to enjoy the fresh air and sunshine in the garden, and to complete the writing of her memories. This last task she was ordered to do by the Prioress at the suggestion of Mother Agnes. She was never to complete this final assignment. When making a reference to it, she laughingly said:

*"I am not breaking my head over the writing of my 'little life.' It is like fishing with a line; I write whatever comes to the end of my pen."*
On July 6, a sudden worsening in her condition brought on a series of hemoptyses which lasted until August 5. After Doctor de Cornière had observed her suffocating spells, her vomiting of blood, and her high fever, he became convinced that she was dying; he stated that in cases such as hers *"only two percent got well."*

When she heard this news, Thérèse was filled with joy. She made her confession to the chaplain and asked him to give her the last anointing, which she desired very much.

In the evening of July 8, she was taken down to the infirmary where she stayed until her death. These quarters were very small. In one corner there was an iron bed closed in by brown curtains to which Thérèse pinned her favorite holy pictures, namely, the Holy Face of Christ, the Blessed Virgin, her "dear little" Théophane Venard, etc. On the same day that Thérèse was brought to the infirmary, the statue of the "Virgin of the Smile" was installed there. Finally, there was an armchair Thérèse used on the few occasions when she could get up. Through the window she could contemplate the garden in full bloom.

On July 9, the Superior of the Carmel decided she was not sick enough to be anointed; and so this was postponed. Thérèse still manifested at times a great deal of vitality and even surprised her sisters with her great cheerfulness. She was living in the constant expectation of the imminent coming of the "Thief," for He is the one who "will break the web of this sweet encounter": this "dying of love" as St. John described it had always been her hope. This is what Thérèse had always wanted. Mother Agnes about this time wrote down the following dialogue:

| Mother Agnes: | "Are you afraid now that death is close?" |
|---|---|
| Thérèse: | *"Ah! less and less!"* |
| Mother Agnes: | "Do you fear the Thief? This time He is at the door!" |
| Thérèse: | *"No. He is not at the door; He has entered.* |
| | *But what are you saying, little Mother? How can I fear one whom I love?"* |

Thérèse never ceased spitting up blood, suffering from her head and her side, and even vomiting the milk prescribed for her by the doctor. During this time her weakness increased considerably.

During the month of July, however, Thérèse still had enough strength to answer the questions of Mother Agnes and her other two sisters; these were questions concerning her childhood; and they also sought her advice. The patient even agreed to the idea of using the notes to compose her obituary notice which was to be sent to the other Carmels. Gradually there was even talk of the eventual publication of her manuscripts on a larger scale. Thérèse confided this work to Mother Agnes and strongly insisted that she complete her unfinished work by the addition of the story of the "sinner who died of love." *"Souls will understand immediately, for this is a striking example of what I am trying to say."* When she referred to her manuscripts, she added: *"There will be something in them for all, except those following extraordinary ways."*

She had a presentiment that her activity after her death would extend far beyond the influence of a book, that it would be worldwide. *"How unhappy I shall be in heaven if I cannot do little favors for those whom I love."* She began to multiply mysterious promises: *"I will return!" "I will come down!"* Then on July 17, she made her now famous prediction: *"I feel that my mission is about to begin, my mission of making others love God as I love Him, my mission of teaching my little way to souls. If God answers my requests, my heaven will be spent on earth up until the end of the world. Yes, I want to spend my heaven in doing good on earth."*

There was a definite worsening of her condition on July 28th. According to her own statement, it was the beginning of *"great sufferings."* The doctor himself was of the opinion she would not last through the night. They went as far as preparing in a room adjoining the infirmary the things necessary for her burial. She was anointed and received Holy Viaticum in the evening.

Contrary to all expectation, including her own, she came through the crisis. These sudden changes in her condition puzzled her greatly. She said to Mother Agnes: *"This evening when you told me I still had a month or so according to Dr. Cornière's opinion, I was absolutely amazed. It is so different from yesterday when he said that I should be anointed that very day! All this, however, leaves me in a deep tranquility. I do not desire to die more than to live; it is what He does that I love."*

In fact, the hemoptyses ceased entirely on August 5, and the patient experienced a short period of relief. Doctor de Cornière went on vacation after having prescribed some remedies on his learning of a lung infection. The calm lasted two weeks. Thérèse was without a doctor when a new attack began on August 15.

She experienced much coughing, difficulties in breathing, pains in her chest, and swollen limbs. She reached a peak in her sufferings between August 22 and 27. Doctor Francis La Néele, Thérèse's cousin through marriage, had to rush from Caen when the Carmel called him. He was the first one to speak about "tuberculosis." This had attacked the intestines. Thérèse was suffering violently at each breath she took, and she felt as though she were stretched out on *"iron spikes."* Then they began talking about the danger of gangrene. *"Well, all the better! While I am at it I may as well suffer very much and all over—and even have several sicknesses at the same time!"* This was Thérèse's comment.

Later on, when she was in a state of exhaustion, she confided to Mother Agnes: *"What would become of me if God did not give me courage? A person does not know what this is unless he experiences it. No, it has to be experienced!"* She even apologized when she cried out with pain: *"What a grace it is to have faith! If I had no faith, I would have inflicted death on myself without hesitating a moment!"*

Then there was a new and unexpected lessening in her suffering in the last days of August. This lasted until September 13. Doctor La Néele said his cousin had only half a lung with which to breathe. She was to live for one more month.

The simple recounting of these sudden changes in Thérèse's condition and her reaction to them cannot possibly bring out the aspects of her personality that her *"last conversations"* and her letters reveal. She wrote her last letter on August 10.

Thérèse was a patient as are other patients; in other words, she was without any lofty thoughts. *"Pray for those who are sick and dying, little sisters. If you only knew what goes on! How little it takes to lose control of oneself! I would not have believed this before."* Someone asked her: "What about your 'little life' now?" She answered: *"My 'little life' is to suffer; that's it!"*

With unaffected cheerfulness, she had a definite *"horror of any pretence whatsoever";* she tried to lessen anything that seemed to overdramatize her condition or anything that would cause her sisters too much pain. There was not the least bit of sadness in the atmosphere of the infirmary. Sister Marie of the Eucharist, Marie Guérin, wrote a note to her parents in which she said: "As far as her morale is concerned, it is always the same: cheerfulness itself. She is always making those who come to visit her laugh. There are times when one would pay to be near her. I believe she will die laughing, she is so happy!"

Thérèse was in possession of a large repertoire that expressed the depth of her character: puns, tricks, mimickings, jokes about herself and the doctor's inability to help. The source of her joy came from her total acceptance of the will of *"Papa, God,"* whom she was about to see face to face. *"Don't be sad at seeing me sick like this, little Mother! You can see how happy God is making me. I am always cheerful and content."*

There existed in this *"sensitive and tender heart"* an exquisite form of consideration for others; she tried to meet each one's needs. She accepted and even begged for a kiss: *"A kiss that makes lots of noise!"* The fraternal charity about which she had written so well in the month of June was now showing the extent of her hidden heroism. The Sisters came to the infirmary purposely to seek her advice or simply to receive a smile from her. Novice Mistress to the end, she was concerned about the tears of Sister Marie of the Trinity and the sadness of her *"Bobonne"* (Sister Geneviève). She even excused the errors of good old Sister Stanislaus, her infirmarian.

Who would have suspected, except for the few who actually knew, that all during this time Thérèse remained constantly *"in the night,"* in that *"underground passage,"* before that impenetrable *"wall."*

The terrible "trial of faith" about which she had spoken to Mother Marie de Gonzague persisted to the very last day of her life. Faced with death, tortured by physical sufferings, Thérèse longed for heaven with all her strength; and yet it appeared "closed" against her! *"It is upon heaven that everything hinges. How strange and incoherent this is!"* Brief confidences made to Mother Agnes came like flashes of lightning: *"Must one love God and the Blessed Virgin so much and still have thoughts like this! But I don't dwell on them."* Through the window she was looking at the garden and could see among the trees *"a black hole."* She said to Mother Agnes: *"I am in a hole just like that, body and soul. Ah! what darkness! However, I am still at peace!"*

Seated alone *"at the table of sinners,"* she was unable to expect external help. The chaplain was frightened by his penitent's temptations against faith: "Don't dwell on them; it is dangerous!" She remained reserved with her sisters regarding these things lest she make them suffer the same torments. Finally she was not even able to depend on the sacraments of the Church. She received Holy Communion for the last time on August 19. "When they bring her Holy Communion, we all enter her room chanting the 'Miserere.' The last time we did this, she was so weak that it got on her nerves just listening to us. She was suffering a martyrdom."

The impossibility, however of receiving Holy Communion did not sadden Thérèse. *"No doubt, it is a great grace to receive the sacraments. When God does not permit it, it is good too! Everything is a grace!"* She offered up her last Communion for an ex-priest, Father Hyacinthe Loyson, a Carmelite. She never kept anything for herself. *"Everything I have, everything I merit, is for the good of the Church and for souls."* In fact, this obsession with sinners and universal salvation was the means of reviving her. She kept up a correspondence with her "spiritual brothers" and even promised them effective help: *"When I shall have arrived at port, I will teach you how to travel, dear little brother of my soul, on the stormy sea of the world: with the surrender and the love of a child who knows his Father loves him and cannot leave him alone in the hour of danger.... The way of simple love and confidence is really made for you."* This she wrote to Father Bellière.

Life in the infirmary had taken on such an ordinary and monotonous appearance that no one could possibly suspect that a saint was dying. Mysterious words from Thérèse, however, occasionally threw a light on the near future: *"Little sisters, you know very well that you are taking care of a little saint!"* And again: *"Gather these [rose] petals, little sisters; they will help you to give pleasure later on. Do not lose one of them!"*

And yet, at the same time, she candidly admits her total poverty. Even when certain dates were suggested as days for her death, Thérèse said: *"Ah! Mother, intuitions! If you only knew how spiritually poor I really am. I know nothing that you yourself don't know! I know only what I see and feel!"*

It was through the grace of God alone that Thérèse had reached this state of absolute surrender to Him. She stated: *"the words of Job: 'Even though he should kill me, yet will I trust him,' always fascinated me in my childhood days. It took me a long time, however, to reach that degree of surrender. Now I have reached it; God has placed me in this degree, for He has taken me up into His arms and placed me there."*

She recognized her own limitations clearly, and she accepted all the humiliations of her state of sickness with its weakness, tears, impatience, especially in the presence of a tiresome Sister. When she was corrected for showing impatience with this Sister, she said: *"Oh! how happy I am to see myself imperfect and to be in need of God's mercy so much even at the moment of my death!"*

She had become perfectly simple: *"Everyone will see that everything comes from God. Any glory that I shall have will be a gratuitous gift from God and will not belong to me. Everybody will see this clearly!"*

After the terrible sufferings at the end of August, the infirmarians brought her bed to the center of the infirmary. Thérèse was able from that position to contemplate the beauty of the garden which was all in bloom. She loved flowers and fruit so much. She was able to see also the material heavens (the other remained closed). She could hear the nuns chanting the Divine Office or sometimes the sound of music coming from a distance. Life seemed to be returning; she was experiencing hunger again. Her Aunt Guérin tried to satisfy her *"desire for all sorts of good things,"* even a chocolate éclair!

On August 30, Thérèse's bed was pushed out to the cloister walk, next to the entrance to the choir which she saw for the last time. Her sister, Sister Geneviève, took advantage of the situation and made a last photo of her sister. In this picture we see Thérèse unpetalling roses over her crucifix, which is always in her hands. She looks emaciated and tries her best to smile.

She celebrated the seventh anniversary of her profession on September 8 and was literally surrounded by flowers. She cried with gratitude: *"This is because of God's goodness toward me. Exteriorly I am surrounded with flowers; but interiorly I am always in my trial; however, I am at peace!"* Out of some flowers she wove a garland for the statue of the "Virgin of the Smile."

The doctor returned from his vacation and was surprised at his patient's condition. A new and final aggravation had appeared after nineteen days of relative calm: the left lung was infected by tuberculosis. Thérèse was suffocating and could speak only by chopping her sentences: *"Mama! earth's air is leaving me.... When will God give me the air of heaven? Ah! my breathing has never been so short!"*

Thérèse reached the end of her way of the cross like a tired traveler staggering at the end of a long journey: *"It is into God's arms that I'm falling!"* She experienced moments of uncertainty as she faced death: *"I am afraid I have feared death. I am not afraid of what happens after death; that is certain! I don't regret giving up my life; but I ask myself: What is this mysterious separation of the soul from the body? It is the first time that I have experienced this, but I abandoned myself immediately to God."*

The agony properly so-called was going to last for two days, but on September 21, Thérèse sighed: *"Ah! what is the agony? It seems I am always in it."*

On Wednesday morning, September 29, Thérèse was breathing with great difficulty. Mother Marie de Gonzague gathered the community, who recited the prayers for the dying for an hour. At noon, Thérèse asked her Prioress: *"Mother is this the agony? ... What should I do to prepare for death? Never will I know how to die!"* After the doctor's visit, she asked: *"Is it today, Mother?"* — "Yes, my child." — *"What happiness if I could die right now!"* And a little later on she asked: *"When am I going to suffocate entirely? ... I can't stand any more! Ah! pray for me! Jesus! Mary! I will it!"*

In the evening, Father Faucon came to hear her confession; when he came out of the infirmary, he was very much moved and said: "What a beautiful soul! She seems to be confirmed in grace!"

Sisters Geneviève and Marie of the Sacred Heart stayed with her that night in spite of her objections. It was a painful night for her. Her three sisters remained with her during the Mass in the morning.

Thérèse pointed to the statue of the Blessed Virgin and said to them: *"Oh! I prayed fervently to her! But it is pure agony; there is no consolation!"*

In the afternoon of Thursday, September 30, Thérèse was able to lift herself up in bed, which she had not been able to do for several weeks: *"See how strong I am today! No, I am not going to die! I still have months, perhaps years!"* According to witnesses, she was then undergoing "the final struggles of the most terrible agony."

Toward 3:00 in the afternoon, seated up in bed, she extended her arms and rested them on Mother Agnes and Sister Geneviève. How could we fail to recall here the words Thérèse spoke regarding the "death of love" she longed for? In June she said: *"Do not be troubled, little sisters, if I suffer very much and if you see in me, as I have already said to you, no sign of joy at the moment of death. Our Lord really died as a Victim of Love, and see what His agony was!"* And in July she said: *"Our Lord died on the Cross in anguish, and yet His was the most beautiful death of love. To die of love does not mean to die in transports. I tell you frankly, it appears to me that this is what I am experiencing."*

Mother Agnes collected the last words of Thérèse and wrote them in a notebook.

*"I no longer believe in death for myself; I believe only in suffering. Well so much the better!"*

*"O my God!"*

*"I love God!"*

*"O my good Blessed Virgin, come to my aid!"*

*"If this is the agony, then what is death?"*

*"Ah! my God. Yes, He is very good; I find He is very good!"*

*"If you but realized what it is to suffocate!"*

*"My God, have pity on me; have pity on your little child. Have pity!"*

To Mother Marie de Gonzague Thérèse said:

*"O Mother, I assure you, the chalice is filled to the brim!"*
*"God is surely not going to abandon me!"*
*"He has never abandoned me before!"*
*"Yes, my God, everything that You will, but have pity on me!"*
*"Little sisters, my little sisters, pray for me!"*
*"My God! My God! You are so good!"*
*"Oh! yes, You are good, I know it."*
*"Yes, it seems I never looked for anything but the truth; I have understood humility of heart. It seems that I am humble."*
*"Everything I have written on my desire for suffering is true!"*
*"I do not regret having surrendered myself to Love."*
*"Oh no! I don't regret it; just the opposite!"*

Mother Agnes relates: "I was alone with her about 4:30 in the afternoon. I thought her end was approaching when I saw a sudden pallor in her face. Mother Prioress returned, and soon the whole community was assembled again around her bed. She smiled at the Sisters; however, she did not say anything until her death. For more than two hours the terrible death rattle tore her chest. Her face was flushed, her hands purple, and her feet were as cold as ice. She was shivering in her limbs. Huge beads of perspiration stood out on her forehead and rolled down her cheeks. It was becoming increasingly difficult for her to breathe. When trying to catch her breath, she uttered little cries."

Thérèse smiled at her sister, Sister Geneviève, who dried her forehead and passed a piece of ice over her parched lips.

When the Angelus bell rang at 6 o'clock, Thérèse looked at the "Virgin of the Smile" for a long time. She was holding her crucifix firmly. As the community had been almost two hours in the infirmary, the Prioress allowed the Sisters to leave.

Thérèse sighed: *"Mother! Isn't this the agony? Am I not going to die?"*

"Yes, my poor child, but God perhaps wills to prolong it for several hours."

*"Well, all right! Ah! I would not want to suffer a shorter length of time."*

Her head fell back on the pillow and was turned toward the right. The Prioress had the infirmary bell rung, and the Sisters quickly returned. "Open all the doors," Mother Marie de Gonzague ordered. Hardly had the community knelt at her bedside when Thérèse pronounced very distinctly, while gazing at her crucifix: *"Oh! I love Him!"* And a moment later: *"My God, I love you!"*

Suddenly her eyes came to life and were fixed on a spot just a little above the statue of the Blessed Virgin. Her face took on the appearance it had when Thérèse enjoyed good health. She seemed to be in ecstasy. This look lasted for the space of a "Credo." Then she closed her eyes and expired. It was 7:20 in the evening.

Her head was leaning to the right. A mysterious smile was on her lips. She appeared very beautiful; and this is evident in the photograph taken by Céline after her sister's death.

According to the custom of the Carmel, Thérèse was laid out in the choir in front of the grille from Friday afternoon until Sunday evening. She was buried in the Lisieux cemetery on October 4, 1897.

While in the infirmary, she had written these lines to Father Bellière on June 9: *"I am not dying; I am entering into life!"*

That marvelous life after death of this unknown Carmelite nun was about to begin.

# APPENDICES

Letter Thérèse Carried on Her Heart
Act of Oblation to Merciful Love
Thérèse's Explanation of Her Coat of Arms
Chronology
**A Letter Sister Thérèse**
**Carried on Her Heart on the Day of Her Profession**
September 8, 1890

O Jesus, my Divine Spouse! May I never lose the second robe of my baptism! Take me before I can commit the slightest voluntary fault. May I never seek nor find anything but Yourself alone. May creatures be nothing for me and may I be nothing for them, but may You, Jesus, be *everything!* May the things of earth never be able to trouble my soul, and may nothing disturb my peace. Jesus, I ask You for nothing but peace, and also love, infinite love without any limits other than Yourself; love which is no longer I but You, my Jesus. Jesus, may I die a martyr for You. Give me martyrdom of heart or of body, or rather give me both. Give me the grace to fulfill my Vows in all their perfection, and make me understand what a real spouse of Yours should be. Never let me be a burden to the community, let nobody be occupied with me, let me be looked upon as one to be trampled underfoot, forgotten like Your little grain of sand, Jesus. May Your will be done in me perfectly, and may I arrive at the place You have prepared for me.

Jesus, allow me to save very many souls; let no soul be lost today; let all the souls in purgatory be saved. Jesus, pardon me if I say anything I should not say. I want only to give You joy and to console You.

## Act of Oblation to Merciful Love

J.M.J.T.

Offering of myself as a Victim of Holocaust to God's Merciful Love

O My God! Most Blessed Trinity, I desire to *Love* You and make You *Loved,* to work for the glory of Holy Church by saving souls on earth and liberating those suffering in purgatory. I desire to accomplish Your will perfectly and to reach the degree of glory You have prepared for me in Your Kingdom. I desire, in a word, to be a saint, but I feel my helplessness and I beg You, O my God! to be Yourself my *Sanctity!*

Since You loved me so much as to give me Your only Son as my Savior and my Spouse, the infinite treasures of His merits are mine. I offer them to You with gladness, begging You to look upon me only in the Face of Jesus and in His heart burning with *Love.*

I offer You, too, all the merits of the saints (in heaven and on earth), their acts of *Love,* and those of the holy angels. Finally, I offer You, *O Blessed Trinity!* the *Love* and merits of the *Blessed Virgin, my dear Mother.* It is to her I abandon my offering, begging her to present it to You. Her Divine Son, my *Beloved* Spouse, told us in the days of His mortal life: *"Whatsoever you ask the Father in my name he will give it to you!"* I am certain, then, that You will grant my desires; I know, O my God! that *the more You want to give, the more You make us desire.* I feel in my heart immense desires and it is with confidence I ask You to come and take possession of my soul. Ah! I cannot receive Holy Communion as often as I desire, but, Lord, are You not *all-powerful?* Remain in me as in a tabernacle and never separate Yourself from Your little victim.

I want to console You for the ingratitude of the wicked, and I beg of You to take away my freedom to displease You. If through weakness I sometimes fall, may Your *Divine Glance* cleanse my soul immediately, consuming all my imperfections like the fire that transforms everything into itself.

I thank You, O my God! for all the graces You have granted me, especially the grace of making me pass through the crucible of suffering. It is with joy I shall contemplate You on the Last Day carrying the scepter of Your Cross. Since You deigned to give me a share in this very precious Cross, I hope in heaven to resemble You and to see shining in my glorified body the sacred stigmata of Your Passion.

After earth's Exile, I hope to go and enjoy You in the Fatherland, but I do not want to lay up merits for heaven. I want to work for Your *Love alone* with the one purpose of pleasing You, consoling Your Sacred Heart, and saving souls who will love You eternally.

In the evening of this life, I shall appear before You with empty hands, for I do not ask You, Lord, to count my works. All our justice is stained in Your eyes. I wish, then, to be clothed in Your own *Justice* and to receive from Your *Love* the eternal possession of *Yourself.* I want no other *Throne,* no other *Crown* but *You,* my *Beloved!*

Time is nothing in Your eyes, and a single day is like a thousand years. You can, then, in one instant prepare me to appear before You.

In order to live in one single act of perfect Love, I OFFER MYSELF AS A VICTIM OF HOLOCAUST TO YOUR MERCIFUL LOVE, asking You to consume me incessantly, allowing the waves of *infinite tenderness* shut up within You to overflow into my soul, and that thus I may become a *martyr* of Your *Love,* O my God!

May this martyrdom, after having prepared me to appear before You, finally cause me to die and may my soul take its flight without any delay into the eternal embrace of *Your Merciful Love.*

I want, O my *Beloved,* at each beat of my heart to renew this offering to You an infinite number of times, until the shadows having disappeared I may be able to tell You of my *Love* in an *Eternal Face to Face!*

Marie-Françoise-Thérèse of the Child Jesus
and the Holy Face, unworthy Carmelite religious

This 9th day of June,
Feast of the Most Holy Trinity,
In the year of grace, 1895.

### Thérèse's Explanation of the Coat of Arms
### She Designed and Placed at the End of Manuscript A

[85v°]

T he blazon JHS is the one Jesus deigned to bring as a dowry to his poor little spouse. The *orphan of Beresina*[1] became *Thérèse of the CHILD JESUS and the HOLY FACE* — these are her titles of nobility, her wealth, and her hope. The vine that divides the shield in two is again [5]the image of Him who deigned to say to us: *"I am the vine and you are the branches, I want you to bear much fruit."*[2] The two branches surrounding the Holy Face and the little Jesus are the image of Thérèse herself who had only one desire: that of offering herself as a little cluster of grapes to refresh the child Jesus, to amuse Him and let herself be pressed by Him according to [10]his whims, as well as to be able to quench the ardent *thirst* He felt during his passion. The harp again represents Thérèse who wanted to sing eternally melodies of love to Jesus.

The blazon FMT is that of Marie-Françoise-Thérèse, the little flower of the Holy Virgin, thus this little flower is represented receiving the beneficial rays of the Gentle Morning Star. The verdant land represents [15]the blessed family in whose heart the little flower grew up; further away is seen a mountain that symbolizes Carmel. On her coat of arms, Thérèse chose this blessed spot to present *the flaming dart* of love that was to merit for her the palm of martyrdom until she could truly shed her blood for *Him whom she loves.* For, in order to respond to all the love of [20]Jesus she would desire to do for Him what He did for her … but Thérèse is aware that she is only a weak *reed*, thus she has put one on her blazon. The luminous triangle represents the Adorable Trinity who never ceases to bestow its inestimable gifts on little Thérèse's soul, thus she will always gratefully remember this motto: *"Love is repaid by Love alone."*[3]

---

[1] M. Martin's affectionate nickname for his "little Queen."

[2] John 15:5.

[3] St. John of the Cross, *Spiritual Canticle,* stanza 9, no. 7, *Collected Works,* p. 506 (see page 195 above). The motto appears beneath the coat of arms, shown on p. ii above.

# CHRONOLOGY

## Alençon

1873　January 2: *Birth of Marie-Françoise-Thérèse Martin, 36 Saint Blaise Street, Alençon.*

January 4: Baptism in the church of Notre-Dame;godmother: her sister, Marie.

March 15 or 16: sent out to be nursed to Rose Taillé, at Semallé (Orne).

1874　April 2: Definitive return of Thérèse to the family.

1875　At this age she thinks: "I will be a religious."

March 29: Voyage to Le Mans.

May 23: Léonie makes her First Communion.

1876　"From the age of three, I began to refuse nothing of what God asked of me."

July 16: First photo: Thérèse is pouting.

1877　April 4: Thérèse's first "letter."

May: She explains to Céline what the word "Almighty" means.

June 18–23: Pilgrimage of Mme. Martin, Marie, Pauline, and Léonie to Lourdes.

*August 28: Mme. Martn dies.*

August 29: Mme. Martin is buried. Thérèse chooses Pauline as second Mother.

## LISIEUX — AT LES BUISSONNETS

1877　November 15: Arrival of Thérèse and her sisters at Lisieux, under care of Uncle Guérin.

November 16: They settle in at Les Buissonnets.

1878　April: Thérèse understands a sermon on the Passion.

|      | August 8: She sees the sea for the first time, at Trouville. |
|------|-------------------------------------------------------------|
| 1879 | Summer (or 1880) Prophetic vision of her father's great trial. |
|      | End of year (or beginning of 1880): First confession. |
| 1880 ti- | May 13: Céline's First Communion, "one of the most beauful days of my life." |
| 1881 | October 3: Enters Benedictine Abbey as a day-boarder. |
| 1882 | October 2: Pauline enters Lisieux Carmel. Thérèse goes back to the Abbey. |
|      | December: Continual headaches, insomnia, pimples. |
| 1883 | March 25 (Easter): While M. Martin, Marie, and Léonie are at Paris, Thérèse gets sick at the Guérins; nervous trembling, hallucinations. |
|      | April 6: Pauline receives the Habit (Sister Agnes of Jesus). Thérèse is well enough to embrace her sister in the visiting room. |
|      | April 7: Relapse at Les Buissonnets. |
|      | May 13 *(Pentecost): Smile of the Virgin, cure of Thérèse.* |
|      | May: Beginning of her spiritual trials regarding her sickness and her vision of the Blessed Virgin. |
|      | Second half of August: Vacation at Alençon, "first entrance into the world." |
|      | August 22: First meeting with Father Pichon at Alençon. |
| 1884 | February to May: Letters of Sister Agnes to prepare Thérèse f or Communion. |
|      | May 5–8: Preparatory retreat. |
|      | May 8: *First Communion of Thérèse at the Abbey.* |
|      | Profession of Sister Agnes of Jesus at Carmel. Quieting of her interior trials for one year. |
|      | May 22 (Ascension): Second Communion, great grace. |
|      | June 14: *Confirmation by Bishop Hugonin, bishop of Bayeux.* |

August: Vacation of Saint-Ouen-le-Pin (Calvados) at her Aunt Guérin's.

1885   May 3–10: Vacation at Deauville (Chalet des Roses); "The donkey and the little pet dog."

May 17–21: Preparatory retreat for renewal.

Commencement of the crisis of scruples, which will last "one year and a half."

May 21: Second solemn Communion.

July: Vacation at Saint-Ouen-le-Pin.

August 22 to October: Voyage of M. Martin to Constantinople.

End of September: Vacation at Trouville with Céline (Villa Rose).

October: Thérèse returns to the Abbey alone, without Céline.

1886   February to March: Headaches; Thérèse leaves the Abbey. Lessons with Mme. Papinau.

Beginning of July: Three days at Trouville (Chalet des Lilas).

Around October 5: Trip of Several days to Alençon, with her father and sisters.

October 7: Entrance of Léonie to the Poor Clares (at Alençon).

October 15: Entrance of Marie to the Lisieux Carmel.

End of October: Thérèse is freed from scruples.

December 1: Return of Léonie to the family.

December 25: *After Midnight Mass,* GRACE OF "CONVERSION" *at Les Buissonnets.*

1887   March 19: Marie receives the Habit (Sister Marie of the Sacred Heart).

May 1: M. Martin has an attack of paralysis.

May: Reading of the Arminjon Conferences.

May 29 (Pentecost): Thérèse receives permission from her father to enter Carmel at age fifteen.

May 31: She is received as Child of Mary at the Abbey.

June 20–26: Vacation at Trouville (Chalet des Lilas).

Spring–summer: Spiritual conferences with Céline in the belvédère of Les Buissonnets.

July: A picture of the Crucified reveals her apostolic vocation.

July 13: Condemnation to death of the assassin Pranzini. Thérèse prays and makes sacrifices for his conversion.

July 16: Entrance of Léonie to Visitation convent at Caen.

September 1: Thérèse reads in *La Croix* the account of Pranzini's execution and his conversion.

October 22: M. Guérin authorizes Thérèse to enter Carmel for Christmas.

October 31: Visit to Bishop Hugonin at Bayeux to solicit the same authorization.

November 4: Departure for Paris with her Father and Céline; then for Rome by way of Milan, Venice, Loreto.

November 20: Audience with Leo XIII. Thérèse presents her petition to the Pope.

December 2: Return to Lisieux (after visiting Naples, Pompeii, Assisi, Florence, Pisa, Genoa, Marseilles, Lyons).

December 28: Favorable answer from Bishop Hugonin to the Prioress to admit Thérèse.

1888    January 1: Bishop Hugonin's answer is transmitted to Thérèse.

March: "One of the most beautiful months of my life."

April 9: *Entrance of Thérèse to the Lisieux Carmel.*

## AT CARMEL

### Postulancy: April 9, 1888—January 10, 1889
### Assignment: Linen room

1888   May 22: Profession of Sister Marie of the Sacred Heart.

May 28: General confession to Father Pichon, freed from trials.

June 23: M. Martin escapes to Le Havre; mental trouble.

August 12: M. Martin has new attack of paralysis at Les Buissonnets.

End of October: Thérèse is approved by the Conventual Chapter to receive the Habit.

October 31: Serious relapse of M. Martin at Le Havre.

1889   January 5–10: Retreat for the reception of the Habit.

January 10: *Reception of the Habit.* Snow. M. Martin's last celebration.

### Novitiate: January 10, 1889—September 24, 1890
### Assignment: Refectory, sweeping of corridors

February 12: M. Martin is hospitalized at Bon Sauveur, Caen.

July: Receives special grace from Blessed Virgin in hermitage of St. Mary Magdalene and under its influence for a whole week.

December 25: End of lease on Les Buissonnets.

1890   During the year she discovers texts on the "Suffering Servant" (Isaiah), and reads the works of St. John of the Cross.

January: Her Profession is delayed.

August 28–September 8: Retreat for Profession; aridity.

September 2: Canonical examination, Blessing of Leo XIII.

*September 8: Profession.*

September 24: She receives the Veil, but her father is not present.

1891    Around February 10: Named aid to sacristan.

April–July: Prays for Fr. Hyacinthe Loyson.

October 8–15: Retreat preached by Fr. Alexis Prou, Franciscan.

December 5: Mother Geneviève dies; was foundress of the Lisieux Carmel.

End of the month: Epidemic of influenza.

1892    May 10: M. Martin returns to Lisieux.

May 12: M. Martin's last visit to the Carmel.

1893    February 2: Composition of her first poem.

February 20: Election of Mother Agnes as Prioress. Thérèse is associated in the spiritual formation of her companions

in    the novitiate.

June: Paints a fresco in the oratory.

June 24: Léonie enters the Visitation convent, Caen, a second time

September: Thérèse remains in the novitiate; named second portress.

1894    January 2: Attains majority.

January 21: First "pious recreation": Joan of Arc; she has main role. In the spring, she begins to suffer from her throat; cauterizings.

June 16: Entrance of Sister Marie of the Trinity; entrusted to Thérèse.

July 29: M. Martin dies at the château de La Musse (Eure).

August: Thérèse changes her cell.

September 14: Entrance of Céline to the Carmel; entrusted to Thérèse.

End of December: Receives from Mother Agnes of Jesus the order to write her childhood memories.

1895 *Year of writing of Manuscript A.*

February 5: Céline receives the Habit (Sister Geneviève).

February 26: Thérèse composes spontaneously the poem titled *Vivre d'Amour* ["Living on Love"].

*June 9 (Trinity Sunday): During Mass, she receives the inspiration to offer herself to Merciful Love.*

June 11: She makes this offering to Love with Céline. A short time afterward when beginning the Stations of the Cross, she has an intense experience of the Love of God ("wound of Love").

July 20: Léonie leaves the Visitation convent.

August 15: Entrance of her cousin, Marie Guérin, to the Carmel.

October 17: Thérèse is designated by Mother Agnes as spiritual sister to Father Bellière, seminarian and future missionary.

1896 January 20: Thérèse brings Mother Agnes her copybook of memories (Manuscript A).

February 24: Profession of Sister Geneviève.

March 17: Sister Geneviève receives the Veil; Marie Guérin (Sister Marie of the Eucharist) receives the Habit.

March 21: Difficult election of Mother Marie de Gonzague as Prioress. Thérèse is confirmed in her role as auxiliary mistress in the novitiate.

*April 2–3 (Holy Thursday night to Good Friday): First hemoptysis in her cell.*

April 3, in the evening: Second hemoptysis.

*April 5 (Easter Sunday) or shortly after: Sudden entrance into the Night of Faith, a trial that will last until her death.*

May 10: Dream about Venerable Anne of Jesus.

May 30: Mother Marie de Gonzague gives her a second spiritual brother: Father Roulland, of the Foreign Missions.

July 3: First Mass of Father Roulland at the Carmel and his interview with Thérèse.

September 7–18: Private retreat.

*September 8: Writing of Manuscript B (addressed to Jesus).*

September 13–16: Letter to Sister Marie of the Sacred Heart (Manuscript B, first part) to dedicate this text to her.

November: Reading of the Life of Théophane Vènard; novena to this martyr to obtain favor of going to the missions; pulmonary relapse.

1897    March 25: Profession of Sister Marie of the Eucharist.

April (end of Lent): Falls gravely ill.

*April 6: Beginning of the last conversations.*

June 3: Mother Marie de Gonzague orders Thérèse to continue her Autobiography.

*Thérèse writes Manuscript C.*

July 8: She is brought down to the infirmary. Has hemoptyses until August 5.

July 30: She is anointed.

August 19: Receives Communion for the last time.

*Thursday, September 30, around 7:20 p.m., Thérèse dies after an agony of two days.*

October 4: She is buried in the Lisieux cemetery.

## POSTHUMOUS CHRONOLOGY

1898    March 7: Bishop Hugonin, bishop of Bayeux, gives
permission for the printing of *Histoire d'une Ame.*

May 2: Bishop Hugonin dies.

September 30: 2,000 copies of *Histoire d'une Ame* are
printed by St. Paul Printing Co., Bar-le-Duc.

1899    Léonie enters definitively the Visitation convent at Caen.

Easter: The first edition of *Histoire d'une Ame* is out of print;
second edition begun.

October: Half the second edition (4,000) is sold.

1899-1902  First favors and cures. Pilgrims come to the grave of
Sister Thérèse to pray.

1902    April 19: Mother Agnes is re-elected Prioress; she will
remain in office, except for the interruption of eighteen
months (1908–1909), until her death, at the express
command of Pius XI (1923).

1904    December 17: Mother Marie de Gonzague dies.

1905    April 14: Sister Marie of the Eucharist dies of tuberculosis.

1906    July 9: François Veuillet, in *l'Univers,* reveals that the
Carmel is busy with introducing the Cause of Sister
Thérèse at Rome.

1907    October 15: Bishop Lemonnier, new bishop of Bayeux,
asks the Carmelites to write down their memories of Sister
Thérèse.

1909    January: Father Rodrigue, O.C.D. (Rome) and Monsignor
de Teil (Paris) are named Postulator and Vice-Postulator
of the Cause respectively.

1910    March 5: Rescript from Rome for the *Process on the
Writings.*

July: In one year, the Carmel has received 9,741 letters from people in France and foreign countries.

August 3: Setting up of the diocesan Tribunal for the Ordinary's Process.

August 12: At Carmel, the first session of the Process.

September 6: At the Lisieux cemetery, the exhumation of the remains of Sister Thérèse; transferred to new vault.

1912    This year Céline draws "Thérèse with the Roses" (charcoal sketch).

1914    July: The Carmel receives an average of 200 letters a day.

December 10: At Rome, decree of approbation of the Writings of Sister Thérèse.

June 10: Pius X signs the Decree for the Introduction of the Cause. He had told a missionary bishop privately that Sister Thérèse was "the greatest Saint of modern times."

1915    March 17: At Bayeux, opening of the Apostolic Process.

1917    August 9–10: Second exhumation and official acknowledgment of the remains of Sister Thérèse at the Lisieux cemetery.

1918    February 9: The Carmel received 512 letters that day.

1921    August 14: Benedict XV promulgates the Decree on the Heroicity of the Virtues of the Venerable Servant of God and delivers a Homily on Spiritual Childhood.

1923    *April 29th: Beatification of Sister Thérèse of the Child Jesus by Pius XI.* The Pope makes her "the star of his pontificate." The Carmel receives 800 to 1,000 letters daily.

1925    *May 17: Solemn Canonization at St. Peter's, Rome.* Homily of Pius XI before an audience of 60,000 people. In the evening, there were as many as 500,000 pilgrims in St.

Peter's square.

1927    January: *Novissima Verba* (Last Words) appears. July 13:
The liturgical feast of St. Thérèse is extended to the whole
Church.

December 14: Pius XI proclaims St. Thérèse of the Child
Jesus Principal Patroness, equal to St. Francis Xavier, of all
missionaries, men and women, and of the missions in the
whole world.

1929    September 30: Laying of the cornerstone of the Basilica at
Lisieux.

1937    July 11: Cardinal Pacelli (Papal Legate and future Pius XII)
opens and blesses the Basilica at Lisieux. Radio message
by Pius XI.

1941    July 24: Foundation of the Mission de France. Its seminary
is established at Lisieux.

1944    May 3: Pius XII names St. Thérèse Secondary Patroness of
France, equal to St. Joan of Arc.

June: Lisieux is partially destroyed by the allied bombings.
The Abbey (Thérèse's school) disappears.

1947    The fiftieth anniversary of her death, St. Thérèse's relics
are brought into almost every diocese of France.

1948    September: First edition of her *Letters*.

1954    July 11: Solemn consecration of the Basilica at Lisieux.

1956    Appearance of the facsimiledition of the
*Autobiographical Manuscripts* (restoration of the *Histoire
d'une Ame* according to the original writings), by Father
François de Sainte-Marie.

1971    July: Appearance of the *Derniers Entretiens* (first volume of
the Centenary Edition).

1972    July: Appearance of the *General Correspondence*

(Centenary Edition).

1973 Celebration of the Centenary of Thérèse Martin's birth

1979 Appearance of the Poésies (Centenary Edition)

1980 June 2: Pilgrimage of Pope John Paul II to Lisieux.

1985 Appearance of *Récréations Pieuses (Théâtre au Carmel)* (Centenary Edition).

1988 Appearance of the *Prières* (Centenary Edition).

1992 Appearance of the "Nouvelle Édition du Centenaire" (New Centenary Edition) in 8 volumes (Cerf and Desclée de Brouwer).

1996-1997 Centenary Celebration of Thérèse Martin's death.

# Index

451

# Biblical Index

The Institute of Carmelite Studies promotes research and publication in the field of Carmelite spirituality. Its members are Discalced Carmelites, part of a Roman Catholic community—friars, nuns, and laity—who are heirs to the teaching and way of life of Teresa of Jesus and John of the Cross, men and women dedicated to contemplation and to ministry in the Church and the world. Information concerning their way of life is available through local diocesan Vocation Offices or from the Vocation Directors' Offices:

5345 S. University Avenue, Chicago, IL 60615

2131 Lincoln Rd., NE Washington, DC 20002

P O Box 3420, San Jose, CA 95156-3420

5151 Marylake Drive, Little Rock, AR 72206

# Notes

# Notes

# Notes

# Notes

# Notes

# Notes

# Notes

# Notes

# Notes

# Notes